Interesting

Interesting

MY AUTOBIOGRAPHY

STEVE DAVIS

WITH LANCE HARDY

EBURY
PRESS

1 3 5 7 9 10 8 6 4 2

Ebury Press, an imprint of Ebury Publishing
20 Vauxhall Bridge Road
London SW1V 2SA

Ebury Press is part of the Penguin Random House group of companies whose addresses
can be found at global.penguinrandomhouse.com

The publisher has made every effort to ensure that all photographers are properly credited,
and, if notified, will rectify any omissions in subsequent editions

Steve Davis has asserted his right to be identified as the author of this Work in accordance
with the Copyright, Designs and Patents Act 1988

First published by Ebury Press in 2015

www.eburypublishing.co.uk

A CIP catalogue record for this book is available from the British Library

HB ISBN 9780091958640
TPB ISBN 9781785030710

Printed and bound in Great Britain by Clays Ltd, St Ives PLC

Penguin Random House is committed to a sustainable future for our business, our readers
and our planet. This book is made from Forest Stewardship Council® certified paper.

To my mother and father.
Jean Catherine Davis and
Henry George Davis (a.k.a Bill)

CONTENTS

1. LUCKY CELLAR DOORS

Do you remember the first time? Well, mine was captured on film! It happened in Sheffield in 1981.

I closed my eyes for a moment to take it all in. Then I saw Barry Hearn charging towards me with his fists and teeth clenched. He hit me like a tank. We had dreamt of this moment for so, so long. Everybody could see what it meant to us. The scene was unreal. I don't think the Embassy World Championship knew what had hit it.

The Brixton riots and the launch of the Space Shuttle dominated the news in April 1981. At the other end of the scale, Bucks Fizz were number one in the pop charts with a song called 'Making Your Mind Up', helped no end by a skirt-pulling dance routine; it was also a Eurovision Song Contest winner for the United Kingdom – that tells you how long ago it was! I was making the headlines on the back pages of the newspapers, too. And Easter Monday would be the day that would change my life forever.

The day before began – as was becoming the norm for me – with a brisk walk after breakfast through the streets of central Sheffield from my rather plush Grosvenor House Hotel down to the Crucible theatre, the home of snooker. Ahead of me was the start of a best-of-35-frames World Championship final against Welshman Doug Mountjoy.

Joining me on the walk – as always – were my father and my manager. The three of us had been on our own little journey for quite a while and the pinnacle was now within touching distance.

Collectively and individually we were chasing a dream. We all had a part to play: my father's complete and utter dedication to his son and an immense love for the game of snooker; my manager's inexhaustible energy, his brilliant eye for business and success, plus an unwavering support of me at all times; and my natural talent, single-minded pursuit of perfection and sheer determination with the help of a pointed stick (made back in the 1950s) with a bit of leather stuck on the end of it and a cube of grit.

We always walk the same walk down to the Crucible, taking care to step on to the big wooden cellar doors on the pavement outside the entrance to the Brown Bear pub, on Norfolk Street, just up the road from the theatre. In the future, these doors will be upgraded to metal due, I believe, to woodworm. Apart from that, this little ritual will remain the same for me as I walk past this popular drinking den for years to come!

A hundred or so yards ahead of the pub is the stage door of the Crucible. It is not yet twelve o'clock on Easter Sunday but already it is packed outside with autograph hunters armed with pens, books, programmes and posters. After decades in the doldrums, snooker is becoming the sport of the masses and it is now on the cusp of hitting boom time.

On any other day during the rest of the season, the rest of the year, the rest of my life, I would be quite happy to stand here and sign autographs all day. But not today, not before the start of the most important match of my life. I can't deal with any distractions. And, to be honest, the last thing I want to do right now is sign an autograph. Let alone a hundred or more.

Despite a relatively low world ranking of 13 – more of that later – I was made firm favourite to win the 1981 World Championship by bookmakers going into the tournament and it has been no different with every round that has passed. On the eve of the final, the best odds you can get on me are 1–3!

I am in a great frame of mind. I have already won four prestigious titles this season and I have knocked out three world champions on my way to the final – Alex Higgins, Terry Griffiths and Cliff Thorburn – as well as the new kid on the block, Jimmy White. I certainly feel that this is my time. Added to that winning momentum, I have a manager who is proudly shouting my name from the rooftops. That helps as well.

I am the hottest name in the game. I can feel there is a tide of expectation building up around me. This has been helped no end by some impressive winning margins in some big matches recently – the pick of the bunch being a 16–6 win over Alex Higgins in the final of the 1980 Coral UK Championship.

As you would expect, Doug Mountjoy has been in good form, too. He defeated six-time world champion and fellow countryman Ray Reardon in the semi-finals, where he also knocked in a World Championship record break of 145 for good measure.

The Welsh Valleys have always been a hotbed of snooker. The Working Men's Club and Institute Union (CIU) scene is strong over there and interest in the sport received an injection of popularity when Ray rose to fame in the early 1970s by winning all those world titles. Doug and Terry are two of the not-so-new brigade to turn professional after years on the amateur circuit. But their ages also tell you how the game is rapidly changing: Ray is forty-eight, Doug is thirty-eight and Terry is thirty-three. I am twenty-three.

This is also Doug's first world final, but he has been around for ages. He is a former world amateur champion and he can be a devastating potter on his day. I was in the audience to watch him beat Ray to win the Benson & Hedges Masters at the New London Theatre on Drury Lane in 1977. He followed that up with the UK Championship title the following year. He has played well in Sheffield – also beating Willie Thorne, Eddie Charlton and Dennis Taylor – and no doubt fancies his chances, too.

Inside the Crucible I have my usual practice session in the rather tight, specially built area backstage. Nearby, a black curtain is all that hides David Vine in the BBC television studio from me. This man is TV's Mr Snooker. And I can hear him clearly as he goes through his pre-programme script. He can hear me as well. At one stage, he refers to me as 'Ice-cool Davis'. No pressure there, then, David? In truth, at that very moment I may just have started to feel my hand shake a little.

The two practice tables backstage are a sanctuary from the outside world for me. They are absolutely perfect with exactly the same cloth as the one that is out on stage; inside that famous, incomparable cauldron a short distance away that will soon witness the biggest match of my career so far. It is a world away from where I started out, playing at my father's working men's club in south-east London.

Sadly, my dressing room at the Crucible isn't as perfect. You couldn't call it glamorous by any means and it certainly isn't the type of place where you would like to spend any amount of time. In fact, it is more like a dentist's waiting room than a dressing room. I suppose that is quite fitting in its own sort of way on a day like this.

Inside this tiny room is a bench, a mirror, a sink, a single coat-hanger and a loudspeaker. It is cramped, to say the least. The toilet is outside. I find that I am in and out of there a few times before I hit the stage! The bench can be a useful tool. I often have a power nap between sessions on it. It isn't too comfortable but when I am in the zone I can easily lie down on it and drop off for a bit until my father pops his head around the door and tells me it is time to get ready for the evening session.

The loudspeaker is the only part of this dressing room that reminds me it is part of a theatre. A feed from the auditorium gives me a sense of the audience arriving pre-match and the excitement starts to build inside when the famous *Pot Black* theme tune – which is a welcome change from that Bucks Fizz song that has been played everywhere during the past fortnight – starts to play. I know that a knock on the door is now not too far away.

With minutes to go before the start of the final, I feel focused. Outside, on the lawns, quite a few fans are gathered, looking up at my dressing-room window and trying to catch a glimpse. One or two of the more agile ones have climbed up trees to get a better view. The whole scene can be a bit like being in a zoo. There is certainly an element of 'Don't Feed the Players' about it all with fans staring at you and watching your every move. I wouldn't say it is the streets of Amsterdam, but you get my gist. Having said that, some players have been known to get spotted up there from time to time in various stages of undress.

I don't interact with the fans. I can't interact with them. I don't even acknowledge them. All I want is to be left alone in my own little shell and prepare for my task in hand. Beyond those fans – across Arundel Gate, the main road that leads into Sheffield's famous 'Hole in the Road' roundabout – is the Roxy nightclub. Tonight and tomorrow will be busy nights in the city as people go about living their normal lives on a Bank Holiday weekend. But tonight and tomorrow are going to be far from normal days and nights for me and my opponent. The two of us are going to be in our own little snooker bubble.

My father and Barry stand in the dressing room with me. These men form my inner sanctum. They are the only two people I can have around me at this time. My father chews on his cigar and doesn't say a word while my manager hardly draws breath, talking about anything other than the match ahead. He is a born entertainer and this pre-match routine is like a shot of adrenaline to me and gives off such positive vibes; something like a psychotherapy session without knowing it.

I do the business on the table and Barry does the business off the table. We have never ever discussed such a plan of action but, instinctively, we have always been on the same wavelength as each other since the day we met. We have such confidence in each other's strengths that it is a perfect match. My father has been my coach since I was a child. He has been with me on the practice table. But his work is done for now. It is all about me.

A knock on the door is followed by another visit to the toilet and then I am on my way, heading into something resembling a rabbit warren backstage with little bits of corridor here and there. I walk alongside breeze-blocks, and yet more breeze-blocks, on my way to the stage.

Soon I am backstage, slipping silently past the black curtains before standing to wait for my cue, so to speak, from the MC. My name is called out and the crowd erupts. My loyal fan club, the Romford Roar, is loud, very loud; the boys give it large.

I walk past the television commentary box – the whispering Voice of Snooker, Ted Lowe, is sitting inside – and go down the small steps into the 900-seat arena. The stage floor is lowered at the theatre during the World Championship to give it the full amphitheatre effect. It works a treat and the intimacy with the crowd seems to magnify the tension. No matter where you are sitting in the audience, you can't make a sound when a player is on the shot. You can hear the back row breathing at times! As always, there is not a spare seat in the house.

The Crucible certainly lives up to its name because it provides a melting pot of excitement that builds and builds. It also has an intimate and intimidating atmosphere with the right acoustics to provide exactly the right setting for a sporting finale such as this. I absolutely love this place. There is no venue like it in snooker. The spectators on the front rows are in your eye line from the off. They have to sit so still. Anybody who dares so much as to open a sweet wrapper in those rows is dead meat. The glare from a player will have them choking on the contents!

Doug and I pose with the World Championship trophy for the assembled photographers, a performance that seems to last an eternity. But at no stage do I make a move to touch the trophy. I know much better than to try and do anything as silly as that! Touching trophies before they are yours is bad – but walking over cellar doors if you want to hold trophies is good, right?

Actually, you can still find some photographs around today that show Doug standing behind the trophy smiling happily for the cameras while I am at his side looking into the distance with my left hand in my pocket. I just want to get the match started! I couldn't wait. I had been waiting for years ...

When we eventually begin, I am on fire. I race into a six-frame lead in just over two hours. I am thriving in this special atmosphere and the unique sense of occasion. Doug is on the rocks, making many mistakes which I subsequently punish with relish. It is nothing special; a few half-centuries. But it is granite snooker.

The game can feel easy at times like this and this was a type of snooker that I had become renowned for: getting my opponent on the ropes from the opening bell and keeping him there. If ever I have my foot on somebody's neck in a match, I never ease up the pressure. Once I have him reeling, I keep applying the pressure – not offering him a glimmer of hope – and, eventually, he will crumple under the relentlessness of it all.

But my momentum is halted in the seventh frame when referee John Williams decides a re-rack is the only solution with just the blue, pink and black remaining. Doug and I had spent 15 minutes and 43 shots between us trying to separate the blue from the black in the jaws of the green pocket. I was narrowly ahead in the frame at the time, 49–48, and although I feel as though I have the upper hand, particularly with such a handsome-looking scoreboard in front of me, that counts for nothing.

This moment becomes something of a turning point in the match. Twenty-five minutes later, Doug wins the restarted frame and subsequently recovers his rhythm to knock in a 76 break to underline he has completely regained his form. The day ends with me holding a slender 10–8 lead overnight. It is still an advantage but at one stage it looked like being so much more than that. I return to my hotel room feeling disappointed with myself.

As a result, I don't sleep too well that night. Breakfast is a big struggle for me the following day as well: I only manage to eat four pieces of grapefruit! The nerves have got hold of me. This isn't the first time I have had a big lead at the Crucible and my opponent has come charging back at me – but it has left me with a horrible feeling inside. It is now a challenge not to let this panic overrun proceedings.

As I push the grapefruit around my plate, I stop for a second to question whether my success throughout the season is eventually taking its toll on me. After all, this is my 67th day in a row without a break. I certainly hadn't expected to be feeling like this midway through the first session. But that seems a long time ago…

We carefully walk over the Brown Bear cellar doors again on our way to the Crucible. Maybe stupidly, I feel better having done so. But, by the end of the first session of the final day, Doug and I have played out another eight tense, cliffhanger frames to nudge the scoreline along to 14–12. The session had been shared 4–4.

The match was turning into another potential marathon for me – just two days after I needed more than 14 hours to see off the challenge of Cliff Thorburn in the semi-finals. I now need four more frames to be crowned world champion; Doug requires six.

That night, I dress for the evening session in the usual attire of waistcoat and bow tie. I am happy with that. I never really felt comfortable in the lounge suit required for the afternoon session; playing in a normal tie, the knot always got in the way of my cue. So, the only way I could work around that was to loosen the tie and yank it to the left of my neck. It looked quite scruffy but it was absolutely necessary for unrestricted cueing.

In my dressing room, Barry holds court once again. This time he tells me about one of the Romford lads, Bill the Cap, losing his cap.

'We have looked everywhere,' he booms. 'He doesn't even look like Bill now!'

I am more than happy to hear about it. The last thing I want to do is talk about the world final.

Barry then asks me to hold my hand out so he can make sure it is firm.

'OK, Davis,' he says. 'Let's see how you're feeling.'

Barry has always called me Davis, never Steve. It is said in an affectionate way. I spread my fingers wide apart. My hand is rock solid. He is happy with that. And so am I.

This is another of our little rituals which we do from time to time. In the early rounds, I might have been shaking a little if he had asked me to do it. The early rounds at the Crucible are always the worst, but by the final session of the entire tournament it is not like that at all.

Looking back, this charade didn't really prove anything to either of us – at least I don't think it did – but it always seemed to provide part of the excitement and preparation before I walked out into the bear pit.

There is one final knock on my dressing-room door, which means one last visit to the toilet for me before I am good to go on stage. I am then on my own again, into the rabbit warren, past the breeze-blocks, through the curtains and into the arena, in front of the tightly packed crowd there to witness my fate. I try not to think about the television audience of many millions watching at home.

High above me, Barry and my father join my mother, my brother and the Romford Roar; the men who have supported me so much over the early years. They are all seated together in the players' guest area up in the gods.

The Crucible can be the greatest place on earth or the worst place in the world for a snooker player. Everything is exaggerated. Win or lose. Within a few hours, Doug and I will experience totally different emotions. For me, I have to make sure that it is going to be the greatest place to be tonight. There is no turning back.

'Go out and do the business,' Barry tells me.

Sure enough, a few hours later I have done the business and I am crowned world champion. There was no turning back: an 84 break won me the first frame of the night, a clearance of 119 won me the next and a break of 44 clinched me the one after that to leave me 17–12 up and just one frame away from the top prize in snooker.

I wrapped it all up with another 44 break in the following frame. By the time I got down to the green, a glance at the scoreboard told me I just needed the brown along the bottom cushion to be almost certain of victory. Once I had got it, the Romford Roar erupted and, as the tension evaporated, the emotions started to rise to the surface.

Live on BBC 2, Ted Lowe told the nation that I was 'breathing heavily'. He was absolutely right. Relief and a little bit of shock had taken over me. All of a sudden it hit me that I had done it. From the moment I potted the blue and scrambled in the pink I felt the tears well up inside me.

Barry's celebration says it all. It epitomises everything about sport: belief, commitment, passion. He punches the air in delight – fists raised in celebration – and shouts out to the Romford Roar, stood high up on the balcony above us.

While I had been practising for something like six hours a day for the previous five years, my manager had been telling the world that I was a future world champion. The Romford Roar had said the same to all their mates and everybody in snooker had been given notice after I had beaten Alex Higgins to win the UK Championship in Preston six months before. This was now Barry's time to announce to the world: 'I told you so!'

The next person I see is my father. I can tell what it means to him just by looking at his face. 'That was good snooker,' is all he says to me. We had worked so hard to achieve this – going all the way back to the start of my teenage years – and we had come such a long way together. This is a very special moment for me. All I can do is grizzle on his shoulder. In a World Championship final, 18–12 is not close. It is a comfortable victory, but nothing can prepare you for such success and you just have to go with the flow.

My mother taps me on the shoulder with a big smile on her face and says simply: 'Well done.' Barry's wife, Susan, hugs me tightly and Keith, my brother, is there, too. Throughout all of this I just stand there – in front of millions of television viewers – and cry like a baby!

David Vine approaches me and confirms the magical moment has really just happened by announcing to the crowd: 'Steve Davis, Embassy World Snooker Champion 1981.' I eventually reply by spluttering out just two words: 'Jesus Christ!'

Of course, this wasn't my planned acceptance speech. Muttering 'Jesus Christ' in front of millions of people live on television isn't too clever. What it eventually means is a lot of work for somebody at the BBC and a shedload of mail coming into Barry's Romford office from irate viewers. In my defence, I was totally and utterly exhausted.

I am presented with a cheque for £20,000 and the famous trophy. The Romford Roar also picked up an estimated £75,000 in bets on me! But the silverware means so much more to me than the money. It always does. Outside, by the stage door, I am now more than happy to sign hundreds of autographs.

A proper Romford Roar party gets underway at the Grosvenor House, courtesy of the sponsors. On the way there, I get down on my hands and knees outside the Brown Bear pub and kiss the lucky cellar doors. We later move on to Napoleon's casino, on Ecclesall Road, where Barry wins a load of cash on the roulette wheel.

The next morning I pose topless in the shower in my hotel room for a photograph that ends up on the front page of the *Daily Star*. Our journey is now well and truly underway. We have made the big breakthrough. Right here, right now. And what a ride it is to be …

2. THE BEER MAT AND THE BIBLE

'Look what I've got here, son!'

I rubbed my eyes together. As I slowly came to and tried to focus in the dark, I saw my father standing at the foot of my bed, grinning from ear to ear. I could see he was holding something in his hand but I couldn't work out what it was.

It was the early hours of the morning sometime in the late 1960s. I was about twelve at the time and I had school the next day. I was fast asleep in my bed at our council flat in Abbey Wood, in south-east London, when I was woken up by a proud and slightly drunk father. At that point, I wasn't entirely sure why.

He had just returned from a night out at the Lee Green Working Men's Club and there was something that just couldn't wait. It was a present for me. But all I could see was a used Watney's beer mat.

I soon found out the reason for his smile. This wasn't any old beer mat. This one – and no other – had Fred Davis' name signed on the back of it!

Fred was an eight-time former world snooker champion. But snooker was at an all-time low back in the 1960s. In fact, between 1957 and 1964 nobody won the World Championship – because there wasn't one. No one thought it worth promoting.

There were few competitions around at this time, so the top players earned most of their money through exhibitions at social clubs. It was customary for professional snooker players to visit these clubs and play exhibition frames against locals. That was part of the game's culture. Breweries sponsored some of these evenings so cheap beer was on sale and everybody enjoyed themselves. Players also appeared at various holiday camps during the summer months, which was also popular and lucrative work for them.

I was to make my snooker competition television debut against Fred on *Pot Black* many years later when he was well into his sixties. But it was his older brother, Joe Davis, who was my father's real hero. This was the man who organised the first ever World Championship back in 1927.

Joe won the world title every year he played in it – from 1927 to 1940 and again in 1946 (when the tournament resumed following the end of the Second World War). He then retired from the event. He remains the only professional never to have been defeated in the competition; a record that is clearly unlikely to ever be matched. He also wrote a book called *How I Play Snooker*. This became my father's bible. He got to know that book from the front page to the last – and so did I!

My life in snooker began as a result of my father's huge affection for the game. This is not unusual: other players had similar introductions to the sport through their own fathers. My father would admit that he wasn't the greatest player around. His highest break is 58.

A 58 break is a lot more than most people have achieved in the game but it is nothing to write home about when you consider my father has spent a lifetime knocking balls around. In comparison to those in the top echelons of the game, a 58-break player is doing just that: knocking balls around! It could be two breaks of 29 joined together by a fluke!

This usually means that so much concentration has been put into the potting side of the game and not too many brain cells have been left to work on the positional side. For the vast majority of club players, getting the ball in the hole is hard enough without having to manoeuvre the cue ball into a position to keep the break going. I am thankful for this – it has meant I have been able to have a job for the last 40 years.

On countless occasions, I have tried to get my father to think more about the positional side of his game but, left to his own devices, he naturally reverts to his ready-made 'pot the ball, walk round the table, and see if there is another one to pot' method. I would love to be able to see what he sees when he plays, just as I would love to be able to see through Ronnie O'Sullivan's eyes and get a glimpse of a true genius at work.

I am regularly asked what makes a champion. Is it practice, determination, technique, concentration? What percentage is nature or nurture? I think the whole thing about ability – from darts to cooking to ice skating – comes down to a freak of nature and an inordinate skill in a focused direction. If that direction means you are exceptional in an area that others can find appealing, then you have a ready-made skill, profession and, ultimately, World Championship trophy on the mantelpiece. Importantly for me, my father loved snooker and he loved to study it even more. That last part was to be absolutely vital in my own success story.

My father was born in 1926. At the age of fourteen with no parents around (his mother died young and his father was fighting in the Second World War), he decided to join the Merchant Navy. He didn't come out until 1947, when he was twenty-one. He subsequently worked for London Transport for 35 years.

A qualified bus driver with a Passenger Carrying Vehicle licence, he could drive anything and he later taught me to drive. I remember his favourite saying: 'You don't use your brake as an engine – so don't use your engine as a brake.'

He spent his early days around motorbikes and, out of necessity, motor mechanics. Two working men's clubs – Lee Green and Plumstead Common – were his life beyond his work and my mother.

It was the working men's clubs that really whetted his appetite for the game. I imagine there wasn't too much for working-class men to do in terms of a social life in the years following the Second World War. My father wasn't a big drinker and he wasn't too interested in pubs either – but he liked having an hour or two down at the working men's club. These were non-profit-making establishments that served cheap beer and by the 1950s it was mandatory for them to have a snooker table and a darts board. Top entertainers also appeared from time to time. I remember Jim Davidson, the comedian, doing a stint at our club shortly after he won *New Faces* in the 1970s.

My father's original game of choice was actually darts. He was a decent club player, too, but, like five-time world darts champion Eric Bristow, he suffered a bout of dartitis – where he couldn't let go of the dart – and, after failed attempts to throw left-handed, he decided to take up snooker. He was soon hooked on the game.

Lee Green – the first club on my radar that my father frequented – had two snooker tables. The game was played there every night of the week with weekly league matches taking place. These were a big attraction and if you were good enough to make the team – and my father was good enough to become a regular – you became a minor celebrity down at the club.

Monday night was games night with a three-man team event in various disciplines, ranging from darts to dominoes and snooker to skittles, which was played against teams from other clubs. Sometimes the winners would be decided by some guy smashed out of his head on ten pints of light and bitter choosing which hand the other team had secretly hidden a small wooden ball in a game of tippit – which was a sort of Call My Bluff contest. It was often difficult to work out which opponent had the ball and in which hand, especially when everybody was too drunk to look like they had a big red arrow over their head! But whoever won the all-important points at the end was a hero for the rest of the night and guaranteed more beer to add to the severity of his Tuesday morning hangover.

My first memory of snooker comes from Lee Green Working Men's Club. Where else could it have happened? It was a Sunday lunchtime and a lot of families were down there, as was usual on this day of the week. At this time women were 'tolerated' in the club (but not allowed on the snooker tables!), the raffle was for joints of meat (at which point, the women were probably expected to take the kids home and cook the winnings and wait for the inebriated breadwinner to stumble through the door).

I was just a little boy, standing two foot nine. This is an important point to mention because, when I stood up, I was still half an inch below the height of a snooker table. On this particular day, I was on a bench seat, watching my father play in a game of doubles, when I saw the black ball rolling towards me. Suddenly, I jumped off the bench, stood on my tiptoes and reached over the cushion to grab the ball. I can still hear the shouts of 'No!' quite vividly. Obviously, I was drawn to the balls – even at that very young age.

My own snooker education of sorts began when, aged eight, I asked Father Christmas for my own snooker table. I received a Joe Davis-endorsed quarter-size table-top version. When it turned up on Christmas Day 1965, Santa had suffered a nightmare! His elves had forgotten to put any balls in with it! Can you imagine that?

Why would Santa be so cruel to do that to me? Maybe it was cheaper without the balls? I don't know. Anyhow, not to worry, the balls duly arrived in the post a week later. In the meantime, I had to make do by walking round the kitchen table, with my snooker table placed on top of it, playing imaginary shots to myself.

Funnily enough, I later read that Joe was only given one ball to play with himself by his father at the very beginning; the idea being that once he learned how to hit the cue ball correctly, he could advance to the next stage. So, perhaps he demanded that the balls for these little tables were sent out a week later to instil the same discipline into his pupils up and down the country? Little did I know that in the future my own name would one day grace the rail of *Pot Black* tables that thousands of kids in the 1980s would wake up to on Christmas Day!

Like most Christmas presents, the six-by-three Joe Davis-endorsed product was a passing fad in my life. From the age of about eight to eleven or twelve, football was my sport not snooker. I enjoyed playing the game and I regularly went to watch Charlton Athletic down at The Valley, which in those days was the biggest ground in the entire Football League with a capacity of 66,000. This was the era of Mike Bailey, Billy Bonds, Mike Kenning and Keith Peacock – all of them were heroes of mine.

I was at the game where Keith became the first ever substitute to be used in the Football League in 1965. I still find it amazing and frustrating that, in a sport run by a committee, certain aspects can take so long to change to common-sense ideas. There were still no substitutes allowed when England won the World Cup the following year in 1966. How ridiculous was that?

Likewise, in snooker, our own rules committee eggheads took ages to address the problem of foul and miss. For a long time, a player in trouble could play as if to hit a red on to the cushion extra thin, safe in the knowledge that if he missed his opponent gained no more of an advantage than an extra four points.

Back to Keith. He later coached me at Alexandra McLeod Junior School, in Abbey Wood, and he would turn up regularly to watch our school team play on Saturday mornings; when, I assume, he was playing in the afternoons for Charlton. It was a different era in those days. Coincidentally, Keith also presented me with my first cue case a few years later after I won a local snooker competition. He was an all-round gent.

A decent right-winger, I was chosen to play for Woolwich and District schools when I was ten but I was cruelly struck down with flu the day before the match and my chance to impress was gone. In hindsight, it was probably the best bout of flu I ever contracted! This was the beginning of the end for my footballing days. I can count on the fingers of one hand the number of times I have been struck down by a virus during a snooker event – luckily it never happened at the World Championship – and I do wonder if the body can sometimes take on an ability to resist such viruses when it really needs to prepare for something.

As it is today, *Match of the Day* was the must-watch weekly sports programme in the television schedule. It started in 1964. But it wasn't until 1969 that snooker got its own regular slot on the small screen. This happened when the BBC launched *Pot Black* to help showcase its brand new toy of colour pictures at the end of the Swinging Sixties.

The funny thing was that most of the country still had black and white television sets. So, take away the black and the white balls and snooker fans had to discern between the remaining 20 shades of grey. We also had to rely on good memories to tell us where certain balls were hiding: the green, the brown, the blue and the reds were dark grey on our television set and even the yellow and the pink could be mistaken for each other.

It was against this background that Ted Lowe gave his famous commentary line: 'For those of you who are watching in black and white, the pink is behind the green.'

Whispering Ted got his famous nickname after commentating on a game of snooker at Leicester Square Hall, in central London, while he was the manager there, for a newsreel item. The film crew asked him to explain the game and he commentated on a match from the back row, hence his need to speak quietly. The style stayed with him.

Ted was the man who provided the players for *Pot Black*. He also worked on the programme as a commentator. He was never a professional player – unheard of these days for a BBC snooker commentator – but he was excellent at setting the scene and painting pictures for fans, particularly those who were drawn to the game in the boom era that followed but didn't fully understand it.

Pot Black was a round-robin competition, with two groups of four narrowed down so that the top two in each went through to the semi-finals knockout stage.

Each match was one frame to fit into a neat half-hour slot in the newly unveiled BBC 2 evening schedule. Nowadays, Ronnie O'Sullivan and Judd Trump could probably fit in a best of three! It was hosted by the ice skating commentator Alan Weeks, dressed appropriately in bow tie, of course.

The programme was an overnight success for all involved. The table fitted perfectly into the television screen and all the different-coloured balls really sold the new technology – if you were lucky enough to have it. Long-term hopes for the show were apparently not too high when it was commissioned but it quickly exceeded all expectations with exceptional viewing figures. Sales of colour television sets increased, too, although what percentage was down to the popularity of snooker is open to debate.

What also became popular was a cracking piece of theme music, which is still played at the Crucible theatre and other snooker venues today. The tune is called 'Black and White Rag'. It was composed in the early 1900s by George Botsford and the version used was recorded by the late Trinidadian pianist Winifred Atwell in 1952.

Pot Black was filmed over a few days at the BBC studios in Birmingham over the Christmas period. But it would run over something like three months from the start of the New Year.

Snooker owes a lot to *Pot Black*. It was really the breakthrough for the modern game. Television viewers got with the bow ties and waistcoats, too. That look had been around since the 1920s. But, at that time, the only people who owned billiard tables were the landed gentry. After dinner, while the butlers cleaned up and the ladies retired to wherever they retired to in those days, the men swanned off to the billiard room. I wonder if the butler was ever called upon to pick out the balls for his master. If so, perhaps he still had his white gloves on from handling the silverware? Then again, perhaps it is all just coincidence?

The *Pot Black* evening dress code worked a treat on evening television. I am sure it helped build an audience for the programme. It also gave the game some respectability after a dark period of snooker halls being associated with many a misspent youth. That expression has always made me grit my teeth. I hate the connotation.

But the irony of a sporting pastime representing a misspent youth suddenly becoming respectable once the evil of money came into the equation meant snooker players had the last laugh! For the general public, the uniform of choice gave the game elegance and respect. While the players were obviously uncomfortable, we got used to the attire.

The show made certain players famous. Whoever won *Pot Black* was considered to be the world champion in the eyes of the public – because it was this competition alone that got the television coverage not the World

Championship. For instance, to the man in the street, Eddie Charlton, *Pot Black* champion, was Eddie Charlton, world champion, even though he never was world champion. He once lost by one frame to Ray Reardon in the world final in Australia in 1975 and that was as close as he got.

Players such as the late Graham Miles, who won *Pot Black* in 1974 and 1975, and Dennis Taylor, who was runner-up in 1975 and 1976, enjoyed substantial boosts to their earnings through appearing on the programme. The offshoot was a significant increase in exhibition bookings. Considering the flip-of-a-coin nature of a one-frame event, there was actually a fair amount at stake for those that took part.

Back in those days, television was a family affair. Few homes had more than one television set so it goes without saying that whatever my mother and father watched, I watched. And there was only one thing that was going to be on our television set when *Pot Black* was on.

Along with my father, it was *Pot Black* that brought snooker into my life. It first aired when I was coming up to twelve – an impressionable age – and it became a must-watch programme in our house from the very start, giving my father his weekly snooker fix.

My first tangible experience of the game on a full-size table came a couple of years later, in the summer of 1971, on a family trip to a Maddieson's holiday camp near the village of St Mary's Bay, in Kent. As fate would have it, there was a snooker room there – overlooking the Romney, Hythe and Dymchurch miniature railway – and children were allowed to play. Approaching the age of fourteen, I wasn't really allowed into working men's clubs or snooker clubs. If I did go into the club with my father, I certainly wasn't allowed to play on the tables. I was under age, simple as that.

My mother didn't get much of a holiday at Romney Sands. She was something of a snooker widow as my father and I played day and night on this full-size table. Although I should mention that my aunt and uncle were there with us, so it wasn't as though she was dumped on the Donkey Derby every day! However, for two weeks solid, the two of us were in this snooker room. I loved every single minute of it. I was now hooked on the game.

Looking back, my father must have been in his element. What could possibly be better than his son suddenly showing an interest in a game that had always been such a large part of his life? He encouraged me every day and he tutored me every day.

The full-size table at the holiday camp lit my enthusiasm for snooker. I began to understand the excitement that the game could offer. And so it was here, on this strip of the south-east coast of England, when Marc Bolan and T Rex were at number one with 'Get It On', that I first began to learn the techniques of the game my father loved so much.

He entered a snooker competition during the first week of our holiday and he won it! His prize was a Thermos flask. It wasn't that I particularly liked Thermos flasks but it was enough to make my mind up that I wanted to enter the competition the following week.

My first ever opponent was an old man who took delight in snookering me whenever he could. He played a lot of safety and annihilated me, unashamedly crushing the hopes of a fourteen-year-old on his holiday. I can still recall him muttering the words 'Snooker's the name of the game' as he walked round the table to once again roll me up behind the yellow.

The defeat seemed to affect me more than it should have done for a kid having a bash on a snooker table at a holiday camp. Most other boys of my age would probably have walked away to find out the times of the crazy golf or table tennis competitions. But I was devastated. I left the snooker room with tears welling up in my eyes. I had to go off on my own to have a little cry.

I didn't want to be seen bursting into tears in front of my father. It was already apparent that I hated losing. I am not sure whether my father was ever aware of how upset I was about it but, regardless, he made it his mission to thrash the old man in the final. He duly did and we finished the holiday with a second Thermos flask! We celebrated his victory with some hot tea and ice cream in the same Thermos flask. Very clever things, Thermos flasks!

I had been well and truly bitten by the snooker bug. As soon as we got home to Abbey Wood, I devoured the Joe Davis book. Absolutely delighted, my father asked Lee Green Working Men's Club committee if they would allow me to play on the full-size table there. Graciously, they agreed but this was only because my father was a member of the team.

Don't be fooled, the standard was not that high: my father has since told me that you could get signed up for the team if you could put together a break of 20! But I would have been snookered without the club's permission. I was still too young to be a member – but I was now given a special concession to play.

Due to being under age, I had spent many frustrated weekends down there with my father watching these grown men knocking balls around in the hope of one dropping in the pocket. Within no time at all, they seemed in awe of me when I made a break of 24! Here was a young kid who was not only able to get the ball in the hole but also seemed to be trying to get the cue ball somewhere near to the next desired ball. When I beat some of the older members of the club, utilising this unusual method of play, they were heard to mumble into their beer that 'it wasn't cricket', which, of course, it wasn't!

When I improved my personal best to 33, my father decided I was deserving of my own cue, in preference to using the ones on the club rack. We headed into London one Saturday afternoon to Bennett and Stevens cue makers, and my parents paid out a large sum of £15 for one. For the record, it was a Power Glide cue. Sadly, it was a disastrous acquisition initially. I couldn't hit the ball straight and kept going in-off. The cue was dead straight and far superior to the ones I had used at the club and I expected to play much better with it. But expectation can be a strange beast and puts undue pressure on people. I was very upset. For the second time, snooker had brought me close to tears!

The Joe Davis snooker table was now in the kitchen all the time, even though I could only play on it from one end. My mother would often complain to me that she couldn't get to the cooker and the cupboards but I was in my own little world and I didn't seem to care about anybody or anything else.

Meanwhile, my father oversaw my technical development and continued to make sure that I did everything according to Joe's book. He always insisted that I cued properly and copied the techniques advised. I listened intently to every word my father told me. One method to ensure I wasn't moving my head on the shot was for him to stand close to me with his cue tip hovering directly over my head. If I played a power shot and my head touched his cue, I had failed.

My father was always determined that I learned all the basics before I did anything else. He was adamant that I should not develop any bad habits whatsoever in my game. My cue action and self-discipline have a lot to do with this upbringing.

I always remember him getting frustrated about not being able to get his own back arm totally in line with his cue. It seemed the best he could do was to get it to run parallel to his cue. Joe stipulated in his book that it was desirable for it to be directly in line. My father was unable to achieve this Zen-like state but I was able to do it with no apparent contortion. We both spent hours in the kitchen checking each other's back arm positions. One was satisfied and the other was puzzled. In hindsight, it was wasted time – as were some other areas of my practice dogma – but, importantly, it focused the mind. Everything was a challenge and every challenge I faced I found that I was up to the task.

I was still at school but snooker was already my life. I had watched news footage with fascination as a young Northern Irishman called Alex Higgins, nicknamed 'the Hurricane', had won the Park Drive World Championship the previous year in 1972. My first memory of the Hurricane was actually seeing him beating John Spencer on TV while wearing a tank-top jumper! I later saw him being interviewed on a news programme and playing a frame against the presenter. These were exciting times: a snooker player making the headlines.

My snooker education quickly moved from Lee Green Working Men's Club to Plumstead Common Working Men's Club, which was much closer to home, after the committee at the former establishment controversially decided to sell one of its two tables to allow them to turn the snooker room into a lounge area to accommodate the growing number of bingo players.

The remaining table was moved upstairs. My father was disgusted by this and immediately resigned from the team. I don't think it made the local paper or the club newsletter but he had been there years so it was a big thing for him to do. But, thinking about it, we were at the stage where we had to move on. To quote Roy Scheider's character in *Jaws*: 'You're going to need a bigger boat.'

Although my father was not a great player by modern standards, he was certainly good enough to be considered one of the better players in the local league in those days and therefore command interest from other working men's clubs. He had the opportunity to join a number of teams in the area – in something akin to an early form of the Bosman ruling – and he went for Plumstead Common after they agreed to allow me to play on the tables whenever they were free.

I was now fifteen, so this was the deciding factor for my father and it proved to be a great decision for me. Plumstead Common had four tables and far superior facilities to what we had become accustomed to at Lee Green. It was a far bigger boat!

This was comfortably the best environment around for me to play snooker and my game really burst into life there. Gradually the members began to defer to me as my overall standard improved and they allowed me to play for longer periods. You put your name down on the board and you would get a half-hour slot. Then the next name took over. As I improved, the hierarchy of snooker friends I was now moving within started to protect me from being kicked off the table.

In essence, I became the resident player on table number one and I probably became a bit of a pest to the casual club player as I started to dominate all evening. I owe all my friends there a huge debt of gratitude for embracing me and understanding my need to occupy the table. I still owe a lot of drinks to a lot of people as well. I was still too young to get a round in myself so everybody else would have to get my drinks for me.

I was hooked on practice and my father continued to be by my side every step of the way offering technical advice. He was keen to improve me in every way as it was becoming obvious that I loved to practise and it felt vital that I did.

I was learning about tactics and positional play as best I could but I didn't really have any good players to copy from at the club. So it was technique, technique, technique – with the Joe Davis book and my father as my guiding lights. While I might have improved far more quickly in an environment of better players, the situation turned out to be a blessing in disguise; I was able to hone the 'perfect technique' first and, therefore, learn to walk before I started to try and run.

Recognising my enthusiasm and commitment, my father kindly offered to pay out again – this time at £10 an hour – for me to have a couple of sessions with Jack Karnehm, a world-class billiards player who, for a long time, was also a famous voice on the BBC's snooker coverage. He was also one of the few professionals who offered coaching lessons at that time.

Jack was impressed with my technique but he also spotted a few flaws in my game that my father hadn't yet noticed. He advised me to play billiards to improve my overall skill set on the table.

Whether this made a difference to my professional development is arguable. I think if you are going to be good at something, you are going to be good regardless. But I enjoyed billiards and it seemed useful as it is a game in which control of the cue ball is essential.

I was maturing as a player and, with my game now being analysed more closely, I also became more analytical myself and, perhaps, more of a perfectionist, too.

Subsequently, I spent the first part of every solo practice session during the school holidays that summer hitting the cue ball up and down the table, watching it pass over the spots on the way up before striking the top cushion, and watching it pass over the spots again on the way down. Said like that it might sound easy. But it isn't – it is a boring but important exercise. It also doesn't do much for your suntan – but with ginger hair and a few freckles that wasn't really a sacrifice.

But this is how you improve: constant muscle memory training. Later on, things began to get really exciting when I started to pot all the colours off their spots and, before potting the black, respotted them all and tried to gain position on the yellow so I could start all over again. I set myself a target of seeing how many times I could do this without missing a pot. When I got to 13 on the trot I felt confident that I had mastered it and relieved the monotony by moving on to some other challenging routines. None of this was monotonous to me at all but I am sure to others it would have been like pulling teeth.

My father and I had built up a marvellous rapport on the table over the years. I didn't enjoy being told what to do but I did it all the same. Yes, we had a few arguments along the way but I suppose that was inevitable. After a good night's sleep, I often conceded that he was probably in the right anyway.

I think there are two aspects to this: one is what a coach thinks a player should do and the other is a coach spotting what a player is doing and noticing over a period of time if things have changed. The latter was indisputable and indispensable for me as I couldn't see myself playing. The former was open to argument and discussion. My father and I usually had good discussions based on subjective stuff. Obviously, I couldn't argue too much about what I was actually doing, although, I think I tried to do so on a few occasions …

The art of being a good coach is to give a strong mental picture of what you want your pupil to achieve. The art of being a good pupil is to take this information on board and put this mental picture to good use. The two of us usually found the correct path sooner rather than later.

Therefore, I rarely suffered any extended loss of form and subsequently with this excellent, solid foundation, I found myself able to improve at a good rate. Arguably, some of the more naturally gifted players who may have poorer techniques have found their own improvement graph doesn't pan out so well. They may never have made the professional ranks, even though to their friends they looked every bit as capable as a Steve Davis or Jimmy White.

The question of natural ability versus hard work and dedication is often misunderstood. The difference is not too great. Some players who are easy on the eye – Jimmy White, Ronnie O'Sullivan, for example – are considered naturally gifted. Others – me, Mark Selby, for instance – are often pigeon-holed differently. It comes down to perception regarding different playing styles. For instance, a player who finds the game relatively easy will play with more fluidity. But he may also have been able to get away without developing a methodical pre-shot routine. Meanwhile, a fractionally less gifted player may have already decided that he needs more method in his game and perhaps has been more receptive down the years to going down that route.

The speed of a player can also have a bearing on how the layman perceives a player's inherent talent: fast equals naturally gifted while slow equals a workmanlike ability. Some slow players, such as the incredibly talented Peter Ebdon, for instance, can play faster and with greater perceived natural ability if they so wish, but choose to play with more control. The secret – in a nutshell – is getting the balance right in your own mind and for your own personality. Get it wrong in either part and you will not be able to allow your true ability to blossom. Get it right and the World Championship is a step closer.

My father was always obsessed with my technique and that became the basis of my natural game. Joe's book remained as important as ever. We would take it down to the club and use it as a reference when we practised. The biggest problem we had was interpreting Joe's dialogue, trying to make sense of what he actually meant. The book can be quite ambiguous and misleading in parts, mainly because of the terminology used.

So while it was our bible, it wasn't particularly clear on how a player should strike the ball. Obviously, it would have made perfect sense to Joe, but we found it difficult to follow. There are no diagrams in the book, just some pictures. As a result, we spent ages arguing about what the master actually meant.

'That is what it says there,' my father would often say to me down at the club.

But my father is not a professional; he is a 58-break player.

Sometimes when I didn't attack the ball with enough punch – the equivalent of a golfer swinging lazily through a shot – my father would tell me that I was 'pushing at the ball'. But I wasn't sure what he was getting at.

'What do you mean?' I would ask.

'You're just not hitting it properly,' he would reply.

'What do you mean?'

'It just doesn't look right.'

And so on, for about half an hour, until I asked: 'So, what if I pull the cue back shorter and then attack it more to get the same pace?'

I would then show him on the table.

'Yeah, that's it!'

My father wasn't necessarily the perfect coach, but we found a way of working together. He would stand in front of me and watch. He became my overseer. I was actually coaching myself to some degree but my father was my eyes because I didn't have a camera!

Essentially, I had to work out a mental picture in my head of what my father wanted me to look like – based on the Joe Davis book. I needed his reassurance every time I did something right and I needed telling whenever I did something wrong. I didn't want to fall into bad habits. We learned together: me as a player and him as a coach.

'Your back arm is not dead straight,' he would tell me.

'Is that right?' I would ask.

'A bit more,' he would say. 'Yes, that's right.'

Then, for the rest of the session, he would stand in front of me and wait to give a 'Yes' before I played; a bit like golfer Nick Faldo's caddie, Fanny Sunesson, did at some stage in the 1990s.

Together, my father and I would share the mental relief of finding the cause and the effect. He could see the effect and I had to find the cause. We worked towards finding a solution in almost robotic fashion – repeating it time and time again once we had found it.

We soon started to learn our new-found trades. And as he got better, I got better ...

For three years all I did was learn. I grafted hard to reach the perfection that both my tutor and I strived to achieve. Technically, my father was as sound as any other decent club player around, but what separates professionals from amateurs is the quality and consistency of the strike and the picture in the brain that tells you where the next shot is coming from. Satellite navigation (for the all-important positional side of the game) is imperative. And these days if you have a dodgy one, you need to upgrade it pronto.

But my father always knew what should be done and how to go about doing it. He was brilliant in that respect. I couldn't have had a better man by my side. The dedication we both channelled into my snooker at that time was extraordinary. Nothing else mattered during those years.

My school friends lived a totally different life from me. I was in my own little world of snooker from now on. There was absolutely no doubt in my mind that this was the game for me. As my standard improved, I started to wonder how good I actually was. Once I turned sixteen, I wanted to test myself in national junior competitions and put my name down for the under-19 English Snooker and Billiards Championships.

The first round took place in Essex and I faced a useful player, who I still keep in touch with to this day, called Paul Smith. His game was handicapped by the loss of an eye in an air pistol accident. I had a chance to win at 2–1 up but I missed a red with the long rest and it cost me. Paul won 3–2. Later on, he beat me in the billiards competition as well! But I never found out how he fared in the final stages of these events. Bad losers never do!

I recorded my first half-century break at Plumstead Common Working Men's Club shortly afterwards. What made it even sweeter was that I did it against the club's best player and a real snooker enthusiast, Bert Steele, who was arguably the biggest snooker fan in the club.

Bert wanted to compete, improve and go to the big snooker events and rub shoulders with the stars. He also wanted to play the shots that the stars played and play the big shots under pressure that he saw them play, too. He loved the game and later opened two snooker clubs of his own, such was his passion for it. Bert was one of the best players in the whole league. I celebrated my achievement with him buying me half a lager and lime and a packet of cheese and onion crisps!

Another regular at the club was Dick Sharples, a kindly old fellow and the only man who had ever made a century at billiards at that place. He had given up playing the game as his eyesight deteriorated with age and now assumed the job of brushing and ironing the tables and retipping the cues.

Dick would watch me play billiards – a bit like Yoda would watch Luke Skywalker in *Star Wars* – and even though his own standard was probably only proficient, he showed me glimpses of how the game should be played and that taught me a lot.

Players used to keep their cues at the club – hung up in metal cases – and Dick knew which cue belonged to which club member. When somebody passed away, he would 'acquire' their cue and so he had quite a collection of them. Every now and again, he would bring out this cue – his prized possession – to demonstrate a few shots for me.

It was a lovely piece of wood. One night, my father unexpectedly came home with it. Dick had told him that he wanted me, and nobody else, to have it. A month later he died. Looking back, I think he always wanted me to have that cue. It became very special to me. It was a Ye Olde Ash made by Burroughes & Watts. It wasn't the top of their range but it was higher up the ladder than the legendary Burwat Champion that some of the other players drooled over a decade later.

I passed O levels in English literature, maths, physics and French that summer, but snooker dominated my studies. Every Monday morning my French teacher would ask me what I'd done at the weekend and I would always reply in French that I had been playing snooker all weekend! *'J'ai joué au snooker,'* was my standard reply. I decided to stay on at school and study A levels in maths and physics. I did so without having any real affinity with either subject, but it meant that I could continue to play snooker far more easily than having to take a job that interfered with my studies of the game!

I took a weekend job in a butcher's department at a local supermarket – working ten hours a day for 28p an hour – to continue to help pay for my snooker education.

After my first week there I realised I had a problem that would afflict me for the rest of my life. With wage packet in hand, I took my first steps into the sordid world of vinyl addiction! I bought 'Heart of Gold' by Neil Young for what I recall was 49p. I bottled getting the album for that was a wage-breaking two quid!

A year on, I thought I had hit the big time. I landed a job in the autumn at Makro Cash & Carry in Charlton. My wages were up to 88p an hour: I was rolling in it. Three months later, I was given my notice. I walked into the manager's office, thinking there must be some mistake.

'No mistake,' I was told. 'You were only temporary staff in the build-up to Christmas.'

I was devastated. Years later, I was back in the same manager's office – after a signing session for *Pot Black* small tables as world snooker champion – for some hospitality sandwiches and tea. I had to say something:

'The last time I was in here, I got the sack!' I said in mock diva style.

The manager looked puzzled. I explained what had happened and he went off to check the old staff registers. Sure enough, he found that I was once a mere barrow boy and he had given me the axe!

I continued to improve on the table and after being stuck on 52 for what seemed quite a while my top break rose steadily through the sixties to the eighties. I remember seeming to be stuck on 88 for what felt like forever! Until, one day, lo and behold, my first century arrived.

I was still sixteen and it came against John 'the Butcher' late one afternoon. I can still remember nervously potting the pink to reach 102. But after sinking the final red with my next shot, the cue ball hit the yellow and went in-off. There was a possible 137 on the table as well! Regardless, I was reeling with excitement afterwards: I couldn't wait for my father to come home from work so I could tell him the exciting news.

I now truly expected the floodgates to open regarding century breaks. My 'breaks book', where I kept a record of 50-plus breaks, was filling up quite nicely. But I had to wait eight months before another century came along. Once again, I found that expectation can block natural ability and trying too hard is how it can manifest itself.

In the spring of 1975, my father and I set off in our C-registration 1965 Mini Countryman for a bone-shaking 90-minute trip over London Bridge and across London, then we were on to the M1 and up the M6 to Nantwich, in Cheshire, for the under-19s British snooker and billiards competition qualifiers.

'I'm Not in Love' by 10cc was number one in the charts at the time. So, 10cc and Minis are forever inextricably linked in my brain. It is also possible that the reason for that is because our 750cc Countryman felt like it was a 10cc as it chugged up the motorway.

I felt pretty raw as I lost to Peter Bardsley. The junior player who cleaned up in both the snooker and billiards competitions was Eugene Hughes, of Ireland, a future world number 20.

The following year, in the same event, I came up against a highly rated young player called Tony Meo at Ron Gross's famous snooker club in Neasden, north-west London.

This place was a hotbed for the top players in London at the time. Roger Brown, Geoff Foulds and Wally West were all drawn to this club, as was Patsy Fagan, who had recently turned professional. These were all big names on the local scene. Big-money matches were lined up for Patsy against the likes of Alex Higgins and Co. and these became part of folklore.

Ron was a real character, too. He was an old-school semi-professional – he won the English Amateur Championship three times – and it would be fair to say that his style of play was … cautious. A bit like Terry Griffiths on Valium!

Ron wasn't helped by the fact that he was born with an unformed left leg and had to wear old-fashioned metal callipers that bent at the knee. He could lock it in to play and this gave him more support. So he effectively played with two straight legs. His body developed natural balance to compensate and his spatial awareness and balance were superb.

Ron was the life and soul of the place and he held court majestically until the whisky finally got the better of him on the night. It was quite common to see him tumble to the floor, falling backwards. But his innate balancing skill, albeit impaired, was of gyroscopic quality. As he fell, he always managed to keep hold of the glass in his hand that at all times during the tumble remained perfectly level.

Tony Meo and I played each other on Grand National day and I remember we were told to stop playing when the race was on – Rag Trade beat Red Rum on the home straight that day to deny him an historic, third win. Rummy would have to wait yet another year for his hat-trick.

Also in the club that day was a thirteen-year-old called Jimmy White. He had a broken leg at the time and was playing shots with a walking stick! Everybody knew Jimmy. He was obviously very special, even at that age.

Both Tony and Jimmy came from Tooting, in south London, and, of course, both of them would become big names in snooker in the future. In fact, in what seemed like no time at all, the three of us would soon be part of the game's new Rat Pack. I beat Tony 3–1 to qualify for the final stages of the English Junior Snooker and Billiards Championship in Leeds.

Off we went in our Mini Countryman again. I was listed as one of the favourites and got as far as the semi-finals in the snooker competition, where I lost to Ian Williamson, 3–1. Three hours later, I beat the same player in the final of the billiards competition to win my first national title.

Once I turned eighteen and was eligible, I entered the English amateur snooker championship, where I lost 4–2 to Brian Tresidder, at the Acton Snooker Centre. I felt I was a better cueist than him but I was still in need of more match experience.

We had a referee in his late seventies and he couldn't see too well. At one stage I had a touching ball on a red, which should have meant an easy safety shot to put my opponent in trouble. But I had to ask for it because the referee hadn't spotted it. He eventually proceeded to take a packet of Rizla cigarette papers out of his pocket, remove a single sheet and – with shaking hands – force it between the two balls and they parted. He pulled up the paper and the balls fell together again. Somehow he declared they were not touching. I didn't argue but, on reflection, perhaps I should have sought a second opinion. However, the marker was even older than he was!

I was now in the Plumstead Common Working Men's Club team in both billiards and snooker. It was a no-brainer once I had turned eighteen as I was comfortably the best player in the league and something of a secret weapon for them. All I could think of doing with my life was playing snooker.

The cost of a light above a table was just 5p for half an hour in those days, so it wasn't exactly costing a fortune for me to play. Social clubs didn't change their prices too much – just enough to keep the tables in good condition – but snooker clubs would charge more.

However, the cost of playing the game has always been relatively cheap – even during the boom era of the 1980s. To some degree the inability of snooker clubs to charge enough to be big, profitable concerns during those boom years ultimately held them back and, with limited funds for renovation, they slowly deteriorated. As the game moved into a new era, rents and rates increased and the luxury of snooker clubs in the high street declined. Sadly, by the turn of the century, a lot of clubs started to close down as a result.

I don't actually remember ever having a serious chat about my future with my parents but, as I reached the end of my allotted time at school, my mother did go to the council and obtained an application form for a clerical appointment in the finance department! She also popped in to the local branch of Barclays Bank to inquire about job vacancies.

Like 99.9 per cent of kids, I didn't really have a clue about what I wanted to do for a living. But I did know that I wanted to play snooker. I was besotted with the game, even though I hadn't even considered if there could be a career in it.

There were so few professional players that it wasn't even on the radar and, to be honest, I don't really remember thinking that I could ever have been good enough to play professionally. I certainly didn't have the dream that a football-mad boy would have of playing at Wembley Stadium. I just wanted to play snooker: full stop.

My father, on the other hand, wanted to give me a proper chance of trying to keep on improving. By now, I was getting a reputation locally as the best player in the area and we were starting to look further afield on an amateur level.

One night, as I was driving my father home from the working men's club with the L plates on (the idea being that he could supervise me learning to drive and get tanked up at the same time!), he shared some happy news with me:

'I've had a chat with Mum, Steve,' he said as he chewed on his cigar while I kept my eyes on the road. 'We've decided to fund you for a year to play snooker. So you don't have to go on the dole and we will see how it goes.'

I was absolutely delighted. But, looking back, I can just imagine my mother going: 'What?'

I am sure this would not have been an easy conversation for either of them to have in our council flat. It wasn't as if there was a pot of gold at the end of the rainbow. I am still not sure what crystal ball my father was looking into – but it turned out he was something of a visionary! This was the best present that I could ever have received from them.

You don't choose your parents and they don't choose you, but each one of us is a blend of both of them. On the surface, my mother and father are normal working-class people and followed normal paths in their lives. They made me what I am.

Our household was a place of common sense and a high standard of intelligence. This provided a solid foundation for me. I owe my parents everything. They gave me a chance to get out of the rat race! I left school the following week and I never looked back.

3. SLIDING DOORS

The first words I ever heard him say were: 'I've heard a lot about you!'

Standing in front of me was a man in a suit and tie. And he did stand out. He was the only bloke in the snooker club wearing a suit and tie so I quickly understood that this was the man who my friend Vic Harris had told me about. Vic called him 'the Governor'.

I was practising on the popular Table 13 – right next to the bar – with Vic at the Lucania snooker club, on Arcade Place, in Romford.

'Vic tells me that you're a great young player,' said the man in the suit. 'Obviously the Lucania Championship is coming up and it's only open to regular club members. But if you're prepared to come over here three times a week, I'll see if I can get you into the event.'

The Lucania Championship was one of the reasons why I was playing on Table 13 in Romford. It was a new one-day amateur snooker tournament that had quickly gained notoriety in the London area with a massive £1,000 on offer in prize money.

'Thank you very much,' I said as I got down and continued my game. The Governor returned to his office downstairs. As first meetings go, it was short and sharp and he did all the talking. A true 'sliding doors' moment if ever there was one.

This was my first encounter with Barry Hearn.

Barry started life as a chartered accountant. In the early 1970s, he was in charge of an investment company and bought a chain of billiard halls for their asset value. He wasn't a snooker fan in those days. He was a businessman.

There wasn't much business in snooker at that time and billiard halls had a reputation for being used by the unemployed and the unruly. Others would go down there to spend their money in the slot machines. In fact, the one-arm bandit was often the lifeblood of these places and kept them going.

During the afternoons in those days snooker clubs were populated by, as well as the unemployed, the self-employed, villains and some good players. The good players were able to earn a fair amount of money for themselves – at least enough to continue playing all day – against some of the less able souls who came through the door. In such circumstances, these players could be viewed as predators with a steady stream of smaller fry to feast on.

Some of these guys hustled, trying to hoodwink unsuspecting opponents by concealing their true standard of play until the final sting. Others pitted their wits fairly and squarely, with perhaps the slightest edge, in organised money matches.

There were numerous handicap systems in place to lure other potential victims: head starts in points, the cue ball not being allowed to hit a cushion, the yellow always being the nominated colour, left-handed, one-handed, you name it. A talented player who didn't want to work in a normal day job because he was so besotted with snooker could find a way to put food on the table in these money-making dens.

I was a talented and besotted snooker player myself, but my situation was quite different from others'. My horizon was to change dramatically with the explosion of live televised snooker in the late 1970s. I was in the right place at the right time. Had I been born ten years earlier, my story might well have been different. As it was, due to circumstances, the most I ever played for was £25 of my own money.

At the time this was the only way for average to lower professional players to make any money from the game. There were hardly any tournaments around and so there was hardly any prize money to be won. Apart from the World Championship for the select few and the exhibition circuit enjoyed by former world champions such as Ray Reardon, John Spencer and the like, the sport was considered a working-class pastime and anybody who was any good at it sadly had the reputation of ... yes ... a misspent youth.

This was the world of snooker that Barry bought into when he purchased the Lucania chain of billiard halls. Most of the clubs were based in London – although there was also one in Hitchin, in Hertfordshire, and Stroud, in Gloucestershire – and stood above Burton's tailors in high streets.

Many of them had town centre locations and so there was the value of the properties to fall back on if it didn't work out. But Barry got lucky, very lucky. At around the same time, BBC television coverage was starting to transform the appeal of snooker and the game suddenly became popular with a new audience. Snooker halls were now in vogue. And the queues began to form...

By the time I reached my late teens, I was ready to venture outside the world of Plumstead Common Working Men's Club in search of more competitive and testing standards. I was hungry for stronger competition. I had only had brief glimpses of these better players during competitive regional matches.

Fate took us over to New Eltham Social Club one night to watch an exhibition match involving the likes of true quality players such as Pat Houlihan, Marcus Owen, David Taylor and the CIU champion, John Beech. Pat and Marcus, in particular, were underground cult heroes in London at the time.

Pat was a bit of a scallywag. He was the Jimmy White of his era. He had the gift of the gab and used his supreme talent to generate a buzz in the clubs. He didn't disguise what he had but he did think of original ways to make money through it. He offered a variety of incentives to unsuspecting prey (or besotted masochists) to relieve them of their hard-earned cash. But he did it in such a way that they would come back with just enough hope for another spin of the double-sided coin! It was either that or to witness a great player at work.

That is how Pat earned his money. Not everybody is a purist who wants to play for the love of the game. Some people get off on having a bet. So part of the history of snooker has always been about people in the club putting a wager on. That will always be there and guys like Pat took advantage. How else could they fund their true passion and talent in life?

Marcus was the most feared of all unofficial professionals and part-time players in London. He was a bit like Dick Turpin in a sense. He also reached the quarter-finals of the Park Drive World Championship in Manchester in 1974.

I was thrilled to be in his company later that night. He invited me over to the Leyton Midland Club, in Leytonstone, where he was based. I didn't need asking twice and so the next morning, with cue in hand, I set off on an hour and a half bus trip to visit him.

What I found when I got there wasn't a pretty sight. It was seedy beyond belief and far more intimidating than the working men's clubs I had grown up with, which in comparison felt totally respectable establishments to me, even bordering on palatial in parts.

This club was squeezed into a narrow archway underneath a railway line and it shook every time a train went over. When it rained water seeped down the walls. Inside this place were four snooker tables crammed into a downstairs area. Rumour had it that there were two more upstairs, but the place was so eerie that I never found out for myself for fear of meeting Freddy Krueger up there, or, more likely, dry rot. I would be surprised if Ron, the owner, possessed a working vacuum cleaner or a table brush with bristles. The place was grim. Money was hidden under the soap.

I loved it! It was a home to real snooker players – not working men's club members who just played for a bit of fun. These men truly loved the competitive challenge that the game offered them. There was no beer around. Just tea and coffee and half a dozen bread rolls that the owner went out to collect at midday from the corner shop bakery. To this day, these rolls remain the best I have ever tasted. There was a choice of ham, cheese or ham and cheese. Sometimes, there was no ham, which made the menu pretty limiting!

When those six rolls had gone, that was it. There was no more. Just a cup of tea with plenty of sugar and snooker talk. We all lived for snooker. But we found that we couldn't really play without having some money on the outcome – not huge amounts but enough to give the game an edge. I couldn't get enough of the place. We were all in awe of players like Alex Higgins and Ray Reardon. I was in there from 12 noon to 6 p.m. every other day. It also took me three hours every day to get there and back.

This was my first regular experience of life on my own outside Plumstead Common. I played a game called Points against a selection of decent players and gamblers, where you earned a tanner a point (probably worth about 20p today) from the previous striker for every point scored. Every shot had to be effectively nominated to prevent any bad feeling surrounding flukes. A double couldn't be a treble and intended pockets had to be named. The order was also changed after every frame so nobody followed the same player twice in a row.

Six months later the stakes had doubled to the dizzy heights of five pence a point. This was a lot of money for me. But I was already considered one of the best players in the club and the handicap system used would never give the less talented players anything more than a little bit of air while they were strangled!

When I made two breaks of 90 and 99 within half an hour of each other, I won nearly £10. I recognised from the reaction of the other players as they threw their money on the table for me to pick up that perhaps this again wasn't quite cricket and that maybe it was time for me to move on and find somewhere else to play.

One thing I hadn't managed on the number one table was a century break. But I knew about a man who had. His name was Vic Harris. He played at the Lucania club, up the road in Romford. The manager there, Les Coates, had once played snooker at Plumstead Common Working Men's Club, too, and he told me great tales about a great man: Vic had been Essex snooker champion four times and was acknowledged as one of the best amateurs in the whole country. Furthermore, he had just whitewashed Wally Broomfield – a player I respected greatly at Leytonstone – 3–0 in the Essex Championship on Wally's home table!

At around the same time, an advert had been placed in the monthly *Snooker Scene* magazine for a one-day event with a £1,000 prize fund – but you had to be a regular member of one of the Lucania chain of snooker clubs to take part. I wasn't but Vic was. I wanted to play against the best players around to test myself anyway and I was finding my feet as a player, gaining confidence and hungry for better opposition. In some ways I was like a gunslinger seeking out the man. So I decided to go over there and try and kill two birds with one stone.

It was an even longer bus journey to Romford than the one I was making to Leytonstone! It was two hours door to door: a bus to Woolwich Ferry, a walk through the ferry tunnel, another bus to Manor Park – the 147 bus also used part of this route and I would dream of making a maximum almost every time I saw it – and, finally, the 86 bus on to Romford.

Wednesdays were carnage. This was market day in Romford and all the eager grannies were out in force. As soon as a number 86 was spotted on the horizon, it was mayhem as they all jostled for position at the bus stop.

Like the young gent I was, I always gave up a seat and stood graciously in the aisle for the whole journey with my one-piece cue case in hand. It was quite common for this to act as a handrail whenever the driver brought the bus to a sudden halt. The fact that it was made of the latest fake black leather plastic made no difference at all when you had hold of a handbag and your best market-day shoes were on your feet.

Vic was about thirty at the time and worked as a lorry driver for a soft drinks company. But he never missed his two o'clock appointment at the snooker club. Les introduced me to him and we got on with each other from the off. After a few frames, we started to play in a much more relaxed manner and chatted about the game in general. Vic wasn't your usual snooker hall hustler. He just loved the game and perhaps he wasn't in need of fleecing his opponents to fund his habit. I think he quickly identified the same traits in me.

In no time at all, the two of us were meeting up there three times a week. Vic was impressed by what I could do on a snooker table, so much so that he told the owner of the Lucania chain that he thought I could be a future world champion. He also told me that he would put a word in for me with the Governor about the forthcoming Lucania Championship.

Les had also raved to Barry Hearn about me. So two credible sources had now informed the owner of the Lucania that something had walked through his doors that didn't walk through his doors too often.

When Barry popped upstairs to see me, I was deep in concentration. As usual, there was a decent crowd hanging around watching as well. Apparently what struck him immediately about me was my clinical approach to the game in what was quite an intimidating atmosphere. The verbal in there could be brutal. Vic, in particular, was a master in winding people up.

Vic and I never played against each other for money; maybe just a cup of tea and the 'tables' (to determine who paid for the lights) but nothing more. We played for the love of the game. I was learning and improving all the time and that was enough for me. Neither of us seemed driven by money anyhow. He earned his living away from snooker and, while he may have taken part in some money matches here and there, I can't recall him ever feeding off the aforementioned fish. Overall, I felt that my standard of play was getting closer to his every time we met.

My standard in video arcade games was also improving. The Lucania always had the latest ones as Barry also now had an interest in a fruit machine company. Defender was my favourite. Obviously, we were all besotted with the original game, Space Invaders, as well. But I used to get very agitated with Pac-Man. It was OK for the first three or four levels and then it started to panic me when they got faster and faster. It was clear that I was much better at games where I decided when the objects should move. We all fell in love with those games in Romford. Every other town and club in the land did likewise.

It was a claim to fame to be the best in the club at Space Invaders or whatever. Nobody knew who this would be until the machine was installed and the next hero recorded a top score. We would then all stand around in awe, watching him play on the machine. It was hilarious, really.

It was like the electronic version of pinball wizard for a while. I was good. I had decent coordination and I enjoyed playing on the machines very much. But I was never quite up to Tommy standard.

The best video-gamer in the club was a young guy we called 'Screwy Louie'. He was also a very talented snooker player. He got his nickname from his preference always to play screw shots. He was brilliant at them. His party piece was to put the ball over a top corner pocket and the cue ball in the jaws of the long diagonal corner pocket. He would then stand on a chair, pot the ball and screw back into baulk.

The games machines made a racket but I never minded the noise. It was all part of the atmosphere. Life in snooker clubs is all about having a bit of a laugh anyway and you can zone in and out of it. I would often be there on my favourite Table 13 – close to the bar and the fruit machines – doing my solo practice when somebody would suddenly scream out that they had just got the highest score on Missile Command and jump for joy.

Largely due to the success of *Pot Black*, snooker had become quite popular and the Lucania clubs had become popular as a result. Barry's idea to hold the Lucania Championship in September was so that players would frequent his clubs in the summer, which was the quietest time of the year for business.

But there were strict rules in terms of entering the competition. It was limited to regular members only of the twenty Lucania clubs. Barry wanted to keep out the sharks, he said, and, while being impressed by my overall play and professional attitude, he recognised that I was very much a new kid on the block. His idea behind the competition was to reward those men who used his facilities throughout the year.

Barry immediately impressed me. I wouldn't say he was overbearing but he wasn't backwards in coming forwards. He organised things with panache as well. He has incredible enthusiasm and is a great salesman with a massive passion for sport. I liked him straight away.

I remained on standby in case anybody dropped out of the Lucania Championship at the last minute. I carried on playing at Romford three times a week, continuing to cross the Thames there and back to play against Vic and some of the other top players in the area. In addition, I was still playing regularly with my father at Plumstead Common Working Men's Club, where he was able to keep a close eye on my technique.

One day, out of the blue, the public address system at Plumstead Common kicked into action with the following words: 'Phone call for Steve Davis.' I was in shock. Who could want to speak to me?

We didn't have a phone at home. My father didn't like them, so I wasn't used to them either. I walked from the snooker room through the lounge area to the front entrance to pick up the one and only payphone in the place, which was manned by the same Jobsworth who checked your membership when you walked through the door.

'Hello,' I said.

'Hello, Steve, it's Barry Hearn,' came the reply down the line – he didn't know me well enough by then to call me Davis!

'Oh, hello,' I said.

'I just wanted to let you know that somebody has dropped out of the Lucania Championship and you're in,' he said. 'We've seeded you at number six. Good luck. And I'll see you next week.'

'Thank you,' I said. I placed the phone down and walked back through the club on cloud nine.

My junior club nemesis, Paul Smith, had pulled out of the competition due to work commitments. True to his word, Barry offered me his place straight away and I was made up to be able to compete against all the other top players around.

What a day it was! Every one of the clubs was represented and supporters came along to Romford to cheer on their men. A couple of the Romford members made a book. Betting was big business. It was like all the local gunslingers had met up in one place to do battle.

Furthermore, while everybody knew the names of the very good players, nobody knew what standard very good actually was. Everybody assumed their man was the best until he was forced to walk away with his tail between his legs, proffering excuses to his supporters who had blown their money on backing him, after coming up against somebody who was found to be better.

The competition kicked off at 10.30 a.m. with eight tables in action for the best-of-three-frames knockout matches. It was by far the most exciting competition I had ever played in. I managed to get down to the last eight, where I came up against Vic, who was seeded two. I suppose it was inevitable that we would have to play each other.

The match was watched by a crowd of over 250 and the tension was tremendous. We were locked at 1–1 and Vic was 23 points ahead with just the colours left. I played a safety shot on the yellow but it struck the brown and trundled into the middle pocket. I cleared the table to win on the black and reach the last four.

In the semi-finals, I beat Wally West, of Hounslow Lucania, 2–0, and then faced Geoff Foulds – father of the future World Championship semi-finalist Neal Foulds – in the final. Geoff was one of the best players in London; very strong tactically and a hard man to play against. In the end, his overall experience proved too much for me and he beat me 3–1.

I received a cheque for £260 (£60 in prize money and £200 in sponsorship for the forthcoming season) and a runners-up trophy. This was my biggest pay day so far. It felt like I had won the Pools. Interest in me at the Romford Lucania started to grow.

The question was: 'How good is Steve Davis going to be?' To a large extent, I now took over from Vic as the local hero. The master could have been forgiven for turning into something of a green-eyed monster at this stage, especially as our match had been decided on a fluke. But, to his credit, he seemed much more excited about my future in the game. He felt I had exceptional potential and that far outweighed any good-natured local rivalry that we had.

There was a further prize in store. Barry arranged for Geoff and me to go on an all-expenses-paid snooker tour of the country, where we could play against the best amateurs around. This is where Barry is different. Any normal owner of a chain of snooker clubs may have done exactly what Barry did: put up a big prize, encourage regular members to compete, create a buzz and generate interest in the brand. But the true entrepreneur thinks outside the box. Barry looked outside of his clubs. He was excited by the game, the atmosphere and the people involved. Snooker talent was starting to evolve in every part of the United Kingdom, although Scotland was a little slow off the mark. The game was gathering momentum and good players were coming out of the woodwork.

Our first stop was Grimsby, where I played Mike Hallett, who was a couple of years younger than me and would one day become world number six. Then we went up to Edinburgh and back down to Dudley, in the West Midlands. We also went over to Bolton, where I met another up-and-coming young player, a couple of years older than me, called Tony Knowles. He was to be another member of the new Rat Pack.

Geoff was from another generation. He had a family and a full-time job and, perhaps, his aspirations for being a full-time professional were tempered by his responsibilities at home. This was the first time I realised that to get to the next level it probably helped if you were young and could play full time.

The tour became a logistical headache for him. He did all the driving on that trip but with the carburettor of our hired car on the blink, it took ages for us to get from one venue to the next. After a while, he suddenly decided that he'd had enough and told Barry that he wanted to pull out.

Barry came up to see us in Birmingham and accepted the situation, but he was firm in his opinion that the show must go on. That was good news for me. I had my cue and wanted to travel. So, he telephoned another player, Russell Jarmak, who lived down in Kent and had been a losing semi-finalist in the Lucania event, and asked him to replace Geoff.

The problem was that Geoff took the spluttering hired car with him, meaning Barry now had the job of driving us to Wales to play against Terry Griffiths, of Llanelli, a world champion in the making and another big name for the future, such was the way the game was developing and transforming itself. When Barry had to return to London on business, Russell and I were left to slum it on the train from then on. So we got on Ivor the Engine at Grumbly Station (minding the big, scary dragon as we went on our way).

More new locations and legends – such as Leeds, where I faced Doug French, and Liverpool, where I played George Scott – followed. We played against two top players in each area we visited. Barry's interest was huge. We checked in with him each morning with a progress report and it felt great to be in a team that was essentially taking on the country. We could feel Barry's enthusiasm and support wherever we went. This was long before the days of mobile telephones as well. The whole experience was a journey into the unknown for me; living the life of a nationwide gunslinger out of a suitcase. I absolutely loved it!

I remained a regular at Romford Lucania and received tremendous support from Barry, Vic and others there, including Mark Lazarus, a former professional footballer who scored the winning goal for Queens Park Rangers in the 1967 League Cup final at Wembley. Mark's brother, Lew, was a boxer who fought for the British welterweight and middleweight titles and Mark's son, Nicky, turned out to be a talented snooker professional for a while, too.

There was always something going on there. Lois jeans were big at this time and suddenly everybody in the club seemed to have a pair! At Christmas, Table 2 was turned into a market stall selling Christmas paper, perfume and Parker pens (these were hot thanks to a television advert that assured everybody you could now write upside down in a spaceship should you find yourself so disposed!).

I was now starting to get some local media coverage, too. This included a rather embarrassing television interview with Janet Street-Porter on *The London Weekend Show*, which was a youth programme for London and the Home Counties.

She was all teeth and glasses, as you might expect, and I was dressed in green trousers with my ginger mop, nervously moving my hand up and down my cue while speaking to her. I suggest you check out the clip on YouTube to get the full effect. I am still living it down!

I was buzzing with excitement afterwards and returned to Plumstead Common with my make-up intact, clutching the script. It is fair to say that eyeliner wasn't too popular among the young males in our community at that time! We were still a few years away from New Romantics and the like so, no doubt, I got some funny looks in the club that night.

I proudly recorded my first ever maximum 147 break in front of my father at Plumstead Common a few days before my twentieth birthday. It was a special moment. For years I had wondered what it would be like to join the 147 Club. I often used to pass that 147 bus on my way to Romford and wonder if it might be a lucky omen of sorts. I had come close, falling just three balls short when I missed a difficult blue on one occasion, and on the day before I achieved my maximum, I hit breaks of 139 and 133 so I knew that I was in good form and that it was, hopefully, only going to be a matter of time.

Tony Meo had made a 147 in practice a few months earlier and was rewarded by appearing on the front cover of *Snooker Scene*. I remember being very envious of that and, perhaps, a little apprehensive that there were other young players around, bubbling under the surface. I also wondered if I would ever get a chance to make it on to the front cover of the magazine myself.

I would practise endlessly. Getting somebody to smash the balls off the black cushion and then try and make century breaks, concentrating on potting the black after every red. While it had no value compared to making a maximum in a competitive match it was excellent practice in itself. If there were fewer than ten reds available, the balls would be set up again and another attempt would be made at a century break.

Solo practice in the afternoons at Plumstead would come with a bottle of Guinness and a cheese and onion roll on offer. I would reward myself with a sip of the black stuff after a 50 break and a bite of the roll when I got to 100. That was how I started to challenge myself. When I practised by myself there was no competition as such so I had to come up with other ideas. It was fun. I couldn't cheat. I wasn't allowed to. I would only be cheating myself anyway.

When making my first ever 147, I sank 15 reds and 15 blacks and was positioned nicely on the yellow. I started to quiver a little inside but I felt fully in control. Funnily enough, the biggest problem I faced was when the rather large wife of a regular member brushed past me on her way back from the bar after being utilised as a waitress by her husband. I was knocked off line as I settled down to pot the brown. I stood up, composed myself and cleared the remaining four balls, shaking like a leaf! My father later told me he would have strangled the woman if I had missed. Although, in a fair fight, I think she would probably have won.

I potted the blue and the pink but left myself too close to the cushion on the black. I was about three inches from the side cushion and dead straight. It wasn't an easy shot at all and I was forced to roll it in. The black hit the near-jaw of the pocket and moved across to the far-jaw of the pocket and hung there for ages before dropping in. I couldn't believe it. I was in ecstasy.

A scorching hot day had turned into a sweltering evening down at the club and the French windows to the snooker room were wide open. Perhaps that helped me make my maximum – for I could now see the balls clearly for a change rather than having my sight obstructed by a mandatory thick smoky haze under the shade that often resembled a bad dose of 1950s London smog.

I celebrated by running out through the French windows and back into the club by the main entrance in an improvised lap of honour. On returning to the snooker room, I was met by rapturous applause and dozens of handshakes. It was great that my father was there to share the moment with me. The first person I called to break the news was Barry. I then celebrated by everybody buying me lagers. I can't remember who drove home that night – but it was most probably via all the back-doubles!

Full of confidence, I was counting down the days to another top event at the Romford Lucania. Barry had well and truly got the snooker bug by now and he was revelling in the excitement of the buzz of organising events. He also played the game most days and it was funny watching the sharks trying to prise a few quid out of him on occasions, thinking he was easy meat. He wasn't. Many times he turned the tables on the hunter. He has a respectable highest break of around 60 and got huge pleasure out of playing the game.

Barry turned his attention to organising a pro-am event featuring Patsy Fagan, Doug Mountjoy, Ray Reardon and Dennis Taylor up against Geoff Foulds, Vic Harris, Russell Jarmak and me. The amateurs were given 14-point starts in each frame. John Smyth was booked as the referee.

We had a ready-made room for such occasions at Romford – away from the main snooker hall that housed 13 tables. There were a further six tables in there but on special occasions five of them were moved out of the way to leave just one main table in the centre of the room. The rest were jacked up and placed against the walls, where they were boarded up with chairs on top of them to create a real match arena.

There was no fire exit and no windows and we had up to 300 people crammed in there; a lot of them were smokers as well. There was a fair amount of wood and flammable cloth, too. Health and safety, eat your heart out!

As these matches became more popular, eventually we were left with just one table in the middle of the room with dedicated seating around it. This room subsequently became known as the Matchroom. Barry's wife would often be the only woman in there. She used to sit quietly while all this shouting and swearing was going on around her. Every now and then you would hear somebody say, 'Sorry, Mrs Hearn!'

I still enjoyed playing in the main hall. All good players gravitate to the tables by the bar in a snooker club and I was no different. It is more fun there and more people are watching you. However, the table in the Matchroom was kept to a very high standard and as time went by I began to realise the benefit of practising on the best cloth in favour of the buzz that might be supplied elsewhere. The room later became a private members' club with mirrors, strip lights and carpet up the walls. It was posh and high class by snooker standards. Obviously, the name of the club has since become synonymous with Barry's successful business empire.

On a very exciting day, when the place was packed to the rafters with raucous Romford support, Geoff beat Patsy, Vic beat Doug, Russell beat Dennis and I completed an am-pro whitewash with a great 3–2 win over Ray. It was unbelievable. The place was going absolutely barmy.

There was a little bit of needle between Ray and me in our match. He snookered me on the last red in one frame but rather than leaving the ball in a potable position, I elected to play off three cushions, knowing that if I didn't hit it, at least I wouldn't gift the game to him. This was in the days before the modern interpretation of the miss rule, of course.

Ray found it impossible not to comment to the crowd about my shot. In a loud voice, he roared: 'And he calls himself a billiards player!' Obviously, he thought that I had deliberately missed the ball. Such tactics had started to become an issue in the game. But this wasn't true. Effectively, the original rules of the game hadn't foreseen any exploitation of its weaknesses and the fact that a player could gain an advantage by not hitting a ball needed to be addressed. The younger players were no different from the older players in this regard: we were all working out the best shot to play in a given situation. If the tactical nuances meant that a player wasn't gifting his opponent the frame, then that would be the right shot for him to play.

To be fair, Ray had been around for years and may have encountered this situation many times before. Maybe he had already seen the implications of it and the shape of things to come. But the new kids on the block hadn't given it too much thought. We played by the rules. As time went on, the interpretation of the miss rule was to come under even greater scrutiny than Ray observed that night.

On a lighter note, as the night continued, Barry came up to me – beaming from ear to ear – and told me that he had placed an even-money bet on an amateur to win the title, had me at odds of 6–1 to win it, and had backed all four of us to win our quarter-final matches before the event had kicked off! Talk about all your bets coming in at once ...

As it turned out, Geoff beat Vic and I beat Russell in two close semi-finals before I got my revenge for my Lucania Championship final defeat by beating Geoff in the final, at close to 2 a.m. The trophy and £200 winnings were mine to keep. Yet compared to Barry's winnings, it was pretty small change. I think it was this night that started off a regular policy of Barry – and quite a few others – betting on me whenever and wherever I played.

It was due to this that I earned my nickname of 'the Golden Nugget'. I was more than happy with that. The Nugget is a famous casino in Nevada. To me, the name translated into money in the bank, a dead cert. The Romford Roar felt that I was such a surefire bet that it was like buying money. I was a sound investment – money in the bank.

I won the Lucania Championship that year. This time I met Russell in the final and I beat him in a very close affair, again in the early hours. I was now definitely the top Lucania dog. Barry was on a roll, too. He told Geoff, Vic and me that he was going to organise matches for us against top professionals in the Matchroom. Before I knew it, I was up against John Spencer, the current world champion. I was given a 14-point start but I didn't seem to need it as I thrashed him, 5–1. This result helped to build my confidence even more and once again underlined that I was one to watch.

It has to be said that these matches were obviously played with me having home table advantage, not to mention most of the crowd on my side. From the professional's point of view, it was a hiding to nothing, really. They were paid to turn up just as they would be for an exhibition. Often, it was just wages for them. I don't think there was any extra on the table for them if they beat me. Their only incentive was pride. Some of them, particularly Alex Higgins, did have a side bet. There was always somebody running a book in some corner of the club.

Barry had a sixth sense of how to generate interest in these nights. He knew they would sell out and that they were great for business. A lot of gamblers were drawn to snooker clubs in those days. So a lot of people were having bets on these matches and the stakes could get very high. The local punters used to love to gamble on me and that brought a lot of excitement as well. But I never had a clue what was being wagered on me. I received £25. Win or lose. I was never interested about whether somebody was winning or losing hundreds of pounds on the side. I know a lot of money was placed on me and I rarely let my supporters down, doing the business for them on more than 30 occasions.

I never had a problem with anybody gambling on my matches; if somebody wanted to have a bet on me that was up to them. It wasn't underhand or anything, it was out in the open. Barry described me as a racehorse who could talk. Although, to be honest, I never said too much! I was just happy to do the business for us all. I was in my element. The money side of things never mattered to me one bit and it never has throughout my career. I just wanted to be a winner: I wanted to be the best.

In what seemed like no time at all, 50 of the hardest, most loyal snooker fans were travelling up to places like the Northern Snooker Centre, in Leeds, and Potters, in Salford, any which way they could – cars, vans, trains, taxis, motorbikes, scooters – to put a few hard-earned – or otherwise – quid on me at pro-am tournaments.

The Romford Roar was born and they were up for the ride! There was the buzz of not only putting their money where their mouths were – after telling anybody who would or wouldn't listen about me – but also to ride a rollercoaster of adrenaline. Snooker is a slow burner of a sport rather than a quick fix one, but it can suddenly erupt into a fever pitch – as it famously did some years later, in the 1985 World Championship final between Dennis Taylor and me when it gripped the nation.

I played John Virgo in a final in Leeds and the support from the Romford Roar made me feel like I was back in the Matchroom. I received ten points per frame from John and the money was stacked up on me from Londoners keen to see me defeat another of the country's top professionals.

The Romford mob pooled their money and presented Barry with a wad of notes, urging him to find somebody to take their bets. The Manchester-based Virgo supporters were not quite as vociferous as the Romford rovers but there was still a sizeable bunch of them. Substantial wagers were struck and I duly won the match 8–3 to ensure that all those heading south left the club in a joyous mood.

John is a great guy. He remains totally passionate about snooker to this day and, like most of us, he has an intense competitive streak. He was also known to have a relatively short fuse in his playing days. This came to the fore in this match during yet another miss episode when he put me in a vicious snooker with reds everywhere. I had no escape other than trying to roll off a side cushion, just ahead of the middle pocket, and lay on a red, dead weight, about a foot from the pocket in open play. Anything other than tight on the red and John would have had a choice of reds.

I succumbed to the difficulty of the challenge and severely underhit the shot, leaving John with the crown jewels in front of him. But, of course, the miss rule was different in those days. If the referee decided that the attempt to hit the ball was not in keeping with the standards of the quality of the player, he could declare a miss and put the cue ball back to its original position.

The foul and miss was rarely called by referees in those days. The benefit of the doubt was the order of the day. But, obviously, if an attempt was so poor or appeared to be blatant cheating then the referee could put the cue ball back if he so wished.

The sensible thought of a discussion with the other player was still to be considered by the vast think-tank that made up the Billiards and Snooker Control Council. Some referees may have taken John's position into account: that he had to all intents and purposes achieved his goal of forcing me to leave him a nice opening red and, therefore, let him play on from where the ball had rested. But not this ref (whose name is being withheld here to protect his grandchildren from embarrassment), who, instead, said to me in a rather fatherly fashion: 'I think you can do better than that, Steve.'

I was in full agreement with him and accepted that I probably could. John also accepted that I probably could and had started to get out of his seat at the same time as the ref had started to move his glove towards the cue ball. As a snooker comedy moment it is ingrained in my brain: a slow-motion image of John reaching out to the ref, who is reaching out for the cue ball while John is screaming 'No!' in super slow motion.

John remonstrated but the ref had already put the cue ball back and wasn't too receptive to his demands. I had another go and played it to perfection. John, much redder in the face, was now whistling through his ears like an old kettle at boiling point. In hindsight, from then on the match was a foregone conclusion. I won the prize money and also received a leather cue case from the owner of the club, Jim Williamson. I used it for many years. But I am not sure whether it was a constant reminder to John about the ref who will remain nameless and his interpretation of the miss rule every time he saw it.

Soon afterwards, I was back in Romford to face the one and only Alex 'Hurricane' Higgins, a brilliant, unpredictable, temperamental, unforgiving foe at the best of times. Tickets were priced at the heady sum of £2 each and they quickly sold out. I received 14 points a frame from him.

Betting was intense – the hard cash ran into thousands of pounds apparently – and it was made even more so by everybody having to hang around as Alex – not for the first or last time in his life – arrived late. Famously, Alex loved a bet. He now wanted to bet heavily on himself against me. He did so and he was left distraught as I triumphed, 5–3. This was the first time I had beaten him. It would not be the last.

Such matches were crucial to my development. My reputation was growing quickly and it was now dawning on me that on my day I was probably already better than a number of the professional players out there, even though I was still very much learning my trade.

Getting guys like Alex to come down to Romford and play me in this type of atmosphere, which was a cauldron of sorts, was superb. Barry invited many of them down to the Matchroom but they didn't all want to come. The matches also started to be reported in *Snooker Scene* magazine and that made a big difference.

I cannot emphasise the importance that this must-read monthly publication had on the game. It has been going since the year dot. Its owner, Clive Everton (a great BBC snooker commentator for many years, far more rounded than anybody else, past or present, in my view), was a pretty decent amateur billiards player in his late thirties at the time I first met him but, much more importantly to me, he was the editor of *Snooker Scene*!

In those days, this was the only regular contact we had with what was going on in the national game. The excitement when it arrived in the post at our house was palpable. Both my father and I were so eager to devour each and every page that we used to fight over it.

Being a fan of billiards as well at the time, I would often drool over Clive's in-depth articles on the Amateur World Billiards Championships and all the professional events as well. Players would also regularly advertise their services for the usual exhibitions, weddings and bar mitzvahs.

So, while these results could, I suppose, get written off by the professionals as nothing more than exhibition matches, at the end of the day they were still results. I honestly think that while these players might have resolved the loss to me on an evening as just a minor embarrassment but a good pay day, it was also the start of the fear factor for when I was soon to turn professional myself.

4. THE POWER
OF PRESTATYN

I didn't own a bow tie, so when I made it through to the final of the Pontin's Open pro-am tournament in the sleepy North Wales seaside town of Prestatyn to play Tony Meo in the spring of 1978 – after beating six-time world champion Ray Reardon in the semi-finals – I had a problem.

Luckily – or unluckily as it turned out – for me, veteran *Pot Black* referee Sydney Lee loaned me this mustard-coloured number. Anybody who saw it wouldn't forget it in a hurry. To make matters worse, the match was shown on Welsh television, although no footage of it has ever surfaced. Perhaps that is just as well …

Prestatyn is full of retirement homes, caravan sites and holiday camps. The Pontin's holiday village was used as a location in the British comedy film *Holiday on the Buses* in 1973. The following year it hosted the first of its annual snooker extravaganzas, the Pontin's Open.

Founded by Fred Pontin back in the 1940s, Pontin's resorts were always popular with professional snooker players, who could supplement their earnings by entertaining a high number of holidaymakers during the summer months. The thinking behind this particular pro-am tournament was fabulous: more than 1,000 eager hopefuls could take on each other and once this huge number of entrants had been whittled down to 24, eight top invited professionals would join in and the competition would then become a best-of-seven contest all the way to the final, which would be best-of-13.

The competition was held in May, which was a pretty unfashionable month in the holiday calendar. So, it filled an otherwise empty week for Pontin's. It also slotted nicely into the snooker calendar – coming just a few weeks after the Embassy World Championship.

Bert Steele, from Plumstead Common Working Men's Club, had gone to Prestatyn the first time the competition was held in 1974 and returned to the club raving about it. Bert's enthusiasm was so infectious that my father and I decided to go up there with him the following year and see it all for ourselves.

And so it was that we found ourselves getting up at three o'clock in the morning for a trip through the deserted streets of central London on to the motorways and up to North Wales. Seven hours later – after getting lost, taking a detour over the top of a Welsh mountain and waiting for what seemed like an eternity while a farmer herded his cows from one field to another – we arrived at the gates of this holiday camp, feeling like three excited school kids.

It was a jamboree, a festival, the Glastonbury of snooker at that time, really. To this day, this event still holds special memories for a particular era of players. It became a big event in Pontin's summer schedule. In the early 1980s, an amateur event was added in the autumn at Prestatyn, which ran for almost 30 years until 2009. The company realised that snooker had a massive following and that it was on to a winner.

The whole week had a great buzz about it. Everybody would hang around in the Clwyd bar. If ever a professional player walked in there, a ripple effect would go around the room. This place was full of snooker fans. It most certainly wasn't a week for the general public. The Clwyd bar was also the place to be where you had to wait for your name to be called out by the tournament organiser and professional referee John Williams, who hailed from down the road in Wrexham.

Each competitor was given a table number and it was every amateur player's dream to be drawn to play on one of the six professional tables in the main ballroom. But this rarely happened. The professionals were almost always given the best tables at Prestatyn.

I remember my first year there very fondly, mainly for following the progress of that great London-based Irish player Patsy Fagan. This man was so popular in the capital that he had become something of a local hero. For a while, he even threatened to take on the establishment and become the Robin Hood of snooker.

Some of Patsy's matches were legendary, including a few big-money affairs. It didn't seem to matter if he was in front or behind, he always played exactly the same game. Patsy also had a superb temperament. In fact, some people said he was a better player when he was two frames behind than when he was two frames in front. His pressure clearances were folklore.

Patsy drew a Welshman in the last 32 in the year I watched him. His opponent, Geoff Thomas, was as popular in the Valleys as Patsy was back at home. This was a meeting of two heroes and it took place in the main snooker hall upstairs, which featured 24 tables in eight rows of three.

The room was packed with people standing on unused tables to get a better view. Being around six foot one, I was one of the fortunate ones, but I could only really see half of the yellow pocket and a little bit of the baulk line myself. It didn't matter. This was London v Wales. It was a big atmosphere with big bets going on.

To my delight, Patsy won. He went on to reach the final where he was unpicked by the brilliance of another Welshman, Ray Reardon. I decided there and then that Ray was to be my new snooker hero, and I wanted to find out what made him tick.

Ray was so interesting to watch. He didn't seem to do anything particularly exceptional but he was always the governor. His tactical nous towards the end of a frame was in a different league from the rest. He also never seemed to get flustered if a player got into the balls first and made a break of 50 or more. He always appeared to have the confidence and ability to turn the frame around.

The other thing about Ray was that he paused at the end of his final pull back of the cue before he struck the ball. I had not seen many players do this – even though the great Joe Davis had enthused about it. Watching Ray dismantle his peers while incorporating some sort of pause into his action was enough to make me realise its value and, during the 1980s, I was destined to reinforce for future generations the potential benefits of the extended pause – I am talking about perhaps half a second – at the end of my final pull back.

I managed to qualify for the last 32 of this prestigious event for the first time in 1977. As well as Ray, the other early winner of the tournament was another Welshman, Doug Mountjoy (as both an amateur and a professional). By the year of the Queen's Silver Jubilee, Prestatyn had become an annual pilgrimage for snooker players and fans alike. During the week, the whole holiday camp was overrun by them.

Cue cases were everywhere. If you were male and didn't have a cue case in your hand there was something seriously the matter with you and if you were female and had a cue case in your hand, you weren't considered to be holding it for your husband or boyfriend either! The likelihood was that you were in the tournament.

It was usually the case that the amateurs who were drawn against each other would play on one of the 24 tables upstairs in the snooker room. The sheer size of this room – jam-packed with all these tables – gives an indication of just how much the game was enjoyed by holidaymakers at that time.

As I have said, once the tournament got down to the last-32 stage, eight professionals joined the 24 amateurs left in the competition. Unless your nickname was the Hurricane, that is. For, in the same year that I reached the last 32, Alex Higgins, although a top professional and one of the biggest names in the sport, was forced to enter in the opening round because he hadn't received an official invitation to play. He still had to give his opponents a 21-point start as an uninvited professional (invited professionals would have to concede 30 points)!

Matches were decided over an aggregate of two frame scores in the early rounds and, in a match against Billy Kelly (later a minor professional), Alex was more than 100 points behind and he still managed to beat him.

I was drawn to meet another former world champion, John Pulman, in the first round proper. This bespectacled Devonian dominated the game for large parts of the 1960s. He was one of my father's heroes – not quite up there with Joe Davis but not far off – and well into his fifties by this stage. By contrast, I was still only twenty at the time.

John had a reputation for being a bit too fond of the whisky – just like Ted Lowe – by that stage of his life but he had got his act together in Sheffield and reached the semi-finals of the first World Championship to be played at the Crucible theatre, where he narrowly lost 18–16 to the eventual winner, John Spencer.

My father and some mates stayed with me in Prestatyn and we were in our element. I got the royal treatment in our cut-price chalet with breakfast cooked for me and no requirement to help with the washing up or the rubbish either. I remember thinking to myself at the time: 'I could get used to this!'

The professional players would not be booked into these chalets. They would lord it in the Grand Hotel instead, which stood just outside the holiday complex on the beach.

The Grand Hotel might as well have been called Buckingham Palace at that time for me. I couldn't envisage myself ever staying there. So, when I did, a few years later, I was left wondering how it had got past the Trades Descriptions Act – while, technically, a hotel, the rest of its title was on very shaky ground in those days!

John had to give me a 30-point start in each frame. I felt pretty optimistic about my chances, very excited and ready to rumble. I was out of my bed like a greyhound out of the traps. I put on my new three-piece suit and tie – bought especially for the occasion – and I looked like a million dollars. Well, more like forty quid after some alterations to the waistcoat!

Meanwhile, John turned up in a pair of crumpled trousers and an inappropriate stripy shirt that looked like he had slept in it! Maybe he had fallen off the wagon after the euphoria of doing so well at the World Championship? Whatever, he absolutely caned me 4–1. He completely wiped the floor with me with some classy snooker. Admittedly, we played the match on a poor table but, to be fair, John adapted to those conditions much better than I did.

I also remember watching Ray Reardon on a table at Prestatyn and noticing how he left himself angled pots in order to make it easier to manoeuvre the cue ball on a slower table. Instead of moaning about the conditions there, both John and Ray adapted to them. It was another important lesson to try and learn.

Typically, Alex (having to give a 21 handicap) won the event, beating Terry Griffiths, who was still an amateur at this time, 7–4 in the final.

I watched the match in awe: Alex totally outplayed Terry with some of the finest snooker I had ever seen. It was a majestic display of true quality. People were hanging from the chandeliers in the ballroom. The atmosphere inside there was something else.

While disappointed with my defeat, I was, more importantly, inspired by what I had achieved in Prestatyn that year. The thrill of watching such an exciting final live whetted my appetite further and I knew that I wanted more. I couldn't wait to give it another crack the following year.

I didn't have to wait too long to enjoy true success in the event. I made it to the last 32 again the following year and this time came up against a fellow amateur, Tony Knowles. Funnily enough, we played on the same table on which I had previously seen Patsy Fagan do the business against his Welsh rival, Geoff Thomas. Now it was the turn of the boys from Plumstead and Romford to put their money up against Tony's supporters from Bolton. My fans weren't disappointed: Tony led for most of the match but I came through in the end to win it.

In the semi-finals, I faced the one and only Ray Reardon. Just a few weeks earlier, he had won the World Championship for the sixth time, a new record in the modern era.

David and Goliath matches were everywhere in Prestatyn. The excitement of this event was for snooker fans to watch their favourite amateurs take on the big boys. Most times, the professionals would quash the hopes of the amateurs but, every now and then, a new hero would pop his head above the table and the fans would be buzzing, wondering if this newcomer could withstand the tactical superiority of one of the best players in the world.

Taking into account the 30-point handicap, the amateur was surely the favourite; or was he? It was a hot topic for discussion and bookmakers really didn't know how to price the matches. It all added to the excitement.

Ray Reardon was the man of the moment and the man to beat. And I beat him. The 30-point per frame advantage certainly helped me but the gap between the two of us was also beginning to close. We could both see that.

I had made it all the way to the final, where I would now face Tony Meo. It would be two London boys together – with me in that mustard-coloured bow tie!

Tony and I played out a terrific match that I eventually won 7–6 after making a vital break of 56 in the deciding frame, made up of all pinks. It gave me by far my biggest win yet in what had effectively become one of the three top events for an amateur to play in.

My prize was £1,500 in cash and a Pontin's holiday. It was actually called a Pontinental holiday! Sadly – or perhaps not so sadly – I never went on it: I sold it cut-price to a friend. Sunbathing in Spain wasn't high on my list of priorities: a) there were no snooker tables; and b) there was sun. As I was fast becoming a snooker vampire, the thought of appearing in daylight was becoming worrisome!

Before the final, I agreed to split the prize money with Tony, which was quite common in sports such as snooker and darts. It was a suggestion from his camp and I was happy to go along with it. There was so little prize money available to us throughout the season that it seemed to be a no-brainer to me. Yet again, I was far more interested in the title than the money anyway.

As somebody who didn't gamble at the time, I didn't fully understand the consequences should this private arrangement ever become public. I am not sure anybody did back then. Over the years, as gambling has become ever more scrutinised, it has become apparent that this was bad practice and, while there may be nothing more involved than players hedging their money like insuring against loss, that is not what the cynical observer or the newspapers could make of such a situation.

When I told Barry Hearn about it afterwards, he wasn't impressed. We discussed it in some detail later on and it was decided there and then that I would never do it again. But that might have had as much to do with what message doing such a deal sent out to my opponent rather than anything else.

Not long after my Pontin's pro-am success, I was practising at the Lucania club in Romford when the manager, Les Coates, told me to pop downstairs as Barry wanted to see me in his office.

'I've had an idea, Davis,' Barry told me when I got down there. 'Summertime is not a busy time in the clubs and I think you need some mobility as well; you can't be coming over here on the bus all the time. You're wasting your time doing that. So I am going to put you on some wages and, obviously, you have got to earn your wages – so I am also going to give you a car to run around in so you can go to all the Lucania clubs and play, practise or whatever there. You will get expenses as well. Are you all right with all that?'

I nodded, feeling pretty pleased with myself and also very excited at the prospect of having my own wheels!

'Great stuff, Davis,' Barry said. 'You're officially on the road. You have transport. I'll work out a rota for you. Go and enjoy yourself.'

Barry was fast becoming an older brother to me rather than an employer. He was also becoming a snooker fan and he was getting excited by everything that was going on around me. He even started to tell people that I was a future world champion! Everybody was now talking about me in the club. I was a minor superstar in a mini way – but soon to be a Maxi way!

So he put me on the payroll. He wasn't stupid. Snooker clubs were always far less frequented during the summer months, even allowing for the British climate. Having the hottest property in amateur snooker turning up on a regular basis was a good draw for these places. But the whole scene also gave me a sense of what was to come: driving to venues, meeting people, being diplomatic and representing the Lucania company name. It was a good experience all round.

It was regular work, too: Monday to Friday, 12 noon to 6 p.m. Apart from my weekend jobs in the supermarket and Makro, this was my first real taste of proper employment.

My wheels were bolted to an Austin Maxi. It was a fleet car from Barry's other flourishing company which supplied fruit machines and video games to pubs and clubs. The car had plenty of miles on the clock. Furthermore, the gearbox was pants. The gear stick was almost as long as my cue! Basically, I got hold of the stick, stirred it up and took pot luck what I shoved it in. Any one of the four forward ones was a result. I just had to hope that I hadn't found the other one! It was a pretty ugly car, too, in all fairness. I would describe the colour as crappy gold. However, I now had what could be classed as a company car of sorts.

Undoubtedly, I was improving immeasurably on the table. Barry now saw to it that I improved off the table as well. Under a fair bit of persuasion from him – it has to be said – I got my hair cut. I finally said goodbye to my Afghan-coated, hippie and Progressive Rock days and went legitimate: I got a new short haircut with a side parting. I went out and bought myself a new top-notch dress suit as well and a black bow tie so that I didn't have to borrow a mustard-coloured one again. I accepted that a good image was going to be very important to me going forward.

I learned a lot just from being around Barry. He is ten years older than me and he became something of a mentor. I watched how he communicated with people and charmed them – whether he needed to or not. Such skills and this type of personality were completely alien to me. It wasn't that I didn't want to be outgoing but I was just so terribly shy. However, that same shyness probably helped me to become the player I was, in all honesty.

My theory is that, in the main, great sportsmen, in particular, are usually born ugly with zero personalities. My reason for thinking this is that when you are sixteen and you start to take an interest in girls, if you are unattractive you find that they take no interest in you. So what are you going to do? Go and practise snooker for six hours a day! That's what I did! And when your mates ask you to go clubbing at the weekend, you tell them you can't because you have some important technical adjustments to work on. You don't tell them that you don't want to because you know you will end the night as Billy no-mates!

Barry came along at the right time for me. We were soon talking to each other every single day. What he saw in me was a single-minded determination and a strong temperament when it came to the competitive stage. I think he admired that. He was also well aware of my talent and potential as well. And, as we all know, the game of snooker was on the verge of explosion, in a way that nobody could ever have predicted. As a result, the two of us were well placed to strike gold together …

5. LEANING ON
A LAMP POST

So this was my dilemma: Barry Hearn – never a man to exude the virtue of patience – wanted me to turn professional and my father wanted me to win the English Amateur Championship; because that was *how it was done*.

It was a hard decision for me to make. My father wanted me to do things properly: win the English amateur title, as Ron Gross, Marcus Owen and Pat Houlihan had done. Then go professional, like Ray Reardon, John Spencer and David Taylor. Terry Griffiths and Jimmy White did it that way, too.

But Barry was far too impatient to wait for that. He wanted me to grab the opportunity in front of me and give it a go right here, right now. I had recently been beaten in the quarter-finals of the English Amateur Championship by Mike Darrington – a very bad day at the office for me, considering the match was played at my home table in the Matchroom at Romford! This was another example of expectation suffocating talent:

I certainly felt under pressure to deliver, particularly knowing what the consequences of winning the event could mean to me.

Recognition had come my way in the shape of an England international call-up against Scotland, played at a snowy Doncaster Racecourse in early 1978, where I was selected alongside the likes of Ray Edmonds, Geoff Foulds and Joe Johnson. I had to wear an England waistcoat, which had previously been used by John Hargreaves. When I got my hands on it, the first thing we had to do was take it out by an inch on either side. Considering I was thin enough to sleep in my own cue case at the time, I reckon John must have had plenty of sand kicked in his face on holidays!

However, professional snooker remained something of a closed shop. There were only a few professional competitions and consequently only a few professional players. The governing body, the World Professional Billiards and Snooker Association (WPBSA), had a committee made up of other professionals.

The WPBSA decided who they wanted in. You might say there was a conflict of interest with all that and gossip abounded with tales of the likes of Patsy Houlihan and Marcus Owen; great players who had been thwarted in their efforts to turn professional by others who considered them to be 'not the right type'. The reality of the situation may have been different but there is no doubt that the system was open to abuse. But some had started to buck the trend: Patsy Fagan, Doug Mountjoy, Willie Thorne and John Virgo, for example, although Patsy was rejected first time round.

Historically, the only way that somebody like me could guarantee a fair hearing was by winning the English Amateur Snooker Championship. The same applied to players from other countries, although why any overseas player would want to turn professional and come over to the UK in order to win zero prize money in a non-competitive scene was anybody's guess.

The situation was slowly changing and although the old professionals didn't particularly want us young whippersnappers ruining their party, they were snooker fans themselves and they loved the game. The times they were a-changin'. There was also a growing interest in the game at the BBC. The WPBSA acted accordingly and eased the criterion for entry into the professional ranks.

Turning professional was a big decision for a lot of people. Not everybody wanted to do it. Terry Griffiths and Doug Mountjoy – two men with family commitments – both had to pack in secure jobs to chase the dream. I only had my cue to support!

Vic Harris, Tony Meo and I had just won the CIU national team championship and I had also just won the CIU National Singles Championship, beating among others the Legend of the Valleys, Alwyn Lloyd, on my way to defeating Jack Fitzmaurice in the final. The CIU nationals were highly regarded titles, as was the popular Pontin's pro-am tournament – and I had now won both of them.

I couldn't see how my application to join the professional ranks could be open to question as I was obviously, at the very least, one of the best amateurs in the land. In fact, I might well have been the very best amateur in the land. I certainly had the CV.

This was the background to a discussion between Barry and my father one night in the summer of 1978, near to the Norbreck Castle Hotel on the seafront in Blackpool:

'I think we should put an application in to go professional,' Barry said, impatient to get the ball rolling.

In between a few chews on his cigar, my father finally replied: 'I don't know, Barry.'

'What difference does it make, Bill?' Barry asked. 'Look, we gave it a good shot at the English amateur. But we got turned over in a best of seven. Who is to say we won't get turned over again in a best of seven next year and, if so, what happens then?

'We have got a good enough case as it is,' Barry continued. 'How long are we going to wait, Bill?'

'I don't know,' my father said again. 'I don't know if he's ready.'

'He might not be,' Barry answered back. 'But we won't know until we find out. If he's going to be good, he's going to be good anyway.'

My father didn't say anything more. It was almost impossible for him to argue. In the end, he conceded and we went Barry's way.

I was standing there silent throughout. I was excited about what was going on and getting off on Barry's excitement. I trusted him. I think my father also trusted that Barry was singing from the right hymn sheet. But Barry still needed to tip him over the edge; giving him a little push from being so conservative to taking a chance and seeing what tomorrow would bring.

Barry managed to achieve that and so I signed a professional contract with him – leaning on a lamp post in the north-west of England – that night. I think it remains the longest sporting partnership in the country. Yet we have never bothered to renew it. This is an example of our true friendship and trusting commitment to each other.

Who knows how long the traditional route might have taken us? For my own part in the triumvirate decision, all I wanted to do was play snooker and test myself against the best as much as I could. My results had been good against every one of the top names in the game that I had played. I now wanted to take that to the highest level and that meant turning professional if I could.

At the heart of it all for me was the opportunity to play against the best players. I didn't look any further than that. I still didn't think I was necessarily going to make big money out of it. Barry might have had other ideas. But even he couldn't have seen what the future would bring. Not at that time. Nobody could have made it up.

Barry submitted my application to the WPBSA and also applied his own method of shouting from the rooftops, which alerted everybody in the game to it and effectively dared the committee to disregard me at their peril. While we waited for their reply, Lucania paid for me to travel abroad for the first time to take part in the Canadian Open in Toronto.

I was excited about going. This was a big thing for me and the first time I had ever flown. I had also read in *Snooker Scene* that it was a big event and I couldn't wait to get out there. Everybody in the world of snooker knew about it. So we all followed the same rainbow even though there was no television coverage and the pot of gold at the other end wasn't that big.

I wanted to go wherever I needed to go, whether that was Romford on three buses or North America by aeroplane. This was also another competition that offered the opportunity for amateurs to take on professionals, but it turned out to be so much more than that. The whole trip was a real eye-opener for me and a learning curve in so many ways.

There was a thriving snooker scene in Canada with some great characters involved, but they had all started off with a different outlook on the game from me. As a result, these men were much more hardened than I was. It was a money-orientated game out there and a tough upbringing for anybody who played it.

The biggest names in Canadian snooker at that time, Cliff Thorburn and Bill Werbeniuk, had both begun their careers playing pool and snooker for money across Canada and further afield. Cliff tells the story of how he once won a lot of money in a match lasting around 36 hours in San Francisco against one guy, who, when it was over, approached him with a gun in his hand. It was one of the reasons why he decided to come over to the UK – to a land where the audience and the sponsors would pay you to play instead. It was another world out there.

Cliff and Bill had become professionals in the early 1970s. Both had performed well in recent World Championships: Cliff got to the final in 1977 while Bill reached the quarter-finals in 1978. Jim Wych – three years older than me and also knocking on the doors of a professional career – was also on the scene, as was the exciting up and coming Kirk Stevens. Yet nobody really knew who these players were in Canada. Imagine the frustration of being so good in your own country and still remaining relatively unknown.

Cliff was a true talent. Of course, he got a reputation for being 'the Grinder' and his late-night finishes at the Crucible are legendary. But he was an old-school player, first and foremost. He never took an undue risk and, therefore, he sometimes took forever over a shot. He understood the tactics of the game and he didn't make it easy for his opponent.

He also played at a time when the miss rule wasn't what it is today. Back in his day you didn't have to hit the ball, provided you made what the referee considered to be a fair attempt. It was a totally different game as a result. But we all did it. All good players were good at what became known as 'the professional foul'. It was part of the game. Safety play in the 1970s and 1980s went on a lot longer because of the miss rule. However, it has to be said that Cliff was one of the cleverest players around. He knew the angles so well. He made very few mistakes and playing against him was always hard. Frames could go on forever.

Slow players are generally harder to play against because they can destroy a fluent player's rhythm. In those days, the speed of play was normally quite pedestrian compared with today. I was able to fit in but, on occasions, got bogged down with tactical play. I preferred to play against faster players and always felt happier playing with fluency and rhythm rather than the nip and tuck of safety play; the problem being it was difficult to force the pace when playing against a genuinely slow player.

Today, even the amazing ability of Ronnie O'Sullivan can be put to the test when he comes up against somebody like Peter Ebdon. You could see him wanting to tear his hair out during one of their most famous encounters. This is actually a very good example because Peter once made a break of 12 against Ronnie that took longer than the 147 maximum the Rocket made in 1997; timed at a breathtaking five minutes and 20 seconds.

Slow play can eat away inside you – and that is coming from somebody who some might think was a slow player himself, even though I am not. But I played a lot of slow players in my career. They don't exist any more. These men would walk around the table, looking at where they wanted to be, even though they knew very well from experience where they wanted to be. This would go on and on and on. To be honest, I struggled with it. The rhythm of my game could be disrupted after being in my chair for far too long. So when you are a true player of speed – like Ronnie is – it must drive you up the wall.

Under pressure, everything is magnified as well. Cliff would go down to play a shot and then he would get up again. I think it became habitual. All those small things add up on the clock. But there was more to his game than that. You have got to be a great player with genuine natural ability to win the World Championship and he did that in 1980. There is absolutely no way you can win it otherwise. But he always took his time. He always took a lot of time.

Bill was a hugely talented and determined player. He was larger than life in every sense. He had a big smile and laughed a lot. Sadly, by the time I got to know him he was not too far away from being an alcoholic and he was expanding because of all the calories. His right arm shook violently when he was in position at the table. It was astonishing to witness and quite amazing that he was able to play at any level at all, let alone a professional one. In time, Bill's problems would be put down to him suffering from what can be a hereditary nervous condition known as essential tremor. Eventually, he tried going down the beta-blocker route to cure it.

It would be hard to believe that a healthier body would have shaken quite so much. Bill's initial remedy for what was commonly called 'the shakes' was alcohol. He would drink plenty before a match to get himself into a fit state – if you could call it that – and then all the time during matches. After a while, he obviously built up a resistance to the amount of alcohol he was able to drink and while he never exactly got drunk at the table, he was always in a relatively happy state.

I briefly made friends with another Canadian called Tony Lemay during my time in Toronto. He was a hustler with a heart and a big name on the Canadian snooker scene. Tony had a sense that I was going to be a very good player. Other than my father and me, he was the first person I had ever come across who eschewed the Joe Davis theory of having your bridge arm ramrod straight. He encouraged me to bend it even further than my father and I had already decided was necessary. He also introduced me into the world in which he lived. It was to be a total culture shock for me. I was still very shy and quite young at the time and, all of a sudden, I was like the Cincinatti Kid.

From what I saw, Canadian snooker players were generally a cross between what I would call proper pool hustlers and proper snooker players. Put those two in a blender and you have a mix of a player who was appreciative of skill but living by his wits. First and foremost, players had to make their reputation as money players. So there were some strong players around and they might have been better money players than tournament players – much better suited to the gamble than an organised competition.

There was no sponsorship out there or anything like that. Nobody was going to give you a wage. Parents weren't financing their kids to play snooker like mine had done. It was a matter of survival. It was a kill or be killed environment. You had to play for money. There was no other way. It was like the high-profile poker player of today: to earn money, you had to put your money on the line first. It was far away from the comfortable life I led at home. Such a scene probably did exist in the UK, particularly for those who didn't have anybody backing them, but I hadn't really had to taste what it felt like.

It seemed that it was all about money not snooker in Canada. It was about what a player could do to get a few dollars – if that was snooker, then that was what you had to do. There were money matches taking place on what seemed like every table in the snooker clubs out there. I saw close up how this world could provide security for such people. This was how they lived their lives – earning cash to justify an existence. I lived the life of the so-called 'down-and-dirty snooker player' with them for a few days. That was enough for me.

All-nighters were the norm. We played these three-red tournaments – with just three reds and the colours on the table – with dozens of players entering. These could go on until daylight. Players would take part in head-to-heads for 24 hours straight as well. The next day, news would surface that one player had finally broken another player and was out gunning for the next victim.

Hustles and tricks of the trade were in abundance. There was a great bet that involved a player placing the black in the middle of the pack of 14 reds, hitting the white ball off three cushions from the jaws of one top corner pocket – in and out of baulk – into the pack and replacing the cue ball and replaying the shot, counting the number of shots it took until the black was knocked into the opposite top corner pocket.

The player would shout out a number and bets would be made – $50 or something – on whether he could do it in more or fewer shots. It was just another way of making money for them. These guys weren't cheats but they did play with an edge. During one practice session, one guy suddenly told me that we were going down to another club to make some money. Nobody knew me so I guess I was a secret weapon of sorts. This was a buzz for a while. But it wasn't for me. I probably came over as a bit wooden to them all but this experience remains the closest I have ever come to the out-and-out hustler.

It would also be fair to say that the Canadian snooker scene back in the 1970s was fuelled by substances that I hadn't seen British players partake of. I am not sure what they were because I ran a million miles from it all, but some of these guys were staying up for two nights solid so it was a way of life for them. I wouldn't call it a druggie scene. It would be wrong to say that. They weren't all stoned out of their brains. But there was something going on; marijuana was popular and there was also probably some use of amphetamines to keep some of them awake.

It was sometimes hard to survive in this environment. The best thing about the whole experience for me was the confirmation from good players that I was a good player, too. That actually meant a lot coming from these hardened individuals who had no choice but to make their money in this way.

Another gentleman I got to know out there was Harvey Rothwell. He was the epitome of the Englishman abroad, even if he was Canadian! Harvey was a cue maker and he adored snooker. He was quite old when I met him. I found it amazing that there were all these people who had loved the game all their lives and yet I didn't even know they existed until I bumped into them overseas. Harvey was another one to take a shine to me and he made me a cue while I was out there. We discussed the theories of the game and I enjoyed those conversations very much. He impressed me with his knowledge. I played with the cue for a day – out of respect – at one of the many clubs I visited and I 'made' a lot of balls with it, as they would say in Canada.

Respect your cue at all times (especially in Canada): Alain Robidoux, who hails from Quebec, started off in the same way as the rest of them. He came over to the UK with cue in hand. He played so well with it as well and looked the business, reaching an all-time high of nine in the world ranking list. His English agents even secured him a relatively lucrative cue contract with Riley's. Part of this deal was to put a Riley's sticker on his cue during televised matches and exhibitions. Alain flew back to Canada with his Canadian cue and, while over there, visited his cue maker and asked him to put a new tip on. The cue maker spotted the Riley's sticker and snapped the cue into pieces! I don't think Alain was ever the same player again!

Another Canadian who deserves a mention here is Bob Chaperon. He was a fantastic talent and, at one time, he put it all together to win the British Open. But, like many others from his country, he didn't seem to possess the necessary discipline. Maybe it was to do with their background? Looking at how nice it is over there, I can understand that homesickness might also have been a problem for some of them.

It certainly was for Kirk Stevens, who was a fantastic player and such a lovely guy. Sadly, he is remembered as much for what happened off the table as for how great he was on it. It is well known that he went off the rails.

Kirk was a crowd favourite with his white suits and stunning style of play. He was in huge demand as a result and he wasn't short of a few quid, either. He was doing exhibitions all over the place – but living out of a suitcase in hotels on his own. That may well have been the undoing of him. He went into freefall. I think he turned to drugs as a crutch and that might not have been the case if he'd had a supportive family and friends around him. He might have been able to avoid that. He might have just needed a strong arm around him: someone to keep him under wraps. If he had got the help he needed, he could have stood the test of competitive time a lot longer than he did.

As it was, he had fallen out of the top 16 by 1987 – when he was still in his twenties – and admitted to having a cocaine addiction. It wasn't nice to witness it. I remember going to India with him on one occasion and he didn't come out of his room for two days. We phoned him up and banged on his door. But he was out of it. It was very sad because he was capable of achieving so much in the game. He burned brightly but not for as long as was undoubtedly possible for him.

But that was all in the future. Back in the summer of 1978, a lot of the top players in the game, including three world champions – Alex Higgins, Ray Reardon and John Spencer – were over in Toronto to play in the Canadian Open. It was an open event (as the name suggests) – but there were no advantages given to amateurs at all. So this competition would provide me with a true test of my abilities against the best in the world. These were not exhibition matches played out in front of my own fans in the comfort of the Matchroom. It was going to be a test of my technique and temperament. It was what I wanted.

The competition was part of the annual Canadian National Exhibition, which was held at Exhibition Place, a vast complex along the shores of Lake Ontario, near to Yonge Street, which was known as the longest street in the world and seemed to go on for ever and ever, which, I suppose, is what is expected of the world's longest street! The downtown part of it attracted the low life and the high life. I loved it there: the Centennial Billiard Hall was open 24 hours a day, attracting gamblers galore; there were lots of cafés and restaurants; and some great second-hand record shops, too, in which, as is my wont, I spent a lot of time.

The whole CNE event was attended by over one million visitors each year, but snooker was not the main attraction. Apparently, the year before, the Canadian Open was staged in a huge marquee with a circus at the other end. Every hour on the hour, a brass band would start up and, when it rained, water would run underneath the boards the tables were standing on. By the time I played there, things had improved somewhat and the competition had been moved on to the balcony area of a huge building.

The tournament organisers must have got some money from somewhere because they didn't charge for tickets. They couldn't do so because it was a thoroughfare. All manner of things were happening below us and there was a lot of music blaring out.

As a snooker player, you have to learn to block out constant noise, or superfluous noise like coughing and rustling sweet wrappers. Obviously, things like the sound of cannon fire going off in the distance every now and then didn't help us if we were at the end of our backswing, but we were all in the same boat.

I did well and made my way through the draw, beating some useful Canadians in the process and also Willie Thorne, who was another example of the growing number of talented British players now trying to earn a full-time living out of the game. I got as far as the quarter-finals, where I came up against Alex Higgins and lost 9–8.

This was one of my best performances against a professional so far, played in front of a packed crowd. I felt like a professional and I felt like I belonged on the table against one of the legends of the game. You can't buy that and the confidence it gives you – it is all part of the education of learning your trade.

The press took notice of me, too. I was absolutely thrilled by the progress I was making but I was also somewhat disappointed to have gone out of such a prestigious competition against one of the very top players in the game after getting so near to the semi-finals.

With time on my hands, I went down to the American border to see Niagara Falls. I should point out here and now that I am not one for sightseeing. One of the common denominators of the ragtag and bobtail mix of those of us who make it to professional level is the lack of cameras hanging around our necks when we go away on tour. But I did visit this natural wonder of the world.

The magnificent Horseshoe Falls – not so much the American Falls or Bridal Veil Falls – are breathtaking with a width of about 2,600 feet and a drop of around 175 feet. But, to be honest, the only sight I really wanted to see was a 12 by 6 foot snooker table with a trophy sitting at one end, waiting for the man who managed to pot more small balls into slightly larger holes than his opponent. The winner of the event was the Hurricane. Given there had been absolutely no handicaps in this tournament, I felt completely vindicated in my decision to apply to go professional.

Back home in England, just a few days before my twenty-first birthday, the WPBSA confirmed my place among the professional ranks. I beat Vic Harris to retain my Lucania Championship title and a small party of us enjoyed a double celebration with a curry at a local Indian restaurant. It was still something of a strange time in snooker with the top echelons of amateur players getting better than a large number of the seasoned professionals that were still hanging around, but there were still some members of the old guard that I needed to get the upper hand over.

First on my list was the Count himself: current world champion, Ray Reardon. We met in the Matchroom again and this time it was over 27 frames and two days. I won the match 14–11 and joked to one of the lads afterwards that it had been good to drink Ray's blood! To be fair, Ray did play on his Count Dracula image and nickname at the time with his greased-back jet-black hair.

This win was another big step for me. I wanted to play Ray because I still viewed him as a yardstick by which to measure my progress, in terms of both match play and tactics. While this match may have had no relevance other than good sparring – because you can't really recreate proper competitive action unless it is actually in a competition – it was a much better feeling for me than for him afterwards. Looking back, it was also the start of the end of an era and the beginning of a new one: Ray had won six world titles in the 1970s. In just over a decade from then, I had won six of my own.

The difference between being amateur or being professional in snooker can perhaps be summed up by the number of chances a player gets in a frame. As an amateur playing against fellow amateurs, I was rarely punished for any mistakes I made. But, at professional level, one error could be costly. Opponents could deliver a knockout blow or, over time, turn a small cut into a gaping wound.

The importance of capitalising on any mistakes an opponent made was dawning on me. Those who consistently took their chances were ultimately the champions. Consistency is a vital commodity in any sport and I was fortunate to have that in abundance, largely due to the manner in which my father and I had approached the game from the start.

I didn't have good players to learn from at the beginning. I had the Joe Davis book and my father's keen eye but the standard of snooker in working men's clubs is relatively poor. However, it turned out to be the perfect route for me. I am not sure it would be today. Nowadays, a player doesn't have the luxury of time. He needs to be fast-tracked in all departments. You have to run very quickly just after learning to walk while at the same time trying to remember how to walk!

If I was starting my career again I would do things very differently. But I can't say – hand on heart – that I would have been more successful! I would have questioned Joe's bible a little bit more – it is my intention to write a better bible in the near future – and I would have spent more time working on the positional side of my game by doing pre-set drills designed to instil better positional patterns in my brain. In essence, a better sat nav.

Winning the Pontin's pro-am and the CIU titles in 1978, plus an impressive performance in Canada and my newly acquired professional status, was to pave the way for my big debut in the must-watch televised snooker competition *Pot Black*.

Barry was instrumental once again, making telephone calls to the BBC in Birmingham and trying to sell them the idea of young Davis versus old Davis on the small screen. Fred was now sixty-five but still remained a mainstay of this popular competition. This was quite a task for Barry as only eight players were invited to take part and invites could be like gold dust. But, now that I had become professional, one big hurdle had been cleared.

Barry had been screaming from the rooftops that I was a future world champion and after a while people started to listen to him. The fact that my surname also held a certain fascination for some probably helped me, too. My opening match was duly against Fred Davis and I am pretty sure that wasn't a coincidence.

This was probably the one and only break I have ever had in snooker: sharing my name with the great Joe Davis – a man once dubbed the Emperor of Pot – and his younger brother, Fred – who was still, somehow, knocking around on the circuit while simultaneously clutching an OAP's bus pass.

The whole series of programmes, which was to be shown on BBC 2 in the early part of 1979, was recorded at Pebble Mill studios in Birmingham over four days between Christmas 1978 and the New Year.

I wouldn't say that the standard of the competition was high. Evidently, some of the players had switched off for the festive season and their waistcoats were struggling to hold the remains of the turkey in place. What mattered to me was that I was in it. The programme provided my big television breakthrough.

However, it has to be said that the Hurricane wasn't too happy about the situation. Alex Higgins had played in *Pot Black* in 1972, the same year that he won the world title, but he didn't like the one-frame format or the fact that it was filmed over two days. He was openly critical about both and neither of those complaints impressed Ted Lowe, the organiser, who held a lot of power at the time.

Alex also claimed to have urinated in the dressing-room sink because he felt the public toilets were too far away. You can imagine the impact this revelation must have had. I am sure that the *Pebble Mill at One* presenters and their guests were not too happy about washing make-up off their faces after a show ever again once they had heard about that! Alex's darkest days were still to come but he was already making headlines for the wrong reasons. On this occasion, he was effectively banned from the competition for the next five years.

He was not welcomed back in a hurry either, despite always providing a huge draw for the viewing public wherever he played. It was only after he beat Terry Griffiths in the final of the Pontin's Open in 1977, with that sensational display that so impressed me, that he found his way back on to the show.

The crowd were yelling for him to be involved in *Pot Black* again that day and Ted and Co. finally relented and invited him back for the 1978 series. Alex subsequently won one and lost two of his one-frame encounters and, for whatever reason, was not invited back the following year. So I took his place.

At twenty-one, I was by far the youngest player ever to take part in the competition. In fact, the player who was nearest my age at the recordings was Doug Mountjoy, who was thirty-six at the time. Otherwise, it was the usual suspects with Fred the elder statesman.

Fred was more laid-back than his brother but he was still a fierce competitor on the table. He was also the beneficiary of a wonderful smile.

Within the game it was said that even if Fred was kicking you in the teeth, he would still be smiling. He was old school and, psychologically, he always tried to get the upper hand on his opponent – a skill that Ray Reardon was always so deft at. Fred once accused the flamboyant Kirk Stevens – a player with a cavalier cue action – of slow play after they ran out of their allotted time during an afternoon session in the World Championship at the Crucible. They returned later that day and, lo and behold, the veteran won the match.

It was a strange experience for me to appear on *Pot Black* after years of watching it on TV. A lot of the old guard were very much still around, but most of these were now dead wood in the game and within no time at all I would be slicing my way through the lot of them. People say you should never meet your heroes. It was to be somewhat surreal not only to meet them but beat them as well!

I beat Fred comfortably, 83–23. But my first year in *Pot Black* wasn't successful. I lost my next two matches, the first against South Africa's Perrie Mans, who had been runner-up to Ray Reardon in the World Championship earlier that year. I hoped to win this match as Perrie was widely regarded in the game as purely a potter with no real cue ball control.

Foolishly, this turned out to be another example of expectation having a detrimental effect on my talent and being an irrelevance when there was a job that needed to be done. Of course, it also has to be said that one frame of snooker is very much a spin of a coin. Regardless, if you go in with no expectations then perhaps you are in a better frame of mind when it starts to go wrong. As it was, Doug Mountjoy also beat me and I was knocked out at the group stage. Ray rounded off another good year by beating Doug in the final.

We were all sworn to secrecy afterwards. I think the powers that be must have got this idea from going to see the Agatha Christie murder mystery play *The Mousetrap* in the West End. The tournament was to run for 13 weeks – a quarter of a year – on BBC 2 and every one of us was under strict instructions not to give the game away.

Of course, in reality nobody can keep their mouth completely shut for that length of time. The butler did it! I told a mate of mine down at Plumstead Common Working Men's Club about it and he used the information to win some money off a few of the other club members. Obviously, I couldn't let this happen again so I told him the wrong winner the following year. He took me at my word, had a few bets and lost. His face was a picture. But word quickly got around. Any bookmaker who was prepared to take a bet on *Pot Black* was not going to be in business for long.

When my match against Fred was finally shown at nine o'clock one cold Friday night in January 1979, the *Radio Times* listed the match as Fred Davis v Steve Davis (no relation)!

I had to laugh when I heard Ted's commentary on one of my shots, so much so that I kept it on videotape for years. It involved me potting a long red down the left-hand side cushion into the top pocket: 'I think Steve will be playing a thin safety shot with a little left-hand side to bring the white ball back nicely down,' Ted said. 'Goodness me, he's potted it!'

It may have been more of an optimistic shot to nothing on my part but Ted didn't know that and you quickly learn never to own up.

After I turned professional, Barry made me VAT-registered. I didn't have a clue what it meant, other than I now had to take a book with some carbon paper in it and write out a receipt after every exhibition. This had become a well-established way of working by the time I started doing some engagements with Tony Meo.

One night, the two of us were sitting in my Maxi as the organiser of the event paid our money to us through the car window. I wrote out a chit, including VAT. So Tony was asked if he wanted VAT as well. After looking at my wedge of cash, he excitedly nodded in agreement and said that he would love some – even though he didn't even know what VAT was and wasn't yet registered!

At this time, the great Ray Reardon walked around a snooker arena as if he not only owned the table but the theatre as well. During a match against him, early in the New Year, in my first proper professional competition, I watched in astonishment as he complained that the reds had not been set up correctly before one frame and warned that he would only break off after they had been reset.

The relatively inexperienced and flustered local referee duly obliged, only for Ray to walk to the top of the table, peer at the reds and complain that they were still not right. The referee started to panic. He fumbled the triangle over the pack, reset them and looked at the reigning world champion for his nod of approval. It didn't come. Ray sauntered up to the baulk line, took a look and slowly shook his head.

The ref was now in bits. He reset them again and desperately pleaded for the Count's approval. Ray stood up, didn't move a muscle and slowly shook his head. The ref dribbled and sweat started dripping on to the balls as he desperately pleaded with them to behave and not go out of equilateral shape.

With a look of increasing terror, he then once again pleaded with Ray for mercy. But this time the Welshman didn't even bother to get out of his chair. He didn't look at the reds; he just stared at the ref – with his arms folded – and shook his head once more.

I was now feeling very embarrassed by this whole situation. I thought Ray was making an issue out of absolutely nothing. If it was all done to unnerve me, then I think it possibly worked: I certainly didn't like the atmosphere that the whole scene created. But it may have been done for Ray's enjoyment. He might have got some kind of kick out of it. Either way, I didn't like it one bit. Whatever his reason, I never held him in the same esteem again. It was either supreme gamesmanship on his part or he was off his trolley! Regardless, he was a great, great player and I don't wish to give the impression that I held any dislike for him. Ray was and still is a brilliant ambassador for the game and a true champion. Maybe he just had a bizarre streak in him.

In total, the balls were reset six times. My concentration was duly shot to pieces by the time we finally got underway and I was beaten comfortably by him, 4–0. It taught me yet another valuable lesson: the need to focus on the job in hand, disregard my opponent and the surroundings, and play the game, mentally, as if it was just me and the table.

Alex Higgins won the four-man, round-robin Tolly Cobbold tournament, held at the Corn Exchange in Ipswich, beating Ray in the final. It was the first tournament he had won in the UK for a year. I defeated Doug Mountjoy in the third-place play-off, but it was Ray who remained in my thoughts afterwards. This former policeman possessed an air of superiority that could certainly unsettle you. He was shrewd as well and the most consistent player around by far at that time. It was no coincidence that he had won those six world titles between 1970 and 1978. But he wouldn't win another one …

Maybe an air of superiority comes with being a multi-world champion? I can empathise with that. A lot further down the line, my own feeling of superiority was probably enough to make other players wilt before they played me. This comes from absolute, pure confidence. At times during my era on top of the game, I felt immortal, like I had a force field around me.

My own air around the table was probably one of aloofness: I never smiled and I was always in control. To some degree, I had to be. I was playing in a gladiatorial setting and it was a stage where my personality had to complement everything else in order for me to win.

I may not have felt too much like a gladiator when I woke up – maybe I had been unable to stomach my breakfast due to nerves – but come match time when the adrenaline was pumping, a true champion can psyche himself into the role of a superhero.

This hypnosis can allay any fears within. I approached my part on this stage as an actor would approach a role in a play. I cut out any negatives that had gone before. This could be a great form of recovery after a bad shot. I had to keep my mind in the present at all times. Believe me, there is nothing worse than thinking about winning your eighteenth frame in a World Championship final before you have won your seventeenth. All successful sports psychologists would agree with me on this, I am sure.

By March 1979 I had featured on three *Pot Black* shows on BBC 2 and my name was starting to spread. More calls were coming into the Romford office to book 'Steve Davis off the TV', as some people were beginning to describe me. Quick as a flash, Barry increased my nightly exhibition fee by 50 per cent up to £75.

Next up for me was a marathon best-of-65-frames encounter against the Hurricane at Romford. It was a four-day match that attracted a lot of attention in the media and, unsurprisingly, every session was a sell-out in the 300-seat Matchroom.

I didn't speak to Alex at all during the contest. It wasn't a social thing for me, it was serious. So I kept myself to myself. I would also be kept away from him. I didn't speak to any of my opponents at the Matchroom. I was like a boxer going into the ring for a fight. The first conversation I actually had with Alex was on a plane some time later and that was only because we were seated together. This was ages after I had first met him as well. Up until then, I never spoke to him at all.

Typically, Alex was Alex that night and placed a lot of money on himself to beat me. What he failed to take into account was that I knew the Matchroom table inside and out. He was to step into a minefield. I won the match 33–23 but only after my opponent had threatened to quit after the forty-ninth frame when trailing 31–18 the day before.

He promptly told the crowd not to bother turning up the next day because he wouldn't be there. Then he charged downstairs to Barry's office and began shouting and bawling. It was a typical tantrum from him. He was in tears as he started complaining to my father that I had Barry to support me while he had nobody.

Interestingly, the influence of Barry was now beginning to have a bearing on the table as well as off it. Not only was I good with a cue in my hand but I also had a manager of growing stature within the game who totally believed in me and bolstered my image at all times when he could. As a duo, we were gathering a true momentum and were now becoming pretty formidable. Regardless of the fact that I was the real deal, Barry's hype could make it all seem even greater. Obviously, this was now getting to some of the players.

The Hurricane walked out of the place into the oblivion of the night and nobody expected to see him again. True to form, an apologetic Alex turned up the next day and the match continued. Furthermore, he was in scintillating form and gave a terrific exhibition of snooker. As we all know, he could really turn it on when he was in form and together the two of us played some unsurpassable stuff. He produced breaks of 132, 93, 80, 75 and 73 and I responded with big breaks of my own: 132, 102, 87, 82, 81, 73, 72 and 71.

As well as the win, I found that I could stay the distance with a supreme talent. I wasn't disturbed or ruffled by him in any way. My self-belief was now very high. As a consequence, I was confident I could brush off any antics that any player willingly or unwillingly tried against me like crumbs from the table.

As for Alex, what can I say? As a player, he was a true genius. Perhaps only Ronnie O'Sullivan has achieved that same style of mercurial ability since. The difference between the two of them is primarily that one has a solid technique – arguably as good as it gets – while the one that came before had a do-it-yourself version. Alex jumped around all over the place during a shot. He looked as if he was trying to head-butt the balls into the pockets on occasions. But by allowing his head to move, his body was on the move as well and essentially this meant an inaccurate cueing action, at least in the sense that there was no consistency in his delivery of the cue.

The end product was, at times, total brilliance – regardless of the head movement – and, at other times, mistake-ridden snooker. Perhaps if he had started his career with a dedicated coach and a Joe Davis bible, the history books might have been different.

The generally accepted argument is that if Alex had been more methodical in his approach to technique, it would have stifled his ability. To put it bluntly, that is total rubbish.

Alex won just the two world titles – ten years apart. He will always be regarded, rightly, as one of the legends of the game. He had tremendous charisma but he was also so often his own worst enemy. As the years went on, the demon drink slowly took over him. I made sure that I kept my distance whenever I could, mainly because it seemed that trouble followed him wherever he went.

But he was a brilliant competitor and a player who entertained millions of people with his swashbuckling style. Nobody is bigger than the game, but some players have played an important part in the development of it and I can't envisage a history of snooker without Alex in it. If there was, it would have been a lot less exciting as a result. Nobody could possibly have filled his boots.

6. DAWNING OF A NEW ERA

In what seemed like no time at all, the floodgates of professionalism opened: Terry Griffiths, the English amateur champion of 1977 and 1978, turned professional just before me and Tony Meo and Kirk Stevens did so at around the same time. Mike Hallett, Tony Knowles and Jimmy White were also waiting in the wings, eager and ready to join the rallying call.

We were adversaries but, together, we became a threat to the established professionals in the game. We were already playing at the high standard – if not higher – of some of the lower-ranked professionals. This was probably due to us having had lots more match play than them, and although we weren't yet at the stage of the cut-throat one-visit-to-the-table wonders of today there is no doubt that, helped by this new wave of young professionals coming into the game, the turn of the decade was to see a big step up in the overall standards of snooker.

My first real experience of this came at the 1979 Embassy World Championship, when I made my debut at the Crucible theatre. The eight seeds were largely from the old guard: Ray Reardon (1), Perrie Mans (2), Eddie Charlton (3), John Spencer (4), Fred Davis (6) and so on. But the qualifying competition featured a couple of the new kids on the block – Kirk Stevens and me – plus the likes of Doug Mountjoy, Willie Thorne and John Virgo, who had all turned professional in the mid-1970s.

I had to win through two qualifying rounds to reach the final stages in Sheffield. I was relatively confident that I would make it and was certainly tipped to do so. Most of the players involved were old professionals still hanging around the scene and they certainly weren't cutting-edge cueists.

My first match was against the Australian Ian Anderson in Leeds. Ian had reached the last 16 when the World Championship was held in Melbourne in 1975. I thrashed him 9–1 and the only frame I lost was on the black.

Next up was Patsy Fagan, the man I had followed with such admiration at the Pontin's pro-am tournament in Prestatyn just a few years earlier. He won the first ever UK Championship in 1977. Sadly, he was now a shadow of his former self. A car accident damaged muscles in Patsy's right arm and he developed a problem that was to wreck his game completely. From then on Patsy seemed to freeze whenever he attempted to use the rest. He tried to sort himself out, but he couldn't. He used to launch himself at the shot and occasionally his cue would end up falling out of his hand and crashing on to the table.

It soon got to the stage where he just couldn't let go of the cue. It was not dissimilar to what happened to Eric Bristow when he developed dartitis. It may have appeared to some as though Patsy refused to use the rest when he played – but he actually *couldn't* use it. On one occasion, I saw him attempt to play a simple pot with it only to give up and end up going off one cushion to hit the red. It was very upsetting to witness the frustration and despair building up inside him. We all felt for him and we all prayed it wouldn't happen to us. Nobody wanted to analyse it too much for fear of catching it!

Today a sports psychologist would have a field day with somebody struggling like Patsy, but I don't think he was necessarily the type of person who would have gone and seen one. The mental side of the game remains something that some people just don't want to talk about. He tried to work around the problem: instead of using the rest, he would go off a cushion into the side of the pack, for instance. Any shot he could reach, really.

When I played Patsy in Stockport, he was already developing these problems. The fluency of his general cueing was also suffering and, as a result, he lost the most important ingredient, confidence. You can't be confident if you can't use the rest and, subsequently, his game suffered dramatically.

So to beat him 9–2 may have been a sign of how good I was but, to be fair, it obviously helped me considerably that he was so limited. It was very sad for me to see. He was such a good pressure player in his day and this problem messed his whole game up. He never overcame it.

I had reached the Crucible. This was only the third time that the arena had hosted the World Championship and the building was less than ten years old at the time. The promoter Mike Watterson had come up with the idea to hold the World Championship there in 1977 after his wife, Carole, saw a play at the venue and suggested to him that it would make the ideal setting for snooker.

I think it is fair to say that not one of us knew that it would become a Mecca. However, it already felt very special. What makes it so unique is the intimidating, intense intimacy inside the arena. This was my first impression. The acoustics also helped. With the right acoustics, you have the right setting for a game of snooker. With the wrong acoustics, it can feel like you are playing in a barn at times. The Crucible was perfect.

It is a venue much more suited to one table than two, but, even with the two-table set-up and the divide in between, it is still a special place to play. The first rounds are always played in a two-table set-up and so this has always been a player's first experience of the place. But the pressure of playing there – simply what it means – can get to you well before you emerge from behind that famous curtain.

Players do freeze at the Crucible. It is important to get a win under your belt. If not, you can feel as if you have never gelled in the place and that can bring even more pressure, which obviously builds over time. Perhaps the Chinese star Ding Junhui is a good case in point here. He has now moved into double figures in terms of world ranking titles yet, at the time of writing, he has reached the semi-finals of the World Championship – and the one-table set-up there – on just one occasion in eight attempts, back in 2011.

There are a lot of players who have never made it beyond the two-table set-up at all and so their experience of the Crucible could be very different from mine. They may perhaps see it as a cramped place to play. They will certainly not have experienced the whole effect. Until that screen in the middle opens up, you can't really appreciate the full value.

It wasn't the best draw for me the first time I played there. My opponent, Dennis Taylor, was seeded eighth and had already reached two World Championship semi-finals in 1975 and 1977. He was one of the tougher seeds I could have faced. He had been professional for seven years and a regular at the Crucible. I was nervous but not fearful at all. However, experience counts for a lot and my opponent had much more than me in this arena.

Dennis was a well-known and popular player who had done very well on the exhibition circuit but he wasn't winning tournaments at the time. He certainly wasn't regarded as a potential winner of the event as – up to that point – his CV hadn't suggested what was, of course, to transpire in the mid-1980s.

He wasn't an aggressive player but he was old school in terms of his shot selection and a clever tactician with bags of competitive spirit. Perhaps he lacked true belief about his winning potential? But he was also one of the great survivors. Snooker was changing into a more attacking game and Dennis was one of the few players who went with it and adapted to the changes. He always had a cool, clever brain. He was always an underrated player in my view as well.

He was also well known for his sense of humour and when asked if his wife planned to come up to watch our first-round match, he wisecracked: 'No, not this one – she's just coming up for the final!'

In a big breakthrough for the sport, the BBC produced daily coverage of the World Championship for the first time that year. But my match against Dennis was confined to highlights only – and the main highlight for the viewers at home was my opponent's century break. As debuts go, it was all too brief for me. I was on my way home after Dennis beat me in a tight match, 13–11.

My main memory of the match is getting hassle for eating a ham sandwich! I hadn't had much breakfast and I was absolutely starving when our morning session extended into the afternoon. With another frame to play, the tournament director, Bruce Donkin, asked me if there was anything I needed.

'Well, I am feeling a bit peckish,' I told him. 'I wouldn't mind a sandwich.'

Out it came. Down it went. And I found myself in the *Daily Star*. In those days, newspapers gave a lot of column inches to the World Championship and one journalist, Ted Corbett, accused me of bringing the game into disrepute for eating this sandwich. There were no rules in place regarding food at the table, but he felt he was right and I was wrong. It was rubbish but also very funny. It must have been a slow day's play for me to be considered such a hellraiser. Perhaps it was the fact that I asked for smoked ham with Lurpak butter that swung it!

After my defeat to Dennis, I remained in Sheffield for a while and watched the tournament progress. It was something of a game changer that year with another Crucible debutant, Terry Griffiths – a 33–1 outsider before the tournament began – winning the world crown just a year after turning professional.

Everybody remembers Terry. He became a star overnight. Due to extended television coverage, this was the first mass public acknowledgement of a snooker player in this way. It was a great story, too: a former postman from Llanelli becomes world champion within a year of turning professional.

Terry came to snooker quite late and perhaps he had a better outlook on life because of that – snooker wasn't the be all and end all for him. He came through the qualifiers and then beat Perrie Mans, Alex Higgins and Eddie Charlton on the way to beating Dennis in the final.

I can vividly remember watching Terry win the World Championship at home and that is saying something! Snooker players are a funny bunch. I was rarely interested in a tournament once I got knocked out. I dare say that, as a breed, all the top players sulk. I know Stephen Hendry is similar to me. Once he was out – nothing; once I was out – nothing. BBC 2 didn't exist and that was it. Although I did usually recover enough curiosity in time to watch the final.

I was instantly made aware of Terry's popularity afterwards. Two days after he won the world title, an open-top car took him through Llanelli and he was cheered all the way as he was welcomed home. I was there too in the thick of it, after being booked to do two exhibition nights with him.

I saw it slowly dawn on Terry that his world was never going to be the same again, not only as a snooker player but also how he was viewed by the general public, stretching into his private life. He was already a celebrity in snooker circles in his own area but the blanket TV coverage of the World Championship to the masses meant that his stock had risen to another level entirely.

There is a sad part to this story: on his first day back at his local club, one of the members shouted out at him: 'Oh, look at this, boys, the world champion is here! Put his name up on the board. I'm not coming off the table to let the world champion on.' I know it broke Terry's heart and he never went in there again. He couldn't accept that his people changed towards him after he had achieved the greatest success of his life.

I could see Terry's life was taking off. But the real story was that snooker was taking off. It was an exciting time. All of a sudden, it now dawned on the powers that be that the World Championship could work as a Wimbledon-style TV event as well, filling the schedules and drawing in big audiences as the drama unfolded. Barry and I would eventually come to coin the phrase 'a soap opera with balls'. The players started to evolve as personalities, whether they wanted to or not; there were heroes and villains among us and our profiles grew every time an event was on television.

By now, John Virgo was making serious moves within the professional ranks. He reached the semi-finals of the World Championship in 1979 and he would go on to win the Coral UK Championship at the end of the year. He was also becoming a funny and popular impressionist with plenty of trick shots to match.

His act really took off once television extended its time slots and people became educated about all the characters in the game: Ray Reardon already had the ready-made image of Bela Lugosi; Alex Higgins was now smoking four cigarettes in one hand; and John Spencer was stopping to sniff before every shot.

John Virgo's impressions became part of the show. Soon, not a year would go by at Sheffield without him doing a turn for the audience after an early finish to a session, which was promptly shown to the nation.

After Sheffield, it was time for the Pontin's pro-am tournament again. This time I played as a professional and so I had to give starts instead of receiving them. It made no difference to me. I retained my title in style, playing brilliantly in the final to beat the much-talked-about, up and coming seventeen-year-old Jimmy White in the final.

Jimmy was very much on the rise and already being compared to Alex Higgins. But I really showed how much I had improved and what my future potential could be against him. Nobody could have envisaged me being able to give such a brilliant player a 30-point start and win but, by the end, I had outplayed him so much that the advantage was irrelevant. I won six frames in a row to trounce him 7–3. Tactically, he couldn't touch me.

Afterwards, in his *Sunday Mirror* newspaper column, Ray Reardon was prompted to write: 'Steve Davis – remember the name! He is my tip to reach the very top in this tough old world of ours.'

For the first time in my career I felt truly invincible. This was to be a real tonic for me. A player is only as good as his last tournament, after all. Therefore, I was flying throughout the summer break, which I enjoyed very much by standing in for Ray at eight Pontin's holiday camps down in Devon.

I filled in for Ray for six weeks in and around Brixham. I had to go to two camps every day from Monday to Thursday and hear a Blue Coat say: 'Good morning, campers! Unfortunately Ray Reardon can't be here today – but, instead, we have got a young, up and coming player to entertain you called Steve Davis.'

I would make my entrance at this point to a series of groans, polite applause and a few people walking out, muttering mild obscenities as they discussed whether they should go to the pool or put their names down for the crazy golf competition!

I had to turn all that around and entertain these people. I still wasn't that well known. I had appeared on a few frames of *Pot Black* and 20 minutes of the World Championship coverage, where I was mainly seen sitting in my chair watching Dennis Taylor pot balls. But it was a good grounding for exhibition work. The ones who turned up for the hour weren't necessarily snooker fans so I had to try and be a jack of all trades for them; knocking a few balls in while avoiding tripping over the kids and making them laugh. It was an enjoyable experience.

I knew that I could entertain them; it would be fun. I had always enjoyed the exhibition side of snooker. I grew up watching other players do them. Once I was out there on my own, I loved it.

This was me learning my trade as an entertainer, which was another big part of being a successful snooker player. Exhibitions are part of the history of the game but at these camps I was often entertaining holidaymakers who were only inside because it was raining outside.

It helped me overcome my shyness. I was a master of my trade with a cue in my hand and half a sense of humour and I found that I could put together a routine of trick shots and a few frames that could make people laugh and enjoy themselves – so much so that they were thanking me afterwards.

I made sure that I had a good time so that the people could have a good time. It was a big breakthrough for me personally to do this. I had developed a strong competitive edge as a player and now I was learning the other side of the coin, which was how to entertain.

It was a buzz, a bit like an actor appearing in a pantomime, I guess. It felt rewarding in a totally different way to the tournaments I had won. It was also an important stepping stone in terms of having the confidence to cope with the growing attention of the media.

There were two journeys going on in snooker at this time: a competitive one and an entertainment one. John Virgo really epitomised that. A large part of snooker's history had always been about exhibitions. This was how the game worked. The holiday camps were good contracts, too. The likes of Ray Reardon didn't make their living from tournament play; the rewards were minimal. They made it from one-night exhibitions. The name of the game was 'Have cue, will travel'. And nowhere was too far.

The excitement was massive. As a new kid on the block I had lots of fun and I made a lot of friends. I realised that people liked me as a snooker player. It was a very important part of my development. It gave me a lot of confidence, too. This was a world where I could enjoy myself without having the concerns and formalities that came with tournaments.

An incident happened to me in the summer of 1979 when I took on Cliff Wilson in the final of a long-drawn-out pro-am tournament in North Ormesby, in North Yorkshire, that I remember to this day. The whole event had taken place over a number of months, but the match – and the entire competition – was to be decided on a respotted black in the seventh and final frame.

Cliff was a whizz-kid player in his younger days and a lot of people in the Welsh valleys thought he had more talent than Ray Reardon. But he didn't turn professional until the age of forty-five, after he had won the World Amateur Championship. He came up to me and asked if I wanted to split the prize money. We had both come so far and there was nothing between us. Looking back, it was perhaps the right thing for him to do in the circumstances, given everything. It was not like there was much cash at stake anyway so he was probably just thinking about the price of his petrol and all that. But he met somebody who was still living in a fantasy land where nothing else mattered other than snooker.

It wasn't in my nature not to play to the limit at all times. The prize money – whatever it was – was meaningless. But I had to play for it. I couldn't allow us to go soft on each other. My opponent remained my enemy until the very end. I had already personally addressed this issue of sharing prize money after my encounter with Tony Meo in Prestatyn. This time I wanted to do what felt right and so I refused the offer.

Cliff, who was no doubt in a totally different place in his life to a pampered young man who had started his snooker life being driven all over the country by his father, couldn't understand. My decision was probably as confusing to him as it was becoming confusing to me as to why somebody would want to accept, given the challenge of the winner taking the spoils on a respotted black in front of an excited crowd.

He tried to cut the black in off the spot straight away in the hope of teaching me a lesson. He missed it and I potted it at my first attempt to win the match.

I wonder what the reaction of the crowd would have been had we agreed to split? There would certainly not have been the same oohs and aahs as Cliff attempted audaciously to cut the black off the spot and the subsequent applause as I mopped up the tears by knocking in a relatively straightforward pot ...

Incidentally, nowadays there are players who consider the cut off the spot as a valid tactical risk. I am still not convinced but it does show the need of an ever-changing game to re-evaluate the cutting edge (so to speak) of shot selection and the realisation that the best form of defence is often attack.

The seventies were coming to a close. The last big event of the decade was the UK Championship, in Preston, which was still a non-ranking event at the time due to it only being open to players from, or resident in, the UK. It was, arguably, second only to the World Championship in prestige.

Similar to the Crucible, the Guild Hall was another venue which had been built in the early 1970s. But this was much bigger than a theatre, about twice the size of the Crucible width-wise with a high ceiling. To give you an idea, David Bowie and Led Zeppelin had played concerts there. It was another great venue for the sport with plenty of seats and a walkway area at the back. When people stood up at the back, the place felt jam-packed.

Terry Griffiths was made top seed but I was heavily backed at the bookmakers, possibly thanks to a massive 13–2 win over him in a best-of-25 challenge match held over two days in the Matchroom a fortnight before and another recent win of mine in Romford over Doug Mountjoy, who had won the UK title the previous year.

However, due to my low world ranking, I had to enter the competition at the final preliminary round and played John Dunning, another member of the old guard: 11 times Yorkshire amateur champion, 1964 CIU champion and 1974 World Championship quarter-finalist. I won 9–3, although it was later reported that John had suffered severe pains in his chest during the match, believed to be a minor heart attack.

I faced the defending champion in the last 16. In a terrific encounter, I won each of the last six frames – just as I had against Jimmy White in the Pontin's pro-am tournament – to beat Doug Mountjoy 9–5. I hardly missed a pot. On leaving the table, the referee John Williams whispered to me that he considered my performance to be the finest exhibition of snooker he had seen since Joe Davis at his peak. I walked away thinking that was a big accolade from somebody who certainly knew what he was on about.

Next up was John Virgo in the quarter-finals. At one stage I missed a shot, sat down and laid my cue on some empty chairs near the table. Just as John prepared to take a shot, the cue rolled off the chairs and crashed on to the floor. John quite rightly gave me one of his trademark glares – he could have moments of getting quite angry on the table – and I have never been so relieved to see my opponent pot a ball and go on to win a frame. He outplayed me in the end and won 9–7.

John then proceeded to go on and win the biggest title of his career, defeating Terry in the final, 14–13, despite being docked two frames for turning up to one session late after the start time was changed for the purposes of television.

A week after Preston, I flew out to Asia for the first time to take part in the Bombay Invitation World Masters, in India, with six other professionals and the crowds flocked to see the likes of Patsy Fagan, Doug Mountjoy, Ray Reardon and Cliff Thorburn in action.

I remember that we played our matches in a gymkhana and the referees had boys on hand to take the balls out of the pockets for them! I beat Doug in one match by taking on an audacious treble. My main memory, though, is seeing the huge differences between the rich and the poor out there.

One evening, we were taken to the sponsors' house – a seven-storey building with one floor filled with antique clocks and another with antique jade – where we were wined and dined in fine style. As we left through the electronic gates, we could see all the beggars, who were a constant feature in the city, waiting for scraps of food outside. It was pretty disturbing stuff. Furthermore, we were told to totally disregard them by our hosts. But that was a difficult thing to do. John Virgo was particularly upset and he wrote a poem about the experience – admittedly from his hotel room in the five-star Taj Mahal!

We were all aware that we were likely to get 'Delhi belly' – even though the event was 700 miles away from the Indian capital. After avoiding non-bottled water, ice, milk and salads for the first few days, everything felt fine. But then we let our guards down around the pool one hot afternoon: Cliff ordered an ice-cream milk shake and we all followed suit. The result was carnage: the snooker was nearly called off that evening as players were running off to the toilet after every 30 points or so while some of us were holed up in our bathrooms; it was a case of alternating between sitting on the pan and kneeling in front of it! I have never, ever felt worse than this. It felt like the bottom had fallen out of my world as the world was falling out of my bottom!

I lost to Cliff Thorburn, who was becoming something of a nemesis, in the semi-finals. (Cliff had also beaten me in the Canadian Open a few months before and was now very much one of the top four players in the world and therefore on my target list.)

Meanwhile, one of the players found out that due to the five and a half hour time difference between Bombay and London, you could tell the time back home if you turned your watch upside down. Patsy Fagan was very impressed by this – even though he had a digital watch!

The new decade began with another 147 maximum in practice on the first day of the year for me. Obviously I was becoming so boring that I wasn't even celebrating the New Year or I was getting so good that I could perform to superhuman levels even with a hangover! Barry had said that he thought 1980 could be the year I won my first major tournament and it had started off well.

I won the Lucania Pro-Am Championship (whitewashing Dennis Taylor 8–0 in the final) and continued my good form with a hat-trick of challenge match wins over successive nights in Romford against Eddie Charlton, Perrie Mans and – at long last – Cliff Thorburn. These matches were promoted as me versus the Rest of the World.

I really rated Cliff. He was a player who never missed a ball through carelessness and I admired that. As his nickname suggests, he was slow and determined, with a tactical game that was second to none. I knew I was doing well if I could beat him.

In fact, I was now enjoying myself a lot and I threw my hat into the ring for the UK Billiards Championship in February. I lost to Rex Williams in the quarter-finals in Leeds. Rex was an excellent billiards player and held the world title on a challenge basis from 1968 to 1980 and won it twice more on a tournament basis in 1982 and 1983. It was no contest as he beat me 1871–862.

In later years, Rex took over as chairman of the WPBSA as he was being eased out of the competitive game. He was a fantastic character and great fun to be around. He loved red wine and would never be able to finish off a joke because he was laughing at it so much.

One night, he unexpectedly provided a comical moment after being called away from his dinner table, after consuming copious quantities of Châteauneuf-du-Snooker, to be an official spokesman on a breaking news story that a player had tested positive for some substance or other in a drug test.

He bowled up at the BBC studio, sat in the chair and David Vine immediately cut to the chase:

'Rex, do you think there is a drug problem in snooker?'

'Well …' a slightly slurring spokesman slowly replied, trying to look studious as he leaned on to his elbow, resting on the arm of the chair. When his elbow slipped, there was to be no Rex recovery. Nobody could remember what he said as the whole studio – and probably most of the viewers at home – were in hysterics.

The first big event of the year was the Benson & Hedges Masters at Wembley. Right from the start, this event was for the crème de la crème of professional players. The world's top ten were invited to take part and Terry Griffiths continued his purple patch by beating Alex Higgins 9–5 in the final.

Rather frustrated, I was champing at the bit to get into this event one day. John Virgo was furious he was not invited to play – just a few weeks after winning the UK Championship – and he let that be known to the powers that be.

The world rankings were calculated over the previous three World Championships and, at that time, the World Championship was snooker's only ranking event. Here was another example of the committee men not reacting to change quickly enough, when perhaps a more entrepreneurial approach would have stirred up a bit more excitement – at the very least.

A lot of new, young professionals – such as me – were coming into the game but our progress was still being stunted in large areas. It would be a little while longer before the whole scene changed for the better.

In the WPBSA's defence, the World Championship was the only event open to every professional. But the thorny issue of the way players were ranked was starting to rear its forever ugly head.

To this day, the ranking list has caused much heated discussion and argument within the game. It has also dictated voting at annual general meetings and caused friendships to be terminated. To the general public, the importance and intricacies of it are irrelevant but to players within the game, hoping, wanting and needing to be inside the top 16, 32, 48 or 64, it is massive.

It was a similar story at the Embassy World Championship. But at least there were preliminary rounds in that event. I had to come through two rounds of qualifiers again; this time I beat former English amateur champion Chris Ross 9–3 and Paddy Morgan, an Australian-based Irishman, probably the only player Down Under who could live with Eddie Charlton at that time, 9–0.

Attention now turned to the Crucible. The favourites were Terry Griffiths, the top seed as defending champion who was in very good form, Ray Reardon, and Cliff Thorburn. Alex Higgins wasn't seeded, having fallen out of the world's top eight after failing to get past the quarter-finals in the World Championship since the event had moved to Sheffield. However, in a television interview on the eve of the tournament he confidently proclaimed it would be the 'Year of the Hurricane'. He was almost proved right.

I met Patsy Fagan again, this time in the first round, and won 10–6. He played much better than in our encounter the previous year, which must have pleased him somewhat, but I was too strong on the day. This was my first ever win at the Crucible. My reward was to hang around Sheffield for three days before my next match – against the tournament favourite.

This was the first time in about two years that I had started a match as the underdog. Terry Griffiths had been given a bye into the second round as the eight seeds came into the competition at the last-16 stage and was strongly fancied, even though the press had already started to dub me 'future world champion'.

I was confident going into the match. By now, every time I played I expected to be able to perform to a high enough standard to give myself a great chance of winning. Nothing is ever certain, though. It was also a nice change for the pressure to be on somebody else.

On the walk down to the Crucible, Barry, my father and I walked over some large cellar doors on the pavement outside a pub called the Brown Bear, on Norfolk Street. We didn't think too much about it at the time …

The Crucible curse – the term ascribed to first-time champions crashing out early doors the following year – looked like it had struck in my favour early on against Terry. I raced into a shocking 7–0 lead and ended the first session 7–1 up. What's more, I was quoted as saying that I felt I could play better!

The back pages of the following morning's newspapers predicted an early exit for the defending champion: 'Champ on way out', 'Champ on brink of defeat', 'Davis has champ on rack' etc. However, by the end of the next session, my lead had been cut to four frames, after a much-improved performance by Terry, to 10–6. I still needed three frames for victory. The back pages of the next day's newspapers now predicted a great fightback by the Welshman.

This was the first time I had gone so far ahead and then seen somebody come back at me, let alone that somebody being the defending world champion. I was beginning to feel the heat and the thought of losing a match in this way – looking over my shoulder and stalling – was my first experience of the horrors that could potentially happen in the game; being in a worse psychological state in front than behind. Added to that, this feeling is much worse at the World Championship than anywhere else.

Going 4–0 up in a best-of-nine and facing a fightback is one thing. But when you have to sleep on it, or you have to wait for the next session after you have let a lead slip, that is a totally different kettle of fish. You begin to feel the heat. Throwing away a lead is the worst feeling. In a way it is worse than getting annihilated. I needed somebody to tell me verbally that, if I did blow it, I wouldn't be a failure. So I went to find my manager.

'Barry,' I said. 'Tell me that I won't be a mug if I lose this one.'

He told me not to be stupid.

'That's not good enough,' I added. 'You have to say the actual words!'

Barry quickly realised that I was at the most important moment in my career so far and that I needed reassurance from him. Looking me straight in the eye, he told me:

'Steve, you won't look a mug if you blow it.'

That was good enough for me. Of course, I was aware that he might well have thought differently but I was happy with what he said, even though he might have had his fingers crossed behind his back! It helped share the load.

On my way down to the Crucible – through the streets of Sheffield – people were shouting words of encouragement and good wishes at me. It didn't feel like I was on the verge of achieving a giant-killing but it probably brought home to me how much the match was being watched on TV. My only contact with the outside world at the moment was walking to and from this theatre. The rest of my time was spent cocooned away from a normal life due to me not wanting to break the spell of being in competitive mode.

Terry made breaks of 95 and 70 to narrow the gap further to 10–8. At this point, both Barry and my father left their seats up on the balcony and went to the bar. Barry was in such a state of panic that he tried to light up a cigarette when he already had one in his mouth! Then he tried to drink his pint while it was still between his lips. His nerves must have been in shreds when Terry won two more frames to level the match up at 10–10 at the interval.

Before the match, Barry and I agreed that he would not visit me in the dressing room while the game was in progress. But at 10–10 my father put pressure on him to do so. He asked him to pass on some tips about where he thought I was going wrong. My father would know that the general ambience in the dressing room wouldn't have been good and also that too many cooks could spoil the broth.

Barry came into my dressing room and found me singing and whistling! Despite losing seven frames in a row, I somehow felt quite calm about it all. It was as if the worry of having to protect a lead had now gone and I could compete as if the scores had been level pegging all along. (I suppose it could also be construed as delirium!)

'I've just come down to find out how you're feeling,' Barry asked.

'I'm OK,' I replied.

'Are you sure?'

'Yes,' I answered.

'Right, then I'll go,' he said. So he left.

When he got back upstairs, my father immediately asked how I was.

'He's whistling,' Barry told him.

'Did you tell him what I told you?' my father queried.

'Yes,' Barry replied.

They both sat there in silence, Barry wondering whether he actually should have passed on the information to me and my father wondering why I was whistling!

The match may well have hinged on Terry's decision in the next frame to try and pot the last red into the top left-hand pocket. The blue was partly covering the hole and it was debatable whether the red would squeeze past it. If the red had dropped, Terry was a certainty for the frame. He struck it well but it hit the cushion just before the blue, cannoned into it but refused to go in. With the red at my mercy, I cleared up to regain the lead. A 116 break in the following frame put me 12–10 ahead and I won the next frame on the colours to win through to the quarter-finals. The world champion was out and, more importantly, I had beaten him.

Media interest in me exploded. I was doing press, radio and television interviews in between grabbing a couple of well-deserved practice sessions with my father and relaxing, in preparation for my next match. I was in the last eight of the World Championship and the telephone in my hotel room was red hot, so much so that we decided to pull a real 'diva moment' and tell reception to block all calls to my room and divert them to Barry's room instead. Mariah Carey, eat your heart out!

Sadly, amid all these interviews, I was badly misquoted in a national newspaper. The quotation attributed to me was: 'People love to hate me because I'm playing perfectly, and I know it.'

This was my first experience of this kind and it upset me a lot. First of all, I didn't say it. Secondly, I still hadn't won anything of note so I am not sure why anybody would think I would say it. I did have Barry in my corner, shouting from the rooftops that I was going to be world champion one day, but there was nothing more than that. Perhaps that annoyed some people in the media. Perhaps it was thought that I had an air of a young person who was full of himself after knocking out the world champion. Who knows?

I do recall getting booed by a small minority as my career went from strength to strength. It wasn't nice. But I always viewed it as a backhanded compliment to how good I was. It took me back to the wrestling on ITV on Saturdays and the way the pantomime villain, Mick McManus (who was a lovely gentleman by the way), was always booed – because he always won.

So part of me didn't mind being seen as the pantomime villain because, at the very least, the audience was buying into the fervour that snooker was now delivering to the nation. In a way it also felt easier than having everybody cheering for me over and above the level of support normally associated with good play.

I knew that no true snooker fan saw me as a pantomime villain – and that was far more important to me. But this is an example of how the public can perceive things one way and a player another way. You turn up and try to play your heart out but the public might have an entirely different agenda. I am not saying all this necessarily started with a quotation that wasn't in 1980 but it wouldn't have helped me that my next opponent, in the quarter-finals, was the People's Champion, Alex Higgins.

I felt that I had been knocking on the door of beating Alex in a major tournament since our very close encounter in Canada in 1978. I wasn't satisfied with my victory in our best-of-65-frames exhibition match at the Matchroom. Although it was serious business for me, maybe it wasn't so much for him as he was being paid an appearance fee. I wouldn't settle until I had beaten him in a top competitive match with everything at stake. So perhaps there was no better place to play him than the Crucible.

Public perception of me seemed to change once I had knocked out Terry Griffiths. I felt there was now something of an expectation on me to beat Alex Higgins as well. A TV crew followed me around Sheffield ahead of the match. They might have been a bit disappointed: all they got were some shots of me practising and taking my expensive silk shirt down to the dry-cleaner's. The piece made out that I was off to the launderette because I hadn't packed enough shirts, expecting not to get so far in the tournament. Looking back, it was probably an accurate assessment! I was learning not to expect anything – only to be prepared for anything!

Alex was always a fierce competitor. He seemed to put on another skin in Sheffield as well. But he wasn't in great form. He had scraped past Tony Meo 10–9 in the clash of the first round.

This was the quarter-final everybody was talking about and everybody wanted to see: a young man tipped to be world champion one day, fresh from knocking out the defending champion, up against the People's Champion. Alex was always an exciting player to watch but he was up and down like a yo-yo. Some thought the kid was going to blow him away. Others thought he would be too clever for me.

I was confident in myself ahead of the match. But, looking back, every contest was still a journey into the unknown for me, especially at this place. We ended our first session locked at 4–4, during which I made a total clearance of 136 to equal the highest break of the championship, made by Kirk Stevens on the first day, and, in the last frame, Alex came close to achieving the first ever 147 maximum at the Crucible. An early safety shot by me knocked the green on to the bottom cushion. Alex followed up with 15 reds and 15 blacks. He continued with the yellow but came unstuck on the difficult green. He tried to double it the length of the table and failed.

I trailed 9–7 at the end of the second session and was always trying to play catch-up from then. In the end, Alex won 13–9. It was the best I had seen him play in years; a performance of self-control and surprising resilience added to his clever tactical nous.

Maybe I still wasn't quite ready to beat the likes of him when they were at their brilliant best in the big matches. But I wasn't far off. It was an exciting match that had definitely lived up to its billing but Alex was fractionally stronger. It later also dawned on us that we hadn't walked over the cellar doors outside the Brown Bear pub on Norfolk Street! Superstition told me that perhaps that was a mistake.

Alex got all the way to the world final, where he twice held commanding four-frame leads but eventually lost to Cliff Thorburn 18–16 in a tense match.

It is an example of the power of advertising at this time that the World Championship was known to a fair proportion of the general public simply as the Embassy, just as the Masters was known as the Benson & Hedges. Even so, the BBC famously had to leave the Crucible during this particular final as the focus switched from Alex's fingers at one Embassy to live coverage of the Iranian Embassy siege down in London.

Cliff's victory underlined the emergence of Canada in the world game. It was no surprise given what I had seen out there myself that the Canadians came of age during those 17 days in Sheffield. Kirk Stevens was a star that year; losing to Alex in the semi-finals after blitzing past both John Spencer and Eddie Charlton. His fellow countryman Jim Wych reached the quarter-finals – where he lost to Cliff – and big Bill Werbeniuk got to the last 16.

Many were sorry to see Alex lose in the final. He was as popular as ever and when he put his mind to it – as he did in this tournament – he was an excellent competitor. But if he was drinking too much alcohol he could never be that player. Alex could do some amazing stuff after a few drinks. The brain tends not to overthink under the slightest influence and, actually, in a bizarre way, it can help matters. But he wasn't too great after too many.

At one time I remember he went on a health kick and was convinced that honey was the solution. Unfortunately he wasn't quite like Pooh Bear in his method of consumption and, instead of eating it out of a jar with a spoon, he was mixing it with half a pint of Double Diamond at the table. You could see globules of honey floating around inside the glass on the table beside him. It ended up looking like a lava lamp! More often, he would drink shorts. Perhaps that way he thought people might think he was drinking water.

Sipping water was my trademark. I would always put the glass to my lips and sip the water. I wasn't one to drink a lot during matches. I would

▲ Me (not exactly) with Joe Davis, the man who started the snooker ball rolling.

◄ The Joe Davis book, *How I Play Snooker*, was my bible as a 16 year old besotted with the game.

► I was probably 18 when this was taken at the Plumstead Common Working Men's Club. My mother insisted I had 'auburn' hair and not 'ginger'! You decide!

▲ Me in a borrowed mustard bow tie being presented with the Pontins Open trophy by Ray Reardon.

▼ Me, Barry and Doug Mountjoy at the Matchroom in Romford, before one of many challenge matches that took place there.

▼ The Matchroom, Romford. Health and safety eat your heart out! 300 people would cram in there, but there was no fire exit or windows!

▲ A publicity shot after I made my first 147 in practice.

▼ Before a recording of Pot Black with (left to right) David Icke, John Williams (ref), Eddie Charlton, Terry Griffiths, Doug Mountjoy, Ted Lowe, Neal Foulds, Silvino Francisco, Cliff Thorburn and Willie Thorne.

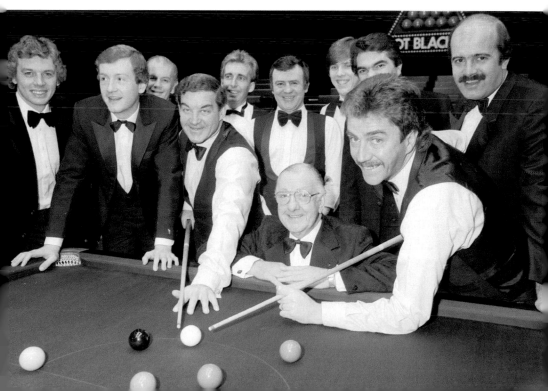

▲ For some reason we threw more than the occasional fancy dress party in Romford – me and Barry letting our hair down.

◄ Barry and I in Vegas, two days before I made the first ever televised 147 at the Lada Classic in January 1982.

▲ My mother and father joining
the celebrations after I won the UK
Championship in Preston 1980.

◄ Another celebration of the UK Championship – my father and Barry pose with the trophy.

▼ My mother and grandmother, Winifred, at Buckingham Palace after receiving my MBE.

▲ Getting my hands on the World Championship trophy for the first time.

▶ It seemed like a good idea at the time, although the table fitter who already had a buyer for the cloth wasn't too pleased!

▲ Still celebrating the morning after my first World Championship title. This picture was on the front page of the *Daily Star*!

▼ Sunbathing before the Matchroom Championship with Willie Thorne, Jimmy White, Dennis Taylor, Neal Foulds, Terry Griffiths and Tony Meo at Cliffs Pavilion, Westcliff-on-Sea.

only sip it to keep my mouth from being dry. It is funny that thanks to all that some sort of image was born ...

I would always smell the glass beforehand as well – to make sure there wasn't the smell of any cleaning fluid left over in there. By the end of the decade, I also recall thinking how easy it could be for somebody to spike my drink during a tournament. That may sound a little paranoid but it was a genuine concern. As a result, I only had bottles of unopened water during matches. Looking back, an unopened bottle of water being a crucial tool of the trade sounds quite funny but it was vitally important to me.

At one time, when I was at my best, it did regularly cross my mind how easy it might be for somebody to sabotage a player's chances in an event in some way or another. As snooker became more and more popular, this minor paranoia began to turn into something of a worry for me.

7. VICTORY IN THE UK

I began to feel in my element during the 1980 Coral UK Championship final against Alex Higgins at the Guild Hall in Preston.

My only problem was that my opponent was moving ice around in a bucket as I played. When it came to etiquette, the Hurricane was never a natural. Whether he was doing this intentionally on this occasion as a form of gamesmanship, I couldn't say, but he certainly couldn't seem to care less. I let him know what I thought of it all by flashing him a look of disapproval – and then proceeded to punish him in the best way possible.

I felt that it was only a matter of time before I was going to win a big one. Something inside me was telling me that, and Barry Hearn kept telling everybody that as well. He believed this would be the year that I would achieve a major victory.

My game had matured a lot in the six months since my Embassy World Championship quarter-final defeat against Alex at the Crucible and, as the competition at the Guild Hall unfolded in the early stages, I began to fully realise this.

I started off with an emphatic 9–1 win over Mike Hallett and when I played Bill Werbeniuk in the next round I was so confident in my ability that during the first interval – with the scores locked at 2–2 – I was able to relax by going on the Defender arcade video game – my favourite at the time – with the Romford Roar in the main foyer downstairs. I went back out onstage and comfortably went on to win the match 9–3 – even though Bill, by now drinking a pint a frame to try and keep his nervous disorder at bay, beat me 9–2 in toilet breaks!

Tony Meo, fresh from knocking out the defending champion John Virgo in sensational style with a 9–1 victory, was a big test in the next round. After 11 frames, I led 6–5. Obviously, the next frame was crucial. I won it after Tony went in-off as he attempted to pot the blue. That was massive. I then pulled away from him and didn't drop another frame, winning 9–5.

I now felt supremely confident that I was capable of lifting the UK trophy. I had a new-found belief in myself that was even stronger than before. It was as though everything was fitting into place.

I can still fondly recall one special morning, lying in the bath ahead of my semi-final against Terry Griffiths, when it dawned on me that I could win the tournament. I actually said the words out loud: 'I can win this!' It was a personal, professional epiphany.

Effectively, overnight I now felt that I was good enough to win a major competition – and this was the second biggest of them all. But it wasn't just that. This didn't feel like it was even a 50-50 chance. I fancied myself so strongly to win it and genuinely believed that I could outplay anybody in the draw. I could see myself not just winning competitions from now on but outplaying my opponents, starting here at the Guild Hall.

Looking back, I might have had blinkers on to a degree but I felt supremely confident. There were some great players around as well. I still didn't really have anything of any real solidity to back up this feeling of superiority within me either, so it was an amazing feeling to have.

Somehow, something had clicked inside me. Technically, I was doing all the right things – but that can come and go at any time. So perhaps I'd moved up another gear upstairs? Jumping up to a new level – mentally – where nobody could get near me? I had certainly jumped up in standard from the improvements I had shown at the Embassy World Championship in April.

I came out fired up like Rocky Balboa in every round, but I was always calm inside. Considering the vagaries of how the balls can run in snooker and the way in which matches can go, plus the fact that all of these other guys were very good players indeed, I must have been in superb mental shape.

I was also quite pleased to be playing Terry. He was always a great player – one of the best around at that time – but his style seemed to suit me down to the ground. I hardly missed a shot and won 9–0.

By winning all eight frames of the afternoon session I required just over 15 minutes of the evening session to book my place in the final. I played consistently solid and hard, tactical snooker and produced a few decent breaks, too, of 72, 91 and 73. My long potting played a big part in such a comfortable victory. My overall play was becoming problematic for my opponents as well.

This was a truly amazing result and one that underlined my new-found feeling of supreme confidence in my game. Afterwards, John Pulman commented on my whitewash on television. It was great to hear him say: 'For years, I have been saying this lad is world class. Now people will have to sit up and take notice.' Even my father couldn't find any faults with my game. That was the greatest compliment of all.

I always felt that I had a good tactical brain but I think one of my greatest strengths was being able to inflict this type of annihilation on an opponent. I could comfortably keep up the mental pressure and never think of easing up. My focus at times was extraordinary. I did let leads slip from time to time – some of them became quite famous – so I understood that any player can suddenly become vulnerable at any time, whatever the scoreboard says.

Frames of snooker are often won and lost in blocks. Therefore, if ever I got somebody on the floor, I would try and hammer home my advantage until they were properly on their back. Put it this way, I never offered to pick them up!

The Hurricane awaited me in the final. The Romford Roar headed north to Preston in their droves with Barry leading the brigade up the M1 and M6. I remember asking him to request they keep the noise level down during the match.

Alex Higgins played to a crowd more than anybody in the game and I feared that a rowdy Romford lot might rouse supporters in his camp. If so, it would undoubtedly help him. Alex tried to counter the Romford Roar by reminding people through the press that, although he was born in Northern Ireland, he lived in Lancashire. He called himself 'LancIrish'!

As expected, his fans were as loud as ever. I led 3–1 at the interval and if anybody had walked into this vast arena for the first time during those opening four frames they could have been mistaken for thinking I was losing 4–0. I didn't like it at all. I met up with Barry and asked him to give the word for our boys to break loose, make some noise and ramp it up a notch. I was winning despite Alex's fans screaming so I was brimming with confidence anyway.

In such a raucous atmosphere, the stakes were raised and, perhaps, the adrenaline levels were, too. I made breaks of 114 and 95 on my way to charging 8–2 ahead. But Alex was never a quitter and he rattled off three frames in a row. He was on fire for a while. I closed the day with the last two frames of the session to lead 10–5 overnight. It was a decent lead and I slept very well indeed.

The next day I sensed that Alex was in a difficult place. He often could be. He smoked and shuffled; puffed and prowled. Smoking by the players was still allowed at this time – although the public would have been prohibited from doing so – and Alex chain-smoked incessantly during matches. The Hurricane was always a fidget in his chair but he appeared anxious and agitated as we continued this match, his face going through a series of tortured expressions. He started to jump up when I was at the table and chalk up when I faced a tricky shot, no doubt hoping that I would miss.

It could have been considered gamesmanship but I would give him the benefit of the doubt and say it was more that he was ignorant of the etiquette required at the time, often defaulting to billiard hall snooker.

In one comedy moment, he also tried to claim a foul after a mistake by the highly respected referee John Williams, who inadvertently picked up the cue ball from the table instead of the pink from the pocket when I was on a break. The look of horror on John's face was priceless. It was a genuine lapse of concentration on his part and I had a laugh about it, but then Alex jumped up from his seat and argued that it was a foul shot; when John explained it was his mistake and not mine, the Hurricane refused to accept it.

The whole scene quickly soured, I asked John for permission to leave the auditorium and was allowed to do so. It was a wise decision on my part as the argument apparently went on for a while. I returned to find everything back to normal and so I continued potting more balls just to rub it in!

It was during another one of my breaks that Alex started digging ice out of his bucket. He was never overly respectful to his opponent, especially when it came down to moving when he was in a player's eye line. He was a bit of a bully when he played so facing up to him didn't do me any harm.

I was finding my feet as a competitor and I had a certain amount of attitude around the table myself, so my disapproving glare at him – straight out of John Virgo's back catalogue – was a sign that I was no shrinking violet around the table.

Admittedly, Alex could be in his own little world a lot of the time. I once did an exhibition with him and while I was at the table, he called over a waitress to bring him a pint of lager. The problem was he was drinking half-pints and he proceeded to pour the contents of the pint glass into the half-pint glass. All eyes were on him as this huge amount of froth flooded out all over the table, dripping everywhere. But Alex, chain-smoking as usual, was so caught up in the moment that he was just oblivious to anything else, including the mess he was making!

Perhaps this shows that gamesmanship was never an intentional part of his tactics at all, that he simply wasn't aware that he could be putting an opponent off. However, having said that, in my opinion at that time it was bad manners. Ignorance could not be an excuse in a match of such magnitude as the final of the UK Championship.

Unperturbed by all his antics – intentional or otherwise – I powered into a 15–6 lead and required just one more frame from the remaining ten. No one had ever lost from such a position.

For different reasons, both Alex and I now left the arena to go for a break. I was in the toilet by my dressing room when a buzzing Barry turned up.

'You've got thirty seconds: make sure you thank the table manufacturer, the cloth manufacturer, the sponsors, officials, fans and the BBC,' he said.

He finished by asking: 'Got it?'

'I feel like I am on *The Generation Game*, but I'll try my best,' I replied.

Then he disappeared.

This moment had been discussed and rehearsed regularly by us during the previous two years. Usually we would be sitting in Barry's office, discussing all aspects of off-the-table stuff and the importance of professionalism at all times when we would go through the motions of who I had to thank when I finally pulled off the first big one.

So, during the afternoon interval I told Barry that, should I get to within one frame of winning the match, I wanted him to come down to my dressing room and remind me of all the people I had to thank. In itself this was a sign of huge confidence on my part as the old adage of not counting your chickens before they are hatched would have been a big red light for me.

I duly went out and wrapped up the next frame to win the UK title, saluting the Romford Roar with clenched fists and a big smile. I was thrilled. I said my thanks and managed to remember them all – although what the cuddly toy was doing in Preston that night was anybody's guess!

I kissed the trophy triumphantly. This was a big moment. I was now a champion rather than a prospect. My form had been exhilarating. To put it in context: this was the first whitewash Terry Griffiths had suffered as a professional and the heaviest major tournament defeat yet inflicted on Alex Higgins. But everything was just about to get a lot harder: I was now the one who everybody wanted to beat.

I won £6,000 in prize money and Barry had £650 on me to win the tournament at odds of 10–1 before it began. So he won even more than me! The two of us were riding the crest of a wave. I was buzzing. Barry was buzzing. Something was beginning to happen. My diary would soon be full with £200-per-night exhibitions.

I had more money than I had ever had in my life. I bought a new car with my winnings. Well, it was a second-hand Rover 3500 but it was new to me and it had power steering and an automatic gearbox. It replaced the tired but trusted Maxi fleet car.

I needed a new car. I now had more exhibitions and challenge matches going on than tournaments and I was driving so many miles that I was on first-name terms with the café staff at Watford Gap service station!

At grassroots level, snooker was bursting at the seams. TV exposure had captured the nation: snooker tables at working men's clubs were in constant use and new snooker clubs were opening up everywhere. The laws of the land were also changing; meaning that many of these were licensed as well.

The result of all this was that the shows were a big success wherever we went. My education at Pontin's holiday camps in the south west of England had been priceless. The telephone was constantly ringing and I made sure that I was a good entertainer and gave value for money at all times. I also stayed on to chat with club members and fans after my trick-shots routine. It was good fun.

Staying on afterwards not only made me feel like I was being a good professional but it was also something that, had the roles been reversed, I would have truly valued. After all, these fans were really no different from me. I was a snooker fan, too. The only difference was I had a better knack of getting the small balls into the slightly larger holes with my pointed stick than they did with theirs!

I didn't mind all the travelling. This was what I did. I had always had a good work ethic thanks to my parents and I came from an era when snooker exhibitions were the places where players earned their crust. Tournaments were still becoming a new way of doing that. The prize money had not yet started to spiral upwards.

It was also still very much the case that you got exhibitions off the back of television appearances and that is why *Pot Black* was such a big competition for the players.

The UK Championship win in 1980 changed all that. It was to signify the start of my domination of the game in the eighties.

I enjoyed playing at the Guild Hall so much. By my second year there I felt I already owned the place. In fact, it would become my home of sorts for years to come – I won there six times over the next eight years. When I walked out into that fabulous arena, it was as though I was back where I belonged. This was my first experience of something like this. During my career, I was to have such a special feeling at three venues – the Guild Hall, the Crucible and Goffs in Ireland – and it was pure beauty when it happened. I didn't want to be anywhere else in the world. I loved every minute of it.

I felt invincible and I started to build up the same superiority complex that had served Ray Reardon so well during the 1970s. I now felt that I was at a level of snooker that was simply better than the rest.

8. CHAMPION OF THE WORLD

Deep inside the cauldron of the Crucible theatre, during my first ever Embassy World Championship semi-final, I fight back from 8–6 down to take an overnight lead of 12–10 into the third and final day of an intense encounter against the defending champion, Cliff Thorburn.

I am ecstatic as I walk off the stage after recovering from quite a painful afternoon where I lost four successive frames. But as the two of us head towards our respective dressing rooms, Cliff suddenly starts having a go at me. He gets quite abusive as well. I don't really understand what he is on about – but I am later told that he had made a complaint about somebody in the audience whistling to put him off at some stage. I am not aware of this. It may have been the case that he heard something but I certainly hadn't.

I would have been disappointed if Cliff genuinely believed that the people who came up to Sheffield to support me were capable of doing something like that – because they wouldn't have been. While the

Romford Roar was made up of a variety of some strong characters from different walks of life – some of them might even have slung you down the stairs if you came anywhere near me or threatened me at that time – these people were snooker fans through and through and always respectful of the occasion and the opposition. When I closed my dressing-room door behind me, the main feeling I had was that I had broken him down. These were not the actions I would associate with somebody who was at one with himself and at the top of his game.

My season went from strength to strength after my triumph in the Coral UK Championship. A few days later I comfortably beat Dennis Taylor 4–1 in the final of the Wilsons Classic in Bolton, taking my prize-winning earnings up to £11,000 in just over 72 hours and adding another trophy to my ever-expanding cabinet. By the end of the week, Yamaha also announced an exciting new £30,000 tournament to be shown on ITV in the New Year. It was to be a Merry Christmas for all of us involved.

But it wasn't a Happy New Year for me. My debut in the Benson & Hedges Masters ended almost as soon as it started with a shocking 5–3 first-round defeat at the hands of 66–1 shot Perrie Mans at Wembley Conference Centre in front of the Romford Roar.

Perrie seemed to rediscover the potting ability that had got him to the World Championship final three years before and he took advantage of a rare bad day at the office from me. I played far too inconsistently but, in my defence, so did lots of players when they faced him because his approach was a bit different.

In fact, Perrie's style seemed more like my father's 'pot one, walk around the table, see where the cue ball has finished and then try and pot another one' approach. And it worked! Compared to the rest of us, Perrie never seemed fazed when he ran out of position. He just got down and knocked in another ridiculous pot from off the cushion, and on the days when he wasn't potting them it seemed that every time you came to the table the balls were all messed up and there wasn't a colour on a spot.

Regardless of excuses, I was out of the Masters before I could fully appreciate the stylish decor of plush seats and smart carpets at Wembley.

My winning streak might have been over but I soon got my season back on track. I beat David Taylor in the final of the Yamaha Organs Trophy at the Assembly Rooms in Derby, 9–6, and followed that up by beating Tony Meo 9–3 in the final of the John Courage English Championship the following week, where I also celebrated another whitewash win, courtesy of a 9–0 semi-final victory over Ray Edmonds. Two more titles were in the bag.

I also very much enjoyed a resounding 6–0 challenge match win over Cliff Thorburn in the Matchroom. Over the years I had beaten all the top players at Romford. This steady run of form on my home patch continued to give me a little boost when I needed it, particularly going into the biggest tournament of them all.

Despite a world ranking of 13 – thanks to a grand total of three world ranking points from my two World Championship appearances so far – I was well on top of the prize money list and made a very strong favourite at 7–2 to win the world title.

Could it be third time lucky for me at the Crucible? Well, we had come up with a new master plan and it didn't involve my cue or technique. It was this: rather than stepping over the cellar doors that we passed every day outside the Brown Bear pub on Norfolk Street we would now step on them; as we had the year before when I beat Terry Griffiths. Simples!

Sportsmen, coaches and their managers really do know no bounds when it comes to silly superstitions! Playing mental games with myself has also been a stupid, occasional habit for me. But is it only me? How many school kids have tried not to step on the pavement cracks on sports day before a big race?

My only serious concern going into the World Championship was the tip of my cue. I was worried it wouldn't last the whole competition. I was now playing in more tournaments than I had ever done in my life and I also had an ever-increasing workload of exhibitions. Therefore, it wasn't easy for me to find the time to put a new tip on and play it in.

Technology-wise, snooker hasn't changed much over the years. While some sports have gone carbon crazy, snooker players still play with a piece of wood with a bit of leather plonked on the end and a bit of chalk to grit up the pointed bit. Over the years, attempts have been made to invent new things: the aluminium cue that didn't warp was great until you leant on it and it bent and it couldn't be straightened out again.

Walk into any snooker club at this time and you would find an Apollo cue (the same brand that made javelins) with a kink in it. Then the carbon cue came along, but it didn't have enough weight so the manufacturers used wood encased in carbon – which defeated the object a little! The carbon had a matt finish but the more you played with it, the more the oils in your hands polished it up, which meant that it wouldn't run through the bridge without juddering. There was also the chalkless tip. This was a great idea but, sadly, no more than that – a great idea! I doubt that even NASA will be able to come up with the requirements that give just the right amount of grip – but not too much – to make us the master of the cue ball.

Then there was my personal favourite: the anti-static chalk! Matchroom actually endorsed it after being assured – close to deadline – that a small flaw would be addressed. It was designed to reduce kicks. The idea behind it was that the chalk wouldn't stick to the cue ball. Therefore, the contact between the balls would always be pure. It worked. It never stuck to the cue ball. The problem was it never stuck to the tip either! So we were caking the stuff on, only to see it strewn all over the cloth by the end of the day's play.

The World Championship was always my priority. Seventeen days plus a good week beforehand of constant chalking meant that little bit of leather was going to get plenty of scraping but the grit makes the physics of the game possible and without it we could never make the ball spin in its different directions. Subsequently, those famous Judd Trump or Jimmy White power screw backs would be spectacular miscues instead.

I agonised for a long time about whether or not the tip would last the distance. Tips always seem to play great near the end of their lifespan but finally I plucked up the courage to cut mine off and put on a new one. Every snooker player will know the dilemma I faced; it was a bit like a long-distance runner – with the possible exception of Zola Budd – hoping their favourite trainers will last until race day.

In the end, I just did it – and whacked a new one on. But I left it until two days before I headed up to the Crucible. A new tip requires a certain amount of time to bed in so I did feel a little bit of trepidation going into my opening match against the highly rated and popular eighteen-year-old qualifier Jimmy White.

In the eyes of the media, Jimmy was the latest new kid on the block, but the two of us had known each other for a long time. It was now five years on from the day I'd seen him play with a walking stick at Ron Gross's club in Neasden.

Since then he had won both the English Amateur Championship (at the age of sixteen) and the World Amateur Championship in Tasmania (at the age of eighteen). He turned professional soon after that. He was young and exciting and had already been talked about as 'the next Alex Higgins'. As a result, Jimmy was also given a nickname that was similar to the Hurricane, 'Whirlwind'.

Later on, Jimmy had his own nickname for me as well. He called me 'Golden Balls' (which I later rented out to David Beckham). Jimmy was spot-on, psychologically, but his connotation was more clouded by his view that I seemed to 'fall on my feet' as a player.

Before Jimmy made his long-awaited debut in the World Championship, he had a makeover – new hairstyle, new teeth and a totally new look. He was also filmed by *Newsnight*, the BBC current affairs programme, posing for pictures taken by Lord Lichfield in a modelling shoot. He was getting attention and rightly so; here was an exciting new talent emerging.

The new look was down to new management. Jimmy had a few managers along the way and this latest one tried to give him a new image, along with the new set of choppers. He was always a good-looking lad but I think they wanted to make him look a bit more photogenic. It was quite funny when he had all this done. He just didn't look like Jimmy for a while and we all had to get used to having this new guy hanging around.

But Jimmy was just trying to move with the times, like the rest of us. He certainly wasn't an old dog at the age of eighteen but he had to be taught some new tricks all the same. It was a new frontier for all of us and we were all going about it in our own way.

The fact that I was young, successful and smartly dressed seemed to bring fresh attention to the sport and the media duly lapped it up. In an editorial on Great Britain for the *Daily Telegraph*, Sinclair Robieson stated that the days of a misspent youth image in the game were over. He cited TV interest as the main reason for the change in opinion. But we all had a part to play – both on and off the table.

A lot depended on who was in your corner, managing you. I was very lucky that I had somebody like Barry Hearn on my side. I actually had 'fallen on my feet' in that respect. Not only was he a great support to me, but as well as coming from the world of accountancy he had experience in the world of design as well. He had a proper understanding of business outside the snooker world. He sold me as a commodity. Of course, Jimmy was highly marketable, too, but we all needed good agents to guide us and a lot of the players were far less fortunate with the managerial hand they were dealt.

The first round at Sheffield is always difficult and Jimmy was on his way to becoming a top-class player. It was a tough draw to get. The snooker cognoscenti remembered our Pontin's pro-am final three years before when I had to give him a 30-point start. But three years in the development of a young player can seem like a lifetime and he was fancied by many to provide me with a huge banana skin in my first-round match.

Jimmy was fast, attacking and often threw caution to the wind and – just like Alex Higgins – he always had the crowd on his side.

Something that has always intrigued me in snooker and sport in general is how fans decide who to support. To be honest, the public don't really know any of us. There could be a mass murderer in our ranks for all they know! You can't get to know somebody just by watching them walk out on stage, bow, smile, play a few shots and do a TV interview.

Obviously if a player has a swashbuckling style, it is an easy decision for them and Jimmy and Alex were both loved by the public for that reason. But what if both players have roughly the same game or style? Take athletics in the late 1970s and early 1980s, for example: what made Sebastian Coe more popular than Steve Ovett? I mean, one of them went on to become a politician!

Jimmy was exciting and a risk taker but at this stage he was still raw and had not yet developed a B game. Safety play seemed to bore him: he wanted to attack all the time. As a result, he was vulnerable to tactical nuances and often got outplayed in that department. As a shot maker, he was simply outstanding. But he hadn't got the balance of his game right yet and he approached it all a bit like a gambler. Given a 50-50 shot or even a 40-60 shot, he would always go for it.

The game was all about potting for the young Jimmy – a natural instinct for a good young player – and when you are so talented you can get results because on some days everything will go in for you. That is why he was such a dangerous player in his early days. It is understandable that somebody with so much natural ability is going to be an attacking player because they find from an early age they can win matches easily like that.

The old guard, still hanging on, struggled to cope with Jimmy the moment he came on the scene. But, obviously, the higher up the ladder this type of player goes so the problems for him to face will be bigger. Players like me – who were effectively far better all-rounders – would usually pick off players like Jimmy. I am proud to say that I had a really good track record against him.

I held a comfortable 8–4 lead, including a 119 clearance early on. But three frames in a row put Jimmy just one frame behind me. This was becoming a familiar feeling for me, reminding me of my match against Terry Griffiths the previous year. But this time I was on my own – Barry had left Sheffield to return home due to other commitments and he was now pleading with the manager of an east London electrical store to switch every television set in his shop to the live snooker so he could watch my match.

I settled down and knocked in a break of 74 to move within one frame of victory. Jimmy came back again to 9–8 but I followed up with a 71 break in the next frame and he finally conceded on the yellow. This was no stroll in the park. It turned into something of a scramble up a hill. I was glad when it was all over. Most debutants could have gone to pieces in a match like that. The fact that Jimmy didn't said a lot about him. He was a warrior and he was going to be a handful in the future.

First-round matches like this can be good for you. I was in the hardest half of the draw and it was good to have been given a tough test. After beating the Whirlwind, I now faced the Hurricane. Alex talked about revenge for my UK Championship win in Preston – but he knew that he hadn't beaten me since our match at the Crucible 12 months before. He admitted to not fancying his chances against me but I put this down to a bit of pre-match psychology. He had been in better form of late and was second on the money list and second favourite for the title.

However, I did notice Alex had the shakes a little during our first session, where I took a commanding 6–2 lead. I saw his trouser leg tremble a few times on the shot. Nevertheless, he responded in typical fashion in the evening with some excellent snooker to reduce my lead to 9–7 overnight. I wasn't that happy with my performance but – as we always say in analysis at the end of a session – I would rather have been 9–7 in front than 9–7 behind!

This happens a lot, especially in the long matches: you come back to the dressing room in bits having lost the last few frames of a session and, even though you are in front, you are acting like you are behind. At times like this it makes good sense to press the reset button; treat every session as its own match and look at the scoreboard and be realistic and optimistic. The following afternoon, I found my A game and resumed control to win through 13–8.

After one former world champion came another: Terry Griffiths was my quarter-final opponent. But the match was no repeat of the 9–0 whitewash I had inflicted on him in Preston the previous year.

Terry had subsequently developed a more careful game plan and returned to a much slower style. He won the World Championship playing this way in 1979 but after criticism from some people for being too slow, he attempted to speed up his game a fraction by trying to take less time studying between shots. This didn't work for him and so he went back to his natural style and played better. Good for him.

As a result, our match was a gruelling affair and it dragged on, so much so that after playing just 14 of the allotted 16 frames – I was leading 9–5 – we were told that we were being 'pulled off' to allow the next session to start on time! In fairness this happened often back then. Not so much these days, but when it does happen, obviously the old football story involving Rodney Marsh, Sir Alf Ramsey and an orange is adapted for the Crucible.

Terry and I shared the first six frames of the following day and then played out another frame that lasted almost an hour. The contest had turned into a real slog. I felt mentally drained by the end and it was with some relief that I finally celebrated a 13–9 win to book my place in the semi-finals. Ted Corbett, of the *Daily Star*, reported that the match was 'a big yawn'.

But just as my match against Jimmy had helped me prepare for Alex, this long-drawn-out affair with Terry now helped me prepare for my next match. I was up against the reigning world champion, Cliff Thorburn. Now I was the one being asked about revenge by the press, given Cliff's victories over me in our last two competitive matches, out in India and Canada. I joked that I would have to make it third time lucky.

The setting for our semi-final was superb. The two-table set-up becomes a one-table affair at the semi-finals stage in Sheffield and in this way the theatre becomes a true gladiatorial arena, the players the centre of attention. No longer are we squashed together, seated in one corner. The table is further away from the players' seats and that means a bit more shoe leather is used but the attention of everybody in the arena is glued to the epicentre of the room – a table with eight legs and six pockets – where this battle to the death will be fought out. This was my first experience of it.

True to form, Cliff kept me in my seat for ages at times during the match. At one stage, I didn't pot a ball for over an hour. The danger with the Grinder was always that you could switch off against him if you weren't careful. At times, you could stand at the table after he had riveted you to the baulk cushion for frame after frame and look at the long piece of wood in your hand and wonder what on earth it was actually for!

Cliff was a meticulous player with certain mannerisms when he took a shot. You had to accept he was a slow player and just get on with it.

That was the way it was. Lots of players had their energy sucked out of them playing him. My recollection of that particular match is that I managed to survive. To quote Nietzsche: 'That which does not kill us makes us stronger.'

Cliff slowly and painfully came from 6–4 down to lead 8–6 at the end of our second session. I was in bits when I got back to the Grosvenor Hotel. The only positive I could possibly focus on was that the session was over and I only trailed by two frames. If it had gone on for any longer, who knows what damage Cliff could have inflicted? I was distraught.

'Never mind,' Barry told me. 'Let's go upstairs and have a best-of-three on Defender.'

He had an arcade video game fitted at the hotel, great fun on my days off at the start of the event, but I didn't expect to be benefiting from it at this late stage of the competition! I tried to find solace with an hour on Defender. It worked a treat. After an hour or so, I felt much better. I ordered a pot of tea and some sandwiches, had a nap, had a bath and got ready for the evening session.

'Let's go to work,' I said to Barry as we walked over the lucky cellar doors outside the Brown Bear pub. 'I want to play some snooker.'

This was all part of the psyching up that went on between us. I had to get into the role. I had to believe I was Rocky Balboa. Therefore, the corny lines had to be said. It was the law!

Despite me being the only Englishman left in the competition – in fact no Englishman had won the World Championship since 1977 – Barry was so annoyed with the Sheffield crowd supporting the underdog against me – whoever he was and wherever he came from – that he decided to drape a Union Jack over the top of the balcony that night. The Romford Roar was in great voice behind it, too. I won six of the eight frames to lead 12–10. The only sour note for me was Cliff's outburst as we walked off the stage.

Looking back, had I known about the background to it I might well have been unnerved by it. I would have hated to think that he thought badly of me and/or mine. So that may have made for a much more difficult scenario in the match because I would have become much more aware of my supporters and, when I was playing snooker, I didn't want to be aware of them. It was great to have their support but I definitely didn't want to be having to make excuses for them.

I don't suppose the scoreline helped Cliff either. He probably felt like I had done earlier in the day. That was my view on it at the time. But I didn't want a confrontation with him. I just wanted to get into my dressing room.

Cliff had smoke coming out of his nostrils! He couldn't handle the pressure, or so I thought. That gave me a terrific boost and it worked to my advantage. I didn't know that there was anything more to it than that. I do know that he didn't win another frame. I won the match 16–10. But it wasn't easy. The last four frames took over two and a half hours. Fortunately, by the time my parents and brother got up to the Crucible – after breaking down nearby on the M1 – there was still some snooker for them to see! Surviving that match was massive for me. I think it essentially won me the world title.

With all due respect to Doug Mountjoy, it had been felt for a long time that the winner of the 1981 World Championship would come from the top half of the draw. I had definitely had the hardest route to the final: beating three world champions and Jimmy White.

I felt very confident going into the world final. Apart from my one-frame defeat to Doug in my first year on *Pot Black* I couldn't recall losing to him since an early challenge match at Romford. But he was in blistering form himself, beating Ray Reardon and setting a new World Championship highest break record of 145 in the process in the semi-finals. On 56 he had played the blue instead of the black so this ruled out a maximum, but 145 was still the highest break ever recorded by television at this time.

Despite all that, I was well aware that I was on the brink of converting all the newspaper talk that had followed me around for the last 18 months or so, and all the plaudits I had got over the past few years, into the biggest single statement I could ever make – something that was tangible, something I could cherish.

Whenever the thought of being world champion had come into my mind, I tried to think about something else – to relieve the pressure. By the time I got to the world final, I was pretty much on autopilot. There was no time to celebrate between the semi-final and the final because the schedule didn't allow it.

My personal schedule was dinner, bed and a good night's sleep. I was tired but adrenaline helped me during those matches. I found I not only survived but thrived on nervous energy. I just had to make sure that I got enough food in my body to keep firing on all cylinders! I also had to ensure I didn't look too far ahead or get carried away with the occasion – I knew full well the importance of it all and what it would all mean if I was successful.

I had to treat every session as a single session: Cliff was yesterday and Doug was today. The transition from one match finishing to the start of another one during the second week at the Crucible is relatively easy to cope with. I was often in such a place that it felt like one long continuation of snooker throughout with no start and no stop. Move on and focus again. I knew that I was in good form and that was very important to me. I was ready to win the world title at last. I now had to make sure that I just kept on playing snooker and didn't start thinking about what might be on the horizon.

I was right on it. I was on top throughout and, although it was quite tight for a long time, duly won it 18–12. I was so caught up with the moment at the end that an overwhelming feeling of emotion took me over. I had a tear in my eye as I knocked in the pink and I looked up to see the people who had been with me on this fantastic journey.

Within a few minutes, I would be in floods of tears. As I wrapped it all up, Ted Lowe described my snooker as 'fabulous and consistent' and spoke of the burden on a young player heavily backed as favourite throughout the World Championship. It had, admittedly, been the hardest two weeks of my life but I had come through it. I had done it!

Barry's bear hug at the end of the match is legendary. We had pulled it off! Our journey hadn't taken too long – five years or so – and there hadn't been too many hard times along the way, but it now felt like we had conquered the world. Well, I suppose we had!

Just after I turned professional, I remember Barry telling me that I had to pull my finger out.

'You aren't winning enough!' he told me.

I thought to myself: 'What on earth are you on about?'

As I was presented with this very special trophy I thought to myself: 'Now I get it!'

Barry's impatience for results felt harsh to me at times. I sometimes tried to disregard it because there were only a certain amount of tournaments I could play in. But all the time he was trying to spur me on. He laid it on the line. I just wanted to play good snooker. But he had a plan – for me to be world champion. That was always his goal. He told enough people that I would be one day. In a relatively short space of time, we had cracked it.

When it comes to individual sports such as snooker a lot of people naturally focus on the player and what makes them so special. Much less is made of family, friends, business partners or agents. Managers can be looked upon as mercenaries more than anything else. But the role that some people have away from the sporting arena can have a massive effect on the outcome. With the right sports psychologist – whether an unknowing friend or a paid professional – you can perform with less pressure and with the right person in any of your corners you can be lifted into uncharted territory. Yes, it is possible to do it all as an individual – but it is far easier and much more fun to do it as a team. My team was absolutely fantastic.

The winning cheque was £20,000 – the same as Björn Borg had won at Wimbledon the previous year – and it took my season's earnings up to £45,000. I later splashed out on a new house for my parents in Plumstead, next door to my father's sister. They couldn't afford a mortgage and I so wanted to say thank you to them in some tangible way for all the help they had given me and all the sacrifices they had made for me in my quest to get here. Whenever I wasn't living out of a suitcase, I was living there – sharing a room with my younger brother by seven years, Keith.

But the money meant nothing compared to the feeling of being crowned world champion. The next day I was on the front page of both the broadsheets and the tabloids. It was also predicted that I would become snooker's first millionaire within a few years. Right on cue, Barry put my exhibition fee up to £1,000 per night.

Television commercials, endorsements and sponsorships flooded in. I even got paid to do a photo session for the computer game manufacturer Atari, which led to the amazing sight of huge billboard posters with my mug all over them. The advertisement even printed my actual highest break on the machine to date: 60,145!

Snooker was flavour of the month. It would soon become flavour of the decade! Sponsors – particularly tobacco companies – loved what they saw and what the game could do for their business. They couldn't get enough of it. It quickly became a very well-paid sport to be involved in.

To that end, my timing could not have been better. They were exciting times, but to walk into a packed room and hear my name announced as the new world champion mattered more. You can't buy that at any price!

This was a team effort by me, my father and Barry. The celebrations at the end said it all. It was the culmination of everything we had worked so hard to achieve. We had done it!

I hope the late Dick Sharples, whom I got to know at Plumstead Common Working Men's Club, was watching from behind those Pearly Gates when I won the world title with his old cue.

9. THE PERFECT FRAME

The Lada was a very popular car in Eastern Europe in the 1980s. It was a solid lump with the front bumper measuring a quarter of an inch. I won one after making snooker history in a tournament in early 1982 and, as I was more than happy with my Porsche 928 at the time, I decided to give it to my parents as a gift.

It had no power steering, no electric windows, nothing. Going round corners could be hard as well and only a bodybuilder could have managed a three-point turn in it. But it never went wrong and it always started first time. I will say that for it. That car always reminded me that I was the first person in history to do something very special.

The euphoria that comes with winning the World Championship – or any prestigious title for that matter – doesn't last forever. I found that afterwards, when I was on my own. It could all feel like a bit of an anti-climax to be honest. I felt flat. I did seem to get quite down on occasions during those long summers that followed because all the excitement connected to winning the world title had gone. It was in the past. All I wanted to do was go out and win it again. Without knowing it, I was already an adrenaline junkie. The exhibitions gave me little hits but it was the competitions that really got me high.

The buzz for me was always about playing the game. I was the total opposite of somebody like Stephen Hendry in that respect. He was all about winning. To be fair, a player is judged as a winner or a loser. It is black and white: winning is everything and losing is nothing.

But, for me, the thrill of winning was just a moment of satisfaction on a particular day. However, it was the thought of winning that was the driving force in the build-up to a tournament. The thrill of taking part was massive, especially as the town or city hosting an event got so involved with it. The practice sessions beforehand seemed to take on more importance. I left on my journey to wherever it was as if I was going off to war.

The thrill of doing something was always so much better than the end product. The end product only mattered because it was evidence that I had done it. That is how I saw it. Winning was only proof of that. It never gave me the same thrill as actually attempting to do it. I think this is where the temptation for a sportsperson to come out of retirement comes from – be it a snooker player, a boxer, whatever. It is the thrill that we miss.

My brain was immersed in the challenge of achievement. During those big tournaments I was so wired about the job in hand. I was playing against some great players and pitting my wits against them. The best way for anybody to achieve success in anything is to enjoy it. For me, that was when winning really became possible.

But once a big tournament was over my mood would sometimes plummet, especially if I had been on a high. The World Championship would always prove to be particularly testing for me because not only was it the biggest event of the season, it was also the final event of the season. The adrenaline and the buzz had then gone.

Snooker is a strange way to earn a living because, emotionally, a player is up and down like a yo-yo compared to other occupations. Of course, people in other walks of life may encounter other problems – they might feel that their lives are not exciting enough, for example. My life was exciting; full of highs and lows but I didn't have too many holidays. Then again, every day felt like a holiday!

That was the pattern of my life. Once the tournaments returned, I was up again. But once the tournaments ended, my mood changed. This was more apparent in the big competitions, but it was still there for any event. Fortunately, there were more and more tournaments popping up as the decade unfolded.

It could be a bit of a conundrum. If something had gone wrong with my game and I had been well beaten, I could be down in the dumps for days on end, upset about my overall standard of play. I would be on the practice table a lot with my father, trying to work out what was going wrong, technically. I would look forward to the next competition in the hope that I could rectify things. I could get so distraught with my game – and this includes lots of times when I was number one in the world!

On most occasions, my problems would be minor. But when I was so caught up in the whole competitive scene, they seemed to be major. The margins at top-class level are so small between winning and losing that the need to find form on the practice table is magnified. So it might have been that I'd perhaps started to miss a shot to the same side of the pocket too often and the cure was probably just a case of adjusting my back arm slightly, usually tucking it in a fraction to get the tip of my elbow in line with the cue.

On other occasions, we found that I had 'lost' the centre of the cue ball and that while I thought I was aiming with my tip at the centre for an intended plain ball shot, I was fractionally to the left or right of the exact centre – even though it didn't look like it to me. This was where my father was invaluable. Hour after hour, he stood behind me, giving me the OK on every shot or doing an impression of a contestant on the *The Golden Shot*! 'Left a bit, right a bit' ...

I would often have to reinforce this by having a whole day playing centre-ball shots – putting break-building or competitive sparring against other players on the back burner until I was satisfied. But this was important to me and it was how I regained my confidence if I had suffered a bad defeat.

I could be very critical of my own game. I was forever trying to stop myself getting into bad habits and sometimes this could feel like pulling teeth. My father was with me all the time. Our often forlorn attempt to crack the code was the challenge we thrived on.

As the press discussed whether I was Mr Cool or Mr Arrogant and became somewhat obsessed with how much money I was earning or potentially could earn in the future, the inevitable lull from competitive snooker continued. There were lots of exhibitions and I was on the road most days and nights. The camaraderie was fantastic and the people I met were terrific. Afterwards, it would be: find the local nightclub, have a great time, wake up, find somewhere to practise or drive off to the next venue and off we go again. I was doing so many exhibitions that I usually didn't have that much time to mope.

While I could have been forgiven for thinking I was getting burnout as the eighties went on, it was so exciting that the word never entered my head. As long as I could get some quality practice in, I would never complain about my workload. I would just have a beer and take the opportunity to wind down.

It was over three months before I could pick up my cue and play a competitive match again. When I finally did, I wrapped up yet another title and a £20,000 cash prize – plus another £2,000 for the highest break of 135 – at the Jameson Whiskey International Open, in Derby, which was the first tournament on the new season's calendar.

During the tournament, I had to jet off to Jersey to take part in a long-standing exhibition commitment. I never stopped at that time. My work ethic was that if people were prepared to pay the premiums that Barry was now starting to charge for me, I couldn't turn them down. The fact it didn't affect my performances in the major competitions says everything about the standard of snooker I was now producing.

Dennis Taylor must have been sick of the sight of me – I whitewashed him again in the final 9–0. So must Alex Higgins, who I beat 9–8 in the semi-finals. The Hurricane tried to goad me into having a £5,000 money match on the side against him afterwards. I declined his offer for two reasons: 1) I had to play in the final the next day; and 2) he would probably have beaten me! I suspected Alex was a far better money player than match player. On the other hand, I felt pretty nervous at the Matchroom when I played for £25!

Alex was also smarting after missing a chance to compile the first 147 ever seen on TV. 'That was a £100,000 shot,' he said to the crowd after missing a red during the break. The stakes to become the first man to achieve the magical maximum on the small screen were getting bigger and bigger – at the Jameson it was worth five times more than winning the tournament!

The honour should have gone to John Spencer at the Holsten Lager International back in 1979 but the television crew were on a break at the time! It still sounds incredible to write that line over 35 years later! I remember sitting at home watching the action on *World of Sport* when, all of a sudden, the presenter Dickie Davies came on and gave us the dramatic news.

They proceeded to show John clearing up the last four colours and the crowd going wild – except they didn't. What they actually showed was a recreation of the break with him going through the motions and the audience going ballistic – as they had been told to do – after he knocked the black in!

I am not sure if there was a prize for this particular maximum but John's break wasn't ratified. The Billiards and Snooker Control Council were no longer involved in the professional game and anyone could see at a glance that the middle pockets were like manholes. It might have been a good idea for the table to be checked before the event took place! These wooden templates were like the Crown Jewels. Sometimes the table fitters didn't have access to them so, effectively, it was guesswork when setting up the table.

My overall success on the circuit was now quite phenomenal and I was able to maintain a strong superiority complex whenever I played. I was riding the crest of a wave. Under Barry Hearn's guidance, I was now the highest earning young sportsman in the country with numerous companies to my name: Steve Davis Limited, Steve Davis Promotions Limited and Steve Davis Properties Limited.

We also bought a forest up in Scotland. Billy Connolly had one next to us! I was the focus of full-page newspaper and magazine articles and interviews in well-respected publications such as the *Observer*, *Radio Times*, the *Sunday Telegraph* and the *Sunday Times*. I also had my own column in the *Daily Star* and I was the subject of a BBC TV documentary called 'Fame'. It was a far cry from one of the first ever interviews I did, which was published in *Penthouse*!

Praise never did anybody any harm. My backroom team would tell me I was the best and I knew I was the best, but my father wasn't so forthcoming in that regard. We were on a purer mission. We were in love with the game and it wasn't solely about winning matches to us. It was about improving my technique so that I could play the best snooker I could possibly manage. The two of us rarely discussed winning or losing – we were just interested in finding perfection on the baize. We enjoyed the good times but we didn't dwell on them.

Before I defended my Coral UK Championship title in Preston, I spent some valuable time in Blackpool at one of the best clubs in the country at the time, the Commonwealth Snooker Centre, which was owned by a lower-ranked professional called David Greaves.

While I was there I also got to know a bespectacled fishmonger-cum-amateur snooker player called Frank Callan, who had started to make a name advising top players on their cue action. I was spending a lot of time in the north-west of England, due to having a girlfriend in Preston at the time, and I enjoyed spending time with Frank.

He was never exactly my coach but we did become friends and it was nice to have somebody around with similar views on how to play the game. He was about the same age as my father but played at a higher level – his top break was around the 140 mark – and this helped me because he knew the game. My father wasn't as knowledgeable about the positional side of play. He couldn't see what the balls did as well as Frank could. I would say that the two of us discussed the game more than anything; I probably helped Frank as much as he helped me. He did offer some good technical advice, though. It was fun getting to know him and spending some quality time with him.

It was reported in some areas (not by Frank or me) that Frank had become my coach, which wasn't the case at all. As a result, for a brief moment, my father may have had his nose put out of joint. I know he felt that I was spending too much time listening to another person. After quite some time I eventually made the decision not to confuse the situation any further and I stayed with what I had. I drew a line underneath it all. It was the best choice all round.

I was in blistering form at Preston in the defence of my UK title, comfortably beating Willie Thorne and Bill Werbeniuk on my way to a semi-final meeting with Jimmy White. The match had been billed as the match of the season so far. It had been given added spice after he narrowly pipped me 6–5 in the semi-finals of the Langs Scottish Masters in Glasgow. He beat Cliff Thorburn in the final to claim his first major title there. A fortnight later, he beat me again, 11–9, in the final of the Northern Ireland Classic in Belfast.

It was apparent that Jimmy was now a handful for anybody. His attacking style of play could have a player on the back foot. If a player showed weakness, he would get swamped by Jimmy's firepower as he reeled off frame after frame in double-quick time. The rivalry between us was building up a head of steam and my matches against him took on extra significance.

This time around the headline writers were to have a ball when I thrashed him 9–0. A few of them carried the word 'whitewash' on their pages. Dennis Taylor had suffered that fate twice from me in the last year and Terry Griffiths had succumbed by the exact same scoreline to me in the semi-finals at Preston 12 months before.

I now faced Terry in the final as I went for my seventh major title in 12 months. I met him in a lot of them. In fact, in this season alone we would contest four individual finals, plus the World Team Championship final at the Hexagon theatre in Reading (when England beat Wales). But I felt that I had now jumped up to a new level and I always seemed to hold the upper hand over him – whereas with Jimmy I was just managing to hold on to a red setter by the tail!

Terry won the first frame of this latest final between us but he was to take only two more as I romped to a massive 16–3 victory with some top-notch snooker once again to retain my UK crown.

My biggest problem in the entire match had been spotting my father sitting in the front row. He knew full well that his place was out of sight and out of mind. He used to sit in the press rooms up and down the country or perhaps the balcony area at the Crucible, so what he was doing there on that occasion, God knows. The last person I wanted to see in my eyeline was anybody I knew well, especially my father. I dealt with it quickly. At the end of a frame I walked over to him and told him to get out or stand at the back. He took it quite well!

There is a big difference between winning the UK Championship and winning the World Championship. You could win the UK title or an event like it quite comfortably – and yet you were still not sure if you could win the world title. So it doesn't always follow that you can produce on the biggest stage of all even though you produced on the second biggest stage of all. However, right now, I fancied myself to produce everywhere I went.

At the annual BBC Sports Review of 1981 show, live from Television Centre in west London at the end of the year, I was tipped as one of the favourites for the Sports Personality of the Year award.

As soon as I came off the red carpet in front of the cameras on my way into the reception area, David Vine pulled me to one side and asked if I had written a speech. I hadn't even thought about it. I knew there had been some calls to the office to make sure I was going to be in attendance. That was never in doubt. To be invited in the first place was such an honour and I made sure my diary was free for this one well in advance. But it hadn't occurred to me that I might have a chance of winning the top prize.

I sat there all night thinking through what I might say if I had come out on top. David's words and the phone calls suggested to me that I might have been close. But I didn't have a speech prepared. In the end, I came second. Ian Botham, who was playing for England in India at the time and couldn't be there on the night, won the award for his amazing performance in the Ashes success over Australia in the summer. Sebastian Coe, who had broken the world mile record twice, came third.

The fact that snooker had been recognised in this way by the general public – who could only vote by taking the time to cut out coupons from the *Radio Times* and post them to the BBC – was amazing. It was further evidence, if any was needed, of where our sport was now at. It was all pretty astonishing, really – just five years before we could get hardly any of the World Championship shown on television! But now snooker had come of age. We had become accepted. The nation liked us.

Snooker was such a big hit on television that it couldn't be ignored. I made regular appearances on the small screen at this time. The pick of the bunch for me had to be appearing on the must-watch *Morecambe and Wise Christmas Show*. This annual hit used to be the highest viewed programme of the year! I featured in a running sketch where I played Eric Morecambe in the final of the World Championship. Ernie Wise was the referee and Ted Lowe was the commentator. I had to make a series of mistakes while Eric walked up to the table and played an incredible range of brilliant shots. This was all edited together nicely so that I could play the shot while they cut to a close-up of Eric's bridge hand! Effectively, I played the part of his double!

I also appeared on *The Russell Harty Show*, *A Question of Sport*, *Blue Peter* and *Tiswas*. The latter was by far the most fun. It was fantastic to go along and get involved with the likes of Chris Tarrant, Sally James and Lenny Henry in all the chaos. It was very daft and very funny and very live: Bob Carolgees, Spit the Dog, the Phantom Flan Flinger … There was no escape. Appearing on *Blue Peter* was a thrill, too. I had grown up with the programme and suddenly I was on it. I also went on Noel Edmonds' *Multi-Coloured Swap Shop* as a guest – not as an item – to promote the *Pot Black* toy table.

Looking back, it is interesting to consider how snooker made such a big impact on children's television at that time. It wouldn't happen today. I say that because children are no longer watching the television programmes that their parents have on in the house. The kids of today are a completely different animal from when I was younger. They want to be celebrities not snooker players anyway!

The year ended with the annual sojourn up to Pebble Mill Studios in Birmingham to take part in *Pot Black* once again. I am happy to say that I finally won the trophy, beating Eddie Charlton 2–0 in the final. The match would not be shown on BBC 2 until the following March.

Ironically, given what had happened to him previously, I played John Spencer in the Lada Classic in Oldham at the beginning of a very cold January in 1982 and, despite being jet-lagged and tired out after a hectic ten-day trip to Australia, during which I signed a contract to play a mammoth, 132-frame match against national hero Eddie Charlton later in the year, and a stop-off with Barry in Las Vegas on the way home, I was to make snooker history.

I arrived in Oldham having not spent one night at home since the turn of the year. The snow was falling and I was a sleepwalking zombie. I struggled through the first four frames against John, which we shared two apiece, and I had to have a power nap in the dressing room during the interval. But this was nowhere near long enough and I came out to play the fifth frame still feeling quite groggy.

John broke off poorly in the next frame and left me with a pot into the middle pocket. After four reds and four blacks, I wondered to myself about the possibility of a maximum as there were no reds on cushions. I then lost position but still managed to double the next red into a middle pocket and screwed the white past the pack to get back on the black and salvage the situation. On my next shot, I screwed the white into the pack but managed to dislodge only two reds.

A series of blacks then opened up the reds nicely for me but, as I was running out of reds, I started to feel the pressure. While I didn't stop getting the pots, I did start to struggle with position. I managed to get just high enough on the fourteenth red into a middle pocket to get somewhere on the black but it meant I had no chance of getting close to the last red. I managed to get the cue ball into the bottom half of the table, between the yellow and the brown, for a long stun shot on the final red.

If ever I needed something special from those endless hours of long, straight potting practice it was now. I just concentrated on keeping my head as still as possible and the ball flew into the top corner. As soon as it crashed into the hole, the crowd erupted.

At that moment, I heard somebody shout out: 'Go on, Steve!'

The angle on the black was pretty good. I knew if I could get a decent position on the yellow, I was in with a chance of making history. My pulse was now moving through the gears. It was a different pressure from the one I had experienced at the Crucible when I won the world title: this time it was just me against the table. I potted the black with a little left-hand side to avoid cannoning into the pink and sent the white rolling down the table.

I didn't get on the yellow perfectly but at least I was on it. The white was just off straight on the yellow. It was a difficult shot. I decided to screw back sharply, taking care to avoid the brown and snookering myself. I got enough screw back on it, especially as it would have been easy to have quit on the shot, but I left myself a fraction short of ideal. I now needed to cut the green in, but I had to sacrifice perfect position. I was now further away from the brown and too straight on it. I had to play a strong run through.

I was shaking like a leaf but felt pumped up. I scrambled the brown in – but was now even further out of position and too close to the side cushion to control the cue ball. I had to cut the blue in the right-hand middle pocket and send the cue ball in and out of baulk and hope to get somewhere near the pink.

I got there but I was in the middle of the table: I now had to cut the pink into the top left corner, using the rest, and also screw the cue ball to the side cushion in order to slow it down enough for me to have a sniff at the black.

I got the screw back on, avoided going in-off in the right corner, and then watched the cue ball travel around the back of the black. I was lucky. The whole colours clearance was a lesson in how not to try and clear them. But now just the black was left between me and a first ever televised 147 maximum break.

The crowd was going wild. I slowly put away the rest and composed myself for the final shot. I stood behind the black and looked at the table. I was enjoying the moment even though I had a difficult final shot in front of me. My palms felt sweaty and I remember blowing on my left hand without even thinking about it. This was something I had seen the great Björn Borg do. I had never done it before and I don't think I ever did it again. But perhaps, subconsciously, it worked for me.

I considered that the only danger was the possibility of a bad contact if I rolled the black in so I decided to stun it in. As I sunk the final ball, I anxiously followed the cue ball with my eyes in the hope that it wasn't going directly towards the yellow pocket. When I was completely sure it was safe, there followed a brief moment of shock as I realised I had done it!

John was the first person to shake my hand. Around us, the crowd almost broke down the hoardings as they tried to get over to congratulate me on my achievement. I had hit snooker's Holy Grail. It was the perfect frame.

I went on to reach the final in Oldham where Terry Griffiths got his own back on me after a string of defeats by winning on the black in the final frame of a best-of-17 contest.

I nearly completed a miraculous comeback after being 8–3 behind at one stage. Terry was squirming at 8–8 and I had the chance of a long black down the side cushion. Safety seemed too dangerous so I went for the pot. It was a good effort – but it wobbled and it wouldn't go down. Terry held his nerve and potted a very missable black.

In the after-match interviews I felt exhilarated, even though I had lost. It had been such an exciting match. Terry had played great snooker and deserved to win, but I had enjoyed an exciting week myself. What's more, I could now leave my Porsche in Oldham and drive home in a new car!

My 147 break was timed at 12 minutes but it seemed to fly by. My prize was a brand new Lada. The tournament before offered thousands for a 147 and the tournament afterwards offered thousands more, but the one I did it in offered a Lada. That didn't matter to me. The true prize was the honour and prestige of accomplishing the unaccomplished.

Lada wanted to take a photograph of me with the car. A mock number plate – SD147 – was ordered to go with it for the photo shoot. They actually tried to buy the real one but the owner, who was driving around in an old Datsun with it up in Scotland, refused to sell. He was offered a brand new car as well – but he still held out.

I gave the car to my parents because I was now driving a white Porsche 928, which looked a bit weird sitting outside a terraced house in Plumstead. To the locals' credit, nobody ever vandalised it, but somewhere down the line somebody did smash in a side window in order to steal a box of home-taped cassettes worth about a fiver! The insurance on my Porsche was £2,500 per year – £1 more than the cost of a brand new Lada!

As for the Lada, its timeline in Plumstead is clouded in mystery and intrigue. When we moved to a farm in Essex some years later, my parents decided that they needed a more robust vehicle – if you could get such a thing! They plumped for a 4 x 4 Jeep and sold the Lada privately to somebody in the neighbourhood. It was later stolen. Obviously the thieves couldn't go around claiming to have Steve Davis' 147 Lada in their possession – even if they knew about it – so it was either demoted to just a normal run-of-the-mill Lada or sent back home to Russia for a tidy sum of roubles.

Many moons later, Ken Doherty came within one ball of a maximum at the Masters and winning a yellow Lamborghini, worth around £80,000. Meanwhile, 147 breaks at the Crucible soon started to carry prize money of £147,000. But I have always been happy with what that Lada represented: there was only ever going to be one man who made the first ever maximum break on television and that was me!

10. THE MASTER

A week before the Benson & Hedges Masters in 1982, I was sitting in Barry Hearn's Romford office when I answered a call from a man with a northern accent. He congratulated me on my 147 break in the Lada Classic and then, in the same breath, told me that the next time I went up north he would break my fingers.

I put the phone down. I can't say he frightened me but I was certainly shocked. I tried not to think too much about it and continued to prepare for the Masters. What I didn't know was that he was telephoning the office sometimes as often as ten times a day and threatening to injure me when I turned out to play at Wembley!

The Masters was the one major tournament left on my wish list. I had gone along to watch it when I was starting out and I had waited patiently for my world ranking to finally justify a place in the list of 12 invited players who got the nod to take part. Now I was keen to add the title to my growing collection.

It was London's version of the World Championship in a sense. The Wembley Conference Centre where the event was held was the perfect setting for it with capacity for well over 2,500 fans inside. It remains a unique competition and it seemed to appeal to a wider audience than other snooker events. It was a spectacle and fans were always guaranteed to see two very good players – among the very best in the world – in a one-table shoot-out.

It was also ahead of its time. The first Masters was held in 1975 – two years before the World Championship moved to Sheffield, so it wasn't feeding off the success of the World Championship and the knock-on effect of television coverage. When the Masters started the World Championship was struggling to find a venue and there was no live television coverage.

So in some ways the Masters was, effectively, innovative in the standards that were set. It was some scene there. The whole front row – containing VIPs and various dignitaries – featured dress suits and bow ties. Flowers were in abundance, too. They were big in snooker at the time – there were bundles of them wherever we went and they were replaced mid-tournament with fresh ones. At the Masters there were so many daffodils around us you could sneeze. But they suited the sponsors' colour scheme so they were everywhere. The local florists had a ball when snooker was in town. Alex Higgins famously found another use for them – but more of that later ...

At this time, the normal dress code for snooker was dinner jacket in the evening and lounge suit in the afternoon, so, as the game started to raise its profile, the players looked to stand out from the crowd – mainly in the shirt department.

Frills were in fashion: big, stupid frills poked out of well-dressed men at posh dinners, so players wore frills, too. This was ridiculous really because the chances of a player fouling the ball were so much higher if he was wearing one of these items. Cufflinks were de rigueur but they could get in the way as well. I wore them in my early days but I realised pretty quickly that there was no point in doing so. Practicality is far more important to a player. As a result, I settled for normal shirts and, looking around at the modern-day players, I realise I was pretty ground-breaking! Long hair could also be a problem, as could beards: in the 2014 UK Championship, for instance, Rory McLeod was penalised by the referee for touching a ball with his beard.

As a venue, Wembley Conference Centre held many more people than the Crucible theatre. If you can play well in certain venues, there is no question that you are a serious player. Wembley was one of those places. There was always an atmosphere there and it could be quite a vociferous one at times, particularly when the likes of Alex Higgins or one of the London lads played there, especially Jimmy White. The Wembley crowd loved Jimmy.

The crowd was always quite raucous there. During this period, any match against Alex or Jimmy was going to be a noisy affair. Everybody had to work extra hard against them where that was concerned. Playing Alex, in particular, could be frightening. Some people who came to watch him – this was particularly true at Wembley – would not come and watch any other match. They had no interest in anybody else. They were fans of the Hurricane not snooker. They liked what they saw in him and they also liked to have a scream-up. So there was a good chance of a rather hostile atmosphere when you put the two of those together. Fireworks were guaranteed!

Perhaps all this was exacerbated at Wembley because of the type of arena it was, circular with a walkway round it so it felt like one of those football grounds with a running track. This gap reduced the feeling of intimacy for me when playing there. Actually, the sheer size of the place made any form of intimacy almost impossible. Some of the crowd were sitting so far back they must have needed binoculars to see. They were just too far away from the table for my liking.

So I never warmed to the arena. Personally, I felt like I needed more time to settle down in a match. The whole place intimidated me. Maybe it was too impersonal. I always felt somewhat exposed there and that made me feel more vulnerable as well. I never really got on with it, not like I did the Crucible. Perhaps I just wasn't a fan of daffodils!

As a result of those phone calls to Romford and without mentioning anything to me, Barry and our two resident staff drivers, Robbo (Robert Brazier) and Ronnie Radley, who had now been promoted to unpaid minders, planned to turn up at every session I played at Wembley that year, tooled up in large overcoats. This says a lot about the Romford lot. These guys would have taken a bullet for me. Well, perhaps a rubber one.

When the rest of the Matchroom members found out about the story, they quickly summed up the situation: had there been any real trouble, one of them would have run away and the other one would have made a book on whether he would get caught or not!

I first noticed something was up when I mentioned I was off to the toilet and, quick as a flash, Robbo and Ron jumped up and said in unison: 'And so am I!' I asked them what was going on and Barry eventually told me the truth. They had all tried to keep it a secret from me – but they couldn't. We all stayed on full alert throughout but nothing happened. None of us really expected this anonymous caller to carry out his threats – but you just never know. I suppose it only takes one moment of madness: Monica Seles being stabbed in 1993 during a tennis match in Germany by a man who was obsessed with Steffi Graf is the frightening proof that it could happen to anybody at any time.

We dealt with the situation although the threats were persistent and quickly went from breaking my fingers to shooting me. The mystery caller started to ring Barry every Monday morning with new threats. In the end

Barry actually had conversations with him and they began to get on famously, so much so that he became a Matchroom fan! He eventually stopped calling. To this day, I have no idea who he was or what happened to him!

In Robbo we had a man with a larger than life personality. He was a lorry driver who spent most of his day in the club at Romford. He was a hardened gambler with not much money in his pocket and gambling was his life: he only ever left the club to go to the betting shop. But he was also a big character in the Romford Roar and he loved it all.

Robbo's life wasn't a success story. He lived from hand to mouth a lot of the time. He started to drive me around the country and became my personal driver of sorts in the end. He was soon chaperoning me all over the place and, because he was a funny character, he was good company. I liked him a lot. He also had a knack of telling you what you wanted to hear. It is always good for a sportsman to have somebody like that around.

I was seeded through to the quarter-finals at Wembley and met Doug Mountjoy – the man I had seen win the competition back in 1977. I won 5–2 with no more damage to my fingers than, perhaps, a bitten fingernail at the interval.

My next opponent was not only a Londoner – who would obviously get the crowd on his side – but also a stablemate. Barry had just signed up Tony Meo but I had to put that to the back of my mind. I knew I was still first in the pecking order. Barry told anybody who signed for him that I would always come first and that was reassuring.

Tony came into the best-of-11-frames match in very good form, having completely dismantled Cliff Thorburn, who was still world number one at the time, 5–0 in just 80 minutes to reach the semi-finals. I knew I needed to start well and a nice 113 clearance in the second frame helped me storm into a 5–0 lead.

I required just one more frame to win but Tony responded in style. As he did so, I suddenly hit a brick wall and 5–0 quickly became 5–4. In the end, I held my nerve with a 75 clearance to rescue a 6-4 win. But it was a tussle. Terry Griffiths beat Alex Higgins by the same scoreline later that night to set up yet another final between us.

The last time we had met Terry had beaten me on the black and at one stage it looked like it could become another classic between us as he fought back from 6–3 to 6–5 in our best-of-17. Although Terry had a great chance to level the match in the twelfth frame – where he led 51–21 at one stage – I made a pressure clearance to regain a two-frame advantage and that seemed to halt his charge. A crisis point had been averted and I continued to control the remaining two frames of the match to win 9–5 and claim the title that completed the grand slam of all the big three tournaments: World Championship, UK Championship and Masters.

Master was an appropriate title, for I now truly dominated the game. I was tipped to become snooker's first ever millionaire at the age of just twenty-four. My prize-money winnings alone in the past 14 months had surpassed £100,000 and I had signed a £220,000 contract for 40 personal appearances with Courage brewery.

I fancied myself to win against anybody at any time and the longer the match, the better it was for me. All that didn't necessarily mean that I would win every tournament, as Terry had proved in the Lada Classic just a few weeks before. But I was the dominant force going into every single event at that time. I still lost here and there. I certainly wasn't bulletproof over nine frames – the likes of Eugene Hughes, Perrie Mans and David Taylor beat me on occasions – but for a high percentage of those times I would cruise through.

While most of the other players were struggling with their own games and obviously having to address the possibility of me becoming nigh on unbeatable, I was enjoying my competitive snooker very much. This made the job in hand doubly hard for them.

The foundations my father and I had put into place over the previous ten years were now really reaping rewards. Whenever I started doing something wrong technically we would correct it as quickly as we could. The conscientious, relentless practice we put in together was now part of the crutch I relied on for my confidence.

I developed a new slant on the 'work hard, play hard' ethic. Work was practice, play was tournaments. I was enjoying my practice sessions more than ever at this time.

With my dominance at a new supreme level, the media asked the question that was on everybody's lips: who would have won a match between the great Joe Davis and Steve Davis? This is something we will never know but for now I will leave the answer to the most respected of all snooker commentators, Clive Everton: 'I think Steve would have beaten Joe,' Clive told Hugh McIlvanney in the *Observer* just a week after my triumph at Wembley. His words were good enough for me.

This question pops up every time we enter a new era in snooker. My answer is always the same: the new era would always have beaten the previous one.

The tournaments kept on coming and so did my victories. I beat Dennis Taylor 8–3 in the final of the Tolly Cobbold Classic in Ipswich in February and Terry Griffiths to win at the Yamaha Organs International in Derby in March, before losing to him in the final of the Benson & Hedges Irish Masters at Goffs in Co. Kildare later in the same month. During the same month, the final of *Pot Black* was at last shown on BBC 2 and, although I had been sworn to secrecy since Christmas, I could now celebrate my victory with a clear conscience.

My only real blip came just a few weeks before the 1982 World Championship in the Highland Masters in Inverness where I was thrashed 6–0 by Ray Reardon, a result that rocked me to the core. I felt as though my game had suddenly collapsed and I couldn't quite put my finger on why this was.

My father and I were at something of a loss on the practice table. The timing could not have been worse either, with the defence of my world title literally just around the corner. I started to become apprehensive about the task that was now looming. Everything suddenly felt magnified as the most important snooker competition of the season approached …

11. THE CURSE
OF THE CRUCIBLE

In an attempt to avoid upsetting the snooker gods I checked into the very same room at the Grosvenor Hotel in Sheffield where I had stayed 12 months earlier ahead of the 1982 Embassy World Championship. I also had access to my own arcade video machine and 40 videotape films of the latest releases to help get me through the expected schedule of 17 days.

Barry Hearn called it the 'Hollywood treatment'. Robbo and Ron were also on hand to peel grapes for me. Ironically, the only movie that we managed to watch was *The Evil Dead*. It was a giggle. We all sat there with the lights off and pretended to be scared. Little did we know that a couple of days later I would be taking part in my own horror movie down the road!

Never before had I felt like I did when I made that familiar journey into the Steel City for the first time as reigning world champion. Driving past the dentist's – otherwise known as the Crucible – and on towards my hotel, I felt more butterflies flapping around in my stomach than ever before.

The pressure of playing in a world final is nothing compared to playing in the first round. When you are defending your world title there for the first time, the expectation and tension are magnified. I can't say why exactly. Perhaps it was because I now knew what it took to win the world crown? Maybe it was expectation? I might have been overawed. I was made the strong favourite again with odds of 2–5 by my name!

Maybe it was the fact that, deep down, I was still reeling from my humiliation at the hands of Ray Reardon in the Highland Masters in Inverness and there were suddenly questions about my form. I certainly didn't feel totally at ease going into the event.

I had been pretty dominant that season so I should have been feeling very confident but I think I let the magnitude of the situation affect me. I could have brushed off losing to Ray in a minor event as a blip – but a 6–0 bashing! You're only as good as your last outing. Confidence, no matter how high, can evaporate in a flash.

Also, when you climb a mountain for the first time perhaps you don't realise how high you have gone and how hard the task is. The second time around you know exactly how high the mountain is and the temptation to look down and see what the fall is like can be too great to resist! Maybe in the build-up to my world title defence I faltered. I became too scared of falling and that was not a good frame of mind to be in. So, the manner of my defeat to Ray combined with this 'looking down' syndrome conspired to make me uneasy.

The World Championship had increased in size from 24 to 32 players this year and was extended to 17 days as a result. As champion, I was named top seed with former winners Cliff Thorburn, Terry Griffiths and Ray Reardon seeded two, three and four respectively. Terry was considered to be my main threat and the bookmakers made him second favourite at 4–1. Alex Higgins, who hadn't enjoyed the best of seasons, was seeded 11. Jimmy White was unseeded, as was my first-round opponent, 150–1 outsider Tony Knowles, who had come through the qualifying competition to get there.

Tony had been knocking around the circuit for some time. I knew him well. I had played him for the first time back in 1977 when I toured the country with my Lucania team-mates Geoff Foulds and Russell Jarmak, playing the best amateurs around. We had also shared a room to cut costs on our visit to Toronto. Well, it cut Tony's costs as I paid the bill. He still owes me £70!

Tony was a couple of years older than me and had won the British Junior Championship twice in the early 1970s. But he was twice turned down as a professional and threatened legal action against the WPBSA at one stage before being accepted at the third attempt. He hadn't achieved anything in the game to suggest he would cause me any problems: I knew I was technically superior and better under pressure than anybody and surely now that I had won all the top trophies I had shaken off his like and jumped up to another level? His odds with the bookmakers underlined that.

As defending world champion I was the first match on. I remember I wasn't looking forward to it too much. I have always hated the first round at the Crucible. It was like a school exam, driving test, job interview and parachute jump all rolled into one. Furthermore, I'd have preferred to face somebody like Ray Reardon, Terry Griffiths or Alex Higgins. With all due respect to Tony Knowles, I probably took it for granted that I would beat him.

It was raining when the Davis camp left the Grosvenor that morning, so we decided to go down there in a spanking new Mercedes with all the trimmings. Obviously it would have been stupid to have asked the driver to take a detour so that I could get out of the car, put a foot on the lucky cellar doors, get back in the car and get dropped off at the stage door, wouldn't it?

The first person I saw once I got inside the Crucible was the BBC's David Vine. This man was the gateway into the game for a lot of snooker fans. While David had presented countless sports for the BBC at Olympic Games level no less, it would be fair to say that he always had a special place in his heart for snooker.

Long after David retired he would regularly telephone Graham Fry, the man in charge of the coverage for IMG on behalf of the BBC, to congratulate or criticise, whether this be about a feature, an interview or a policy decision regarding an incident that had unfolded during the event. His reason for doing this was always the same: to show snooker in the best possible light.

While some in the media have been guilty of treating snooker as a low priority, David was proud of the sport and his involvement in it. In turn, I would like to think that we were proud of him. Now that we have established a Hall of Fame within the sport, I think the one person who should be posthumously inducted is David.

David had a problem. He was a smoker. Back in the day, that was pretty normal in snooker but that may also have exacerbated his problem. It can't have helped that cigarettes were thrown around like confetti at tobacco-sponsored events. Furthermore, all performers felt nervous at the Crucible: I couldn't stay out of the toilet until I went out to play and David would chain-smoke his way up to transmission. The closer it got to going live, the more he would cough to try and clear his throat. The tales of him clearing his throat before going on air remain the stuff of legend.

On many occasions I would be in the practice room, behind the black curtain that gave David a modicum of privacy, trying to hit some balls in between his coughs. In fact, I would be trying desperately hard to concentrate around David's coughs. As the clock ticked down, all you could hear was the click of the balls and David's coughing as he moved up the gears. With one minute to go, David would hit overdrive and the coughing would reach fever pitch, sounding like somebody trying to start a lawnmower. By this stage my father and I would be laughing so much that we'd collapse on the table in tears, unable to see the balls we were trying to work with, let alone focus on important parts of my game such as eye sequences during long shots. All of a sudden, bang! David goes live to the nation and there is not a cough to be heard. There is complete silence around him apart for some uncontrollable giggling from behind the snooker table and the ever-professional floor manager Dave Bowden trying to hush us up.

On the morning of my first defence of the World Championship title I was in the same practice room doing a routine where I lined up all the balls across the middle of the table for long pots. It was a good way to test myself: the equivalent of hitting balls with your driver on the practice ground before a round of golf. I sank 16 or 17 of the 21 balls, which is a really high percentage. Willie Thorne was standing there watching me and he commented on how well I was hitting the ball. I was happy with my technique but deep down I still felt apprehensive.

The first frame can often be the most important one of a match. I potted some good balls in my opener against Tony Knowles – but he took it on the colours after I had fouled by feathering the cue ball while lining up to pot the blue. He then won the next three frames to lead 4–0 at the interval, by which time I was in my dressing room feeling punch drunk!

Tony was a great front-runner. He fed off confidence. He was much better when he was in front than behind. More so than most, I reckon. He seemed to get an injection of confidence once he got his nose in front in a match. It was the fifth frame before I got on the scoreboard. By the end of the first session, I was 8–1 behind.

I was in shock, completely put off balance by the way Tony had started bossing the table. He possessed a trademark spin of the cue – a bit like a cheerleader with a baton – and that was agony for me to watch because I could see how in control he felt. He usually reserved it for exhibitions but he did it against me in one frame when he was clearing up. His obvious enjoyment of the occasion made it much worse for me.

It was clear to me by now that this was his moment and it wasn't going to happen for me. Tony required just two more frames out of the next ten to win. Mentally, that is a huge lead. I knew he wasn't going to stall and I wasn't ready to pick up the pieces even if he did. I also had to deal with the expectation of the crowd, willing the favourite to get beaten by an unknown outsider. Everything weighed on my mind. I wanted to crawl away.

I walked back to my hotel with my father, 8–1 down in a match I had expected to breeze through. I was devastated. My whole world had evaporated in what seemed like the time it had taken to lose the first frame. I had turned up there like a giant piece of porcelain but with one small knock I had shattered into a thousand pieces. Usually, I would respond to a losing session in an important tournament by coming out with all guns blazing, but this time around I was inconsolable.

In the end I was basically waiting to lose. I don't think I even bothered to go to the practice room with my father before the second session the following day. I just wanted to hide away from everything. I had capitulated and I was ready to be punched with my hands hanging by my waist. Tony completed a 10–1 humiliation in what somehow seemed to be no time at all yet an eternity at the same time.

On reflection, I just wasn't mentally strong enough to deal with it all once it started to unravel and go so wrong. It was a weird experience for me anyway, coming in cold to a red-hot cauldron with all eyes on me and, of course, Tony played the best match of his career up to that point. Make no mistake about that. Yes, he had nothing to lose but he was fired up and when I showed weakness he was ready to jump on it.

Tony later told the press he had been in a nightclub until two the night before the match! I had been tucked in bed well before midnight.

Perhaps I should have mentally prepared better for what to do if he got off to a flyer in the way that he did? But I didn't. I was in the wrong frame of mind to cope with it. What more can I say? The pressure got to me. The Crucible curse had struck again.

At the time of writing, no first-time world champion has yet managed to defend his title successfully at the Crucible. I was the fifth man to win there and Mark Selby was the nineteenth in 2014. It remains to be seen what happens to him ... The eighteen who came before all failed to retain their title. A few, like me, even crashed out in their first match – Terry Griffiths, Dennis Taylor, Shaun Murphy, Graeme Dott, Neil Robertson ...

It is a phenomenon. Why have we all been so vulnerable? I wonder if it was our understanding of how hard it was to win the trophy coupled with being defending champion and the level of expectancy heaped on us. Did we all put too much pressure on ourselves?

For the record, I defended the world title six times and I never felt under as much pressure as I did that first time. I was a winning machine. But I really started to feel the heat when the World Championship came around. I think that was largely down to knowing what was required of me.

A sports psychologist should have a look at this. My view is that when the World Championship comes around everything intensifies and, subconsciously, the first-time world champion puts too much pressure on himself. The thrill of going for the crown the previous year quickly turns into the fear of not being able to keep it. The Crucible becomes a beast. Too many of us have collapsed in this way for it all to be a coincidence.

I simply froze. I didn't like the situation I was in: defending world champion, first match, first out to play. It was horrendous. I was in freefall and powerless to do anything. The hardest part of it all was going through the motions. In boxing you can throw the towel in. In snooker, you can't. I had to wait until Tony had won his tenth frame – because there was no way I was going to win a second!

In life people tend not to remember good moments as much as the bad and some of us aren't allowed to forget certain bad moments either. This was my first experience of this. Losing 10–1 to Tony has stayed with me. As for my opponent, he was a great player with lots of ability and he was always going to have his day in the sun. This would be the start of a purple patch in his career. He won the Jameson International later that year and got to number two in the world. He also went on to play in three World Championship semi-finals.

Looking back, Tony was probably much more talented than we all gave him credit for at the time. It certainly wasn't the case that I got beaten by somebody who couldn't hold a cue, so it could be argued that he was a difficult first-round opponent. But from experience I would add that every first-round opponent at the Crucible is difficult. It is just one of those places. I never once felt comfortable playing in the first round there.

I stuck around in Sheffield for a while afterwards. I went on a bender. The therapy that came with that did help me for a while, but only long enough for me to forget there was a tournament going on a few hundred yards away from the nightclubs! It actually turned out to be one of the best: Alex Higgins beating Ray Reardon in the final with a 135 break to win his second world title ten years after his first.

The scenes at the end where Alex called for his baby, Lauren, to be taken to him onstage are the stuff of folklore. His match-saving clearance of 69 against Jimmy White in the semi-finals was the moment of the tournament. It remains the number one bottle clearance in the history of the game. It should also be considered the most amazing moment that has ever happened at the Crucible – and it would be if a stupid incident three years later had not raised its ugly head and swayed public opinion!

It may well have been a defining moment in Jimmy's career as well. If the Whirlwind had just lost the match, perhaps it would not have been so defined. But the Hurricane's brilliant and ridiculous clearance – the most amazing the game has ever seen – made that impossible.

Alex was in his element, enjoying every moment, looking up to the commentary box, feeding off the crowd's excitement and producing daredevil shots the nature of which if any had gone wrong would have handed Jimmy a place in the world final against Ray Reardon and, possibly, the old master would not have been able to hold the Whirlwind – or perhaps he would?

Either way, the history of snooker would have been very different. What would a parallel universe look like in which Alex Higgins made a single mistake in that break and Jimmy White went on to win the world title in 1982? If ever you wanted to believe in fate, that one moment in the Whirlwind's career would perhaps make you a believer.

The experience of crashing out in the first round seemed to affect me more once the season officially ended and I faced the dreaded two or three months without a competition to play in. I hid away for a while. I beat myself up a bit, too. My mother – my staunchest supporter – even wrote in the scrapbook that she loyally kept of my snooker career: 'May 1, 1982: Defeated by himself!'

All these years on, the attention to detail that my mother put into those loving scrapbooks of hers has helped me fully appreciate her involvement in my career and what it meant to her. She was as proud as punch and, should somebody dare to criticise me, her protection of her son was extraordinary. But her honesty, exemplified by that comment in her scrapbook, came from the heart.

Since becoming a parent myself and having children, who are now themselves trying to make their own way in life, I have come to understand a lot. My mother was something of a silent supporter during my career. While my father went everywhere with me as my coach, she was the true parent in a sense: sitting at home, watching the matches, supporting from afar, buying the newspapers the next day ... I know it meant just as much to her as it did to him.

I thrashed Alex Higgins 5–0 in an exhibition match in Warrington just a few days after his world title triumph but it was small consolation for me as the Hurricane was, quite understandably, on a celebratory bender – I know I used to be immediately after winning the World Championship – but it still felt therapeutic, especially given that some exhibition matches were reported at a local level as if they were actual matches.

Helping my recuperation was the fact that I hit form again a few weeks later when I beat Ray Reardon 9–4 to win the Pontin's professional tournament in Prestatyn. I also played some exhibitions in the summer and these were an important way for me to get out of my shell and back in the saddle. These events always helped to lighten the load of anything negative that might have happened to me. I couldn't sulk forever and I found that snooker wasn't so bad after all.

But I wasn't going to forget my first-round defeat to Tony Knowles at the Crucible. There were reminders at every exhibition with fans wanting to know exactly what had happened. There was no hiding place: a woman came up to me in the local supermarket and asked for my autograph. I happily obliged. She asked if I could write it out to her daughter, Toni Knowles!

12. SNOOKER IS BETTER THAN SEX

Snooker had gone global by the summer of 1982 and I was at the forefront of it. The new season began earlier than usual with a trip Down Under to play in the Winfield Australian Masters, a competition organised by Eddie Charlton.

I had to beat Eddie to win it. A further series of 13 exhibition matches followed between us all over the country. This was Australia v England and so the contest was dubbed 'the Ashes' in the media. As well as a handsome cash prize, the winner got to keep the ashes of a burnt cue case. You get the connection.

Eddie was quite a character and the most successful Australian snooker player until the emergence of Neil Robertson many years later. He was also a man from another era, almost 30 years older than me. He was always jetting back and forth between Australia and the UK. In that sense, he was the fittest player on the circuit, which is fair comment because he'd been both a boxer and a surfer and remained a keep-fit fanatic. He certainly looked after himself in an age when some of his counterparts were knocking back the drink and piling on the pounds.

He considered himself an unlucky player or, should I say, he considered his opponents to be lucky players. If it wasn't for that fact alone he would have won more honours in the game – or so he believed. He never won the World Championship himself but he came very close, losing by just one frame to Ray Reardon in Melbourne in 1975 in a tournament he helped to organise – and one where he managed to avoid the best players in the draw until the final! He was also runner-up in the World Billiards Championship and remains the only player to have reached both finals without winning either of them. In the UK he was most famous for winning *Pot Black* on three occasions, which at the time earned the winner more publicity than winning the world title anyway.

So Eddie invented his own version of *Pot Black* and made sure there was no luck involved in the outcome. Players had to nominate all shots, including attempts at doubles, trebles, plants, combination shots and anything else that could otherwise be construed as a fluke. He was obsessed with trying to eliminate any luck whatsoever from the game because he felt he would then have a better chance. Of course, it didn't make a blind bit of difference. While he may have thought he was unlucky, he wasn't.

Whether the constant travelling put him at a disadvantage compared to his British-based rivals is debatable. He was a good player but he wasn't as naturally gifted as the likes of Alex Higgins, Ray Reardon and John Spencer and played a solid but uninspiring game. His best days were behind him by the time I played him and his technique was being overrun by the new, aggressive style on the table. He never seemed to be adventurous enough with the cue ball for my liking but maybe jetlag did have something to answer for, because when he did manage to get the World Championship moved to Melbourne in 1975 – and very nearly won it – it showed that his game still had genuine strengths.

On one occasion later in his career, while snookered during a doubles match against Dennis Taylor and Cliff Thorburn, Eddie muttered the words 'lucky bastards' to himself when he walked to the table past the referee, who unfortunately was miked up. The whole room heard it. It was hilarious. Both Dennis and Cliff struggled to play on amid the laughter while Eddie stood there unimpressed, cursing his bad luck again. He was always a very serious player, even in a fun event like the Hofmeister World Doubles.

Eddie also raised a smile when he had a hair transplant late in his career when well into his sixties. He turned up at one event with these big holes – where hair had been planted – across his forehead. The BBC production team made a very funny music item to 'The Way We Were' by Barbra Streisand, featuring Eddie past and present with hair, no hair and, suddenly, more hair than ever.

To sum Eddie up: he was a trier and a trooper. He was a good player for his time and he grafted his way to some good results. He had a fantastic work ethic but, as a natural talent, he wasn't in the same bracket as somebody like Ray, who was always the master. Try as he might, he just couldn't get the better of him. Ray always had something extra in the tank when they met. I never struggled against Eddie either.

By the early 1980s, Eddie seemed to me to be punching well above his weight. He reached three world finals and a further six world semi-finals in his career, the last coming in 1982. But he continued to play on the exhibition circuit back home and died following a heart attack at an event in Palmerston North, in New Zealand in 2004, aged seventy-five. Bizarrely, six months later, when the following season's ranking list was issued, Eddie had gone up two places! Either that said a lot about the state of organisation at WPBSA HQ or I had severely underestimated his talents!

Back in the UK, the WPBSA was unhappy with my decision to withdraw from the forthcoming Langs Scottish Masters in September and the Professional Players Tournament in October. My decision was for business reasons: I wanted to do the best business I possibly could on the table! With a growing number of tournaments on the calendar and a burgeoning exhibition scene, it was impossible for me to do everything. My priority was to make sure that I was in peak condition for the big tournaments and so I didn't need to play for just a few grand here and there.

WPBSA company secretary Mike Green subsequently warned that I might not be eligible to play in the Embassy World Championship if I withdrew from certain events on the calendar. As bluffs went, it wasn't the worst, but it was certainly in the bottom three I had ever heard.

Due to demand and some nice letters from snooker fans I did play in the Scottish Masters after all and won it, beating Alex Higgins 9–4 in the final. But I didn't change my mind about the other untelevised event – it was to take place too close to the Coral UK Championship for me.

My intense tournament schedule continued with a long journey from Glasgow to Derby immediately after the Scottish Masters so that I could defend my Jameson International title. In addition to the World Championship, the WPBSA was now in a position to award world ranking points to some other events on account of them being open to all professionals and this was one of them.

But I didn't win it. Tony Knowles beat David Taylor 9–6 in the final to claim his first major title. It did Tony the power of good. By the end of the season, helped by a strong performance at Sheffield, he was up to fourth in the world rankings.

Tony was now in the big time, but his success and fame were to backfire when he was fined £5,000 by the WPBSA for bringing the game into disrepute after doing an article in a national newspaper in which he revealed he had dressed up in his girlfriend's underwear. He was later to claim that his game deteriorated from that point in his career. His world ranking subsequently slid downwards from an all-time high of number two.

Newspaper talk also surrounded my own world ranking at this time with the somewhat extreme speculation that I might even have to qualify for some competitions the following year if I didn't quickly rediscover my winning touch in the big events. To counterbalance this, Doug Mountjoy did an interview saying I was still two blacks (14 points) better than anybody else as I approached my quest to win a third successive UK title in Preston.

Such comments never did me any harm, not least for the effect it would have on my opponents; I don't suppose it would have gone down too well with my nearest rivals. So, if somebody like Doug was saying something like that it was priceless. The superiority complex was well and truly under reconstruction.

Important tournaments took over my life. Everything revolved around them. Once there, I couldn't have a cameraman clicking away or anything like that – even after I had played a shot.

I don't know how other players deal with it but for me the big matches were draining. I couldn't do anything on the day of a match. If it was at night, the daytime would be purgatory. In my pomp, I became snappy. It was only after the match had finished that the relief or agony took over.

I wouldn't say that I was a temperamental player but I did need everything to feel right. I think this was mainly due to the pressure of being the number one player in the world. I couldn't really relax. There were too many eyes looking out for my results to make it anything other than high tension every time I walked out to play.

Despite being seen as the man to beat, I would still feel nerves against a big rival such as Terry Griffiths, who I played in the quarter-finals at Preston that year. I was no doubt pacing the floor before I got into the arena. With good reason as well – on this occasion Terry beat me 9–6. My hopes of an unprecedented hat-trick were over.

Terry went on to win the UK title for the first and only time, beating Alex Higgins in a pulsating final, 16–15. I think this was probably the happiest I had ever seen him. Even though he is habitually an early riser and certainly not a night owl, it was cause for much-deserved celebration. I doubt he went to bed that night until five or maybe six minutes past midnight.

In addition to the change in ranking events, the other innovations in the snooker calendar were a doubles tournament and a national three-man competition. My partner in the doubles competitions was my new Matchroom stablemate Tony Meo. The first event we played in together was the Hofmeister World Doubles Championship at Crystal Palace where we hammered Terry Griffiths and Doug Mountjoy 13–2 in the final. The two of us absolutely cleaned up in the World Doubles – winning four of the first five annual tournaments. The one year we didn't win we sat in the hospitality room together and got wrecked. It would have made a good advert for the sponsors. Or not!

Tony seemed to me to play far better in the doubles set-up than he did on his own. Maybe there was less pressure on him because we could share the load as a team? He was also able to enjoy himself. He could get himself into a bit of a state before a match and this affected his game for he was far more talented than the general public probably ever realised. He did win tournaments – but nowhere near the number he was capable of winning in my opinion. He could be a very dangerous player on his day.

When we played together, Tony was often the match-winner. I used to say to him: 'I'll do the safety, you do the potting!' He seemed quite happy with that. I enjoyed watching Tony pot balls for us, too. I enjoyed taking a bit of a back seat and, as the event took place just before Christmas, watch our winnings roll in. It was a great buzz playing in a partnership with him. The record books show that we were nigh on unbeatable. Our strike rate was phenomenal.

There was always the possibility of trying to play tactically in doubles, especially changing the order at the end of a frame. I decided to let the other team do all the worrying. Therefore, we just played in whatever order they wanted. Then we would watch them discuss whether they should change it after they had lost a frame.

Alex Higgins and Jimmy White played together once, a pairing that had the potential for great things or the world blowing apart. Jimmy has told me that Alex's idea was to allow each of them three 'kamikaze' shots during a match. Halfway through the first frame, Alex had already had four so Jimmy said to him: 'I thought we were having just three each?' And Alex replied: 'No, we'll scrap that idea.'

I also enjoyed the World Team Cup. I won four World Cups with England. The first of these was with John Spencer and David Taylor against the mighty defending champions Wales (Terry Griffiths, Doug Mountjoy and Ray Reardon). It was some match and we won 4–3.

I felt a different type of pressure in a team event representing my country than I ever did playing on my own or at a doubles event. I also realised how nail-biting watching snooker could be when you had an interest in the outcome.

On one occasion I remember watching John Spencer – who had been struggling with his form of late – make a superb pressure clearance. It was purgatory! I had no control over proceedings and just had to sit there, suffering. I had not been more nervous in my life. Now I knew what my father had been going through all those years. Players' parents must suffer more turmoil and agony than anybody else. I wouldn't wish it on anybody.

I successfully defended my *Pot Black* title by beating Ray Reardon in the final just after Christmas – I took the oath of secrecy on pain of death once again for another three months. I also won the first event of the New Year – the Lada Classic – and a £16,000 cheque by beating Bill Werbeniuk 9–5 in the final.

Having no need – or desire – for a second Lada, I successfully avoided another 147 and set my target on the more unusual 146. There was actually only one century made in the whole event and that was a 101 by Bill, so that gives you an idea of the average standard of snooker back in those days. Unless, of course, everybody was trying to avoid winning the car.

Incidentally, at this time, Yugo – a Yugoslavian version of Lada – started to produce cars in the UK as well. It also started to sponsor snooker events. These were dangerous times to be a player. If Ronnie O'Sullivan had been around back then, he would probably have ended up with a fleet of scrap metal on his driveway.

Doug Mountjoy beat me 5–4 in the quarter-finals of the Benson & Hedges Masters the following month, meaning I had now lost all three of the Triple Crown titles I had held a year before. The *Sun* posed the question of me: 'Superstar or Fallen Star?' The British press have a reputation for knocking down sports people when they are at the top but that never upset me. I usually wouldn't read the newspapers anyway. If I did, it was mostly after I had won. If I had lost, I wouldn't even turn on the TV. Therefore, I wouldn't know when stuff was being put out there. Also, I was always sensible enough to realise that it was just stuff ...

I packed my bags for a mid-winter break and another overseas trip after the Benson & Hedges Masters, this time to the Persian Gulf with Terry Griffiths. Barry Hearn was now beginning to set his sights on taking snooker to different parts of the world. Bahrain and Dubai were two new territories for us to explore. It was always exciting to go to brand new places, play in front of new faces and try to sell the game. The local people were pleased to see you and, particularly in the 1980s, it was a terrific experience. We were there as ambassadors and I found that much easier and far nicer than the yo-yo mentality involved in competitions. Being out there as something of a pioneer was both rewarding and special.

The break seemed to do both of us some good. A week later we contested the final of the Tolly Cobbold Classic at the Corn Exchange in Ipswich and I won 7–5. This was the sixth time Terry and I had played each other in the final of a major competition.

Meanwhile, some rather ridiculous awards started to come my way off the table, including Head of the Year from the National Hairdressers' Federation, which I shared with the TV presenter Selina Scott. This led to a photo shoot that made most of the next day's newspapers with me standing behind Selina with a comb and a pair of scissors in my hands!

Looking back, it is hilarious to think that I won this award when I had ginger hair and a side parting with a smidgen of dandruff. I remember I was interviewed and asked a lot of serious hairdressing questions, such as:

'How much do you think you spend on your hair in a year?' and 'Who does your hair?'

My answers were: 'About fifty quid' and 'Julie in Romford.'

I also won Rear of the Year, sponsored, I believe, by a clothing manufacturer. It felt terrible being used and abused in this way but, let's face it, you don't win such awards for nothing! I suspect I was respectable eye candy for the older lady viewer. Having never viewed the male of the species as particularly attractive I really didn't see the fascination myself. For me, the thought of somebody such as Tony Knowles cocking a leg over the table meant it was a difficult shot to reach! Naively, I suppose, I never understood the fascination it held for women!

I had to pose for a picture (from behind) with my fellow winner Su Pollard, from the TV sitcom *Hi-de-Hi!* Dancer Vincent Simone also won it quite a few years later and the two of us compared backsides during boring moments while filming *I'm a Celebrity … Get Me Out of Here!* in 2013. The general consensus was that his was far cheekier than mine but I felt slightly aggrieved that age wasn't taken into consideration.

My next success on the table came at the Benson & Hedges Irish Masters at Goffs. The venue was actually situated in a place called Kill. It was to be a place of pure beauty for me and 1983 was the first of an amazing eight wins I had over there. Winning so many times in what is still arguably the best snooker venue the game has ever had remains one of the proudest achievements in my career. I played some of the best snooker of my career there, too. It was just perfect for me, certainly a case of horses for courses …

In the heart of the Irish horseracing and breeding industry, Goffs sales ring was turned into a fantastic snooker venue with seating about 320 degrees around the table creating an amazing atmosphere. There was standing at the back there as well in the 1980s – long before health and safety decreed it to be unsafe. There was always something special about a venue where people could only get their hands on standing tickets. The place would heave. It felt like the snooker was the hottest ticket in town and the players responded accordingly.

I excelled in that environment. Strangely, the floor around the table wasn't perfectly level so whenever I played a shot off the rail I could feel that I was a little higher than I would be if it was normal flooring.

Watching today's players – some of whom have dismissed the theory books and the advice of getting the cue as parallel to the table as possible (they prefer to raise the butt of the cue up in the air in order to give themselves the room to not get the cue trapped between their chin and the cushion) – perhaps that was a reason why I played better at Goffs than at other venues.

I felt very much at home at Goffs. Similar to the Crucible theatre, it was a real melting pot and it 'out-Crucibled' the Crucible in the way that it was the amphitheatre of all amphitheatres in which to play snooker. It was electric. I never felt more gladiatorial than when I played at Goffs. No doubt, the bloodstock fraternity were outraged but, once again, a venue that had been specifically made for one purpose was hijacked by snooker and became much better known in Ireland as a result.

I absolutely loved it from the first time I played there. The previous year I had reached the final, where I lost to Terry Griffiths. But this time around I dominated in all my matches and comfortably beat Ray Reardon 9–2 to claim the £12,000 first prize. This victory meant an awful lot to me. It came at exactly the right time, too, setting me up perfectly for the forthcoming World Championship, which began a fortnight later.

When I arrived in Sheffield, it felt like a weight had been lifted from my shoulders. The feeling of the dentist's waiting room was still there but it wasn't quite the same as it had been 12 months earlier when I returned as defending champion for the first time. First-round nerves still abounded but I no longer had the albatross of retaining the world title around my neck.

I was made the clear favourite again, this time with odds of 5–4 next to my name. The usual suspects were behind me: Terry Griffiths (6–1), Alex Higgins (7–1), Ray Reardon (8–1) and Jimmy White (10–1). Alex, the defending champion, was placed in the top half of the draw as top seed with Ray, seeded two, in the bottom half. I was seeded four and therefore set to meet the Hurricane in the semi-finals – if we both won through our early rounds.

The big shock of the first round was Tony Meo knocking out his mate Jimmy White, 10–8. Otherwise, all the seeds went through. I defeated Rex Williams 10–4. In the last 16, I met Dennis Taylor – sporting a new pair of glasses for the first time – and despite trailing 4–3 after a very tight and drawn-out first session, I did enough to win through 13–11 – the exact reversal of the scoreline of the previous time we had played each other at the Crucible in 1979. I had a much more comfortable time in the quarter-finals where I beat steady Eddie Charlton, 13–5.

Elsewhere, the big story came in the Cliff Thorburn v Terry Griffiths match, with Cliff eventually winning it 13–12 at 3.51 a.m. More importantly, in one of those 25 frames Cliff made the first ever 147 maximum at the Crucible. His fellow countryman Bill Werbeniuk was playing David Taylor on the other table at the time and famously poked his head around the dividing wall to watch him do it.

BBC commentator Jack Karnehm spoke for us all with his words: 'Good luck, mate' as Cliff approached the final black.

The sight of Cliff sinking to his knees after sinking the black was brilliant. I must admit to feeling a slight pang of jealousy about his achievement at a venue where I never came close to making a maximum. But my exclusive TV 147 Club of one now had a new member. Cliff won £25,000 for his break – enough to buy ten Ladas!

The other man making the headlines was, once again, Alex Higgins, who, it was claimed, had called his second-round opponent, Willie Thorne, a cheat during his 13–8 victory. The miss rule – or lack of it – had been the catalyst.

'Somebody should do something about him – at times he gets away with murder,' Willie said afterwards. But he decided not to make an official complaint, although he would have been entitled to do so. Never one for an understatement, Alex fired back: 'It's only because I am Alex Higgins that this has blown up into a nuclear explosion. It's a dog-eat-dog situation here.'

Alex beat Bill Werbeniuk 13–11 in the quarter-finals to set up a semi-final clash against me. His wife, Lynn, was then asked for her opinion on a tongue-in-cheek comment I had made about snooker being better than sex.

'If he gets more of a kick out of playing snooker than making love, I feel very sorry for him,' Lynn was quoted as saying in the *Sunday People*. 'He must lead an incredibly empty life.'

These comments were in response to another quotation attributed to me in the same interview saying I liked to play Alex because I found him 'obnoxious and very ignorant'.

For what it is worth, I had been asked in an interview for *Woman* magazine if snooker was indeed better than sex. This is the sort of inane question that is thrown at people in the public eye from time to time by the media. It mattered little to me. I can't even remember if it was a male or female interviewer who asked it. I responded by asking what was more important to them, their job or sex?

In general, snooker players agreed to do most interviews that came our way in the 1980s and we took a chance that the writer wasn't going to have a pop at us. Most articles concerning sports people are intended to be positive and, unless you were obnoxious during the interview, that was how it stayed. Occasionally, there would be a negative piece but that probably said more about the interviewer or the publication.

After a while in the business, you more or less know that you are going to get misquoted every now and again. So you have three choices: 1) you don't do interviews; 2) you demand absolute control; or 3) you stop caring because, as Oscar Wilde said: 'The only thing worse than being talked about is not being talked about!' On this occasion, I did the last one.

I thrashed Alex Higgins and, for the record, I probably enjoyed it more than anything else I did that week. I took the first three frames and led 5–2 after the opening session. By the end of the second, I was 10–4 ahead. I played solid snooker while Alex looked forlorn as he downed his lava lamp of lager and honey. The following day, I won the required seven frames to wrap up a pleasurable 16–5 win.

The headline writers then struck again: 'If Steve Davis says one more rude word about my Alex, I'll stick a knife in him,' the *Daily Mirror* reported Lynn to have said. All these years on, it is worth reading that again word for word. It had now gone crazy. It is also an example of how interested the newspapers felt the nation as a whole was in the snooker-loopy 1980s.

Cliff Thorburn was my opponent in the final after he fought through two more marathon matches. There was a 13–12 win over fellow Canadian Kirk Stevens in the quarter-finals, ending at 2.12 a.m., and another late night/early morning 16–15 win over Tony Knowles in the semi-finals. Tony missed a pink to win that match as well. Cliff's stamina was amazing but all this meant that he would have been pretty tired by the time he walked out to play me the next day.

I often didn't bother to return to my hotel between sessions and put my head down in the dressing room to get a power nap. It was an effective way for me to recharge my batteries. An hour was all I needed to switch off and back on again.

I led Cliff 12–5 overnight and lost just one frame of the next seven the following day. Once I got to 15–5 in front I actually set myself a personal target of keeping ten frames clear of him. That was a game within a game for me. To think that I had a lead of ten frames over somebody like Cliff in a world final is incredible.

But it helped me to keep my concentration as it gave me something to aim for. It is laughable really but, having had leads evaporate before, I was very conscious that I knew all about losing a big lead. In fact, for that to happen to me early on in my long-frame match professional career reinforced my desire never to take my foot off the gas in situations such as this. Having said that, desire is one thing and achievement is another.

It was nice to include a tournament-best break of 131 to clear the table in the fifth frame of the day, too. I wrapped up an emphatic 18–6 victory against him with a session to spare.

Regardless of the scoreline, I still flung myself up in the air when I sunk that respotted black in the final frame. I think that was all to do with the relief of getting my world title back. Right on cue, I blubbed with relief on the Crucible stage again. Live on TV once more in front of an audience of millions. The winner's cheque was £30,000 but it felt almost incidental. The only thing that mattered was getting that famous trophy in my hands again.

Memories matter. The nicest ones are those moments where I felt totally dominant and I was actually enjoying myself. That win over Cliff Thorburn would certainly fit into that category. I felt so in control. I would look around the theatre and think to myself: 'There is nowhere I would rather be right now than here.' I was able to play my game with pure freedom and to do that on the biggest stage of all is the biggest statement you can make. It is quite something to be able to play like it means nothing when it actually means everything.

Regaining the world title was perhaps the biggest hurdle I had faced so far. Many players have won the World Championship, but to become a multiple world champion effectively moves you into a different league. For the second time in my career, I was on top of the world. Perhaps this time around I was better placed and mature enough to use it as a springboard to even greater performances in the future.

13. NUMBER 10 AND ALL THAT

There I was sitting on the back of a dray, being dragged through the streets of Reading by two shire horses during a promotion for Courage brewery, when suddenly a house brick was flung at me. Luckily it didn't connect. While it might have been thrown by an Alex Higgins fan, the reality is it could also have been politically motivated.

A week after my second World Championship win I was a guest of honour at an evening reception at 10 Downing Street held by the Prime Minister, Margaret Thatcher, and her husband, Denis.

In 1983, both Barry Hearn and I epitomised the working class made good. We were both apparently millionaires and – in the eyes of the marketing people – probably summed up perfectly the positive side of 1980s Thatcherism. The General Election was a month away and the Tories were pulling in as many supporters as they could get. It was Barry's idea to join the bandwagon and I went along with him. As did the majority of the country – Mrs Thatcher was re-elected with 397 seats in the most decisive election victory in the UK for almost 40 years.

And so just four days before the election I found myself on the platform at a youth rally held by the National Union of Conservative and Unionist Association, at Wembley Conference Centre, a venue I knew well from playing at the Benson & Hedges Masters. But this time I was wearing a 'Maggie In' badge on my jacket! The Prime Minister was there as well, giving another of her tub-thumping speeches before posing for pictures with us all for the press afterwards. I stood in a long line of people and was introduced to her as if she was the Queen. I remember she told me that she admired my professionalism. That was it, ten seconds and gone.

I trusted Barry's judgement on absolutely everything and I would say that he very rarely got it wrong. This was probably a good move for all sorts of reasons. But, from my own perspective, affiliating myself to one political party when I really didn't need to be involved in politics at all was, in hindsight, a mistake.

Politics alienates people and it alienated people regarding me. Thankfully, it didn't cause any long-lasting problems but it wasn't nice for a while. As part of a new contract with Courage brewery, I took part in a lot of exhibitions for John Smith's bitter in the north of England, sometimes visiting towns and cities that survived on coal mining. Within a year of the election, the miners had begun their year-long strike against pit closures. Suddenly I was in a very uncomfortable situation. These people had long memories …

I would walk into a pub or a club in South Yorkshire or somewhere and it would hit me straight away that certain people in there were having a very bad time of it. Fortunately, snooker won through because of the love that people have for the game, but I didn't feel good in myself at all given my, albeit brief, support of the Conservative Party the previous year.

I can only assume that brick was thrown at me by somebody who hated the Tories. He might also have been a big snooker fan. Sadly, he might also once have been a Steve Davis fan.

I was reminded in the strongest way possible that snooker is a classless game and that is one of the great things about it. Snooker has working-class roots. I began playing it at a working men's club, so even if it had become upwardly mobile it didn't have to be thrust down the working man's throat. I learned a lot from it all. I have never been one to try and show off about the fact that I have earned a few quid in my time. As I have mentioned, the money never mattered to me. But I was always aware that there were people far less fortunate. I showed a lot of respect to a lot of people and it was never about me, it was always about snooker. I had to protect the game as well as promote it. The credibility and integrity of snooker has always been very important and remains so.

The passing of time changes a person as well. Perhaps when I was younger I might have thought of myself as a private enterprise – you make your own luck and all that. A lot of people were thinking that way at that time because they voted the Tories back in by that strong margin, so it wasn't an unpopular view in 1983. But things have changed enough to tell me that it causes serious problems. I don't like 'them and us'. I never have.

I was so fortunate to be able to make a living out of a pastime that I loved. It would have been unthinkable in the 1950s, 1960s and most of the 1970s that a player could earn in the region of £1,000,000 in prize money. But I have to thank snooker and the people who loved the game for that. So, to even upset one of them because of my involvement in a political publicity stunt was a big mistake.

I should have sat down and thought it all through. Sometimes going with the flow is not the right way. The other part of it all that grates is that snooker was obviously seen as a sport that was getting a lot of publicity and for the Conservatives to have the world champion on their side was an astute tactical move. I wonder what they would have done if the election had been in 1982? But, essentially and importantly, snooker isn't political and it shouldn't be used as a political tool. I sincerely regret it all and apologise to all those people for connecting myself in any way, shape or form to a political party. I didn't enjoy it. I actually disliked being involved in it. From then on, there was also an element of people trying to get me involved again. But I didn't want to know any more. I decided never to get involved in anything like it again.

I never enjoyed playing the game of the A-list celebrity anyway and in the UK in the 1980s snooker was A-list. It is quite nice to now be seen as a C-list celebrity and I much prefer being invited somewhere I am wanted as opposed to somewhere that somebody can have a photograph taken with me. Thankfully those days are gone.

Visiting Northern Ireland at around that time wasn't easy either. On one occasion, in Belfast, I came out of a television station after doing a live studio interview and there were loads of kids, aged between about six and fourteen, hanging around outside. There was a car waiting for me and all these kids started calling out to me: 'Mister, can I have your autograph?'

So I happily signed some autographs for them. All of a sudden, I felt one of them kick my ankle. Then another obviously thought that was 'a good game' and did the same. There was no security around. I decided to get in the car quickly. But as I tried to shut the door, they held it open between them and began spitting at me. These were hard kids living in a tough area but I hope that in their own way they were just trying to find some form of entertainment. It was a bit more boisterous than Hampstead!

After the General Election, I was off overseas again with a month-long trip to Hong Kong, Bangladesh, Singapore, Australia, Dubai and Dallas, Texas. When I returned to the UK, I made my TV presentation debut on *The Sports Quiz with Steve Davis* on Anglia television. This was basically a sports version of *Mastermind* with some of the hottest quizzers in the land. I generally found the whole experience to be a bit out of my comfort zone: I was more uncomfortable with an autocue to hand than my snooker cue – but I tried my best. I am not sure what I really learned from the whole experience other than how to pronounce some obscure Russian shot-putters' names and when to throw the questions open to a bonus point, but it underlined once again how in vogue snooker and I were at the time.

There was also a show called *A Frame with Davis* which was something of a rip-off of *A Round with Alliss*, a popular golf programme at the time hosted by Peter Alliss. Each programme featured two celebrities and me having a knockabout on the snooker table and a chat. I would ask some questions, show them some shots and give them a chance to entertain the studio audience. The guests were certainly not C-list either: Les Dawson, Bobby Davro, Jimmy Greaves, Dennis Waterman and Norman Wisdom all appeared, to name a few. It was good crack but I can still remember my horror in front of a live audience when I stumbled over Richard O'Sullivan's name time after time. I soon realised that, while I might be a good snooker player, I certainly wasn't a natural TV presenter.

In order for the producers to make the programme, they had to convince the powers that be that the show was educational so that it could go through on that particular budget. However, I am not sure that watching Norman crawl under the table to play a shot rather than walk around it could come under the label educational! It was amazing to rub shoulders with all these multi-talented entertainers. Perhaps even more amazing was that one of the runners on the show – basically the person who gets the crew food and drink when they snap their fingers – was, I believe, a certain Jonathan Ross!

I am pleased to say when it comes to television I have improved with age and learned an awful lot since those days. At least I had the comfort of a snooker table in *A Frame with Davis*. I was out of my comfort zone with the sports quiz. I think that was the hardest work I have had to do in my life. I didn't like it one bit. Thankfully, I wasn't asked to do it again. But the amount of television I was doing at this time was beyond belief and stretching well beyond snooker.

In fact, it was reported that, apart from newsreaders, my face was the most seen on TV this year. I was asked to play the piano with Leo Sayer on his BBC show due to an off-guard comment I made that I was trying to learn the piano! I also did a comedy sketch on *Cannon and Ball*, which was performed in front of a live studio audience and, to this day, remains one of the most exciting moments off the table that I can remember. From learning the script to performing it as live was such a buzz. I probably had to wait until the excitement of *I'm a Celebrity ...* to achieve that again.

Throughout all this I would still be putting in the hours at the snooker table. I needed to maintain my technique and I found that there were a few parts to practising: 1) the guilt (I had to put the hours in because somewhere, somebody else was putting just as many hours in – if not more); 2) the flow (a player needs a certain amount of hours to keep their standard up to a high level); and 3) technique (I wasn't really interested in playing the game as much as keeping on top of the technical part of my game). After I had done that, I could relax and have a game or two.

The next phase was trying to see if I could assimilate all of the above into my natural game under the scrutiny of a competitive environment akin to a boxer sparring. The final phase would be making it all become habit. All of this was going on behind the scenes while I turned up on TV to play the star of the show. There was no time to relax. After a very busy summer, I was happy to get back into the regular swing of things.

I started off by successfully defending the Langs Scottish Masters in Glasgow, beating Tony Knowles 9–6 in the final. I followed that up by regaining the Jameson International with a 9–4 win over Cliff Thorburn and the highest break of the day every day of the competition. My winnings totalled £25,500 for the week. Alex Higgins called me a 'lucky bastard' after I beat him 5–1 in the quarter-finals! Maybe I was – but I had read that Gary Player quote somewhere down the line and regurgitated it for snooker: 'The more I practise, the luckier I get!'

Afterwards, on the long drive south from west Scotland to mid-Wales, where I was heading for an exhibition, I was lucky to escape with no injuries after I was involved in a car crash on a notorious bend 70 feet above the River Wye near the village of Erwood. Ron Radley was driving me down there in my Porsche – and he almost drove us over a ravine!

We were on our way to the Professional Players Tournament in Bristol via an appearance for Courage in Newtown, in Powys. My one-piece aluminium cue case, which was placed in the footwell of the car by my feet, rising past the handbrake between the two seats, was wrecked but miraculously my treasured cue was undamaged.

I was the map reader and I had mistakenly directed Ron to another place called Newtown, on the outskirts of Cardiff. Once we got there, we soon realised that we had made a mistake. Somebody told us about the other Newtown – the one where we were meant to be – and by that time it was 6.30 p.m.! We set off as fast as we could but the road got narrower and narrower and it became more and more windy. In the end, we were on Mission Impossible.

Ron told me not to worry and proceeded to drive like a maniac so that I could make the exhibition on time. But the roads were awful. We hit this accident black spot just outside Builth Wells, lost control on the adverse camber, went straight across the road and hit a wall. Our immediate reaction was panic – but for slightly different reasons: Ron was trying to open his jammed door, fearing the car would explode like it does in the films, while I immediately opened my door and got my cue case out, just in case the car tipped over the edge and fell down the mountainside. As it was, both of these were unlikely to happen as no part of the car was actually over the edge. Nor did it catch fire, let alone explode.

'Steve, I can't get out,' Ron shouted. 'I can't get out.'

I was already 'out' with my cue case safely in my hand. But the four cases of whisky I had won from making the highest break every day at the Langs Masters had been thrown forward on impact along with our luggage and something had jammed on to the end of my cue case, which was now severely bent.

I wasn't concerned at all about Ron but I was in a total panic about my cue. I was sure it was broken. I opened it up and was greatly relieved to find that my cue was in one piece. Only then did I hear Ron's cries. I now rushed around to the driver's door to try and help prise it open.

Once we were both out of the car we looked over the wall and saw this sheer drop into the water below us. In the end, only one headlight made the river. Happily the car had been saved by the stone wall.

I still made the date at the venue by taxi, albeit a couple of hours late. There were a few boos when I arrived. Few people believed our story but after the newspapers found the written-off vehicle at a local garage and published photographs of the wreckage the following day, the severity of it all hit home. We had been very lucky.

I was asked to have my picture taken with the bent cue case! One photographer wasn't too impressed with the state of the case and asked if he could perhaps bend it a bit more! Obviously, I was going to buy a new one anyway – so the two of us got to work on it. And that was the photograph that made most of the newspapers. When I later showed the picture to my cue it was most impressed by what it had survived and asked to be named Houdini instead of the name I'd previously christened it with: Fred!

The shock of the accident didn't really hit me until I played Mike Hallett a few days later in the Professional Players Tournament and found that I couldn't concentrate properly. He beat me 5–2. By that time, everybody knew about the accident. 'Steve's lucky break' was the headline of choice.

As for Ronnie Radley, he lived off the stories for a while. It got to the stage where, back at the Matchroom, he was telling it like this: 'I felt the car go and I knew that I only had two choices – to try and keep it on the road or aim for the wall. I thought the wall was the best in the circumstances.' As if he had time to even think! Basically, he lost control of the car. That was the end of the beloved white Porsche, too. I replaced it with a silver one. It seemed like a good workhorse to have, especially after I was left completely uninjured from such a major accident.

The following month it was the time for the Coral UK Championship again. I was installed at 4–5 as the firm favourite again, ahead of Tony Knowles, Terry Griffiths and Alex Higgins. Alex's odds were interesting because, by his own admission, he was out of sorts with his game at the time.

I beat Willie Thorne 9–3 in the first round and progressed to the final with two comfortable 9–4 wins over Tony Meo and Jimmy White respectively. There waiting for me – as per script – was Alex.

I blitzed him 7–0 in the opening session with some great snooker that included five breaks of 60-plus. He was on his knees. I was in dreamland. What followed was a nightmare. By the end of the first day, my lead had been cut to 8–7. I plunged from perfection to panic.

Alex was constantly asking the referee – the larger than life Len Ganley – to clean the cue ball. At one stage he was doing this nearly every other shot. Regardless of Alex's image, this was pretty disjointed stuff. I doubt it was gamesmanship but he slowly but surely played his way back into the game. By the standards of today, Alex wasn't actually a fast player but his antics and mannerisms made him far more watchable than most.

I was beating myself up inside. I had been here before, most notably against Terry Griffiths at the Crucible when I needed Barry Hearn's assurance to help me get through to the end. Playing catch-up – with nothing to lose – in these circumstances is always a much simpler task than playing out in front, looking over your shoulder and trying not to get caught.

The crowd can be another factor. More often than not they will shout for the guy who is behind – even more so if that guy happens to be called Alex Higgins. All these things come into the equation and in this match I stalled completely. As soon as a player can't start the engines there is instant pressure and that becomes constant pressure. As is well known, I certainly wasn't immune to this type of thing happening to me and it was a horrible feeling.

I completely collapsed in this match. The Hurricane smelt blood and no doubt got a big kick out of it as well. Once he hit the comeback trail, he could be a fiercely competitive animal. In fact, if he had possessed the cue action, dedication and temperament of Ronnie O'Sullivan he would have been unbeatable – just like the Rocket!

To sum Alex up, he is the only player I have ever played against where, even if he needed snookers with just one red and the colours left, I wouldn't necessarily feel that I was the favourite to win the frame. He could be very clever as a safety player. He was also one of the best I ever encountered at getting snookers and he was excellent at containing a situation until the moment to strike was ripe. A lot is made of him being a brilliant potter but he was also an astonishing, innovative all-round talent on his day – and on those occasions you felt that you were in the presence of a true genius.

I led 11–9 but soon trailed 12–11 and then 14–12. I won three frames in a row to lead 15–14 and stand just one frame away from victory. But Alex levelled and then raced into an unsurmountable 77–0 lead in the final frame to win 16–15. I conceded and he celebrated one of the biggest wins of his career.

A lot of people ask me why Alex didn't win more titles in the game. I think it boils down to the fact that his cue action was somewhat erratic and his lifestyle was far, far worse than that. To win a snooker event, a player has to be consistent throughout the week. I doubt whether Alex had a consistent week in his entire life. Therefore, while he might have been able to get things right for a match, more times than not he wasn't able to get things right for a whole tournament.

For Alex to produce the performances and results he did is testament to the strange sort of brain he must have had to have been able to compartmentalise all of the problems in his life and produce such brilliance on the table every now and again. Perhaps when he played he could forget all of his worries and be in the moment?

The one famous story on the circuit that stands out to me more than any other about him is the one when he apparently whacked his girlfriend in front of a crowd during a match and then went to the table and proceeded to knock in a break of 130. I mean, how can anybody be so out of control one minute and so in control the next?

Obviously, Alex's life was in complete turmoil a lot of the time but I personally never knew the extent of all that during his career. There were times in his life when he had been banged up in a cell the night before and then came out and played a match, which is incredible.

I retained the Lada Classic – which had become a world ranking event – a few weeks later by beating my doubles partner Tony Meo 9–8 in the final in Warrington. Tony could easily have won it, too. He was trailing 45–33 in the final frame but was put off while taking on the yellow by somebody in the crowd shouting out, 'Come on, Tony'.

I have no doubt that he would have beaten me but for that. Referee Jim Thorpe snapped: 'I hope you are ashamed of yourself!' I wasn't delighted to win in such circumstances, although I did try my best to pot the remaining six balls.

While Tony and I were dominating the World Doubles, his old sidekick Jimmy White was on the verge of his first major title breakthrough. It came at Wembley in the Benson & Hedges Masters. His semi-final clash against a white-suited and booted Kirk Stevens (who had beaten me in the quarter-finals) was sensational. Jimmy led 3–0 and Kirk fought back to 3–2 before Jimmy unleashed a great break of 113. Kirk fired back to 5–4 with a fabulous 147 maximum. It was the best and most accurate 147 there had been up to this point – mine featured a double after I lost position while Cliff Thorburn's started off with a fluke.

Not to be outdone, Jimmy rounded off the match with a fantastic break of 119, finishing with eye-catching shots to pot both the pink and black to rapturous applause. Jack Karnehm was lost for words in the commentary box so he made one up. 'Fantabulous!' was added to the commentators' lexicon. It was a delight. The cue power Jimmy could produce at times was simply astonishing. It has taken a couple of generations to produce players who can generate enough cue speed to outscrew the Whirlwind. The likes of Neil Robertson and Judd Trump have astonishing cue power but Jimmy, in his youth, was as good as it got.

I think it might be fun to have a mini screw back competition one day – a bit like the popular Puissance event in showjumping on TV in the 1970s when Eddie Macken and Boomerang used to leave others in their wake as they jumped over a giant wall.

After beating Kirk 6–4, Jimmy defeated Terry Griffiths 9–5 in the final to claim the Masters trophy. This was the tournament at which the Whirlwind came of age and the Wembley roar was truly born. It seemed at its loudest when Jimmy was in town, arguably eclipsing the support Alex got. Of course, I wasn't watching any of it. I refused to accept that TV existed until the event had ended. All good winners are bad losers and, perhaps, even greater sulkers!

I was licking my wounds in preparation for the next tournament. I responded by winning the Tolly Cobbold Classic again in Ipswich (8–2 against Tony Knowles), the International Masters in Derby again (against

Dave Martin and John Dunning in a three-man final group) and also retained my Benson & Hedges Irish Masters, making eight breaks over 50 in a 9–1 demolition of Terry Griffiths. Yet again Goffs had provided the perfect warm-up for me ahead of the World Championship.

A number of players made their debuts at the Crucible theatre in 1984, including men who would go on to have successful futures in the game – Neal Foulds, Joe Johnson and John Parrott. Neal and John were aged twenty and nineteen respectively and were the next wave of young professionals coming into the game. They both enjoyed good wins in the opening round by knocking out Alex Higgins and Tony Knowles respectively – but went out of the competition in the following round, to Doug Mountjoy and Dennis Taylor. Joe was a lot older than both Neal and Tony and was already in his thirties. His day would come but he was thrashed 10–1 by Dennis in his first match at the World Championship.

Much, much older than Joe was the evergreen Fred Davis, who was making his last ever appearance at the Crucible at the ripe old age of seventy years and 253 days. Bill Werbeniuk beat him 10–4 in the opening round. Fred was no longer a hot prospect to win the world title, of course: he was there to make up the numbers. But it was still an astonishing achievement for him to be there.

I think it will be impossible for anybody to repeat that feat in the future. It was the end of an era as well. To a certain degree, Fred extended the Davis legacy that had been left by his late brother, Joe. It must have been frustrating for him to have always played in his brother's shadow and he showed an astonishing commitment to stay in the game so long.

I was up against another debutant, Warren King, from Australia, and found it pretty easy going for a first-round match at the Crucible, winning 10–3. I was still glad to get it out of the way. I enjoyed a comfortable victory against my second-round opponent, former world champion John Spencer, to set up a quarter-final clash against Terry Griffiths.

Terry was back at his best in this match after that crushing defeat I had inflicted against him at Goffs. Despite losing the first three frames, he hit back with five in a row to lead 5–3 after the first session. We often had some really good battles against each other and, when he was firing on all cylinders, he was a very difficult opponent.

This was one of the best matches we played. Terry won the first frame of the second session to move three frames ahead before I came back at him and turned the tables by winning four frames in a row to move back in front. Terry seemed to evaporate under the pressure for a while – which often happens at the Crucible – but he got one frame back before I powered back with a 73 break to lead 8–7. Another terrific fightback by him levelled the scores overnight.

It wasn't necessarily quick snooker but it would have been intriguing to watch for the neutral. What modern-day TV audiences would make of it is another matter entirely but in those days television viewers were more patient souls.

The second day went in my favour. I took hold of proceedings early on and made life difficult for Terry with some good safety play. By the afternoon, I had won through to the semi-finals, 13–10.

Next in line was another familiar face, Dennis Taylor, who had knocked out Doug Mountjoy 13–8 in the quarter-finals. This was our third meeting at the Crucible and we were level at one win each going into this match. Both of the previous encounters had ended 13–11 but this one was more one-sided with me having the edge, 16–9.

I was through to my third world final in four seasons and I felt good. I'd only been asked the question once, in my match against Terry, and I responded in championship-winning style.

The bottom half of the draw had thrown up some great matches with Jimmy White's 13–8 quarter-final win over Cliff Thorburn being the pick of the litter until the Whirlwind surpassed it with another semi-final thriller against Kirk Stevens, which he won 16–14, to reach his first ever world final.

Jimmy was a very popular player wherever he went. Playing him was a lot like playing Alex Higgins, but without the aggro. The two of them were also very close friends at this time, so much so that Alex was starting to appear as something of a mentor to Jimmy. He would be by his side during the final.

By contrast, I was becoming a little unpopular at this time in certain quarters. I started to receive odd things in the post, including forms of hate mail addressed to me either at the office in Romford or courtesy of the Crucible. The worst of the lot was probably a soiled nappy with words to match: 'This is what we think of you!' I'll always remember the look of disgust on the face of the secretary who opened up that particular parcel.

Anonymous mail is a strange one. Fans sending in photographs and things like that can be flattering to start with. It is always nice to receive good wishes and everything, but you can never afford to get too involved. If a player ever decides to befriend a fan, it can turn out to be dangerous. People can always make something out of nothing. Some celebrities are criticised for appearing standoffish but it is a difficult balance.

Nowadays, every 'celebrity' gets abuse via Twitter and, of course, the powers that be have a tough job in responding to these bad apples. But, eventually, everything finds a balance.

I was booed from time to time during my career but I never really minded it. I considered it the ultimate compliment. Playing against Jimmy White in a World Championship final, I had to accept that some of the people present at the Crucible were going to be vehemently opposed to me winning because they so wanted to see my opponent win.

I understood that. I also understood that the fervour of supporting one player over another could lead to people getting so caught up in the moment that they could boo you. It might sound odd but I found it exciting in a way that people could get that involved with snooker. So, I certainly never took it personally.

The nappy was slightly different – obviously that was meant for me personally (even though it wasn't my waist size!). You are always going to get cranks! So, playing against Jimmy was just going to be one of those things. I was also a man with a reputation. I was at my peak. I was there to be shot at. Being the favourite isn't always easy either. The word alone brings a certain pressure with it. I never thought about it too much because I only had to think about playing a game.

How other players viewed me at that time I don't really know. I was still a relatively young player in 1984 and it might have been the case that I appeared aloof around the table. I have been told that. Perhaps the aloofness was me trying to remain in control – not just of the balls on the table but also of my facial expressions, knowing full well that the cameras were on me.

I had a fair amount of nerves. I had a lot of them at the Crucible. But if I didn't show that, I felt I could remain in control. That was my thinking. It wasn't necessarily how I was feeling. But that is how I dealt with it. Perhaps other players considered me mentally stronger than I actually was in the circumstances, which is an interesting thought. Maybe they saw this mystical aura which actually didn't really exist. The mind can play tricks, after all. Tales gather momentum, too. Apparently, I always practised wearing my dress suit, bow tie and, especially, my dress shoes so that I felt that I was at the right height when I played!

Jimmy White was firmly the fans' favourite going into that final. Thunderous applause and some tears had greeted his semi-final win over Kirk Stevens. As a result, I knew that it would be handy to get off to a good start to negate not only Jimmy's momentum but also the crowd's excitement. I achieved that by dominating proceedings and building up a 12–4 lead overnight.

However, as I have mentioned before, having a big lead and having to sleep on it can play nasty tricks on the mind. If we could have continued playing that evening, I think I would have run away with it. But every session during a match can have a different story line just the same as different chapters in a book.

As a result, that evening I had one of the worst night's sleep I think I have ever had. All I could think about was the possibility of Jimmy coming back at me. I knew that he was capable of doing so. I also knew that I wasn't immune to comebacks.

Furthermore, part of me was becoming a little scared of them. To some degree, I was the first player to have really experienced these comeback scenarios on a regular basis because I was the first player to be able to play relentlessly strong enough snooker to actually build up a massive lead. Therefore, I was also the only player in a position to suffer with the unusual psychological tricks this could play on the mind.

And so it proved. The second day of the final was a totally different story. Jimmy began with a break of 119 and lived up to his nickname by taking seven of the opening eight frames. To say I was shell-shocked as I left the theatre that afternoon is an understatement.

Perhaps I asked for it? Whatever it is that the public sees as an image – I was the Ice Man at this time – the people themselves may not necessarily have the same perspective. The scoreline flashed its way from 12–4 to 13–11 in no time at all. I just sat there staring and watching a formidable talent at work while rooted to my chair.

The game of snooker can be a strange beast. In some individual sports, players get equal shots. But sometimes in snooker a player just has to sit there while the other guy keeps knocking the balls in. Once you are sitting in that chair and your opponent is at the table, the longer he can keep you there the more 'out of stroke' you become. So, even if you are a long way in front, the reality is he has the upper hand – and there is absolutely nothing you can do about it. If you have been kept in that chair long enough and you do eventually get up to play a shot again, it can feel as if you haven't held a cue for a year!

So, this was exactly what I had been dreading. Here we go again, I feared. This was the same type of lead I'd held against Alex Higgins in the UK Championship final in Preston and it had been followed by the same type of comeback from a similar player in similar swashbuckling form with the crowd cheering him on all the way.

I was scared out of my wits. The camera would pan across to find me looking like a rabbit caught in the headlights. That was a true reflection. Once again, I had gone from playing brilliantly to playing as though I had a lead weight on my arm. Both Jimmy and the crowd would have sensed that, too.

Sometimes in snooker you can be reeling so much that you just can't wait for the bell to ring. That 'bell' is either the interval or the end of a session. Both can be lifesavers if you need to regroup mentally. Mini-sessions of snooker are little chapters in a match and there have been many occasions when things have turned around after an interval or the end of a session.

Thankfully, the evening session started better for me. I won the first frame. However, the two of us were still locked together as the match wore on. At one stage, I started to edge ahead but after three frames in a row from Jimmy it was suddenly 16–15 with just a maximum of four frames left to play.

A vital clearance of the colours put me one frame away from victory at 17–15. Back came Jimmy again with a match-saving 65 clearance to make it 17–16. I was involved in a thriller. I opened the thirty-fourth frame with a break of 32 and Jimmy replied with a break of 40. I held my bottle to build another break of 25 but missed a vital brown into a corner pocket. I led by 17 with just the colours left and I finally staggered over the line.

A disconsolate Hurricane was on hand to comfort the Whirlwind. But he couldn't hold back his tears as he did so. It would be six years before Jimmy reached a world final again.

I could now feel the relief once more. But it was a totally different emotion from the one I had felt 12 months earlier against Cliff Thorburn. This time I had so nearly crumbled in the final, but to be the first player to have retained the world title at the Crucible while feeling very much on the back foot is something I am very proud of.

To pull it off was tough. The walk to the table took forever at times. Clearing the colours felt like climbing a mountain. At those moments I believe the hours of practising with my father got me through. Deep down, I had a built-in resistance. The nation might have viewed me as somebody who was rock-solid but I felt far from it at times. I was always vulnerable in those situations. I believe most top sportsmen suffer like this on occasions. In fact, I would love to have been a fly on the wall in various dressing rooms over the years to witness the self-doubt that captures us all, even the most formidable.

I was king of the castle again. Fittingly, two days later I celebrated by buying a seventeenth-century farmhouse for all the family, set out in 100 acres of arable land on the outskirts of Romford. My manager was just down the road as well so it was perfect.

My father supervised the building work on the property for me. At around this time, I retired him from his job at London Transport. I remember being paid a fee of £10,000 to do an exhibition. At the same time, my father – who was approaching sixty – was still grafting his balls off twelve hours a day. It made no sense. I told him to pack up working there and then. He had done more than enough. I had one demand for the new house: I made sure my brother – who was set to become Riley's senior table fitter for the south of England on his twentieth birthday – and I had separate bedrooms this time! I also had a practice room fitted, although this was more for my father than me. Well, who wouldn't want a snooker room if they had the space!

In the meantime, snooker continued to go global. The summer saw new exhibition events springing up in Thailand, Singapore, Malaysia, and Hong Kong. The Far East was taking the game to its heart and we were always astonished by how well known we were out there. Nobody really knew just how many people all over the world watched the BBC's snooker coverage, either live or via aftersales.

Out of the blue, Barry Hearn received a telephone call from a TV company in Thailand about the possibility of Tony Meo and me going out there to play some matches. They had seen us on the small screen and now wanted to meet us in the flesh.

Seeing as I had spent most of my teenage years studying the layout of a snooker table before that of the globe, I didn't even know where Thailand was. As a snooker nation, it didn't exist. We were asked to do just one thing out of the ordinary for them: dress up in white suits with dark sunglasses when we arrived at the airport!

We flew first class on Cathay Pacific – I had never turned left after boarding a plane before! When we got out there, we felt like we were the Beatles. Some 300 girls had been hired to greet us at the airport. There we were, three likely lads from Plumstead, Dagenham and Tooting thrown into a whole new world without so much as a rehearsal.

We were given the best suites in the top hotels plus chauffeurs, police escorts and security. We enjoyed ourselves. We met some nice people, played some fun exhibitions and sold snooker to the masses, which was our reason for going out there.

The Thai people loved it and they seemed to love us. But just as we were about to leave to return home, we were escorted to a police station in Bangkok. When we got there, we had to go down three or four floors deep into the basement. We didn't know what was going on. But there was only one thing we could do: let Barry do all the talking...

Tony Meo was very worried but all I could do was giggle. After a week of adulation and seeing my face on billboard posters, I believed we could walk on water. What could they do to us? We were untouchable.

'Don't say a word,' Barry told us. 'I'll do all the talking.'

He was asked how much money we had been paid for coming to Thailand. He said nothing. The story was that we were there to publicise the game and we were sticking to it. This went on for something like two hours until he'd had enough and decided to call their bluff:

'This man here earns eight million baht a year,' he said, pointing at me. 'This man here earns four million baht a year and I earn two million baht a year. We don't need this. We came here to spread the game of snooker. If you can't accept that, fair enough. Do what you like with us but we will not be coming back to Thailand.'

The police officers went into a huddle for a few moments until one of them said: 'Thank you for answering our questions, you are free to go.'

Meanwhile, a suitcase full of cash was sitting in Barry's hotel suite. Before the days of electronic payment, we needed the money up front. So we got it up front. We managed to get out of the country with it as well!

Thailand would become one of the emerging nations in the game. The Thailand Masters, in Bangkok, became a regular and successful event on the calendar from 1984. The country also produced James Wattana, one of the top players in the world in the 1990s, who rose to a best-ever ranking of three and became a national hero when he won in his own country in 1987.

On the table my only success in the Far East came in the Hong Kong Masters. Terry Griffiths seemed to clear up with wins in both Singapore and Malaysia. Considering how much he hated travelling and his dislike of anything that didn't taste like lamb, it was a mystery why he did so well. Some years later, the same could be said of John Parrott, whose track record abroad was superb even though he always hated to be away from his beloved home town in Scouseland!

The domestic calendar resumed in Glasgow with another final between Jimmy White and me. I won again, 9–4, to make it three Scottish Masters titles in a row. A few days later, the tour moved down to Newcastle, where I retained the International Open with an emphatic 9–2 win over Tony Knowles.

Then it was down to Reading for the first edition of a new tournament called the Rothmans Grand Prix. It replaced the Professional Players Tournament and carried record prize money of £45,000 for the winner – £1,000 more than I got for winning the World Championship. It was held at the Hexagon theatre, which had previously held the World Team Cup. The venue was now to join the list of regular homes on the circuit. Overnight, the Grand Prix became one of the big competitions to win and the Hexagon became another name synonymous with snooker.

I reached the semi-finals there, where I lost 9–7 to Cliff Thorburn, my first defeat in a major championship since Kirk Stevens had knocked me out at the Masters nine months before. I had almost forgotten what losing felt like. Dennis Taylor beat Cliff in the final to claim his first major honour in the game at the age of thirty-five. It was a very emotional win for him as it came just three weeks after the sudden death of his mother and his family had to persuade him to play in the competition. He was a very popular winner. It was to be some season for him ...

14. THE BLACK BALL AND THE MISSED GREEN

In hindsight, I believe the turning point was a missed green by me in the ninth frame when I was 8–0 up.

It is the 1985 Embassy World Championship final at the Crucible and my opponent, the bespectacled Dennis Taylor, is sitting motionless in his chair as I comfortably work my way towards a 9–0 lead.

I am in full control of the match as I decide to take on a pot down the side cushion to secure, most likely, another frame. My thinking is that, if I miss, I might be safe anyway as the brown is close to and covering the same pocket. So, I talk myself into going for it and – at 8–0 up and cruising – what could possibly go wrong?

I miss it. Dennis, who has been struggling to find the end of his tip with the chalk – never mind the pockets – drags himself up from his chair and proceeds to win his first frame of the match. Relieved, he enjoys the moment and the crowd cheer his valiant effort, happy for him that he has at least one frame on the board.

I sit in my chair and shake my head. I know I have let him off the hook. What I don't know is that the whole story of the match is just about to change …

Thirty years on, I still wonder if World Championship history would now be different and whether the most famous match in the history of snooker – the black ball final – would have played out the way it did, if I had just played safe on that green?

Improvements to the world ranking system had been a long time coming. It was also vital for the powers that be to recognise that the Coral UK Championship was outdated. It was a closed event for players from the UK. The likes of Cliff Thorburn and Kirk Stevens – ranked third and fourth in the world at the time – couldn't play in it on account of being Canadian. It was backwards thinking and it needed to change. Thankfully, it did. In November 1984, the event became a ranking tournament for the first time and it was now open to all players from all nations. It was not a year too soon.

All the players had reluctantly accepted the previous situation but I don't think any of us thought it was right. The Benson & Hedges Masters was invitation only but that competition had its own identity. The WPBSA statement behind changing the UK Championship to an open event was an acknowledgement of what had to be done for the future of snooker. It was a massive turning point. A lot of us had fought our way – tooth and nail – past draconian, historic rules and regulations as amateurs to get to where we were and we were still fighting for more changes to be made at professional level.

This was a significant step in the right direction and Barry Hearn was instrumental in persuading the men at the top to change the system. It effectively marked the start of the world ranking list being taken more seriously and soon we would have a provisional world ranking list; a 'what if' projection of what the list would look like at the start of the following season. It was interesting to note that while the world ranking list remained static for the whole season, both the media and the players now started to take more notice of the provisional rankings.

There was definitely an added buzz in and around Preston with the likes of Cliff Thorburn and Kirk Stevens being there. Both of them did well, too, reaching the semi-finals. Tony Meo pushed me hard again in the opening round and required just two frames to beat me when leading 7–4 before I rattled off five frames in a row to triumph 9–7, including a tournament-best break of 134.

I progressed more comfortably past Jimmy White (9–4) and Kirk Stevens (9–2) to secure my fourth final appearance at the Guild Hall. My opponent turned out to be the same as the previous year: Alex Higgins.

Although I didn't rattle off the first seven frames of the final this time around, I did come close by leading 6–1 at the interval with some solid snooker, including two century breaks. I was determined not to make the same mistakes as 12 months before. But Alex put on a much better performance in the evening, including a strong break of 124, to make it 9–5 overnight.

Déjà vu can happen in life and it can happen in snooker, especially against somebody like Alex. The Hurricane was in his element in major finals and the crowd were on their feet as he took the first three frames of the second day to narrow my lead to just one frame at 9–8.

But I had slept well and was able to stay focused this time. In fact, I was so pleased with the character I brought to my game in this match that I would rank it as one of my best. I won the last four frames of the afternoon session and the first three of the evening session – seven in a row – to complete a resounding 16–8 victory. I didn't do anything differently from my match against Alex the previous year – but I was less shocked by the comeback this time around and, therefore, I was more prepared for it!

Alex cited the crowd as the reason for his defeat: 'It doesn't help me when they are baying for Steve Davis' blood,' he said afterwards. 'It is all right being the People's Champion but it is a very hard burden to carry now. They are no help to me at all. They don't realise how it works against me but it also works in favour of Davis. All the noise makes me lose concentration. I have to keep pausing and reassessing shots whereas Davis plays in perfect silence. I think it is about time we passed the People's Champion tag on to Jimmy White so that I can get on with my game.' Alex did give me a rare accolade as well: 'At the moment he is the number one and I will just have to settle for being number two,' he said before roaring back with usual headline-grabbing timing: 'But I will be back.'

The Mercantile Credit Classic was born in 1985 (replacing the Lada Classic) and although I had never seen a Mercantile Credit on the road, I was eager to get behind the wheel! Seriously, this was a new development in the world of snooker sponsorship with a financial institution using the game to announce its presence to the general public.

It was held in Warrington at the start of the year and it gave Willie Thorne the only world ranking title of his career. Willie started his career in the same way as John Virgo; playing money matches, gunslinging and taking part in a few gambles here and there. That's how it was in the 1970s. There were few tournaments for amateurs and, therefore, there was little prize money available. He showed his capabilities in amateur competitions and when the game opened up he was one of the first from that scene to turn professional, in 1975.

Willie was known in the game as Mr Maximum such was his prowess in practice at making maximum breaks. He made over 200 of them, which at the time seemed like an astonishing number. It also seemed a bit strange to me for him to keep count for that long but, nevertheless, it was impressive. In comparison, I had made a dozen or so, perhaps not even that. Admittedly, I wasn't going out in every practice session with the aim of making a maximum but, again in hindsight, maybe Willie had a point – the crystal ball of the future would have told us that break-building was going to be the key to unlocking the next level of the game.

While I was certainly no slouch in this area, there are two types of accurate positional players: those who play the correct percentage positional shot and those who can put the cue ball exactly where they want it, regardless of whether there is an element of risk should they get the weight of the shot wrong.

All players have a built-in sat nav system in their brain but some are more accurate than others. Mine was OK but I also relied on superb cue ball control. Willie probably had an upgraded version of the sat nav but perhaps less cue ball control, particularly under pressure.

We all had to wait until the arrival of Stephen Hendry before we saw somebody who had both of these talents plus a top-notch temperament. Then we saw the ultimate maximum-making machine. The fact that Stephen held the record for the most centuries in the game for so long is testament to his prowess, both as a break-builder and a winning machine.

There are two things I would have liked to have experienced as a player: 1) looking through Ronnie O'Sullivan's eyes during a game; and 2) having Stephen Hendry's sat nav hot-wired into my brain!

Along with Willie's big breaks, his instantly recognisable bald head made him a popular character on the circuit. He was also famously popular with the bookies – and unpopular with his bank manager – as he infamously racked up large debts from time to time.

I almost celebrated a maximum of my own in Warrington – three years after I had achieved one in the Lada Classic – in my last-16 match against Alex Higgins. I rolled in 13 reds and 13 blacks but fell short on the next red to record the most frustrating 104 break I have ever made. I beat Alex 5–2. After the match, he endeavoured to tell me where I had gone wrong in trying to get position on the fourteenth red. I knew he was right but I didn't want to listen.

In the quarter-finals, I defeated Ray Reardon, who was still ranked fifth in the world at this time, 5–1. I now faced Willie in the semi-finals. I built up a 7–5 lead in our best-of-17-frames match but a couple of trademark big breaks by Willie levelled it and a couple of mistakes by me were punished with two quality breaks of 44 and 79 to put him in front. I managed to stop the rot by drawing level at 8–8 and take the match into sudden death, where a break of 62 put Willie in charge but a missed red let me in. I comfortably put away the first two reds and blacks but then missed a red myself to hand the initiative back to him. It was nip and tuck until the colours when he did enough to get over the line.

In the final, Willie beat Cliff Thorburn 13–8 and, therefore, his long-standing supporters were finally able to stand in the queue at the bookmakers to receive a small percentage of the money they had punted on him over the years.

The Benson & Hedges Masters remained an invitation-only event for the top-ranked 16 players in the world and therefore remained non-ranking (as it does to this day). It was still London's snooker event and the one that continued to attract a loud crowd that was both unique and ubiquitous. This whole atmosphere reached a new level for me when, for the fifth time that season, I played Alex Higgins. My record against him was four wins out of four.

It was the first time we had ever met in the competition. All 2,692 tickets had sold out well before Christmas. The cheers that greeted Alex's entrance were up a notch on anything I had heard before. When I walked out, I received a mixture of cheers and boos – something that was, by now, quite normal whenever I played him. Being a Londoner in London counted for absolutely nothing in this situation. Alex would raise a fist to the crowd and a fair number would return the gesture.

Since the beginning of the decade I had won 13 of our 15 matches. The big disappointment for me was the 16–15 UK Championship final defeat at the end of 1983, where I had blown a 7–0 lead.

On this occasion, he just got the better of me, winning 5–4 in a tense, mistake-ridden match. As the crowd erupted at the end, Alex fell into a group of fans in the first few rows, absorbing handshakes and pats on the back all round. He was fired up, so much so that he appeared to yell out the words: 'I'm fucking back!' It was picked up on television. The BBC received complaints. Quick as a flash, Alex protested that he had actually said: 'I'm fighting back!'

There was no doubt about what he said on *TV-AM* the following morning. 'I hate Steve Davis' was the headline. He was well and truly pumped up again. But, once more, his form on the table didn't last. Terry Griffiths beat him 5–1 in the next round. Cliff Thorburn beat Doug Mountjoy 9–6 in the final.

The following week, I was involved in another sudden-death encounter, against Tony Meo, in the semi-finals of the Tolly Cobbold English Championship in Ipswich. I won through 9–8, continuing my run of close victories against him. In the final, I romped to a 9–2 win over Tony Knowles. It was my first title of the year. Little did I know that it would be my last for the season.

I lost 9–7 to Kirk Stevens in the semi-finals of the British Open. In the final, Kirk was beaten 12–9 by South African Silvino Francisco. This was Silvino's only major tournament title but it was somewhat marred by his accusation that Kirk had played the match under the influence of drugs. He was subsequently fined and penalised two world ranking points. So they really stuck it to him! However, Kirk later admitted that he had a drugs problem, and the penalty was reversed. Ironically, Silvino was later convicted of smuggling cannabis into the UK and served three years in prison. Sadly, the whole incident did little good for the image of the game.

Drug testing was introduced at the World Championship for the first time in 1985. I think there were two main reasons for this: 1) to try and keep the game clean; and 2) to make it suitable for inclusion in the Olympic Games. Thirty years on, we still wait for the latter. Snooker has been part of the Asian Games since the late 1990s but the earliest it could now be considered for the Olympics would be the 2024 Games.

The drug test was simple enough: we had to urinate into a bottle. But it was quite difficult to do that when you had a doctor watching over you. Since then, it has obviously become a bit more sophisticated but they still have to watch you do the business. In the early days, a doctor would accompany you to the toilet and, at places like the Crucible, this could be a small toilet. After unnervingly peering over your shoulder, it would be his job to put a cap on the jar and take it away. As with other players, my biggest problem was that once a match had finished I relaxed. Beforehand, I would have been a leaking tap – but afterwards I was like Fort Knox!

The system soon progressed to them splitting our samples into two bottles. One doctor would now double to two doctors – a bit like two policemen corroborating your speeding offences. There would be sheets of paper and plenty of ticks and crosses for them to fill in. This was a procedure that had to stand up in a court of law if required so there could be no cutting corners for the doctors of drug testing. The urine we produced also had to be the right strength. If it was too concentrated or too diluted it was no good.

We would have to strain to drain every last drop to produce the minimum quantity required to supply two sample bottles and then we would watch as a bit of litmus paper was placed in it and wait to see it change colour before being held up against a chart. When I was once told that mine was too concentrated, I almost hit the roof. But I ended up having to guzzle down water for another hour until I felt the urge to go to the toilet again. There was now also the risk that I wouldn't be able to stop mid-stream and my second sample might overflow. For me, the whole saga was a total waste of time – but sadly, it is a necessity.

We went along with it and we had a good laugh about it, too: Terry Griffiths used to study the jar from every possible angle, as if he was playing an intricate snooker; Tony Knowles, being a bit flash, was so confident he used to do it at the table straight after a match; and Bill Werbeniuk required a bucket not a jar to give his sample! Fred Davis was actually brought in for drug testing once. He was well into his seventies at the time and Ann Yates, the WPBSA official, was understandably embarrassed to ask him to produce a sample. He was clean, of course, but the joke was that he had actually tested positive for Sanatogen multi-vitamins!

I find the whole drug-testing world today rather hypocritical. Some snooker players have tested positive – but they weren't trying to cheat. They have been caught with a substance in their bloodstream. Alcohol may also have been found in their bloodstream. But that doesn't carry any form of penalty. Neither does coffee. Yet testing positive for something like marijuana can end a sportsman's career.

Regardless of the substance a sportsperson is tested positive for, they will always be labelled as a drugs cheat, especially in the tabloid press. However, there is a big difference between a person who uses a particular drug – be it alcohol or another substance – for personal or social use and a person who uses anabolic steroids or blood doping to gain an advantage in their chosen sport.

It is also ironic that one of the worst drugs out there, in my view, is alcohol. It destroys people. It certainly destroyed Alex Higgins. Yet some mellow people are walking around smoking marijuana, not doing any harm to anybody, and they are considered sports cheats. If we are going to do drug testing, I think we should also do breathalysing. However, drinking alcohol doesn't make you a cheat. Alex was a drinker, but he was a far better player when he was sober. He was just such a great player that he often played well when he was drunk.

At one time there were a lot of arguments regarding beta blockers. Bill Werbeniuk famously took them. I never for one moment thought that he did that so he could cheat. Surely a better way forward would be to say that if somebody is found to have any substance in their body they will be disqualified from that event. Even so, that would only come down to giving the game a good image. It has absolutely nothing to do with cheating in my view. The WPBSA said as much when the drug tests came into the game, talking about the necessity of preserving the good image of snooker – particularly with a view to getting the game into the Olympics in the future.

Manoeuvring my way around the demand for urine samples, the time had come for me to attempt to win the world title for a third successive time. This had not been done since Ray Reardon won his fourth title in a row in 1976 and it had never been achieved at the Crucible. I was the top seed again and for the fourth year in a row the bookmakers made me clear favourite at 11–8 for the new record first-prize money of £60,000. Despite that, the fact was I had won just one of my preceding seven tournaments leading up to the big one.

My first-round opponent, Neal Foulds, was, I thought, rather unfairly priced at 300–1. He was a very tough first-round opponent. After all, he had knocked Alex Higgins out the previous year. Son of former Lucania champion, Geoff Foulds, Neal would soon rise to number three in the world rankings and reach the World Championship semi-final in 1987.

This was the first time we had played against each other on such a stage. Being first match on meant an early start, live on BBC 2. I prepared by getting up and out of bed before eight o'clock every morning for a fortnight leading up to the championship.

The defeat by Tony Knowles was a one-off. It happened and it was gone, over, in the past. But the famous theatre could still send a shiver down the spine, especially to the defending champion in those early stages of the opening round.

And so it was that we shared the first six frames of the match, during which Neal knocked in a break of 101. The last two frames of the morning and the first of the evening put me 6–3 up, and I also led 7–4. Neal levelled at 8–8 but I dug deep to produce an important 39 break in the next frame and got over the line with some consistent snooker. A win is a win but 10–8 is a little too close for comfort. Furthermore, my highest break in the match was 67. I knew that I would have to improve on that.

My normal fluency returned in my next match, against David Taylor who I beat 13–4. I was now quite pleased with my form going into the last eight, where I faced the number seven seed Terry Griffiths.

I suffered a nightmare start against Terry after going in-off the final black to lose the opening frame. I was reeling at 4–0 down. This was now pressure of a different kind. But I mentally regrouped during the interval and overtook him with consistent, high-quality snooker, winning six frames in a row and nine out of ten in total to turn the tables completely and hold a 9–5 lead overnight.

The next day I continued this run of form with four of the next five frames to secure another win over the popular Welshman at the Crucible, my fourth out of four against him.

My opponent in the semi-finals was that other wily Welshman Ray Reardon, who was still going strong at the age of fifty-two. He was playing in the semi-finals of the World Championship for the first time in three years and bidding to become the oldest winner of all time. His 13–12 victory over a young and very promising twenty-year-old Liverpudlian

John Parrott was a Crucible classic: Ray won eight of the last 11 frames in that match to progress so he still had the game to beat the stars of the future. But I was now a very different player from the one he had brainwashed at the Tolly Cobbold Classic in Ipswich on my professional tournament debut in early 1979.

I took a 3–0 lead but some fine snooker by Ray brought him back to 3–2. However, solid breaks of 80 and 47 helped me flatten any early initiative he showed and pushed me into a commanding 5–2 lead at the end of the first session. I won the first two frames of the next session to go 7–2 ahead and while Ray won two of the next three frames – either side of a 72 break by me – I produced my best break of the tournament so far with 106 to nudge into a 9–4 lead. A 72 break by Ray brought him back to 9–5 but from then on I was unstoppable. An 82 break won me the next frame and some more impressive, albeit not massive, scoring by me put paid to a fantastic effort by a great former champion. I won seven frames in a row to cruise into my fourth Crucible final, where I met Dennis Taylor.

The Northern Irishman had quietly and comfortably progressed with wins over Silvino Francisco (10–2), Eddie Charlton (13–6), Cliff Thorburn (13–5), and Tony Knowles (14–5) in the semis. There were so many early finishes at the Crucible that year that John Virgo was working overtime with his impressionist repertoire, which now included a giant pair of upside-down glasses in the style of the pair that BBC commentator Jack Karnehm had designed for Dennis.

I don't think snooker fans ever really appreciated just how good a player Dennis was. He was a very clever tactician and had lots of cue power when he needed it. On most occasions, I had got the better of him. My record stood at 12–2 against him going into the world final. There may have been a flaw in his technique regarding body movement but he always had a great understanding of where the ball was going and there was no doubt that from 1984 to 1986 he got his head down and improved his technique. He introduced a pause at the end of his final pull back, which stopped the jerkiness. Suddenly, he seemed like the man who had everything in his game. His timing was spot on. He was in the form of his life.

I felt mentally strong going into the final and could not have asked for a better start, winning all seven frames of the first session and the first of the second session as well. At around 7.30 on the night of Saturday, 27 April 1985, I was on top of the world, 8–0 up and apparently cruising to my third successive world title. Dennis couldn't get out of his chair. He sat motionless in his corner and could be seen talking to himself on occasions. He later touchingly revealed that he was, in fact, having a conversation in his head with his late mother.

So, when I now think about that missed green in the following frame, my feeling is that most – if not all – of the top players around today would have chosen to take it on as well. It wasn't about that for me. The way I played snooker was different. I had only been able to build up big leads by playing a psychological percentage game as well as a shot-based one.

Depending on the state of the scoreboard, players will either decide to take on a shot or play safe. The best players are the ones who make the most correct decisions. However, since turning professional I had quickly worked out that in long-frame matches there were other factors to consider: if you held a massive lead there was less incentive to take risks; if your opponent was stuck in a hole, the worst thing to do was give a helping hand. So, instead of trying to make the hole bigger for him but take the risk of him getting hold of the spade, perhaps it was better to sit back and let him flail around in panic and dig himself deeper.

That is why it is sometimes better to play a defensive shot even when the odds are, say, 70–30 in your favour. It is a fine balance. It is impossible to know the right course of action because nobody can watch two different outcomes play out. So, we are back in the world of sliding doors …

I would love to know what would have happened had I played a safety shot on the green. I think there is a good chance that eighteen and a half million people might have had a better night's sleep the following evening if I had!

That is the shot that I beat myself up over. When a player looks back on a match, certain moments pop up like big flashing neon signs and that missed green in the ninth frame is my big flashing neon sign of the black ball final. In hindsight, I could have opted to play a safety shot. Dennis might have potted the green and gone on to win the frame and come back to win the match anyway, in which case I might have been left saying: 'Why didn't I go for the green down the cushion?'

A player lives and dies by the decisions he makes on the table and, in the history of the game, there have been lots of cases of players winning frames in blocks during long-session matches. This is to do with how one player can start to feel comfortable as his opponent starts to feel uncomfortable and vice versa. At the moment Dennis made it 8–1, I sensed that the dynamic had changed and I suddenly stalled.

Snooker isn't just about potting balls. It is as much about playing the right shot at the right time. That was my game. That is how I won so many matches by so many frames. Not only was I very accurate on the table but I also made the correct tactical decisions, based on the psychology of the game. I understood that it wasn't about going for a risky shot – it was the consequences of what subsequently happened to the other player's morale. In every match there are decisions that will effectively win or lose a match. Although I didn't know it at the time, I had just made a fatal one.

The tide was about to turn. Dennis had endured his bad period and it was now going to be my turn. Although I produced a decent half-century break in the next frame to regain my seven-frame advantage, it would be my last of the session. At the end of the night, Dennis had cut my lead to 9–7 with six frames in a row. He had gone from managing a total of 67 points in six frames in the afternoon session to making breaks of 61, 98 and 70. By contrast, I had gone from making breaks of 87, 55, 66, 58, 64, 57 and 57 in the first ten frames to not being able to make a single one over 40.

I left the Crucible shell-shocked. I wanted the earth to swallow me up. I knew that it was going to be an uncomfortable night. While 9–7 was still a lead in my favour, the story of the day was not about a tight affair. It was totally different from that. Going from 8–0 to 9–7 in an evening session was only good news for one of us and that was my opponent. I had steam coming out of my ears as I walked back to the hotel with Barry and my father. Neither of them dared to say: 'Well, it is better to be 9–7 up than 9–7 behind.' I was inconsolable.

I didn't feel good in myself the following morning but I had to put the previous night behind me. It looked like I had managed that when a break of 46 helped me to win the second frame of the day and a pressure black – after Dennis had missed it for the frame – put me further ahead at 11–8. But Dennis came back again with breaks of 48, 57 and 55 to level the match at 11–11. He also made a break of 44 in the next frame, but I clung on to win it and get in front again. I also took the final frame of the session to lead 13–11. We had just half an hour to ourselves before we were on the table again.

Average frame times were longer in those days. One reason for that is that the current interpretation of the miss rule means that it is a much quicker game nowadays. Safety could go on for ages back in the day. I sometimes wonder if I would have won more or less in my career with the rules of today: I was the most consistent and accurate potter around under pressure. On the other hand, you could argue that certain styles of play suit a set of rules more than others. One thing is certain – the modern-day style of play and shot selection would have definitely arrived a lot sooner!

Barry and my father popped into Dressing Room 6 to see me before the final session. The pressure was now showing on my face. David Vine caught me for a comment in the corridor live on BBC 2. I don't think I made much sense to him.

Somehow, I produced the highest break of the match in the first frame of the final session – a stylish 86 – to settle my nerves a little and move into a 14–11 lead. The fact that neither of us had made a century shows that both of us were feeling the heat. I now needed just four more frames for the title. I knew that the next one would be vital; the difference between 15–11 and 14–12 in a world final is colossal. But Dennis took it with a break of 61. However, a break of 66 in the twenty-seventh frame re-established a three-frame advantage for me at 15–12. The winning post was almost in sight.

Holding his nerve, Dennis then produced three fine breaks of 70, 57 and 79 to draw level at 15–15. It was now essentially a best-of-five-frames match. I won the next two to lead 17–15 so I needed just one of the next three frames to be crowned world champion.

Dennis responded superbly and made breaks of 42 and 57 to level the match at 17–17 with one frame to play. The stress was overwhelming. My father retreated to the dressing room. Unable to watch, he would follow the match – not really knowing the score – for the next hour or so by listening to the PA system amplifying the voice of the referee John Williams just calling out the breaks. Barry was standing nearby, peeping from behind a curtain backstage like a child watching a horror film. Even he couldn't watch in the end. I was on stage – I so wanted to be anywhere else in the world but there.

The final frame summed up the match in terms of quality: there wasn't much of it. I was well placed on a couple of occasions. At one time, with plenty of reds available on the table, I missed a blue into the corner pocket. I also missed a shocking pink that I reckon my father would have knocked in!

Dennis wasn't playing any better than me. We were like two men having a game down the working men's club, knocking the balls around for the price of a pie and a pint in front of one man and his dog, never mind playing for the World Championship in front of a record eighteen and a half million people live on BBC 2. The safety play was better than the potting and at times tension can provide high entertainment – and so it proved.

I led 52–44, with one red left. I potted it with the rest and ran off the side and bottom cushions back up the table. But it wasn't enough. When the referee came to collect the rest from me, I wouldn't let it go; pulling at it as if to pull the cue back for my next shot. For a few seconds the two of us were involved in a tug o'rest at the top of the table.

I was now forced to play a safety shot instead of having a possible colours clearance. Anybody who knew me could probably tell that I didn't really know where I was. I was on autopilot. We both were. The only difference was that my face was getting whiter while Dennis' was getting redder! After a bout of safety and a lot of hitting and hoping, I somehow fluked the green in the centre pocket while trying to play safe. Another bout of safety ensued. I had a couple of half-chances on the brown – while Dennis was sunk in his chair, muttering to himself again. I was 18 ahead with 22 left on the table. I needed just one ball to leave him needing snookers.

A game of cat and mouse ensued until Dennis pulled out a stunning shot down the cushion to pot the brown in the yellow pocket. He then knocked both the blue and pink into the green pocket to move three points behind me as we reached the point when Ted Lowe's dulcet tones set the scene perfectly for those watching at home:

'The final frame, the final black.'

At this point, Dennis went over to the World Championship trophy and kissed it. With the black close to the middle pocket, he elected to attempt an audacious cross double. He later said that he couldn't live with himself if he hadn't tried to pot it. So he went for it. He missed. But it went safe.

I played a tough up and down safety, which I was delighted with, only for Dennis to try another audacious long double with an element of safety thrown in for good measure; this time into the top corner pocket. He missed again. But again it went safe.

The tension was now intense and, instead of driving the black on to the right-hand side and top cushions to get it back into baulk with lots of distance between the balls, I mishit my next shot so badly that it hit the opposite side cushion and eventually collided with the cue ball.

Dennis now had the first realistic chance of clinching the title. It was about a three-quarter ball black to a distant pocket with some two feet between the balls. He got down, struck the cue ball with power and missed the pot by miles. So much so that his elbow could have taken somebody's eye out in the front row! He walked back to his chair and covered his eyes.

The crowd was now completely caught up in the drama as I was left with a chance of a pot into a top-corner pocket. As the balls started to slow down, I realised there was a possibility of the black cutting into the top-right corner. However, it rolled a couple of revolutions too far to make it a 'gimme' for me. The crowd was now screaming …

I got out of my chair with legs like lead. They didn't feel as if they were mine. Neither did my arms. Neither did my cue. Getting up to the table seemed to take me a lifetime.

As I got down to play the shot, I was only focusing on potting the black. It was a relatively thin cut – although it probably looked easier on

TV due to the table looking like a square to the viewer at home – and, to my credit, I didn't undercut it. When a club player misses a cut they are usually too afraid to catch it thin enough so, in my defence, I did play it better than a club player! The trouble was, being a professional, such criteria didn't matter!

Instead, I overcut the black massively, so much so that it didn't even wobble in the jaws of the pocket. My right arm had now disowned me. In fact, it wouldn't have been inappropriate for the theatre's PA system to have burst into life at this moment with the words: 'Would Mr Davis please come to the stage door to collect his elbow!'

With the black missed thin, the cue ball had more speed on it than I had designed. So, instead of staying in the bottom half of the table, it went in and out of baulk and left Dennis with a relatively easy pot. As I watched where the balls were going, I realised that I had blown it. I put my hand to my head and looked up towards the Romford Roar. I couldn't believe it and I am sure they couldn't either …

In a split second, the crowd fell silent. You could hear a pin drop. Dennis got down, took his time and put the black away. The Crucible erupted. Dennis famously celebrated by raising his cue above his head with both hands. He then wagged his finger as much to say 'I told you so' to his good friend Trevor East, at the time ITV's head of sport, who was sitting in the press seats.

We shook hands and, while we were waiting for the dignitaries and the BBC team to come on to the stage, Dennis famously kissed the trophy again. This was perhaps the most well-deserved action of the day. What a performance and what a test of character from him to come from 8–0 behind in a world final. He fully deserved his success and he was to become a very popular champion. For me, it was all a blur.

David Vine asked me to come forward and say a few words live to the watching all-time record audience on BBC 2.

'Can you believe what has happened here tonight?' he asked.

I replied with a moment of ironic humour: 'Yeah, it happened in black and white.'

I was emotionally, mentally and physically wrecked. I had been one ball away from securing a hat-trick of world titles. I had worked all year to do that and I was now left with nothing at all in the cruellest way possible. Dennis had not been in front in the match until the very end. It was a shock to the system. But that is snooker. At the time it felt like the worst moment of my life. Of course, I look at it all very differently nowadays.

First of all, there are those amazing television figures: the highest ever number of people watching TV after midnight in the UK and the highest ever number of people watching BBC 2 at any time. You can't buy that. That frame is the most famous frame that has ever been played. It was another sliding doors moment for the game. Would eighteen and a half million people really have stayed up until gone midnight to watch me beat Dennis 18–12? It had to happen in the way that it did to have the impact that it did. It was a brilliant moment for snooker. It also did Dennis the world of good. As he always said, a player only has to win the world title once to be remembered as a world champion.

I am also very proud that I helped create something that remains in the memory for so many people. I have been told many touching stories over the years. My favourite involves a young schoolboy who loved snooker but had to go to bed at about nine o'clock that night. He secretly watched the latter stages of the final unfold on a tiny black and white TV in his bedroom with the sound turned down. At 17–17, he heard his father – who was watching the match in the living room downstairs on colour television – coming upstairs, so he turned the TV off and pretended to be asleep. He heard his father open his bedroom door, close it and return downstairs. The boy switched his TV on again and watched the rest of the match. The following morning, his father couldn't contain his excitement over breakfast, telling him how the match had been won on the final black: 'I'm so sorry you missed it. I did come upstairs to tell you about it so you could come down and watch it with me. But you were fast asleep and I didn't want to wake you!'

Thirty years on, I am not sure if winning that final would have ultimately changed my life in any way. If I had done it, would I have gone on to win another three world titles or would I have ended up as a four-time rather than a six-time world champion? Maybe I would have become an eight-time world champion? If ever anybody invents a time machine, my choice will be to go back to the 1985 world final and find out what the outcome would have been had I played safe on the green – or potted the black!

The missed green at 8–0 was just one moment in a 35-frame final. If I had won the world title, it wouldn't have been an issue. But when you look back in life, you reflect on moments that appear to be crucial and you place a lot of emphasis on them. The crucial moments are the ones that stick out. If you had a choice to make and you chose the wrong path, you beat yourself up. I had a choice on the green but I didn't have a choice on the black. Subsequently, my decision to play the green sticks out to me far more than the missed black that everybody remembers.

If I had my time again, would I go back in that time machine and try to rectify the outcome? Of course! After so many years, I still think about it. However, the most important factor is that it was only a game. Yes, a player has to commit everything and the winner is destined to be elated while the loser is inconsolable, but it is only a game. We both won a lot of prize money and I certainly lived to fight another day.

15. THE MATCHROOM MOB

'What's the worst that can happen, Davis?' Barry Hearn asked me. 'It bombs and nobody knows it ever came out?'

'No, Barry, the worst is it comes out, everybody knows about it and my street cred – or what little I have – is in shreds!' I told him.

And so it came out! The silly world of novelty records was on its way to Romford!

A week or so after Dennis Taylor had beaten me in the final of the 1985 World Championship, Barry signed him! There I was, sat in the Matchroom office, looking for a shoulder to cry on when my best mate gave me another boot in the groin: the one person's name that I didn't want to hear for a while until my shredded nerve endings and pride began to heal was Dennis Taylor's. For a moment, I thought my life was falling to pieces.

'I am going to need to sign up another player, Davis,' Barry told me. 'Snooker is getting so popular that I need more players.'

His words didn't really register with me until the very end: 'I have signed Dennis!'

Those four words hung in the air. How uncaring! Surely, this was not what best mates were meant to do? However, I had enough understanding of the business world to quickly accept that it made total sense. Barry needed the world champion – and I was no longer that man.

First and foremost, Barry's support for me was never in doubt. That was always the case. But he told me that he wanted to sign other players and overnight Dennis became the most popular player on the circuit as well as the new world champion. So, it was a no-brainer for any manager to want to sign him, including the best in the business. With Tony Meo and Terry Griffiths also on side, Barry now had a team of top snooker professionals.

The four of us were all ranked in the top ten in the world at the time. It seemed natural that Barry was going to be the manager of some of the best players in the game: he was the man who could do the best job for them. He was always trying to promote snooker and his business interests as well. But doing it this way was ultimately going to mean there would be an inevitable power struggle within the game sooner or later.

Under Barry's guidance, snooker started to explore exciting new experiences and territories. I spent the summer of 1985 getting to know Dennis Taylor as the two of us joined the referee Len Ganley for a promotional tour of China.

Len was a formidable character, a large jovial man who took no nonsense. He did a good job of being a referee and a personality at the same time. He also was respected by the players because of his talent with a cue and once recorded a break of 136. We felt that he understood the game, rather than just calling out the scores and respotting the colours.

He was a famous face as well. He featured as the referee in a popular Carling Black Label advert in which he appeared to crush the cue ball, and he was also immortalised in the song 'The Len Ganley Stance' by the post-punk band Half Man Half Biscuit. Brush the baize and keep the crowd in check …

Our trip to China came just a few months after Wham! had made history by becoming the first pop group to play a concert over there. It was now up to Dennis and me to try and wake them up to snooker. It proved to be a ground-breaking trip and it paved the way for a massive surge of interest in the game that continues to grow.

The reception we got when we arrived in Shanghai was fantastic. Sadly, the same couldn't be said for the food in the hotels. I lived on tomato soup every day because everything else the chefs served up 'wasn't food as we knew it, Jim', to borrow from Leonard Nimoy.

However, I don't remember Len complaining too much. Maybe he was given better food? He was definitely given better accommodation. He had a suite in all the hotels where we stayed because he was considered the official. The same luxuries didn't extend to Dennis and me; we were just the players. There was often brown water coming out of the taps in our rooms.

From the moment we arrived at customs we realised we were entering a different world. Although we had special treatment, we could see that everything was regimented. People either travelled by bicycle – all of which looked exactly the same, by the way – or public transport. Nobody had cars.

I saw a massive pile-up of bicycles one day. I was gazing through the window of our coach while we were being taken to another top restaurant for another official lunch of baby birds in goo and sea slugs, when, suddenly, in what was a one-way sea of bicycles, somebody decided to turn right. The ensuing carnage would have made YouTube gold as more and more bicycles piled into the damage ahead. A crash at the Tour de France had nothing on this.

Expecting to see a certain amount of rage aimed at the offending cyclist who had not used any hand signals, I was astounded to see that they all just got back on their bikes and started pedalling again. Nobody had a go at anybody. It was just assumed they would all now return to business as usual.

So they did. They straightened up their handlebars and wheels, picked up their shopping or children off the floor and off they went. I didn't see a shred of emotion on any of their faces. Obviously, it was a daily occurrence.

The Chinese came out in their droves to watch Dennis and me play. The standard among the local players was low: the best of them could hardly put a break together of over 30, at least in front of a crowd. But their enthusiasm and interest was palpable. Thirty years on, China and snooker has become a success story that none of us on that trip could ever have predicted at that time.

Barry had us touring everywhere in the 1980s: Tokyo, Singapore, Kuala Lumpur, Hong Kong, Bangkok, you name it. The world was our 12 by 6-foot oyster. We would use the close season to take a couple of months off and travel. Being born in August, I spent my birthday in a few exotic locations over the years. On one trip I remember a large Japanese crowd singing happy birthday to me while a cake was brought to the table.

Snooker was played predominantly in Commonwealth countries but we came at it from all angles and tried to take it to new nations as well. We were doing what we loved to do. I loved to play snooker and Barry could see business possibilities opening up before his eyes.

We had Camus Cognac sponsoring us on the Asian tours. We got so many free bottles of the stuff we couldn't get rid of them. Money seemed to be no object wherever we went. First-class air travel was mandatory, especially as somebody else was picking up the bill! We never stopped to consider it might one day end.

We also went out to Brazil on a promotional tour after another international telephone call and invitation straight into Barry's office in Romford:

'Do you manage Steve Davis? We have a guy in Brazil called Rui Chapéu – Rui the Hat – and he has been unbeaten in snooker for so long now that television viewing figures are beginning to drop. We would like to invite Steve out here to come and play him.'

The deal was quickly done and so we flew out to more uncharted territory to basically have another holiday while I played some random player who, we presumed, would probably struggle to make a break of 30!

How wrong were we! While the game was called snooker out there, it was not snooker as such. All the colours may have been on their spots – but there was only one red! The table was also a lot smaller and the pockets were very tight, making it impossible to play anything other than a slow roll along a cushion. The rules were so different that I had effectively to learn a new game and new tactics. The partying would have to wait!

Rui and I played in front of a crowd of around 1,000. He was an interesting character: he was about 20 years older than me and wore a white cap – probably to cover a receding hairline – and white trousers. Local folklore had it that Rui had never been seen without his cap (this sounded familiar!) and that he would only remove it if he was beaten on TV. So, although there was no prize money on offer, the challenge to remove his cap was like a red rag to a bull. What could be under there?

Evidently, it was no foregone conclusion that I would win. Rui knew the game he played inside out and I had two days to learn all the nuances. In a race to nine, I was 3–0 down. My opponent was giving it large and his supporters were goading me in Portuguese: 'So you call yourself a world champion?'

When the MC pleaded with the crowd, I thought he was asking them to be more respectful. I asked Barry to find out what had actually been said and Barry asked one of the TV guys, who was brutally honest with him with the translation: 'Look, we know he is rubbish, but he has travelled a long way.'

I was inspired to beat this guy, who really was at the top of his game, on his own patch. I won the next frame and began to find my feet. With the match in the balance, I played a shot that by normal standards in snooker would have been a standard power run-through, but on the tight pockets of this Brazilian table it was outrageous. The crowd went ballistic. The contest had turned and no doubt the betting had swung violently. I think that one shot broke Rui's spirit.

I had come out to Brazil for a holiday and yet I found myself in full competitive mode in a red-hot atmosphere that would have given the Crucible a run for its money. In the end, I was the victor with a couple of frames to spare. I remember it as one of the most exciting matches I had ever participated in even though technically it wasn't actually a snooker match!

The match became folklore in Brazil with parents telling their children of the moment when the famous Rui the Hat was finally beaten on TV. I actually met up with him again a few years ago when I went out to play in a snooker event out there. He is a lovely guy. But, as far as I know, he never took the cap off!

Meanwhile, Matchroom joined forces with the cosmetics firm Goya to provide new sponsorship for the former Jameson International. It was renamed the Goya Matchroom Trophy and moved from Newcastle to Trentham Gardens, in Stoke-on-Trent. Cliff Thorburn beat Jimmy White in the final.

Dennis Taylor and I played each other in the finals of the next two competitions on the calendar. The press had now dubbed us 'the Robot and the Joker'. The pick of the bunch was a gruelling and thrilling 10–9 win for me in the Rothmans Grand Prix in Reading. I led 4–0, 6–1 and

7–4 but Dennis fought back once again – as he had in Sheffield – to draw level at 9–9 and leave us playing out yet another nail-biting sudden-death frame in the early hours live on television for the £50,000 first prize.

At 10 hours and 21 minutes, it was to be the longest one-day final in history. But this time I won, surviving a black ball finish in one frame when – with my legs shaking like jelly as the nightmare loomed in my mind once again and a whisper went around the room – I managed to sink an easy black. The sense of relief that flooded through me as I saw it drop in the pocket was immeasurable.

Then it was a flight out to Toronto, where Dennis beat me 9–5 in the final of the Canadian Masters. His standard at around this time was superb. These days some people think, unfairly, that Dennis just got lucky in one big event but for a period of time in the mid-1980s he was outplaying all of us!

We were denied a third successive final meeting when Dennis lost 9–7 to Willie Thorne in the semi-finals of the Coral UK Championship in Preston. My own route to the final saw me beat Tony Meo 9–5 and Barry West 9–1 before I met Jimmy White in a noisy encounter.

I was jeered early in the match after claiming a free ball following a foul by Jimmy. Referee John Smyth disagreed with me at first but then changed his mind, something that proved highly unpopular with the Guild Hall crowd. The match was level at 5–5 before I moved into top gear and took the last four frames to win 9–5. But I certainly didn't have the crowd on my side.

Meanwhile, Willie fought his way through a tough draw, beating both Terry Griffiths and Dennis Taylor. He was in good form again and looking to end the year how he had started it, after his success in the Mercantile Credit Classic in January.

After throwing away big leads in previous major finals, it was a nice feeling to reverse that trend and come back from 12–6 down against

Willie to win 16–14. It was some fightback, too: I lost the first four frames of the second day and, despite winning two of the last three frames of the afternoon session, I still trailed 13–8 at the interval.

The match turned on the first frame of the final session. Willie missed a very easy frame-ball blue off its spot when clearing the colours. That shot haunted him. I think he took it for granted that it would go in. We all take it for granted that shots like that will go in. But sometimes they don't and that can immediately wreck your concentration. The look on Willie's face was one of total shock. I got up from my seat, won the frame and got down to business. He did apply some pressure with a break of 96 but I won the last three frames quite comfortably to claim my fourth UK title.

A few boos could be heard as I lifted the trophy. I had to face facts: I was certainly not the most popular player in the world. I'd always known that. But I also took strength from it as a compliment – a back-handed compliment maybe – but I felt that I was being booed because I was consistently getting to finals and winning prizes.

It was a successful time for all of us at Matchroom. The following week, Tony Meo and I won the World Doubles for the third time. Later that month, Dennis Taylor beat me 9–5 in the final of the Kit Kat Break for World Champions – an invitational event held in Nottingham for eight winners of the world title.

By Christmas, Matchroom players had won more than half the titles on offer so far that season. But I wouldn't say that I ever felt part of a Matchroom team. There was a certain amount of camaraderie between us, of course, but, apart from when I played with Tony in the doubles, the other players always felt more like acquaintances to me than team-mates. I actually couldn't imagine being massive friends with anybody on the circuit. I wanted to keep my distance, just in case it compromised my ability to deliver the killer blow in a match against them.

These days it is a different scenario. The game has come of age in so many ways and a lot of players find the balance between being friends and smashing each other up on the table the next day.

The Matchroom name was going from strength to strength, but Barry needed more players to help fulfil the intense demand he had for more bookings. So, he signed Neal Foulds and Willie Thorne. A little bit later, Jimmy White and Cliff Thorburn joined up as well. We even had a record in the top ten!

'Snooker Loopy' was Barry's idea. He phoned up Chas Hodges, of Chas and Dave, and suggested we did a song with them. They had a lot of success in the late 1970s and early 1980s and famously recorded a couple of hits with Tottenham Hotspur FC.

As a Magma and avant-garde progressive rock fan who at the time was massively into soul music, I would have to say that Barry's musical taste was rubbish! Basically, he liked country and western and that was it. If the lyrics didn't involve somebody losing their dog it simply wasn't music as far as he was concerned. I would trust him regarding business decisions every day of the week but that wouldn't extend to music. So, when Barry told me about this my heart sank.

By now, my Porsche had a mobile phone in it. I vividly remember the day I got the call from hell from my manager:

'We're making a record, Davis, and it is brilliant,' Barry said. 'We are going to do a video and everything.'

I went cold. 'Who is making the record?' I asked.

'Chas and Dave and us,' he told me.

I slumped further into my seat. I didn't say anything for a second. And then I announced: 'Barry, I'm not doing it.'

'Trust me, Davis, it is great,' he snapped back. 'Look, I'll get a demo tape sent to you. Take a listen before you say no.'

I played the demo in my car – it was Chas and Dave doing the vocals at that stage – and, after a few listens, I thought to myself: 'Actually, this could be quite catchy' – albeit like penicillin on a lump of bread. I decided to bite the bullet and went with the exuberant flow of a man to whom it was very difficult to say no.

We had a good laugh doing it. A film crew recorded us in the studio and we later did a video for it down at the Matchroom, too. Barry was in it, of course. Then – horror of horrors – a few DJs picked up on it and, before we knew it, we were in the charts. It was poptastic!

Every week, Barry was on the phone to me: 'We are up to number seventy-six, Davis' and 'We've hit the top forty'.

Once we got into the top 30, the video got played on *Top of the Pops*. The record sold well. The fact it got to number six is hilarious. I am not sure what Madonna, George Michael or Whitney Houston made of us as we climbed above them in the charts! We were now officially pop stars!

Unfortunately, that success led us into the world of the inevitable, difficult follow-up single. Chas and Dave gave it their best shot and out came 'The Romford Rap'. It bombed. At that stage, Barry's vision of the breakthrough album and the framed gold disc finally bit the dust!

Thankfully, there was never an LP. God knows what other songs we could have put on it! Barry might have tried to sneak 'Old Shep' on there somewhere or perhaps the tale of Tony Meo's dog, which gets stuck down a mineshaft and we all think is dead. But, while Tony cries his eyes out in grief, Terry Griffiths gets out his old miner's helmet and rescues the dog and we all end up in tears.

When I did *I'm a Celebrity* … in 2013, 'Snooker Loopy' was played one night on a jukebox as part of a game. I had to stand up and sing it to people who had clearly never heard it before. Get me out of there!

Funnily enough, the only reason I knew the words to the song after so many years was that when my children were growing up I used to play the record for them and they thought it was brilliant. I wrote all the words out for them and they took the record into school and played it to their mates. So 'Snooker Loopy' had something of a resurgence in the late 1990s and made the Brentwood primary school charts!

The only good thing to come out of 'The Romford Rap' was probably the video. This time we went into a proper studio and some money was thrown at it. It featured a giant snooker cushion and 15 dancing girls in red. The Matchroom Mob all had different-coloured suits on: Neal was in yellow, Dennis in green, Tony in brown, Terry in blue, Willie in pink and I pulled rank and wore black. Jimmy was, obviously, dressed in white.

At one stage, we all had to walk precariously along this four-foot-high cushion, while looking at the camera. Willie was at the front, leading the way but, because he couldn't guarantee the direction he was walking in was going to be perfectly straight, he veered off-line and fell off the edge, dragging a couple of players with him. That was as exciting as it got. The record didn't sell and we soon accepted that the game was up on the record front. It was back to the day job.

Something that did work was that the more players Barry got into his camp, the more clout he had. Another successful business initiative came with the Goya Matchroom aftershave range. In the jungle, Joey Essex, who had just brought out his own range, was quite puzzled when I told him that I had beaten him to it by about 25 years! He couldn't get his head around a fifty-six-year-old snooker player having an aftershave endorsement. It does seem bizarre but back in the day that was the fervour that snooker somehow dragged with it.

It was all done properly. We spent a fair amount of time down at Goya HQ in Amersham because it was felt to be important that we all chose an aftershave that we liked. We were handed four different samples – labelled A to D – and we had to decide about a month or so later after trying them all out which one we preferred. So, we all immersed ourselves into the heady world of perfumery.

I remember getting in a hotel lift one morning to go down to breakfast and Tony Meo was in there with a random guest. The two of us started smelling each other:

'Which one have you got on?' he asked me.

'I am wearing B today,' I replied. 'What do you think?'

I am not sure what the other guy in the lift made of the aftershave, but he probably thought he had quite a strange story to tell his mates when he saw them. But we had to wear the stuff. It was expected. There was no end of products coming out at that time: Matchroom slippers, Matchroom duvet covers, Matchroom pillowcases. The world had officially gone mad. C won it. Personally I felt B was more subtle. Sadly, it lost out in the second ballot.

Back with the snooker, my next success came at the Dulux British Open in Derby in February. There was a certain irony that we were playing in a paint-sponsored event when some fashion magazine at the time had intimated that our latest Matchroom product was only one molecule removed from turps!

My opponent in the final was, once again, Willie Thorne, but the story of the match was somewhat different from our clash in Preston. Despite losing the first frame, I won the next eight frames of the opening session, including a 127 break at the end, to lead 8–1. Despite a decent fightback from Willie, I triumphed 12–7 to claim the £55,000 prize, taking my season's prize-winnings to over £200,000 and – along with Willie – helping to set a new tournament high for Matchroom earnings of £111,000.

I felt in good shape going into the Benson & Hedges Masters where I met Willie again, this time in the quarter-finals, and beat him again,

5–4, in a match involving some great breaks from both of us – 132 from me and 138 and 110 from him. But I came unstuck against Jimmy White in the semi-finals and lost 6–3. It was a popular victory for the Whirlwind – although he subsequently lost 9–5 to Cliff Thorburn in the final. Cliff's winner's cheque was for £45,000, an increase of £7,500 year-on-year and another example of the booming business snooker had now become.

The build-up to the World Championship took place over the Irish Sea at Goffs. I had won the Benson & Hedges Irish Masters in 1983 and 1984 and it remained one of my favourite events on the calendar, but this time, with a heavy heart, I decided not to enter as it was scheduled a lot closer to the World Championship than usual. My priority was to try and win my world title back. Over in Ireland, the Whirlwind beat the Hurricane in the final, 9–5.

In keeping with other tournaments, the winner's cheque at Sheffield was also increased – up to £70,000 – to make it, rightly, the richest prize in the game. Dennis Taylor, defending the title, fell victim to the Crucible curse and lost 10–6 to Mike Hallett in the first round. But Mike was then knocked out in the next round by a man who had only just scraped into the top 16 the previous year – and it had taken him six years on the professional circuit to get there.

Joe Johnson had never won a match at the Crucible before the tournament began but, after beating Mike, he continued his progress by shocking Terry Griffiths 13–12 in the quarter-finals in an amazing match where he fought back from 12–9 down. He followed that up by knocking out Tony Knowles 16–8 to surprisingly reach the world final.

As world number one I was the second seed and, after comfortable wins over Ray Edmonds and Doug Mountjoy, I faced Jimmy White again in the quarter-finals. With the form we were both in, I thought it was obvious that whoever won would become the favourite to win the World

Championship and I said as much to the media. I couldn't see anybody stopping whoever progressed, not least because the confidence gained from beating the other would be huge.

The first frame is always a big one in a match like this and a 134 clearance was a great way for me to start. Another century break at the end of the session gave me a 5–3 lead at the break. As expected, it was a tight match but I felt good. I felt even better after I won the first four frames of the second session.

This period in the match was to be massive psychologically for me and it put me in total command at 9–3. Jimmy could only muster two more frames and I won through 13–5 without ever feeling at all troubled during the match. I was made the firm favourite to win the world title. Regardless, I just focused on my next match. That meant Cliff Thorburn.

In terms of world rankings, Cliff and I were the top two players in the world, but I always felt confident of beating him, particularly at the Crucible. However, it was always tough against him. Our previous semi-final there, back in 1981, was a mammoth encounter and so I prepared myself for the task in hand. I was ready for plenty of hours to be clocked up against the Grinder around a single table in the centre of the cauldron.

There were a few errors by both of us in a match of nail-biting snooker. I was 6–4 up when a mistake by Cliff handed me the eleventh frame, but I returned the compliment and handed him the twelfth. A 56 clearance from Cliff reduced my lead further and we shared the last two frames of the day; Cliff was the last to leave the arena with a grin on his face but I held a narrow 8–7 lead. It was hard work and it had only just begun.

The first frame of the third session summed up just how tight it was. I started off well with a break of 62 but Cliff came back to win it on the black. After over eight hours of play, we were locked together at 8–8. He moved ahead with a break of 65 in the seventeenth frame but back I came to level at 9–9. Cliff responded with a break of 89 to win the following frame but I replied with a break of 112 to level at 10–10. Cliff came back again with a break of 44 to go 11–10 in front before I levelled once again at 11–11 at the interval.

It was draining stuff – mentally as well as physically – and so now was a good time for a nap in the dressing room. I needed to recharge for the evening session. Everything was pointing to the ultimate test of wits in another late finish.

Meanwhile, Joe Johnson had quickly won the two frames he needed to defeat Tony Knowles. The Yorkshireman – well known for being a singer in a local band, Made in Japan, in his spare time and a 150–1 shot for the title before the tournament began – could now put his feet up and watch Cliff and me slug it out.

Two more quality breaks in the opening two frames of the night – 79 from me and 104 from Cliff – made it 12–12. We now both required four frames for victory.

I got in front again at 13–12 by winning a half-hour frame and the next was the most crucial of the match. Cliff made a mistake on the green when he was well placed to draw level at 13–13 and the green and brown were enough for me to and take the frame, which was the longest of the match at 62 minutes, and move into a 14–12 lead.

It seemed to be the killer blow. Cliff looked deflated, but he was never beaten until he was beaten. I pressed home my advantage: breaks of 42 and 45 won me the next frame, and 44 and 77 in the one that followed made me the winner at 16–12. It was as tough a test as I could have had from Cliff – perhaps even more draining than my 16–10 win over him five years before.

Like the previous year, my final against Joe Johnson was billed as something of a David and Goliath affair. This was fair but many knew just how talented my opponent was and anybody who had watched Joe perform in the earlier rounds would not have been so ignorant to think that was the case.

Joe and I had known each other from our amateur days and we turned professional at roughly the same time. Joe did so after reaching the final of the World Amateur Championship, where he lost to Cliff Wilson in 1978.

Whenever I played Joe I always thought what a naturally gifted player he was. He was also a really lovely guy. He hadn't been seen much on TV so viewers at home probably wondered where he came from but those of us in the game knew all about him.

Something just hadn't clicked for Joe until now. This is not unusual. There are a lot of good players who never win tournaments. But every now and again, they have their moment in the sun. However, this doesn't often happen at the Crucible. Joe managed to do it on the biggest stage of all.

I felt that I started well in the fina, winning the first frame and pulling out two century breaks of 108 in the third frame and 107 in the fourth frame to lead 3–1 at the mid-session interval. If nerves had affected Joe in the early stages, he soon put them right. He reeled off three frames in a row to lead 4–3 at the end of the afternoon.

I levelled at 4–4 and then followed up with three more frames to lead 7–4. Joe responded in some style by winning four frames on the trot to lead 8–7. I produced a quality break of 81 to draw level at 8–8. There was nothing between us.

The first session of the second day finished with Joe 13–11 ahead. A 100 break in the last frame of the afternoon kept me in the hunt. However, in the evening session there was no contest: Joe went into overdrive with some astonishing free-flowing potting of the highest order and wrapped up victory by winning five of the six frames that were played that night. I had no answer.

The final was a fairy tale for Joe. I can't offer any excuses. My shot selection was fine but his was better. My potting was OK but his was better. He simply outplayed me. He deserved his title and he was a popular world champion.

My post-match interview with David Vine summed up the difference between this world final defeat and the previous year's. While I had been unable to get more than a few words out after the black ball final, I was much more accepting of the situation this time around. So, while the pill was still bitter, I could at least swallow it! I was left to lick my wounds again but there was no feeling of devastation when I left the Crucible – that was to happen the following day, once the adrenaline had subsided and the reality of the situation kicked in!

My statistics at Sheffield were still very good: I had now made five world finals in the 1980s; won three and lost two. The numbers remained in my favour. But for another 12 months I would again have to be introduced as the world number one but not the world champion wherever I went. I just had to get my head down, wait for the new season, and get back in the saddle again.

16. PUBLIC IMAGE

'Jimmy's got a name, "Whirlwind"; Alex's got a name, "Hurricane". Why haven't I?' I asked.

'OK,' Barry replied. 'We'll call you "Very Good". How's that: Steve "Very Good" Davis?'

'Nah.'

'All right, "Extremely Professional": Steve "Extremely Professional Indeed" Davis,' he said. 'That's a good 'un.'

'No, it's not. It's boring,' I replied. 'I'm sick of being a boring one. I don't want to be boring. I want to be flamboyant, different, exciting …'

'All right, Steve "Boring but would like to be Exciting" Davis?' he suggested.

'Nah, look, I want a name that captures the real me.'

'Plumstead!'

'What?' I asked.

'Steve "Plumstead Boy" Davis.'

'That's not the real me. I want a name like Whirlwind or Hurricane.'

'Windy!' Barry said.

'Windy?' I questioned.

'Very Windy!' he added.

'I've got it: "Interesting Davis".'

'Steve "Interesting" Davis!?' Barry exclaimed.

'It's mad. It's devil-may-care. It's interesting!' I declared.

And, with that, I had a new nickname.

The British public love an underdog. A plucky loser who fights until the end seems to appeal to them much more than a cocksure champion who doesn't seem to have to try too hard. Losing two world finals in two years didn't necessarily make me the most popular player in the world, but it might well have made me more popular than if I had won them.

I was always passionate about being professional. I did the right thing at the right time. I was a winning machine. This earned me the tag of boring. People were bored of me winning all the time. They became so bored that apparently I became boring. There wasn't too much I could do about it. Luckily for me, I was soon to connect with the audience in a more positive way without doing anything about it at all. A single moment changed my profile overnight and it was created from the fact that I didn't have a personality!

Spitting Image was a popular satirical puppet show on ITV on Sunday nights. It launched the careers of many top British comedians – among them Steve Coogan and Harry Enfield – who featured on it as voiceover artists. The programme writers focused initially on politics but after a while they turned their eyes on sport.

I did a TV interview in Romford with Jan Ravens, who also worked as a voiceover artist on the show. When I told her how much I loved the programme, she told me: 'You'd better watch it next week, then!' I immediately knew exactly what she meant.

I felt myself go cold. *Spitting Image* hadn't touched sport before but had ruined people in politics. So, I had a week to try and imagine what they had in store for me ... Barry Hearn closed down the Matchroom club and we decided to make a party night out of it, watching the programme go out live to the nation at 10 p.m.

The sketch involved Barry and me in a snooker club. In it, my puppet was very upset about both Alex Higgins and Jimmy White having nicknames while I didn't. Barry was portrayed as the archetypal manager with cigar, gold chain and sheepskin jacket but I was the one – with cue in hand and rifle sight attached – who piped up with the immortal word 'Interesting'. And so my favourite nickname Steve 'Interesting' Davis was born ...

We all collapsed laughing in the Matchroom when we saw it. I didn't analyse it. I never considered whether or not my playing style was negative to my personality in any way. It was certainly true that I wouldn't crack a smile while playing unless something extraordinary happened. The game was far too difficult for me to do anything other than focus all the time.

I actually thought the sketch summed me up perfectly, especially from the public's side of their television sets – and despite being the latest victim on the show, it somehow worked in my favour. How does that happen? Forget Sports Personality of the Year and those other awards, this was *Spitting Image*! It was monstrous. The nickname stuck and 'Interesting' became my moniker overnight. It confirmed the public's perception of me and, in turn, that seemed to lift all the pressure off me.

It was a gift. The puppet was only interested in snooker and so it was the best back-handed compliment I could have had. I mean, what other personality was a twenty-something snooker player who practised eight hours a day so that he could just win tournaments going to have? Barry and I learned the entire script from that sketch off by heart so that we could do it to order in the club.

In a bizarre twist, it also fulfilled a role regarding an image that the media could never find for me as well. It made light of a situation that for some reason had become an issue. 'Snooker is better than sex' and all that nonsense ... Nobody could suggest I was boring any more. I wasn't, I was interesting ...

Spitting Image was another chapter in the snooker success story. From *Pot Black* and one frame per week on the TV, via more coverage on the box than the Prime Minister, to now having my personality analysed in a satirical puppet show!

Barry actually got me the puppet for a fortieth birthday present so I have had it for some time now. It is made of foam rubber and latex. In the first year I had it I used to have him lurking around in different places in the house, just to scare the crap out of the cleaner I had at the time. Nothing works quite like a life-size torso hidden in a wardrobe! He is in a bin liner at the moment, slowly rotting away. His eyelids have gone a bit now but he is apparently in good nick compared to some of the others and he turned up as a studio pundit on the BBC coverage of the UK Championship in 2013 while I was out in the jungle!

It has crossed my mind from time to time that if I had my moment again – and I knew beforehand that I was going to be as successful in the game as I became – would I have been able to come up with an image to go with it all? Maybe I could have worn a mask, like Kendo Nagasaki? It would be nice to walk around for the rest of my life as an unknown. Some of the wrestlers managed that gimmick. I could have played on it too and informed the media that I wouldn't take my mask off until I had won seven World Championship titles. In the meantime, Barry could have hired a few masked reserves to put people off the scent ...

But, seriously, any sportsman has to be very good at what they do to make any sort of image work for them. Whenever I walked out to play I was always in the zone and I dared not do anything to break that concentration, never mind consider what my image might have been. That would have been a distraction. In sport, there are only a few winners who are also personalities. My life was: wake up, practise, go to bed, repeat. Nobody becomes the best player in the world in any sport just by having a personality. It is probably far better not to have one – having one will most likely mean that you won't be a winner in the first place!

After the TV show came the book ... I was subsequently involved in compiling a brilliant literary masterpiece called *How to Be Really Interesting* with one of the main writers on *Spitting Image*, Geoff Atkinson. It was done in silly *Monty Python* style and it was so much fun to do. I still enjoy reading it today. I gave Geoff as much information as I could to help him take the mickey out of the other players on the snooker circuit as well as myself.

Everybody was stereotyped. There was the Bill Werbeniuk Health Workout featuring cartoon drawings of him knocking back the beers; Tony Knowles' favourite food was a sausage; Terry Griffiths' favourite holiday destination was two weeks under a hairdryer; Willie Thorne's hobby was modelling men's bathing caps while Alex Higgins' hobby was the same as his favourite food and drink: lager.

It was so corny and stupid that it was pure genius. Looking back, the thought that we could actually compile a whole book about somebody who was boring but actually thought they were interesting is just surreal. Some of the players got upset about it but I never understood that at all. It wasn't as though I didn't make fun of myself! I ripped myself to pieces. A list of my best chat-up lines included: 'Would you like to hear about my break of 137 against Doug Mountjoy?'

The success of the book put me in an even stronger position. If ever the subject of being boring was brought up again, I could always revert to the puppet's mentality of believing that I was interesting! I had some strong ammunition, too: 'What type of chalk do you use?' and all these great, daft lines that were in the book. So, there was no point in anybody having to go any further down that particular line.

Bizarrely, *Spitting Image* was a definitive moment in my career. The book was also a definitive moment because when it gets to the stage where you can laugh at yourself you have cracked it. *How to Be Really Interesting* underlined how the game had captured the imagination of the public to such a degree when it became a Christmas bestseller.

Not that everybody got the joke. I went on a daytime TV show and was asked about how I had managed to turn my life around after being so boring. It quickly became clear that the interviewer hadn't actually read the book and had got completely the wrong end of the stick. I sat there and was interviewed as if I'd written some sort of self-help book!

Spitting Image is long gone but my nickname remains. It is by far my favourite of all of them. The Nugget is endearing but Interesting is just so good. To go down in history as the most boring/interesting sportsman in the world is just great. Although, obviously, I still have to fight off aspiring newcomers in this department: Nick Faldo tried to claim the title and Andy Murray has also been knocking on the door a few times …

Back to the boring stuff – or should that be interesting?! The first big event of the 1986–7 season was the Rothmans Grand Prix in Reading when former world billiards champion Rex Williams turned back the clock to beat me 5–1 at the age of fifty-two before losing 10–6 to Jimmy White in the final. The following week, I beat Willie Thorne 9–3 to win the Canadian Masters for the first time in Toronto. This came just a few weeks after Willie had beaten me in the final of the Matchroom Trophy in Southend. In all, a record number of 30 tournaments would be contested during that whole campaign – there would never again be so many until Barry's revitalisation of the game in the recent years.

My toughest opponent at the Tennents UK Championship at the Guild Hall came in the shape of a young Maltese player called Tony

Drago. He was even faster around the table than Jimmy White! I couldn't shake him off and only won through 9–8 after he missed a shot with the rest due to an unusual grip, something with which he was always prone to error.

In the semi-finals I comfortably swept past Alex Higgins 9–3 after another eventful week in the life of the Hurricane, in which he head-butted WPBSA official Paul Hatherell. He was later fined £12,000 and banned for five tournaments. The last, sad chapter of his career was beginning.

At around this time players would often go outside into the auditorium and sign autographs after an exhibition or tournament. So Alex decided to buy himself a gold pen and a silver pen to sign – and sell – his posters. A silver Hurricane autograph would cost £1 but a gold Hurricane autograph from the People's Champion would set you back £1.50.

After that little money-making venture, Alex went one step further and realised that time is money, and that if he could speed up the process he could pocket even more. So he got himself a basic printing set. The stamp he used didn't even bear his signature. Instead, it just had 'A. HIGGINS' in capital letters. There he would be sitting, grinning like a Cheshire cat, with his ink pad stamping these posters. Boom, boom, boom ... Fans walked away with these purchases, trying to work out what had just happened. There was the occasional angry face but, generally, it was utter bemusement.

My opponent in the UK final at Preston was Neal Foulds, who had recently won the International Open and reached the semi-finals of the Grand Prix. He would go on to finish the season ranked third in the world. But even after winning the first two frames he posed little threat to me on this occasion. I led 10–4 overnight and 14–7 after the first session of the second day. Breaks of 124 and 66 in the first two frames of the final session earned me a comfortable 16–7 victory. The £60,000 first prize took my total career tournament earnings past the £1 million mark. More importantly to me, it was my fifth UK title.

Another Christmas bonus came in the shape of the Hofmeister World Doubles Championship with Tony Meo in Northampton. Then it was time for the last *Pot Black* in its current format. The success of the competition had paved the way for the success of the game in the 1980s but it had become hard to include it in the annual schedule because of the growing number of tournaments on the calendar. Jimmy White won the event, beating Kirk Stevens in the final. *Pot Black* would return in the early 1990s for three brief years and, again, in the late 2000s for the same duration. But its glory days were in the past.

Pot Black now had something of a nostalgic appeal but it didn't have the same pivotal significance in the calendar. To a degree it had served its purpose, but its place in history cannot be overestimated. Every snooker fan owes *Pot Black* and the people who gave it the go-ahead in the first place a massive debt of gratitude.

The Whirlwind was having a good season and the two of us met in an exciting final at the Mercantile Credit Classic in Blackpool in January, which I narrowly won 13–12 after trailing 35–0 in the final frame. Jimmy left me with a chance to pot a long red, which I took. It was my most important shot of the season, a sink or swim moment. I sank it and swam successfully to shore.

My father and Jimmy's father, Tommy, were now starting to see a lot of each other in the players' rooms on the tour. Both of them did their best to be 100 per cent committed to their son when we played each other without being disrespectful to the other. At 12–12, Jimmy's father was apparently jumping around the place, thinking that his boy was going to do it, while my father just chewed more furiously on yet another cigar stub. Then, moments later, it was Tommy who was looking subdued as my father returned to normal, watching me take control of the final frame.

Before the final, I had to beat two outstanding young players. The first was the well-respected twenty-one-year-old John Parrott, who I just managed to beat on the final black to win 5–4 in the quarter-finals. The second, in the semi-finals, was the new name on everybody's lips.

Stephen Hendry was just seventeen but he had already won the Scottish Championship and set a new record for being the youngest player ever to reach the final stages of the World Championship – he famously lost 10–8 to Willie Thorne and was then applauded off the stage by his relieved opponent. He reached the quarter-finals at the Grand Prix and, by the time he played me at Norbreck Castle, he was already being tipped to be the youngest player to win the World Championship one day.

I won 9–3 but Stephen certainly showed enough talent to suggest that he could be a major headache in the near future. His arrival on the scene was an example of how quickly the game was progressing. Young players like him were learning fast and, while I could still find the right tactical shots to win these matches, I also knew that I was starting to be pushed by a new breed of player and, to some degree, I was being forced into helping them learn the ropes.

I had now won four tournaments in a row and felt I was on a roll. But that came unstuck at the Benson & Hedges Masters when I lost 5–2 to Doug Mountjoy in the first round at Wembley. Dennis Taylor put on an amazing performance to come from 8–5 down in the evening session to beat Alex Higgins 9–8 in the final and win the £51,000 prize.

Fortunately Goffs always suited me much more than Wembley and so it was that I regained my Benson & Hedges Irish Masters title with ease after crushing Willie Thorne 9–1 in the final. It was the perfect build-up to the Embassy World Championship in Sheffield.

As I had done in 1984, I met Australian Warren King in the first round there. It was to be a much closer contest this time around but there was to be no shock and I happily progressed, 10–7.

Next up for me was my childhood hero Ray Reardon, who was still seeded at 15 despite being in his mid-fifties at this time. The Count proudly rolled back the years to lead 3–1 at the interval. I was pretty dismayed. At the break, I mentioned to my father that the table was so fast that I couldn't control the cue ball.

'Perhaps you're pulling the cue too far back,' he told me.

I wasn't aware, but he had spotted something from the press room. I rushed to the practice table to see if that was the case and quickly discovered that I could easily cut down the pull back and therefore hit the ball more positively and still cope with the speed of cloth.

I went out and pulled the cue back over a shorter distance and, immediately – even under the tension of the match – it felt that I had much more control. The boost in confidence it gave me was extraordinary. It was a comfortable 13–4 win for me in the end.

However, in the penultimate frame of the match, Ray made a wonderful century break, the last one he would ever achieve in the World Championship. None of us knew it at the time but this legend wasn't coming back to play here again.

Without doubt, the match of the quarter-finals was played between defending world champion Joe Johnson and Stephen Hendry. Joe was seeded number one for the tournament as defending champion but he'd had a relatively uninspiring season – yet his success at the Crucible the previous year was testament to his ability. When you saw him play you could see that the game came easily to him. His cue action seemed completely natural and he had this wonderful flowing style with a beautiful touch. But Joe didn't seem as motivated as other players for some reason. He also always struck me as too nice to be a relentless winner. I think he would have needed to have been more selfish and a little nastier, perhaps? I believe the top players have got to have those characteristics. The margins in talent at the highest level are not that great. But what does make a difference is a player's mindset, tactical knowledge and how he performs under pressure.

However, Joe was shining again. The Crucible curse didn't seemed to haunt him. But Stephen gallantly fought back from 12–8 down to level at 12–12 before losing 13–12 in a terrific match. In the semi-finals, Joe beat Neal Foulds 16–9 to reach a second successive world final. I reached a fifth successive world final by defeating Terry Griffiths 13–5 in the quarter-finals and Jimmy White 16–11 in the semi-finals. So the 1987 world final was a repeat of the 1986 world final. The winner's cheque had been increased from £70,000 to £80,000 to remain the biggest prize in the game.

I started well with a 127 break in the first frame to get off to the perfect start. However, some solid break-building by Joe put him 3–1 ahead at the end of the afternoon. But I still had the better of the first day and led 9–7 overnight. I nudged that lead up to 14–9 the next day and then watched in horror as Joe fought back to 14–13.

I was sitting there thinking to myself: 'Not again!' But breaks of 64 and 40 in the next frame and a 30 and 73 in the one after took the pressure off at 16–13. By winning two of the next three frames, I clinched the match 18–14 to become world champion for the fourth time.

For a first-time champion, Joe came as close to retaining his title as anybody. He certainly hadn't suffered from any form of Crucible curse. But his career sadly faded away and over the years he also suffered a number of heart attacks. He managed one other notable victory in the Langs Scottish Masters, but in terms of the main professional events on TV, he seemed to disappear as quickly as he arrived. He didn't really capitalise on his success. I don't think he really wanted to go on the road and travel too much.

After losing two successive world finals, it was a case of third time lucky for me. My retired father was, as usual, an ever-present in the press room backstage every day I played, chomping on his cigar and watching my every move, and he was delighted. We all were. It had been three long years since I had last held the trophy and it was great to have it back.

My final triumph in another successful season came in the inaugural Rothmans Matchroom League, a non-ranking round-robin competition with £500,000 in prize money for top invited players, which had been created by Barry. I beat Neal Foulds in the final to bring my season tally to eight titles – my best record in three years.

I really enjoyed the Matchroom League – or Premier League as it became – and won the first four of them. It ran for 25 years and was an event tied up with the fact that Barry was now moving his business interests into creating sports events. Ultimately he was a salesman so that was a natural progression for him. He also saw the potential of satellite television and indeed Sky took over coverage of the Premier League in the 1990s.

It was this event that also helped to introduce Allison Fisher to a wider audience. She was signed up by Barry and became the general public's first experience of seeing a quality female player in action. She was an exceptional talent with a great feel for the game. There is no question that she got a certain amount of fast-tracking into the league set-up but she proved her worth by beating Neal Foulds and drawing against Tony Meo. I also played with Allison in a mixed doubles event at the World Masters at the Birmingham NEC, which was Sky's first foray into snooker, and we won it.

Allison played on the professional scene for a while, too, but she never made it through to the televised stages of an individual event. At one stage, I think she was ranked in the mid-200s which, while it might not sound too great, was actually a very proficient standard.

She won the Women's World Championship seven times but she became frustrated with the women's game and felt she was banging her head against a brick wall trying to make it pay. There was little sponsorship and I think it would be fair to say that the general standard of play – apart from her – wasn't that great. In the end it had to be accepted that people just didn't want to watch it. They wanted to watch Allison but that was it. Nicknamed the Duchess of Doom after moving over to the USA to play on the nine-ball pool circuit, she has done far better for herself than she could ever have imagined by staying in the UK and has won dozens of titles out there.

The Matchroom League was another big hit for Barry and, at this time, his snooker interests were going from strength to strength. Matchroom players earned well over £1 million in prize money between them that season and we would provide all four World Championship semi-finalists the following year.

But the powers that be were getting uneasy. Barry definitely made some enemies. The main issue seemed to be that he told people what they didn't want to hear. This didn't go down too well at the WPBSA and it all got quite tedious in the end. This was frustrating for me because I am sure he could have taken the game forward so much at that time – if he had only been allowed to do so.

The WPBSA couldn't stop Barry creating and selling events but they hated the fact that the Matchroom League largely showcased Matchroom players. So they were caught between a rock and a hard place. The fact that I use the word 'they' to describe the WPBSA says a lot about the mess the game had got itself into – I don't use the word 'we' here, even though the players were the members who voted on who was on the board!

The governing body always seemed to be the players' enemy. Barry also sat on the board in the mid-eighties as well. It could get ridiculous. Mike Watterson, the promoter who brought snooker to the Crucible in the first place, was putting on the World Championship for us and one day at the start of the boom decade we all sat down as a committee and asked: 'Why are we letting this man make money out of us?' So the WPBSA booted him out.

From then on, the membership was trying both to run and promote the game. Any outside promoter was seen as a competitor. But they were offering to put money into the membership's pockets! Obviously, the WPBSA tried to represent all players but the TV companies were very interested in invitation events that supplied top players. The WPBSA was always trying to block these invitation events and promote open events that were more often than not doomed to fail. They just didn't want entrepreneurs like Barry knocking on the door. This was to be an ongoing problem when Stephen Hendry's manager, Ian Doyle, also built up his own stable of players.

Barry has always been his own man and he always stood up for what he believed to be right. He had caused some controversy earlier in the season when he pulled out all of his players from the Belgian Classic because it clashed with Matchroom League fixtures and another promotional trip to China. But the WPBSA knew about those dates beforehand and Barry also hoped that the Ostend event could be rescheduled. However, the WPBSA refused and it was lost from the snooker calendar.

The WPBSA seemed to dislike the fact that there was somebody on their patch who they couldn't control and therefore an unfortunate and unnecessary negativity started to grow in some quarters. In the end, Barry's days on the board were to be numbered. I don't think he could be bothered fighting the board all the time. So he stopped trying to be involved in the snooker world so much.

He still put on a couple of events but, basically, he gave up trying to work alongside what he felt were a bunch of amateurs on a committee that would have struggled to manage a corner shop. The vast majority of the board was made up of players, past or present, whose main skill in life was getting a small ball into a slightly larger hole with a pointed stick. Managing a worldwide professional sport was not their forte. Furthermore, it was unrealistic to expect any more from them. But that was the way it was: it was written into the constitution of the WPBSA that the board must include a certain percentage of players.

Subsequently, we were constantly hampered in any quest to allow proper professional people to take over the game. From the moment Mike Watterson was booted out in 1983 – regardless of whether or not he was going to become a future Bernie Ecclestone – the seeds of future rifts, mismanagement and emotional turmoil were sown.

It is ironic that, after Barry stopped being so involved, he went into the world of darts and the success that sport has enjoyed under him has been extraordinary, including a very successful PDC World Championship and its own Premier League, shown on Sky. Tickets for both events are like gold dust.

But that shouldn't have come as a surprise. He is an astonishing man who has lived life at the pace of two people. He is also a great example of what a person can do if they really set their mind to it. I have been blessed to have had him in my corner throughout my career. He tried absolutely every sport going at school to try and become a winner at something. He entered a walking race once – but he couldn't resist breaking into a run at the end and was disqualified!

When the 1990s came along there was the big satellite television boom. But snooker was now sadly largely without him. He had gone off to focus on other sports and making Matchroom one of the biggest independent production companies in the world of sport. He achieved this and it remains a hugely successful operation, involved in something like 40,000 hours of television. Behind it all, his principles of having fun have remained.

Our trip to China in 1987 was ground-breaking stuff once again. The country's leader Deng Xiaoping specifically asked to be shown the art of billiards during our visit and so Barry invited a master of the game, Rex Williams, to come out with us on the trip.

The whole Matchroom Mob also took part in a TV event against eight of the country's top amateurs. I played against a sports centre employee called Wang Lin while Jimmy White took on a chef called Zhang Yanbin. Neither of them had made a break over 60 before, but the big deal was that these matches were watched by a TV audience of well over one hundred million people! Live coverage of any sport in China was rare – but snooker was new and fashionable. Willie Thorne won the event, becoming something of a pin-up overnight!

Then it was off to do some sightseeing ...

Sadly, I had no interest in seeing these places. Such a feeling is common among most players. We all got taken to the Great Wall of China and none of us wanted to go. Barry might have wanted to do it, but none of the players were in the slightest bit interested. We would much rather have been practising back at the hotel.

It took over two hours on a bus to get to there and we played cards and liar's dice on the way. I would much rather explain the rules of liar's dice here than talk about the trip to the wall. We got to it, looked at it, I think Jimmy actually had a sneaky wee up against it, had photographs taken by it and went back to the hotel.

We also visited the Forbidden City. I had a walk around. It was all right but it was missing a snooker table! What can I say? I have been to all these places around the world and not really seen any of them. Don't feel sorry for me, I am just not bothered about it.

We are all the same. On a later trip to China, we got dragged along to see the world famous terracotta army – dating back to the third century BC – in Xi'an. After about 20 minutes there, Stephen Hendry asked me: 'How long have we got to be here?'

He was as bored as me. When he got back home to Scotland, he was asked during a radio interview how much he had enjoyed his cultural trip to one of the most amazing archaeological finds of the twentieth century – a discovery that would have had the *Time Team* dribbling with excitement.

'It was OK if you like looking at a load of old plant pots!' was Stephen's reply. That summed it up perfectly for me. Move on …

I refer any interested readers to the holiday section of my *How to Be Really Interesting* book. Every day spent in Romford was a holiday for me!

17. BULLETPROOF

I was now at the top of my game. To dominate matches in the way I did and record emphatic, enormous winning scorelines was a statement in itself. I was always prepared to take total control in a match and – like a boxer in a ring – once I could smell any weakness, I was totally focused and afforded no sympathy whatsoever to my opponent.

I was always the same. I never changed. To whitewash a top-ranked player was always a very proud moment. But when I was in the zone, competitive snooker was becoming a far easier proposition. I was now at a level that was well above the rest. It felt as though nothing could stop me.

The World Championship, UK Championship and Masters are the three big competitions in snooker. In the eyes of both the players and the British public that is still the case. For how long, we don't know. But it is a major honour to win one of these trophies and to win all three in the same season is very special. The Triple Crown is the Holy Grail. But you only need one off day and the dream is shattered.

Until 1988, nobody had yet achieved it. I had come close before, winning two of the three titles in three previous seasons – 1980–81, 1981–2 and 1986–7 – but was denied by two Northern Irishmen: Alex Higgins (who won the Masters in 1981 and the World Championship in 1982) and Dennis Taylor (who won the Masters in 1987).

The 1987–8 campaign began with the World Series, involving showcase events in Hong Kong, Tokyo and Toronto, and I defeated the fast-improving Stephen Hendry 9–3 in the final of the Hong Kong Masters. A few weeks later, I beat Cliff Thorburn 12–5 in the final of the International Open at Stoke-on-Trent, to take the £40,000 top prize and the first ranking title of the season.

Cliff had beaten Stephen 9–1 in the semi-finals to inflict the heaviest defeat so far in the youngster's professional career. But the eighteen-year-old – now up to 23 in the world rankings – recovered in some style to record the best win of his career so far in the next event on the calendar just a few weeks later – against me in the Rothmans Grand Prix at the Hexagon theatre.

We met at the last-16 stage over the best-of-nine frames and he won 5–2. As I had predicted, he later admitted he had watched the video of my 9–3 victory against him in the Mercantile Credit Classic earlier in the year many times and decided to change his game accordingly. His safety play was much improved. This was the most balanced snooker I had seen him play. With me out of the way, he went on to win the competition, beating Dennis Taylor 10–7 in the final to claim his first ranking title.

But I had a reason to disregard my defeat to Stephen as a blip. In my previous match – against Jim Wych – my cue started making some strange noises, as though the ferrule was loose or perhaps something worse. I was handy enough to put a new tip on myself – something many other professionals couldn't do – but to make running (or even static) repairs was beyond me.

But I knew a man who could. A number of years earlier, a bloke had pestered the life out of me, saying he wanted to make a replica of my cue for me to use as a spare. I finally agreed and he came along to an exhibition at Dartford to measure it. I thought nothing more about it until this cue was delivered to me. It was absolutely brilliant and, while I didn't actually use it, I wrote out a cheque to him for £200 – even though he hadn't asked for a penny from me! John Parris still hasn't cashed the cheque – it is up on the wall in his workshop!

So, after my cue had started to make these odd sounds at the Hexagon, I got straight on the phone to him and then straight in the car to see him in Bromley for a diagnosis. The news wasn't good: the wood inside the ferrule had cracked and, in order to repair it, I had to lose a ferrule length. I gave John the nod and he did a great job on it by taking roughly half an inch off the length of the cue.

The problem was I needed it to feel exactly the same as the one I had used since the very early days of my career – the cue with which I had won four world titles. And it didn't. In that match against Stephen, I felt as though I was all over the place; the length had only been reduced by a small amount but it felt like I was playing with a toothpick not a cue.

After losing to Stephen, I went back to see John that night and we discussed our options again. In the end, we decided to splice more ebony on to the butt of the cue to restore it to the original length.

At around the same time, a new generation of cues had started to come on to the market. Both Alex Higgins and Jimmy White had been seen playing with a new-style three-quarter-length two-piece cue. Instead of using half-butts that resided along the length of the table, below the cushions, they were now adding a longer piece to the butt section and, therefore, obtaining more reach – but more importantly they were still playing with their own shaft and tip instead of the inferior ones on the residential half-butts.

The results were much better. I had made do up until this time with a Heath Robinson extension that clamped and tightened on to the butt. It was never totally solid and, therefore, couldn't be trusted on a power shot. With my cue in need of repair anyway, I now had a chance to bite the bullet and make a change.

We decided to turn the old one-piece into a two-piece. With my nervous blessing, John sawed it in half at its balance point and inserted a join. I was pacing up and down in his house as he went to work in his shed. He later told me that he felt like a brain surgeon as he worked on this precious 40-year-old piece of ash for me – and that he had never felt pressure like it. It was now up to me to get used to it. I had every belief that I would.

When I got the cue back and played with it, I immediately noticed that the weight had increased dramatically – in snooker terms at least – by about a couple of ounces. It now felt like a tonne weight in my hand. In fact, my wrist was aching at the end of my first practice session with it. But the results were very impressive. It felt a better cue than before, certainly on power shots, and I was so impressed with it that, a few months later, I asked John to add even more weight to it.

The power game that is played today provides an interesting dilemma for the modern player. The mass of the cue multiplied by the speed you can deliver at the moment of impact on the cue ball determines how fast the ball leaves the tip of the cue. So, while a lighter cue can perhaps be accelerated quicker from its starting position at the end of the final pull back, I assume a heavier one needs less acceleration. To my knowledge, there has never been a proper study into the optimum weight of a cue for a player. I suppose trial and error has probably resulted in the correct parameters but it would be nice to know; especially if the study reported back that all players would be well advised to do intensive weight training sessions as a result!

The 1987 UK Championship was the first time I was able to put my remodelled cue to a proper test. My opening match was against Alex Higgins, who was all over the newspapers yet again on the eve of his return after his five-tournament ban for head-butting a WPBSA official at the Guild Hall 12 months before. My cue felt good as I crushed him 9–2 to move into the last eight.

With Stephen missing from the televised stages in Preston, I beat John Parrott 9–5 in the quarter-finals and Willie Thorne – who made the first ever 147 break in the tournament the week before, albeit untelevised – 9–2 in the semi-finals to set up another final against Jimmy White.

The Whirlwind was now ranked number two in the world, but my record against him at the Guild Hall was excellent with four wins from four matches. We had enjoyed some good battles in recent matches and this would turn out to be the best contest we had ever played there.

It was a test of sheer willpower as well as skill. I took the first frame with a break of 106 but Jimmy hit back with breaks of 91 and 139 to lead 3–1. He was 5–2 up after the first session but I then won five of the seven evening frames, making breaks of 107 and 98, to end the first day at 7–7.

Jimmy won the first two frames of the next day but I won the next four to lead 11–9. Back he came again with three in a row to go 12–11 ahead. I drew level with a century break and won the next frame on the black to nudge ahead at 13–12. Jimmy levelled again at 13–13 before I produced a break of 110 to go 14–13 ahead at the mid-evening interval. He levelled again at 14–14 with a maximum of just three frames left to play.

But I didn't need three. A break of 108 put me 15–14 ahead and a 42 clearance won me the match 16–14 and the winner's cheque for £70,000. It was my sixth UK Championship title. When it mattered, I had delivered again.

I was very happy with my overall form. At the next ranking event, the Mercantile Credit Classic, I didn't drop a frame in the first three rounds, including a 5–0 whitewash of Alex Higgins in the last 16. In the quarter-finals, I faced Stephen Hendry and, with my 5–2 defeat against him at the Grand Prix fresh in my mind and a remodelled cue in my hand, I was pleased to beat him 5–3. My semi-final opponent was the Welsh player Steve Newbury, who had surprisingly knocked out Terry Griffiths in the previous round. I brushed him aside 9–2. Waiting for me in the best-of-25-frames final was the former *Junior Pot Black* champion John Parrott.

Although this was John's first major final, he had already made his mark. The twenty-three-year-old was fifth in the provisional rankings for the following season thanks to some strong performances, including a semi-final appearance at the Grand Prix. He had also beaten both Jimmy White and Tony Knowles so far in Blackpool.

He made me fight, too. I led 9–5 overnight but John played excellent snooker to win six of the first seven frames the following day and lead 11–10. He was a few in front in the next frame as well before missing a tricky red. I rescued the frame with a break of 83 and that was the catalyst for further breaks of 68 and 99 to wrap up the match 13–11. It was another trophy in the sideboard but, at the same time, the tournament had announced that yet another new kid had arrived on the block.

The Benson & Hedges Masters had continued not to be a good competition for me. I had only managed to get beyond the quarter-finals once since my victory there in 1982. Compared to my four World and six UK Championship titles, it just didn't stack up. Due to my poor form there, I tried to change my routine a little this time around and booked into a hotel for the first time, sadly leaving my mother's home cooking behind but gladly doing without the regular one-hour commute as well.

The bookmakers, seemingly unworried by my previous form at Wembley, still made me the man to beat as 6–4 favourite. My main rivals were likely to be Cliff Thorburn – who was aiming for a remarkable fourth Masters title in six years – and crowd favourite Jimmy White. There was no Stephen Hendry (still ranked outside the world's top 16 players), but John Parrott was there and Alex Higgins was also around.

Defending champion Dennis Taylor crashed out in the first round and Alex Higgins went out in the quarter-finals. The man who beat them both was world number 16 Mike Hallett. I had played Mike way back at the start of our amateur days when I toured the UK with Geoff Foulds. At the age of twenty-eight, this was to be his breakthrough tournament.

Mike faced John Parrott, who had shown impressive form again by knocking out Cliff Thorburn 5–4 in the quarter-finals, for a place in the final. Mike won the match 6–5 in thrilling fashion after requiring four snookers in the final frame. He was now through to his first major final after nine years on the professional circuit.

My own route had been rather more comfortable, beating Dean Reynolds 5–2, Terry Griffiths 5–0 and Joe Johnson, the conqueror of Jimmy White, 6–3 in the semi-finals. For the first time in six years, I was in the final at the Masters again.

I remember there was some talk about me and my Wembley jinx before the match, but that couldn't have been further from my mind as I demolished Mike 9–0 in the final. It was only the second whitewash ever recorded in a major final – my 9–0 defeat of Dennis Taylor at the Jameson International Open in 1981 had been the first.

I was thrilled. I played solid snooker throughout the match while Mike just lost the plot. It was something of a stroll by the end. I was the Masters champion again. It seemed a long time since I had whitewashed a fellow professional. To do it in a major final was very special. To do it in the Masters was even better. As well as the £55,000 top prize, I picked up a further £6,000 for the top break of 126 in the tournament, which I recorded in the final. This took my season's earnings up to close to £300,000. I was now established as the highest earning sportsman in the UK again.

A few weeks later, I secured a fourth Benson & Hedges Irish Masters title with a 9–4 victory over Neal Foulds at Goffs and went up to Sheffield in defence of my Embassy World Championship title feeling as good as ever. The Triple Crown was on …

I felt that I had matured from the player I had been in my early years. I had taken a few knocks along the way, especially at the Crucible. Winning the world title back after those two losses to Dennis Taylor and Joe Johnson had left me feeling in a much stronger position.

At the age of thirty I felt comfortable with myself going into that particular championship and that was such a great feeling. I was playing some strong stuff in matches while still endlessly searching for perfection on the practice table. I was also in a position where I was thoroughly enjoying the competitive snooker arena. The Crucible was feeling less like a trip to the dentist and more like a day at the office – my office!

The prize money at the World Championship was on the up again, rising to £95,000 for the winner – a massive increase on the £7,500 Ray Reardon had picked up as world champion just ten years before! I was the top seed and favourite again.

Stephen Hendry, currently ranked third in the provisional world rankings and second-favourite with the bookmakers, was unseeded again due to his current world ranking and, as a result, could have been placed anywhere in the draw. As it was, he was in the opposite half to me. His second-round match against Jimmy White turned out to be a Crucible classic.

My opening match against John Virgo was one of those first-round struggles at Sheffield for me. I was 9–5 ahead and required just one frame for the match but John clawed his way back to 9–8 and subsequently had a chance to draw level after I missed a pink. But he couldn't take advantage and I managed to crawl over the line 10–8.

I was back in my usual stride for the second round where I obliterated the challenge of Mike Hallett 13–1. He must have been sick of the sight of me. Mike was a fantastic striker of the ball with loads of cue power and a beautiful touch. But he rarely brought the killer instinct with him to the match table.

Jimmy came out on top in a brilliant match with Stephen, 13–12. The 25 frames were completed in just over four and a half hours. It was exhilarating snooker with 21 breaks of over 50, including three centuries. Afterwards, Jimmy's odds to win the title tumbled from 8–1 to 6–4. But I was now the 10–11 favourite.

In the quarter-finals, I met twenty-two-year-old Tony Drago, who was enjoying a rich vein of form after knocking out both Alex Higgins (10–2) and Dennis Taylor (13–5). He was now after a hat-trick of world champion scalps.

I always treated the Tornado with the greatest respect. His talent and knowledge of the game have always been immense and are reasons why he has enjoyed such longevity in snooker. In this match, however, he struggled to keep up with me in terms of break-building. I made 11 half-century breaks in a comfortable 13–3 victory.

And so from arguably the fastest player on the circuit to certainly the slowest: Cliff Thorburn was to be my World Championship semi-final opponent for the third time. Apart from the odd defeat in the Matchroom League it had been four years since I had lost to The Grinder. My record against him at the Crucible was unblemished, too, with one final victory and two semi-final victories against him from our previous three encounters.

▲ The beginning of the end for our pop star journey – recording the video for 'The Romford Rap' … The difficult second single!

▼ Me and Stephen Hendry during the Dubai Classic. The crowd was a bit sparse but it was nice to see they brought their own drinks!

▲ Quite a reception on the first of our many visits to Thailand.

▼ A visit to the zoo in Bangkok. Not sure who was keeping an eye on the tiger though!

◄ Me with Pele during a publicity day for Madame Tussauds, when we were both being unveiled as new waxwork figures.

▼ Suzanne Dando (gymnast), Brian Jacks (judo champion) and me, all caught up in the Conservative spin machine.

▼ An exhibition evening with some of the Liverpool FC giants of the eighties.

▲ Me playing Eric Morecambe in the World Championship final, with Ernie Wise refereeing.

◀ Tongue tied as presenter of my own TV show, *The Sports Quiz with Steve Davis*.

▼ Spot the most boring one! Me and my *Spitting Image* puppet.

▶ Difficult to know whether I was in the zone or under pressure at the Crucible!

▼ Alex Higgins could be a difficult character and we didn't always see eye to eye, but he was one of the genuine superstars of the game.

◀ Me and Joe Johnson, probably before he demolished me in the final in 1986. By this time I'd started wearing a bow tie for afternoon sessions.

▲ A begrudging handshake for a great performance by a superb player. Dennis Taylor, 1985 World Snooker Champion.

◀ The young pretender, Stephen Hendry. Little did I know he'd one day take my crown. This was taken to publicise an exhibition tour around Scotland.

▲ I got out of there! On the other side of that bridge was an interview with Ant and Dec, a glass of champagne and some FOOD!!

◄ My sons, Jack and Greg, at Buckingham Palace on OBE day.

▲ On top of the world! Me, Barry and a selection of silverware.

Both of us made a steady start. I led 4–3 at the end of the opening session and the second session put me 8–6 in front. But I went into overdrive in the third session by winning the first three frames as Cliff potted just five balls. I ended the night 14–8 up and I rattled off the two frames I needed in just over an hour the next day to record a fine 16–8 win. In the other semi-final, Terry Griffiths caused a minor surprise by beating Jimmy White 16–11 to reach his second world final nine years after his first.

At one time Terry and I were competing against each other in quite a few finals so it was nice to turn the clock back again. My Crucible record against him was even better than my record against Cliff with five wins from five, the first of those coming back in 1980. Terry's image had changed a fair bit over the years. He had now developed a rather striking bouffant hairstyle for which he got a fair amount of stick. His talent on the table was never in doubt. He was a great player. He was also a big smoker.

Smoking was part of the game in those days. As a non-smoker, I just had to get on with it. I was obviously sharing a lot of other people's smoke when I played at the working men's club or the Matchroom but during tournaments up and down the country it wasn't a problem because the players were seated apart. However, the Crucible was different. Sitting next to an opponent during the two-table set-up at Sheffield was particularly difficult. In fact, it could be horrible. David Taylor objected so strongly to it that he once asked for another chair to be placed at the other end of the table behind the BBC cameramen. I never went that far but that is not to say that I was happy about the situation either.

Nowadays, it seems like another age but back in the day it was accepted that players who were non-smokers had to politely sit there while smoke was puffed into their faces. Fortunately, because of the one-table set-up that we had in the final stages at Sheffield I was able to sit far away from Terry in the other corner during that final. Of course, it wasn't just him: Alex Higgins, Jimmy White and a lot of other players were also big smokers. There was also the inescapable fact that so many tobacco companies were involved in the game as well. We had big sponsors in Embassy, Benson & Hedges and Rothmans. There was always a pack of 200 waiting for you in your dressing room. But I couldn't complain – smokers were paying some of my wages!

Terry took the first and last frame of the opening session but I won the other five. I also won two of the opening three frames of the evening with an 81 break moving me into a 7–3 lead. But the rest of the night was a totally different story as he stormed back with three frames in a row to trail 7–6 and then won two of the last three frames of the session to level at 8–8 overnight. Here we go again…

Fortunately, I won the first three frames of the first session the following day and six of the eight overall – finishing with a break of 92 – to go into a 14–10 lead before taking my now regular final-day dressing-room power nap. It was to do the trick yet again. But Terry will have kicked himself after letting the first frame of the night slip away. He was 32–0 up when he made a mistake on the blue. I gratefully capitalised to take the frame.

Terry's mood was probably summed up when he rather comically reversed himself into the giant globe that was positioned below the world trophy and knocked it down amid roars of laughter. It was to be the only ball dropping for Terry in that final session! I was firing on all cylinders by now and made two devastating breaks of 118 and 123 to move to within just one frame of victory. It was no contest in the end and I comfortably claimed my fifth world title 18–11. The Triple Crown was also mine!

What a season! Terry and I embraced each other at the end. If I had to pick anybody I wouldn't have wanted to have beaten in a world final it would always have been Terry. That is how much I respected the man. But for me to have won five world titles at the age of thirty also felt amazing. The newspapers were now calling me a legend. Some of them also jokingly suggested that I should retire! But I was far too interesting to ever consider doing something like that.

I continued my domination of the game in the first ranking event of the following season, too, by beating world number two Jimmy White 12–6 in the final of the International Open in Stoke-on-Trent. I was in blistering form again. I won the first seven frames and made four century breaks while Jimmy didn't score a single point in eight frames! By early October, I had also won the Matchroom Trophy by beating Dennis Taylor 10–7 in the final.

Later that month, I also regained the Rothmans Grand Prix title with a 10–6 win over a resurgent Alex Higgins in the final. Talk about not being able to keep a good player down: Alex had talked a lot about getting back to his best since his five-tournament ban but few believed he could do it. It was five years since his last major title but fine victories over Dene O'Kane, Neal Foulds, Rex Williams and Alain Robidoux got him to the final.

However, I was in no mood to show any mercy. I started off with a 137 break and was 6–2 up at the interval. I won the match 10–6. But my opponent showed he still had enough about him to make a challenge on his day. Furthermore, the £39,000 runners-up cheque was his biggest ever pay day, such was the growth of prize money in the game. For the record, the winner's cheque was £65,000.

Ten years after I had first turned professional, I felt I was walking on water. I had been world number one for six successive seasons, won over 40 titles and earned an estimated £5 million. Life could not be any better.

But I was about to get a wake-up call from a young pretender to my throne. My winning streak suddenly ended when Jimmy White beat me 9–4 in the final of the Canadian Masters the week after the Grand Prix. However, my game felt all right in the early rounds of the following tournament – the UK Championship in Preston – but I was nowhere near my best. I still beat Warren King 9–7, Gary Wilkinson 9–3, Danny Fowler 9–6 and John Parrott 9–4 to reach the last four again.

But Stephen Hendry was becoming the danger man and he had shown better form than me, beating Willie Thorne 9–4 and Cliff Thorburn 9–2 in his previous rounds. In fact, Stephen won all seven frames of his afternoon session against the Grinder. He then confidently predicted to the press: 'I can beat Steve Davis.'

It seemed that he had made both me and my status his new goal. He had certainly moved up another level. And so it was that he defeated me 9–3 at the Guild Hall. I played well but he played much better. The fact he did this to me in an arena where I had played some of the best snooker of my career and dominated year after year hurt a lot. It also set off more than a few warning bells in my head. It was just one match at the end of the day but I knew this kid was now getting to be very good. Ironically, he didn't go on and win the competition – not this year anyway.

Doug Mountjoy pocketed the £88,000 first prize with a 16–12 win in the final in the twilight of his career, at the age of forty-six, ably aided by a new-found confidence after employing Frank Callan as his coach. Frank's stock was about to rise and more players flocked to him. Meanwhile, Doug continued this unlikely purple patch by going on to win the Mercantile Credit Classic as well.

After that, it was back to normal. Whatever Doug had found with Frank seemed to disappear as quickly as it had appeared. The elusive form book in sport can be so fragile. And so can the role of the coach. Various players have won the World Championship with a coach by their side, only to kick him into touch further down the line. One minute a player is raving about the help he is getting and then, in no time at all, he is with a different coach!

I didn't stay down for too long. I beat John Parrott 9–5 in the final of the Everest World Matchplay in Brentwood and defeated Jimmy White 5–4 in the final of the Norwich Union Grand Prix to take my season's tally to five trophies. But I missed out on the Masters after a second successive defeat to Stephen Hendry, 6–3 in the semi-finals. This time he did go on and win the title.

I missed out on the Irish Masters as well – after another defeat to Stephen in the semi-finals by 6–4. But a rejuvenated Hurricane beat him 9–8 in the final.

In some ways this win might even have eclipsed the magical clearance Alex made against Jimmy White on his way to winning the 1982 World Championship. Alex's leg was still on the mend after he had broken it falling from the window of his girlfriend's flat, but he continued to play with a plaster cast on it. While obviously hindered by this and in some discomfort, he still managed to beat the man who was fast approaching the start of his period of domination. It was a truly incredible achievement.

My main memory of the Irish Masters that season was one of embarrassment when I miscounted against Mike Hallett. I cleared all the colours up to the black when the referee coughed to get my attention. He glanced towards the scoreboard and I discovered that I was eight points behind! I left the black on the table and walked out of a packed house, straight to the toilet and – while recovering from shock – started to think about how stupid I was going to look when I walked back into the arena!

As I passed the press room on the long walk back to the stage, I noticed that all the reporters were buzzing about what I had just done. Then I had a brainwave: I popped in, picked up a calculator and walked back out into the arena with it in my hand! It is always good to laugh in certain situations and on this occasion the crowd laughed along with me. It was too late to save the frame but luckily I was able to win the match.

I also crashed out of the Anglian Windows British Open with a 5–1 defeat to eventual champion John Parrott in the quarter-finals. But the one player occupying most of my thoughts at this stage was Stephen Hendry. He now seemed to be consistently beating me in major competitions and that was becoming a worry. I could also see that his confidence was growing season by season as well and I knew that I needed to find an answer – and quick.

Yet despite Stephen's form and run of results against me, the bookmakers kept faith with me at the Crucible and installed me as 5–4 favourite to win the World Championship again, which this year carried a prize of £105,000. Stephen was listed as second favourite behind me at 5–1 with John Parrott 7–1 and Jimmy White 8–1.

I successfully began the defence of my world title with a 10–5 win against Steve Newbury. Tragically, between our two sessions – played in the morning and evening of Saturday, 15 April 1989 – the Hillsborough disaster was taking place just a few miles away at the home of Sheffield Wednesday FC during the FA Cup semi-final between Liverpool and Nottingham Forest. In total, 96 people would lose their lives.

The atmosphere at the Crucible around that time was like nothing I have known before or since. There was a minute's silence before the evening session and John Parrott, a proud Liverpudlian and an Everton fan, wore a black armband during his match against Steve James the next day.

All of the players and officials also went to Sheffield Town Hall to sign the book of condolence. It was a terribly sad time. As a professional sportsman, I somehow had to remain in my own little zone during it all. That was difficult with a tragedy such as this taking place so near to where we were. It affected us all in different ways. I know it affected John very much.

I beat the relatively unknown Steve Duggan – ranked 50 in the world – 13–3 in the second round with a session to spare. I repeated that emphatic scoreline against Mike Hallett in the quarter-finals. I had dropped just 11 frames on my way to the semi-finals.

The next day, Stephen Hendry beat Terry Griffiths 13–5 to set up a mouth-watering semi-final between us. But this time it was going to take place on my treasured patch and it was one that I knew I really had to win for all sorts of reasons.

It was so important to start well. Two half-century breaks of 50 and 60 helped to win me the first two frames. Stephen's break of 75 in the next frame reduced the arrears but I kept producing with consistent breaks of 55, 31 and 32, and 68 winning me the next three frames to put me 5–1 up. Stephen replied with a 74 break of his own but I responded with five frames in a row – including breaks of 48 and 62 – to lead 10–2. Stephen rallied by taking the last two frames of the first day with breaks of 42 and 64 but, particularly given my recent history in matches against him, a 10–4 advantage was a great lead for me to hold overnight.

Perhaps inevitably, Stephen came out snapping at my heels the next day. He quickly won the first two frames to reduce my lead further to 10–6 after, effectively, a four-frame winning stretch. He then produced a break of 68 to lead the next frame by 51 points with 51 left on the table. The pressure was on. I kept my composure to sink the remaining three reds, three blacks and colours to tie and force a respotted black. This was now a massive moment for both of us. And it went my way. I potted the black to go 11–6 up. A rarely seen clenched fist celebration from me summed up to the crowd just how I was feeling at that moment.

The next two frames were shared before Stephen made a magnificent clearance of 139 to apply more pressure and then won the following frame as well to apply a little more. At 12–9, the final frame of the day was a big one. I held my nerve in a tense frame to go into the next day 13–9 ahead. That was to prove vital.

The following day, Stephen scored just eight points in three frames as I rattled in breaks of 63, 71, and 54 and 40 to clinch a 16–9 win. I was made up with the way I had finished the match but, once again, getting off to a good start had been crucial.

Regardless of the form Stephen had shown in other events, as far as the press were concerned the World Championship was the important one and the older master had put paid to the young pretender when it really mattered!

The surprise package at Sheffield that year was probably the unseeded Tony Meo, who found himself in the semi-finals for the first time after wins over former world champion Joe Johnson, the evergreen Eddie Charlton and Dean Reynolds. But he came unstuck pretty easily against John Parrott 16–7 in their semi-final.

A lot was expected of John. He was up to second in the provisional world rankings for the following season and he had done well at Sheffield, overcoming Steve James 10–9 before beating Dennis Taylor 13–10, Jimmy White 13–7 and Tony Meo. This was his big moment and he was under pressure. But it was a big moment for me as well – a win would mean I would equal Ray Reardon's modern-era record of six World Championship titles.

I clinched the opening frame after a 34 break and doubled my lead with a 51 break in the following frame. John got off the mark after hitting a break of 49 in the third frame and a couple of decent breaks saw me into a 3–1 lead at the interval. When we returned, three breaks of 30 or more pushed me to 4–1 ahead and a break of 61 extended my lead further before John reduced arrears with a 46 break of his own.

But I went into overdrive from the eighth frame onwards and John seemed to have no answer. The high point was a break of 112 in the tenth frame. Suddenly I found myself 9–2 up. Meanwhile, John was struggling to pot a ball in some frames and when he did manage to put some shots together, such as a 52 break in the twelfth frame, I responded with a 60 break of my own to snatch the frame from his grasp. He found some form with a 68 break to win the fourteenth frame but I took the last two frames of the day with breaks of 80 and 68 to lead 13–3 overnight. It was the most comfortable lead I had ever held at this stage of a world final.

The following day was rather easy work for me. I didn't really have to break into a sweat at all to reel off the five frames I needed in no time at all. John seemed disconsolate and ready to throw the towel in. But I probably felt more comfortable on the table than I ever had before in that final. I loved almost every minute of it. I felt untouchable. It was as though John was going to break down every time he started to put a break together and I was going to mop up every time.

So, to finish a somewhat difficult season in this style was terrific. I had despaired at times but I now felt like Superman. It was as though I had a force field around me again. It was great to have got that feeling back. I admit that I had questioned myself a lot. I didn't think my technique was perfect going into the tournament and that affected my confidence. It unsettled me.

But any fears I might have had at the start of the World Championship felt a million miles away as I strolled through that world final with embarrassing ease. Both John and I knew that he hadn't played well and for me to win 18–3 was magnificent for me but also crushing for him in equal measure. But that was the record scoreline that I had now placed in the history books along with equalling Ray Reardon's record of six world titles. I would now go in search of a seventh.

18. HONOURED

My nan had the best seat available. She was a little bit frail but so proud that she was placed down at the front, about 20 feet away from the Queen. I bowed and took two steps forward. The Queen pinned on my medal, shook my hand and said very quietly: 'Prince Philip and I were away at the weekend and so we didn't see the final. Did you win?' I couldn't believe it. The Queen was a snooker fan! My jaw was on the floor. 'Yes, Ma'am,' I replied with a smile. 'Well done,' she said. And then gave me a little push …

The popularity of snooker was at its highest level. As world champion and world number one, I was inevitably the main ambassador for the game and the man who received personal recognition for its success. It was a position I was proud to hold.

The first major honour bestowed on me was the MBE in 1988. The first I knew of it was when a letter arrived from Buckingham Palace signed off by an official there as Your Obedient Servant. It was a far cry from life at the working men's club in Plumstead. But, without sounding unappreciative or making light of the whole Queen's honours lists, I was quite ambivalent about it all and remain so to this day.

I recognised that the award was all down to the popularity of snooker and that was a statement in itself about how much entertainment the game had brought to the public. I was, therefore, honoured for services to the community. But it would have been more accurate to have honoured me for services to me – I wasn't doing anything for snooker or the community, I was doing it all for me. It was my hobby. I played snooker because I liked to play snooker.

So, the day after I beat Alex Higgins in the final of the Rothmans Grand Prix in Reading – there surely couldn't have been a greater contrast – I was off to Buckingham Palace. I decided it was a girls' day out so I dragged my mother and nan along with me. We had a lovely day.

When I got to the Palace, a rather posh chap came to the waiting room and informed me and a long line of other people what was going to happen. We were essentially part of a big conveyor belt for the Queen to meet, greet and hand out medals to. We were told that when it was our turn, we would be required to walk forward, turn 90 degrees, face the Queen, bow (or curtsey), take two steps forward, wait for the Queen to pin on the medal, a handshake would follow and perhaps – if we were so fortunate – have a brief conversation. Whether she spoke or not, we would know when it was time to leave because her handshake would slowly turn into a gentle push. Nobody ever sees the push but each and every one of us who has ever received such an award will have felt it. That is the sign to leave, which means taking two steps backwards (being careful not to turn away), bow, turn and off you trot. Then it is time for the next one on the conveyor belt.

When it came to my turn, the Queen pinned on my medal, shook my hand and said those glorious words that confirmed to me that I was the best thing since sliced bread. And then there was the push ...

Buckingham Place is not a place that is set up for the general public. There was nowhere to get a sandwich or a coffee. We were also hanging around for ages afterwards. I was absolutely starving during the official photographs outside, so much so that I had to get the Matchroom limousine to stop off at a well-known burger chain on the way home. I went in there and bought a hamburger in my morning suit! But I couldn't wait to get back to the Matchroom and tell my mates about the Queen being a snooker fan who watched me on TV. I mean, does it get any better than that?

A few months after being honoured by the Queen, I was honoured by the British public. After making the top three on three separate occasions, I was voted BBC Sports Personality of the Year in 1988. Me? A personality! Can you imagine? The man who'd had a charisma by-pass was now officially Sports Personality of the Year! Olympic swimmer Adrian Moorhouse, who won the gold medal in Seoul in the 100m breaststroke, was second and golfer Sandy Lyle, who won the US Masters, came third. Both of them must have been gutted – never mind the sportswriters who would always favour Olympic events or outdoor sports. But this award was voted for by the public. It was a great honour that they'd voted for me and, more importantly, it was a fantastic result for snooker.

After years of attending this prestigious live TV event in London, when I finally won it I was a little disappointed to be playing in an exhibition match in Milan! I would have loved to have been in London to receive the award, but there was no way that I could break the engagement and fly back to the UK.

I missed out on the drama as well. I was already aware that I had won before it was announced to the nation because the BBC had organised a live link-up and halted the exhibition to speak to me. So, obviously, something was up! While I watched presenter Des Lynam on a small monitor below the camera focusing on my mugshot, I also noticed the trophy being placed in front of me on the cushion rail!

Des was the smoothest TV presenter in the land and now he was going to come over to me live in another country in front of millions of viewers. I said thank you down the lens – looking into a very dark screen, as it happens – to the British public and as many sponsors as I could remember and then got back to my game. The after-show party went on without me at BBC Television Centre.

Personally, I was never too bothered about winning any awards. They were nice to receive but they never turned my head. I don't have any awards on show at home, for example. But I felt that this was a magic moment for snooker. It was treated as second class by some people in the media but here was the British public sticking two fingers up to them! So, it was great to make history. This was the first (and only) time that a snooker player had won the award. I didn't view it as an award for me so much as an award for snooker. It underlined again just how popular the game was, particularly with TV viewers.

But, of course, it is nice to be liked and it meant a great deal to me that so many people could spend their time filling out those little forms in the *Radio Times*, cutting them out and posting them in. It took so much more effort in those days than sending a text or a tweet today. It also made me realise that I was actually a popular snooker player. Although I might have received a few boos at Wembley and other places at times, particularly when I came up against Alex Higgins or Jimmy White, I was also liked, perhaps by a silent majority? There was also the fact that after years of having the 'boring' tag and now the rather brilliant 'interesting' tag around my neck, I had now pulled off the best gag of all time by winning a personality award. Mr Interesting was now Sports Personality of the Year! You couldn't make it up.

Over the years, this prestigious BBC award has not been without controversy. It is rumoured that Red Rum received the most votes in 1977 after his hat-trick of Grand National wins – but he was ineligible for obvious reasons. Wimbledon champion Virginia Wade picked up the trophy that year. Fans of world champion fisherman Bob Nudd also campaigned long and hard for recognition of his achievement but it never happened. The Olympic figure skating champions Jayne Torvill and Christopher Dean won it, joined at the hip as a single unit.

Nowadays, ten people are nominated for the award by an independent panel. Subsequently, the general public can only vote for somebody on that list of names. Disappointingly for me and snooker, Ronnie O'Sullivan has not been nominated so far. Then again, it took 15 world titles before somebody thought it was about time to put darts player Phil Taylor in there. Hopefully it will happen soon.

I also got the ultimate accolade of being cast in wax at Madame Tussauds! I went along for a 'sitting' and, stupidly, put forward the suggestion that instead of just standing there chalking my cue, I could be sitting on the table rail – or handrail as it turned out – playing an unusual massé shot (where the cue is at 90 degrees to the table and you hit down on the cue ball to make it do a U-turn)! 'Great idea,' said the photographer and artistic director.

So, I modelled this pose for over two hours while they took photographs from 360 degrees. By the end of the session, my back was breaking! I was in there for a number of years but sometime during the 1990s I was melted down and turned into one of Steve Redgrave's oars!

Two more ranking titles came my way before the eighties were out. The first was against Stephen Hendry in the final of the International Open in Stoke-on-Trent in September. I was behind early on but turned things around from 6–4 and won the last three frames to secure a 9–4 victory. It was another sweet success for me. The following month, I played even better to retain the Rothmans Grand Prix in Reading. After a tricky start, where I sneaked past Neal Foulds 5–4, I thumped Jason Smith 5–1, Tony Knowles 5–2 and Danny Fowler 9–2 to set up a final against British

Open runner-up Dean Reynolds, who had enjoyed a decent tournament with wins over Warren King, John Parrott, Dennis Taylor and James Wattana. But he had never beaten me and it soon showed.

I think the pressure of it all got to Dean and he crumbled. The Hexagon played host to another Davis whitewash without me ever really needing to get into top gear. My highest breaks in a 10–0 win were 82, 52 and 48. My third Grand Prix crown earned me £70,000 and it was my fiftieth major snooker title. The whitewash was also my third in major finals after crushing Dennis Taylor 9–0 in the International Open in 1981 and Mike Hallett by the same scoreline in the Masters in 1988. Nobody else had yet achieved it.

I had started the 1989–90 season in dominant style and I had no reason to suspect that things were going to change. I now travelled up to Preston in search of my seventh UK Championship title of the 1980s. I hoped it would be the perfect way for me to finish off the decade. The early rounds were no problem for me and I comfortably catered for Tony Chappell 9–3, Cliff Wilson 9–3, Willie Thorne 9–4 and Mike Hallett 9–5 to reach the semi-finals. Up against me was another one of the growing, chasing pack of young players now on the scene, Gary Wilkinson.

I knew a bit about Gary. But the general public had just found out the most important piece of information: he was a player in form. His name and photograph were on the back page of most of the national newspapers after he inflicted a 9–0 whitewash of his own against Jimmy White, knocking in six half-century breaks in the process. Gary had started the tournament as a 400–1 outsider but after wins over world number three John Parrott in the last 16 and Jimmy in the quarter-finals, his odds were slashed ahead of our match.

It was the first time we had played each other. Gary won the first four frames of the opening session. I trailed 5–2 at the interval and 6–2 after the first frame of the next session. But I dug deep to find some big breaks and fight back to win five frames in a row to go 7–6 ahead. Two frames on the trot put Gary 8–7 up and left him just one frame away from victory. He powered into a decent lead in the next frame as well and left me requiring two snookers to save the match. It seemed that I was soon going to join John and Jimmy on the scrapheap.

I managed to get one snooker but with just the pink and black left I still needed another. Gary wasn't snookered. The pink was on the top cushion. I watched in amazement as this player, who had hardly made a single mistake throughout the match, completely missed the pink. I was back on target. I potted the remaining two balls to draw level at 8–8 and, in a real cliffhanger, snatched the final frame to go through 9–8. Gary had simply miscounted – just as I had done against Mike Hallett in the Irish Masters. He was so involved in the climax of the match that he simply forgot to check the scoreboard. He thought I could win by potting the remaining balls. This miscalculation cost him the match.

With Gary's help in not securing the padlocks, I had performed something of a Houdini act. My reward was yet another meeting with Stephen Hendry in the final. Still only twenty, he had been denied in the final at Preston 12 months before by Doug Mountjoy after he had memorably (and annoyingly) knocked me out in the semi-finals.

My record against Stephen over the longer distance was good and the final of the UK Championship was the best-of-31 frames – the same total as the World Championship semi-finals where I had beaten him 16–9 earlier in the year. So, I felt my chances of winning were good, especially at a venue which was a personal favourite. I knew that he would be tough to beat and I was aware of his great ability but I fancied the job; I was the reigning world champion and I also knew I had a better tactical game.

At the Crucible earlier in the year I had romped into an early 5–1 lead. At the Guild Hall, it was almost reversed as Stephen steamed into an early 4–0 lead. During the interval, I tried to mentally regroup. I showed a bit of character by fighting back with breaks of 46 and 60 to quickly cut the deficit in half. I won the next frame as well to be breathing down his neck at 4–3.

What followed was a mini exhibition of the finest snooker from Stephen, reminding me more than ever of his enormous talent. In terms of breathing down necks, this man was now right on mine. It was during this match that I could truly sense that my position as world champion and world number one was going to be seriously under threat from him. Stephen made breaks of 55, 88 and 64 to stretch his lead to four frames again at 7–3. I responded by winning the next two frames but it felt like a real fight to do so. He responded with two more high breaks of 75 and 91 to lead 9–5 overnight.

I had to play patiently and wait for any chances I could get. But the first chance of the second day went to Stephen and he pounced to go 10–5 in front. It was now or never for me. I held my nerve and pulled the score back to 10–8 by winning three frames in a row and, while Stephen took the next one, I followed up with two more straight afterwards to get back to 11–10. I had won five frames out of the last six. Now I just had to win six frames out of the next ten …

But this was as close as I got to Stephen, who responded like the champion he would soon become. He made breaks of 123 and 112, and, with me suddenly reeling at 13–10 down, he clinched the twenty-fourth frame as well.

I was now staring down the barrel at 14–10 down. I struck a tournament-best break of 138 in the next frame – beating my own top score of 136 in the process – and clawed another frame back to go to 14–12, but that was all I could manage. Stephen was so strong in the next frame and finished me off with a break of 66 to beat me 16–12. As he lifted the trophy towards the group of photographers in front of him, I was in no doubt that this was the best player I had come across since I turned professional. Ultimately the 1990s would belong to him.

19. END OF AN ERA

Just minutes after Stephen Hendry had beaten me 16–12 to win the 1989 Storm Seal UK Championship, the two of us walk into the BBC TV studio at the Guild Hall in Preston to be interviewed by David Vine.

At first, David almost congratulates me on coming second. Tellingly, he then turns away from me to speak to the new UK champion. His opening words to him are like a dagger to the heart: 'It is the end of an era …'

It is the last month of the 1980s and these words will turn out to be prophetic as we head into the next decade. The 1990s will be difficult for me – and that is largely down to the young man who is sitting to my right with the prestigious trophy that I have won six times in the past on his lap …

After this defeat to Stephen, it would be four months before I reached another final that season. Various tournaments seemed to pass me by as titles were shared out by an assortment of players: Jimmy White won the Everest World Matchplay, Stephen Hendry won the Benson & Hedges

Masters (again) and John Parrott won the European Open. The less well-fancied Steve James and Canadian outsider Bob Chaperon also got in on the act, claiming their only ranking titles in the Mercantile Credit Classic and Pearl Assurance British Open respectively.

It was turning into a bad season for me. I felt out of form, regularly recording bad results in a way that I had so rarely suffered before. I lost in the first round of the World Matchplay to Dean Reynolds and crashed out of the British Open to world number 19 Steve Newbury. My best performance over the winter months was to reach the semi-finals of the Classic, where I lost 6–4 to Steve James.

Although I was still the reigning world champion, my winning confidence had been shaken badly enough to mean that there was not only a new kid on the block but a queue of more kids behind him, trying to get on that block. They all seemed to fancy their chances and I was beatable like never before. While at one stage in my career I was the best thing since sliced bread, now it seemed that I was the bread – and everybody was having a slice of me.

I lost my affirmation that I was head and shoulders above the pack by starting to lose too often. I had also lost confidence in my cue action again. Nothing I tried on the practice table seemed to work in the match arena. Added to the fact that players were starting to fancy their chances against me, this meant that I was now in a vicious circle of losing even more confidence.

The effect was that I was now putting pressure on myself to score in matches when I was among the balls – something that a player in form revels in – but I was struggling to make regular sizeable breaks. So my confidence was dented again. I was beginning to spiral out of control in all areas of the game. In a nutshell, my feeling of supreme confidence was in tatters.

Perhaps the hardest part in any sport is trying to regain confidence after you have lost it. In many ways, it is obtainable by only a few. In other ways, those who have attained it have perhaps an even harder task to try to rediscover it. My father and I worked tirelessly on the practice table to try and find a solution. But it was becoming a conundrum – and one that I hadn't encountered before. My confidence was possibly at its lowest ebb since I had turned professional back in 1978.

With the Embassy World Championship around the corner, I went over to Co. Kildare to play in the Benson & Hedges Irish Masters at Goffs badly in need of a confidence boost as much as anything else. I so wanted that title back.

I scraped past Willie Thorne 5–4 in the quarter-finals and then took my place in the bear pit by sneaking into the back of the TV commentary box for the much-anticipated all-Northern Ireland clash between Alex Higgins and Dennis Taylor. I rarely did so – but this was a match that nobody wanted to miss.

Although I had a long history of what might have appeared to be personal confrontations with Alex, it was mainly played out in the newspapers. I had always kept my distance from him. However, Dennis had to spend time with Alex in international matches and during a bitter war of words between them – after a match for their country against Canada in the British Car Rental World Cup in Bournemouth the previous week – Alex allegedly threatened to have his team-mate 'shot' the next time he returned to Northern Ireland. So, this clash was billed as the grudge match of all time. It was a sell-out. The place was heaving inside with people stood three deep on the balcony in parts. The atmosphere was intense.

I think the bookmakers were even laying odds on whether Alex and Dennis would shake hands before the match. But the offender offered the offended his hand and it was accepted. Dennis won the clash 5–2 in determined fashion. It meant an awful lot to him to do so. He followed it up with an exciting 6–5 win over Jimmy White in the semi-finals.

Meanwhile, I defeated Terry Griffiths 6–3 to reach the final at Goffs for a sixth time. Moreover, I had finally reached my first final of 1990 – on the first day of April. Dennis, without a tournament victory himself for three years, certainly had the crowd on his side in our match. But I played solidly, making four half-centuries, including a highest break of 84 in the last frame, to win 9–4.

It was my fifth Irish Masters title. The press boys – some of whom had written off my chances of winning a seventh World Championship title – were now reporting that I had indeed gone on to win at the Crucible after each of those previous four occasions! It was a nice reminder for me in the circumstances and although such records actually count for nothing, there was no doubt that my week in Co. Kildare had done me the world of good.

The stage was set for a cracking tournament in Sheffield: I was aiming to become the first man in the modern era to win seven world titles – beating the record I shared with Ray Reardon – while Stephen Hendry was in a position to win the Triple Crown (just two years after I had achieved the feat) after claiming the UK Championship and Masters trophies that season.

My nerves going into the first round there were nowhere near what I had known in 1982 – when I defended the world title for the first time against Tony Knowles and was promptly crushed 10–1 – but, as defending champion at the Crucible again, they were probably at their worst since that day. I had heaped more and more responsibility on to my technique again. In reality, there was probably nothing different about it but it was certainly coming under more scrutiny as I was losing much more often.

In the 1980s, I had always gone to the practice table in moments of trouble to regroup. That was my medicine. Relatively quickly, I found that I could get back into winning ways. However, things were changing: the general standard was improving and maybe I had got to the stage where I just wasn't able to improve any more.

In hindsight, perhaps this would have been a good time for me to see a sports psychologist – but I wasn't of that persuasion or ilk and so that thought never crossed my mind. No! My answer was to take my supposedly failing technique back to the practice table. I had to improve it!

Despite my win at Goffs, I didn't feel the problems were over for me. But at least I had greater peace of mind. The bookmakers didn't know about any of these concerns, which is probably why they made me the clear favourite again at 2–1.

My first-round opponent was Eddie Charlton, who was now in his sixties. I wasn't tested at all by him and cruised through 10–1. My next opponent would be sixteenth seed Steve James, who had beaten me on his way to winning the Classic in January, and had come through an infamous first-round match 10–5 against Alex Higgins, who had to qualify for the World Championship on account of his declining world ranking.

Their match was straightforward enough but the post-match press conference wasn't. Clearly much the worse for wear – after sitting in an empty arena by himself while he finished off his drink – Alex hit out at anybody and everybody. He said that he hated snooker. He said that the game and everybody in it was corrupt! He also announced his retirement. He would soon return ...

Even by Alex's standards this felt a bit more than just another one of his drunken rants. By this stage of his career, he was effectively finished as a player. He was no longer a force in the game and he was attracting more and more controversy wherever he went. Looking back, he was going off the rails. But I couldn't feel sorry for him. I had been in his company too many times where he had treated people appallingly. So, to me it just felt like karma. What goes around comes around...

I will say this: when Alex was in control, he could be a very dangerous player. But he couldn't handle his drink and he couldn't stop having a drink. However, it would also be fair to say that I wasn't in the best position to see the good side of him. Around the competitive scene, he was using alcohol as a crutch and it was alcohol that was making him more and more obnoxious. I never saw the more relaxed side of his nature.

Looking at that footage of Alex sitting there in his match chair today, I regard it all as a very sad moment indeed. Maybe if snooker had introduced breathalysers as well as drug testing, it might have been the Hurricane's salvation. He would then have had to play sober or not at all. He had no resistance to alcohol and it ruined him.

I started in style against Steve James with a 117 break but only led 5–3 after the first session due to another miscounting mistake that handed him the fifth frame. Luckily it didn't affect matters and, feeling much more relaxed about my game as a whole, I booked my place in the last eight with a 13–7 win.

Steve had a cavalier style of play. We had a black ball frame early on in this match where I played a great safety shot, leaving the black an inch off the side cushion on the baulk line with the cue ball near to the jaws of the black pocket in a dead straight line with the yellow pocket. I walked back to my seat feeling happy that I had the advantage. But before I could celebrate my trap, Steve jacked the cue in the air and stunned the black into the yellow pocket at 100 miles an hour. As the crowd erupted, I slumped into my chair and Steve returned to his seat and said to me, in total honesty without a shred of gamesmanship: 'I couldn't think of anything else!'

My quarter-final opponent was the unseeded Neal Foulds, who had knocked out Dennis Taylor and Willie Thorne in the previous rounds. I started well and breezed into a 6–1 lead before he took the final frame of the first session to trail by four frames. All looked good for me but the second session turned into a nightmare and, after some fine snooker from Neal and some rather clumsy snooker from me, we were all square at 8–8 at the end of the day.

It is likely that I would have been behind in the match had referee Len Ganley not awarded a push-shot against Neal in the eleventh frame. This turned out to be the only frame I won in a run of eight, during which I never made a break of more than 30.

Happily, I rediscovered my form the next day and five frames without reply booked my place in the World Championship semi-finals for an eighth successive year.

I was now aiming for an eighth successive world final. The prospect of a first Davis v Hendry world final was also as close as it had ever been but we both faced difficult semi-final opponents. I was up against Jimmy White for a fifth time in Sheffield after four wins from our four previous matches. But this was our first meeting there for three years and the number four seed had seemingly eased his way past Danny Fowler, John Virgo and Terry Griffiths and looked to be in good form. Meanwhile, Stephen was playing the number three seed John Parrott. It was a quality last-four line-up.

Jimmy came out looking fired up. For the first time in our five meetings at the Crucible, he won the first frame. I came back with breaks of 58 and 51 to win the next two frames and, while Jimmy levelled at 2–2 at the interval, three more strong breaks of 68, 81 and 47 earned me a decent 5–2 lead at the end of the first session.

The next day saw Jimmy looking even more determined. He made breaks of 64, 42 and 56 to come back to 5–4 after little more than half an hour. He then proceeded to make further breaks of 50 and 66 in two of the next three frames to level the match at 6–6. I raised my game to produce two quality breaks of 69 and 112 to steer myself into an 8–6 lead, but I couldn't shake him off. He put together another three-frame run with half-century breaks in each to lead 9–8. A 66 break from me levelled it up again but then he produced a four-frame winning streak to lead 13–9.

Suddenly, I felt as though I was on the rocks again. I had never been in this position against Jimmy in Sheffield before. Equally, he had never been in this position against me. I felt the match was slipping away. I required seven of the last nine frames to win. That was soon to be six out of the last seven as Jimmy led 14–10. Time was running out for me, and fast …

I made a break of 59 to make it 14–11 and one of 77 to make it 14–12. The twenty-seventh frame went down to the black and I won it. It was now 14–13. The next frame was massive and, crucially, Jimmy took it. Despite hauling myself back to 15–14 it was to be too little too late for me. Jimmy got over the line. I lost the match and my world title 16–14. I lost my number one world ranking later that night as well after Stephen Hendry beat John Parrott 16–11. It was the first time I had not held the top spot in the rankings list since 1982.

These were crushing blows. The 1990 World Championship final was the first I hadn't contested in eight long years. I had little interest in it, to be honest. For the record, Stephen beat Jimmy 18–12. He now had the Triple Crown of World Championship, Masters and UK Championship as well as top-ranked status.

It was to be a long summer of contemplation for me. I got married and my life changed. On and off the table, everything was now different. But, as I have said, while the press started to speculate about whether all this had contributed to my downfall, the true reason was that the players were just getting better. After years of being the king of snooker, I had suddenly been dethroned.

Throughout the 1980s, I always felt that I was the best winning machine out there and also the best pressure player and the best match player. I wasn't complacent. But I never looked to the future and I hadn't really considered the possibility that sooner or later somebody would come along and rock my boat. It happened so quickly and so ruthlessly that it took a long time for me to cope with it all.

Stephen Hendry completely changed the game of snooker. He introduced a new attacking style that we had never seen before. But it wasn't just about attack. There had been attacking players before – but mainly ones that bordered on a suicidal style of play which lacked any instinct of self-preservation. This was different. Terry Griffiths eloquently summed it up: 'Steve used to slowly strangle you to death whereas Stephen would steamroller you!'

It was now a case of kill or be killed. Some players adapted to that change better than others. Moreover, up and coming players had already adopted that style of play as well. As a result, some of the older professionals faded away. Just as the eighties had seen a massive change in snooker, so would the nineties.

Stephen would become the dominant force in the game in a similar way to how I had been a decade before. At twenty-one he was of a similar age as well. I had been twenty-three. But I was now going on thirty-four. Within no time at all, it felt as though the rest of us were left to fight over the scraps …

I didn't have a clue what to do about it. It came as a complete shock. I grew up in an old-school world of snooker thinking, namely not overly extending oneself in the risk-taking department. It was all about not giving your opponent an easy chance as a result of taking on a risky pot. But the game was changing and players were realising they could take on more risks than previously considered tactically sound. The rewards were huge – they could win the frame in that visit.

Stephen wasn't playing tightrope-walking stuff. He was playing good, attacking, opportunist match play that unleashed the potential to take on what appeared to be a risky shot in such a way that there was an element of insurance built in. The only ball that was going to be left on was the one he was playing and there was no guarantee if he missed it that it was going to be left on anyway. He had a much more aggressive shot selection.

Part of that came from his confidence. He looked super-confident. The other part was down to his incredible talent.

The next season didn't start well for me and I crashed out of the Rothmans Grand Prix 5–2 at a very early stage to the unfancied Nigel Bond, ranked 38 in the world. Having said that, Nigel went on to reach the final – where he lost to Stephen. He also later reached the world final as well – where he also lost to Stephen. I reached two finals of my own in the autumn of 1990 but lost them both: John Parrott beat me in the final of the Norwich Union Grand Prix in Monte Carlo and Stephen thrashed me 9–1 in the final of the Dubai Classic. He then told the press that he was disappointed not to have won 9–0!

I did make a century break in the one frame I won but, admittedly, the rest of the match was just pure domination by my opponent. I might as well have not bothered turning up and stuck my *Spitting Image* puppet in the corner! Perhaps the puppet could have done better.

All the players were treated well in Dubai and we each received a superb watch for taking part in the event. As the losing players started to trickle home that week, customs officials at Heathrow airport randomly stopped Neal Foulds and a couple of other players and discovered these top-notch watches, which weren't being declared by these criminally minded players.

Neal alerted the rest of us to these potential checks. So, on arrival at Heathrow, all but one of us queued up in the red zone, ready to declare our watches and duty-free purchases. Meanwhile, Stephen Hendry boldly went through the green door, only to get stopped by a smug-looking customs official, who most probably thought he had landed a big fish red-handed and couldn't believe his luck.

'Anything to declare, Mr Hendry?' he asked.

'No,' Stephen replied.

'No watches by any chance?' the official inquired.

'No.'

'We are aware that everybody in the Dubai snooker event received watches,' the smirking official continued.

'The watches were consolation prizes,' Stephen fired back, with the trophy distinctly visible for all to see.

'Oh, my apologies,' the embarrassed official said.

And Stephen continued on his way.

The watch presented to the winner was, of course, the best one of all!

Stephen was the new king of snooker. His hero was Jimmy White. But while he admired the Whirlwind's style of play, he identified that my application was going to be an important attribute if he was going to be the best.

He was a lot younger than me and we never said much to each other. I wasn't the most social person and it didn't feel as though we had a lot in common anyway. I had my own friends around me and would never socialise with other players unless I was abroad with them. So we didn't have too much to say to each other.

When I went out to play him I felt that I was fighting an uphill battle with myself against a player who was producing top-quality snooker that I just couldn't handle. The balance of power seemed to change almost overnight. This was a standard of snooker I hadn't encountered before and I didn't like it. I was stretched to a limit where I felt uncomfortable. I felt inferior in enough departments to feel that I was drowning in the tide.

So, it became increasingly difficult to play against him and I admit that I struggled mentally. I knew he fancied the job too much in the same way that I had fancied it a decade before. It reached a crescendo when he thrashed me 9–1 in Dubai. When you are fighting against sheer embarrassment, it is a bad place to be …

Once Stephen established himself as a champion, I felt far more vulnerable playing him. While he was measurably stronger mentally, I had also suffered a blow that had injured me. That changed the equation. My shield of invincibility was gone and his was now in place.

Along with his manager, Ian Doyle, Stephen mapped out a single-minded route to success. Ian probably studied what Barry and I had done more than Stephen did. I think he tried to copy Barry's modus operandi. His management company, Cuemasters, became the 1990s version of Matchroom. It had successful sponsorship deals with Sweater Shop and Highland Spring. It was apparent that whoever had the world champion in their camp had the bragging rights in the snooker business to some degree.

I felt a long-frame tournament was my best chance of turning my fortunes around. I had changed my grip slightly and found a bit of form at the UK Championship in Preston, beating Willie Thorne 9–5, Nigel Bond 9–7 and John Parrott 9–6. But I was still some way off feeling that my game was in as good a shape as it had been for a while – and I both wanted it and needed it to be. My opponent in the final at the Guild Hall was none other than my nemesis, the wonder bairn, Stephen Hendry.

The start was ominous. Stephen hit breaks of 63, 42, 71, 78, 55 and 91 to lead 5–0. The third frame took him just seven minutes. I broke my duck with a decent reply of 77 in the next frame but Stephen took the last frame of the session to lead 6–1 at the break. It looked like another drubbing might be on the cards.

However, the evening session was much better for me. After sharing the first two frames, I reeled off four in a row to trail by just one. Stephen did win the last frame of the day after a break of 59 but the 8–6 overnight scoreline was as healthy-looking as I could have hoped for earlier in the day. I enjoyed a good night's sleep, too, probably due to not having to look over my shoulder.

It was now imperative to get a good start the next day. It didn't happen. Not for me anyway. Stephen knocked in a classy break of 122 to extend his lead to three frames. I hit back with a break of 62 in the next frame but he regained his three-frame advantage with a 64 break. A 43 clearance in the following frame made it 11–7.

Back I came with decent breaks of 89 and 73 to narrow the deficit to 11–9. An 87 break in the next frame from Stephen put him 12–9 up but I was undeterred. This rediscovered fighting spirit closed the gap further with a break of 102 winning me the twenty-second frame and determined breaks of 37 and 42 were enough to take the next as well. I was now right back in it at 12–11 down.

We shared the next two frames and after Stephen missed a fine cut on a red in the twenty-fifth frame and I cleared the table with a break of 36 to snatch it, the scores were level for the first time, at 13–13. I was beginning to fancy that I had turned the match in my favour.

Although Stephen regained his lead in the next frame, a strong break of 90 brought me level again and two breaks of 44 and 51 in the twenty-ninth frame put me in the lead for the first time in the match at 15–14.

After four successive defeats by Stephen, this match was turning into both my best performance and the most pressure I had applied on him in well over a year. I was now just one frame away from what would surely be the sweetest UK Championship title I had achieved since my big breakthrough against Alex Higgins in 1980.

So, the next frame was going to be the most important for me since I had lost my top spot in the world rankings. I started well in it and found myself 45 in front. The winning post was in sight. Stephen took on a cut red near to the pink spot, into the left centre pocket from off the top cushion. It hit the far-jaw and came back towards the top cushion to meet the cue ball, which had gone in and out of baulk.

I suppose I now trusted to luck a bit too much; that, after potting the red, I would be guaranteed to be on a baulk colour, especially as the brown was close to the green pocket. But I snookered myself on it –

ending in line with the green. Either side of the eventual path of the cue ball would have been fine – but I potted the red like my father would have and didn't guarantee position.

Looking back – sliding doors-style – that was the moment! Instead of having a great chance to clinch the match, I could only put the blue safe for a bit of insurance. I did have another opportunity – that resulted in three extra points – but that wasn't the point. My real chance was the one where I failed to play the correct shot when it mattered!

I then had to suffer and watch Stephen clear to the blue before audaciously slotting it down the rail with the rest and knocking the pink in to level the match at 15–15 and take us into sudden death.

I was in bits! I felt I had missed my big chance. On my first visit to the table in the final frame, I missed a long pot by miles and scattered the reds everywhere. Stephen proceeded to make a break of 98 to clinch the title. It was worthy of winning such an outstanding match.

I took great pride in pushing him so close but I also knew that ultimately I had blown it by not taking my golden opportunity in the penultimate frame. The standing ovation I received from the packed Preston crowd at the end was small consolation.

Afterwards, Stephen said he had never played in a better match than that. I knew what he meant. I also felt that I had answered a lot of questions – not least from myself – with that performance. All those epitaphs seemed premature. This was about as good as I had ever felt – playing standard-wise – after losing a match, even though my run without a ranking title now stood at 14 months and counting ...

Regardless, I was distraught. I knew in my heart that I had played a great game of snooker and nearly turned around a match in which my opponent was in front for a long time. But, as well as I could have done at a venue where I had dominated in the 1980s, Stephen was now playing at a new level. He was the new winning machine in the game.

I privately feared that I was losing touch with his level of play. I was struggling mentally and on a long, winless streak. Suddenly, competitions weren't enjoyable for me. I found that it was nowhere near as much fun to play snooker when I wasn't winning. But that was probably something that I had just taken for granted for so many years during the good old days.

This is the nature of sport: the new champion replaces the old champion, reflecting the hierarchy of the animal kingdom. It actually did feel like that. I already knew that I was losing my grip on the game and that largely came through losing regularly to Stephen. I had beaten him a few times when he was a teenager. It was never the case that he wasn't talented but I could just play the right shot at the right time and that was often enough to beat him.

But, like all great champions, Stephen learned so fast. He spotted that he could play snooker in a slightly different way from players of previous generations. I suppose in a way I taught him how to beat me. I was effectively part of his apprenticeship in the same way as Ray Reardon had been part of mine.

Every new generation of players had always taken the good pieces of the snooker jigsaw puzzle from the previous one and then added new pieces to it. The attacking element was about to be correctly assimilated into the game by Stephen.

It was indeed the end of an era.

20. A TIME TO PONDER

Throughout the 1990s, I explored every possible technical adjustment without making any real changes to my game. Looking back, I now wonder whether anything was wrong at all. Maybe all I had to do was realign the expectations I had and lighten the load I was carrying. As it was, I didn't do that. I beat myself up a lot.

It shouldn't have been the end for me but it certainly felt as though it was at times. Perhaps I felt I had reached my limit of performance and I couldn't get any higher? Perhaps there was nothing else left in the tank? Perhaps it was a step too far to go up to the next level? Maybe I had already made the most of everything I had?

My coach couldn't help me. My father and I only ever worked on my technical ability. He was expert at spotting my technical set-up. If I started to change anything, he could notice it immediately. This stood me in good stead. But the challenge was now completely different. His strength wasn't in the positional side of the game and teaching an old dog some new tricks was going to be hard.

Stephen Hendry was to remain the top player in snooker until the end of the nineties. What he had that made him so special was the consistent ability to be more aggressive than anybody else and keep applying the pressure. So much so that he asked big questions of his opponents to produce the goods whenever they got rare chances. More often than not, his opponents – including me – felt the heat too much, knowing that any miss could lead to being steamrollered into the ground.

Until Stephen came along, my game had the cutting edge when it came to accuracy and tactics combined. I was also the best pressure potter out there – my strike rate on the game-ball shots was very high. Alex Higgins and Jimmy White were probably playing more exciting snooker than me but their games were more about gambling and therefore more prone to error.

When I got on the table in my heyday, it seemed like I was going to clear all the balls. Sometimes it didn't work like that but if my break ended I would never push the boat out for a desperate or risky shot to keep going. I played safe and left no breathing space for my opponent. I used to enjoy cutting off their oxygen supply.

Stephen played a more accurate positional game than me. Subsequently, he won more frames from one visit to the table than anybody had ever done before. Similar to my time of domination ten years earlier, he was still learning parts of the game as he went on but his potting was very accurate, he had fantastic bottle and he became so good that his chances of being punished were minimal.

He was a strong break-builder and while I was a great match player and a very good tactician, my own break-building was very much the 1970s and 1980s model. Looking back, I think I should have sought ways to improve in that department. Instead, I probably sat on my laurels for far too long thinking I was untouchable.

Stephen became the first of many great players who were able to successfully adopt this new style. Ken Doherty was not far behind him. Within a few years, the floodgates opened and there would be this group of youngsters – who had been busily practising while I won one world title after another during the 1980s – set to pounce. Top of that list would be a young prodigy from London town that Barry Hearn was just about to sign up who went by the name of Ronnie O'Sullivan.

As players, we all continue to learn from our peers. That is why the development of the game has been so exciting and why its future is difficult to predict. The old-fashioned way of colliding with the corners of the pack to dislodge a few reds was now being superseded by a new generation who were playing to open the pack with much more force. Stephen was at the forefront of this, even though I had personally seen the benefits of it myself a number of years before. But what he did was to take that part of the game and become the number one exponent of the art.

If a player gets a chance today, his first consideration is: how do I turn this into a frame-winning break? The old-school professional would mop up the loose reds and try to open the pack afterwards. This often went wrong and he would then have to play safe, leaving himself open to a possible counter-attack. The modern player looks to open up the pack as quickly as possible to create a frame-winning chance there and then.

Progression is natural. But from my perspective – sitting at the top of the tree in my own little world for so long – it was always going to be a bitter pill to swallow when it happened. If I could have my time again, I would have tried to do something about future-proofing my game. That is easier said than done. I was always working on my technique and trying to keep that as strong as it could be. So, maybe I am being a little hard on myself?

If I could have had somebody like Stephen Hendry coaching me at break-building in those days, I sense I would have been an even stronger player. But I didn't realise it was going to be a problem at that time. In hindsight, I can compare how I played the game to how the modern-day game is approached. Back then, however, I would never have considered showing any sign of weakness by asking a fellow professional for advice. Neither would I have expected any of them to help me, particularly my biggest rivals.

So, my way was to go back to the practice table. I was always trying to work on my technique. I always felt that I struggled with it, even though it was considered to be the best in the game. Perhaps that is the madness of a perfectionist? I felt that all I could do was to try and upgrade my standard in practice. So I focused on changing my grip or altering my eye sequence or changing my stance. Anything that felt like it might maybe make a difference. I think I tried absolutely everything by the time the century was out.

It wasn't all doom and gloom. It was only that I was being ultra-hard on myself. I knew that I was still a force to be reckoned with – even if this super Scot had nicked the keys to my sweet box!

I reached the semi-finals of the last tournament of 1990, the Coalite World Matchplay, losing out to Stephen Hendry 9–6 in Brentwood after being level at 6–6. But Jimmy White surprised him in the final with a fine 18–9 victory. While I was struggling with my game, the mercurial Whirlwind was maturing and showing signs that he could maybe be the one to challenge Stephen's grip on the game.

In the New Year, Stephen retained his Benson & Hedges Masters title at Wembley in an astonishing final against Mike Hallett, when he came from 7–0 and 8–2 down to win 9–8. To this day, this match was perhaps the most amazing comeback that we have ever witnessed in snooker. It also probably didn't do any of the other top players much good to witness Stephen somehow turn around a match where Mike had managed to snatch defeat from the jaws of victory. Stephen was only human – or at least I think he was – but after this match his superiority complex no doubt grew another layer.

The next time I came up against him in a world ranking event was in the semi-finals of the Pearl Assurance British Open in Derby. He beat me 9–6 before defeating Gary Wilkinson 10–9 in the final. He was always there or thereabouts – just as I had been for so long.

However, he did suffer a dip in form when he was surprisingly beaten 5–0 by the relatively unknown Mark Johnston-Allen in the European Open in Rotterdam. Mark went on to lose to Tony Jones in the final but, uniquely, holds the enviable record of being unbeaten against Stephen. He played him three times and turned him over on every occasion!

My first title of the season came at my favourite playground of all, Goffs, in Co. Kildare, when I beat John Parrott 9–5 to retain my Benson & Hedges Irish Masters crown. Stephen lost to Dennis Taylor in the quarter-finals but was still very much the man to beat going into the 1991 Embassy World Championship. This meant that for the first time in over ten years I didn't go to Sheffield as favourite. The world number one justifiably had that honour.

Approaching the tournament with the heat off (to a certain degree) was a strange feeling. I didn't have the pressure on me to live up to top billing but in its place there was this feeling that all eyes were on me to see how I coped with being dethroned.

All things considered, it was business as usual. I had a difficult first-round match against the highly regarded and up and coming Irish qualifier Ken Doherty, winning through 10–8, and progressed to the quarter-finals after beating Tony Meo, 13–6.

I then had a magical moment ahead of my quarter-final against Dennis Taylor when I walked out on to the stage as a bleary-eyed, proud new father. I had been up and down the country to be present at the birth of my son, Greg Robert, and the next day MC Alan Hughes announced the news to the Crucible crowd.

Alan was a great character and popular among the players. Like Willie Thorne, he loved a bet on the horses. We all thought the two of them were the unluckiest gamblers around. They never seemed to have a good day! Alan used to tell us about his bad bets. Perhaps he had some sort of masochistic tendency to tell everybody about it and that was part of his therapy? He once backed a horse that was leading on the flat and it fell!

It could only happen to Alan. I once watched a race with him on a TV monitor by a betting stand at a snooker venue. He was cheering his each-way bet to what looked like a certain victory when – at the last moment – the camera pulled out to reveal three horses on the nearside of the track out in front. It meant another torn-up ticket for our MC. Honestly, he was so unlucky that if he ever bet on you to win a match you realised you had lost it before you even picked up your cue!

Alan left the snooker scene in the 2000s. He was getting older and it was decided that the game needed a fresher face. But he was a lovely guy and his thoughts and words that day gave me an amazing feeling inside – so much so that I couldn't pot a ball for the first two few frames! I eventually got my game together to win 13–7.

In hindsight, the whole thing was thoroughly unprofessional on my part: knowing the gestation time of the human race, what was I thinking of, timing the birth with the most important event of the year? In my defence, Greg popped out of the oven two weeks early on 29 April 1991!

As well as Stephen Hendry coming on to the scene with all guns blazing, there were other significant changes in my personal life. I was now married with a child. But life goes on through such changes: I was still a selfish snooker player pursuing my own goals and everything continued to revolve around that. Snooker was always more than just a game to me – it was my profession.

My win over Dennis hardly made headlines. That is because the newspapers focused on the sensational 13–11 quarter-final defeat of the world champion by Steve James. Like the rest of us, Stephen had fallen victim to the Crucible curse.

Steve was a fearless potter with a fiercely attack-minded game. He didn't try and out-think himself. He just saw a shot and pulled the trigger. We all knew how dangerous he was but I don't think anybody gave him a chance against Stephen. However, Steve thoroughly deserved the win. He took the last four frames of the match to leave Stephen looking shell-shocked. In fact, this would be the only defeat Stephen would suffer at the Crucible between going out in the semi-finals in 1989 and losing in the final in 1997. That says such a lot about Steve's performance in that match. Perhaps it took somebody with a game and attitude like that to actually outplay Stephen at that time?

As for the defeated world champion: we had all been there. As a result, the World Championship was blown wide open: Steve James versus Jimmy White and John Parrott versus me in the semi-finals.

My record against John was good. I hadn't lost to him in a match over more than best-of-11 frames before. But, regardless of the thrashing I had inflicted on him two years earlier in the world final, he reached new heights at the Crucible that year and I was powerless for much of the match. He led 9–2 at one stage and this meant that when I did manage to produce a run of three frames in a row, I only pulled the scoreline back to 11–7. The gap proved too much and John deservedly won 16–10.

Jimmy, who beat Steve 16–9 in the other semi-final, was to face a similar fate to me in the final. John won the first seven frames and then they shared the following 22. John won 18–11. John was a worthy world champion. He had grown in every department since he turned professional. He had experienced disappointments along the way and I think that might have made him stronger. He was always a positive hitter of the ball with a strong cue action and he was one of the best off-the-cushion players around. He also had plenty of guts and determination. So it was all there. For the second time in two years we had a new world champion. For the third time in a row, Jimmy had finished runner-up.

Stephen Hendry remained world number one and I remained world number two for the new season. I was to meet him no fewer than six times in finals and – after what felt like an awful lot of one-way traffic in our own personal encounters – I managed to beat him in some of them.

A revised and rejuvenated *Pot Black* series was the first (although I would never count that event as too competitive). I also beat him 6–3 in the final of the Thailand Masters in Bangkok and 10–9 in the final of the Belgian Challenge in Antwerp with a clearance of 66 in the final frame. In between these matches, Stephen beat me 10–6 in the final of the Rothmans Grand Prix in Reading.

Our next meeting came in the best-of-17-frames final at the Mercantile Credit Classic at the Bournemouth International Centre in early 1992. Despite winning the first frame of the match with a 73 break, I was 3–1 down at the interval. I recovered to play some of the best snooker I had produced against Stephen for a long time. Strong, consistent breaks of 41, 48, 67 and 43 won each of the next four frames to put me 5–3 ahead. But, perhaps inevitably, Stephen came back with some good breaks of his own, including a fine 108, to level at 6–6.

I hit a break of 67 to lead 7–6 and, in the next frame, a break of 99 put me one frame away from victory at 8–6. Stephen made breaks of 99 and 82 to level the match once again at 8–8 and take it to yet another sudden-death decider between us.

In a situation like this it is all about who can hold their nerve and produce at the table. On this occasion, a 57 break from me would ultimately be the difference between us. I won 9–8. Incredibly, it was the first world ranking event I had won since the Rothmans Grand Prix in 1989. I was ecstatic.

This was the final year of the Classic before it was discontinued and replaced by the Welsh Open as a world ranking event from the following season. It had been a great competition for me personally, producing six wins and that first ever televised 147 when the event was sponsored by Lada. It had now duly signed off with another important moment in my career.

What was also nice about that win was how the crowd had changed towards me – I seemed to become far more popular in tournaments once I stopped winning them all! Sometimes, I found the crowd being on my side quite difficult to deal with, particularly if I was playing badly. The worst feeling in the world is to struggle to try and play when people are cheering for you because they feel sorry for you. I often wanted the ground to swallow me up on such occasions. It didn't help me at all. I now realised how Alex Higgins and Jimmy White had probably felt in these situations.

But in Bournemouth it all clicked for me. I was playing well and the crowd was on my side. Stephen Hendry was the new pantomime villain. Similar to me, I think he quite enjoyed it because he saw anything less would be an indication of him not being the one to beat. Actually, I was rather envious: I would have loved to have turned the clock back and rediscover boos!

Stephen responded to that defeat in usual style with his fourth successive win in the Masters at Wembley, beating John Parrott 9–4 in the final. He had already surpassed my record there. I was beaten by Neal Foulds in the quarter-finals this time around.

Stephen also won the Irish Masters, beating Ken Doherty 9–6 in the final. It was at this tournament that I suffered an embarrassing early-round defeat.

When the miss rule interpretation was changed at professional level, the WPBSA got its major players together and bashed out new guidelines for referees. The one big change was if a player could see a full ball and missed it three consecutive times, he would forfeit the frame. I didn't agree with it – but it was voted in. During the discussion, I remember Neal Foulds asked who would be stupid enough to miss three times in a row if the frame was at stake. Doh! Homer Davis, that's who!

Ken Doherty and I were locked together at 4–4 in a best-of-nine in front of a packed and partisan Goffs crowd. There were about four or five reds left on the table when crafty Ken got me into all sorts of trouble. I could see the reds but there was no safe path back to baulk. I felt that the only thing I could do was to play a long roll up to a red on the top cushion. I played it and missed it. The cue ball rolled off course a fair bit. It was replaced and I played it again, only to see the cue ball once again veer off the right line by a good half a ball.

Ken asked for the cue ball to be replaced once again. At that point, the referee, John Street, announced those now all-too-familiar words to me: 'Steve, I have to warn you: If you miss for a third time, you will lose the frame.'

'OK,' I said. So, I aimed full ball and watched in horror as I saw the cue ball go down the table and roll off even more.

I turned and shook Ken and John by the hand and then walked out of the arena as quickly as I could – as the vast majority of the crowd tried to work out what had just happened!

To this day, I still believe a frame of snooker should be won by the player himself and not by the other guy making a mistake. The problem is that nobody has yet come up with a better solution than the current set of rules that doesn't significantly change the game!

I was still reaching finals and winning world ranking titles: I lost 18–11 to Gary Wilkinson in the final of the World Matchplay at the Dome in Doncaster but beat Alan McManus in the Asian Open final in Bangkok. However, as the World Championship came around again, I felt that I was still struggling with my technique.

I was up against a relatively unknown qualifier at Sheffield but young Peter Ebdon – fully equipped with a ponytail – was to exude supreme confidence from the moment he walked down the steps into the cauldron at the Crucible to play me. He bowed to the crowd, milked their applause and then set his mind on putting me to the sword.

It was a year for brash debutants. Mark Johnston-Allen played his first match there the day before, wearing black and white quartered trousers! Tony Knowles beat him 10–4.

A few players have walked out on their debuts and made a statement. When the flamboyant Jimmy Michie qualified, the two of us were present at the live draw for the first round on the BBC.

Jimmy was full of it. 'I can't wait,' he told me. 'I'm going to turn up in a limousine and wear a wild waistcoat.'

'It's tough out there,' I told him. 'It's hard enough standing up sometimes and it can be difficult getting your cue moving so the best thing you can do is to try and go under the radar. Don't draw attention to yourself. No flash clothes. Just play your game.'

He thanked me for my expert advice.

Come the tournament, I was in my hotel room watching the snooker on TV when I saw Jimmy step out of the longest limousine imaginable with a sparkling waistcoat, posing for the photographers, who duly snapped away.

Jimmy subsequently collapsed in his match. He couldn't pot a ball.

I think Mark King probably wore the best waistcoat of all time early on in his Crucible career. He looked like The Joker with an exclamation mark on one side and a question mark on the other. It was a great design – but it really is tough enough playing in the first round of the World Championship, without drawing any extra attention to yourself.

Peter Ebdon was something of a stallion in his younger days. He was a fast player and with his ponytail bouncing around the table he was a sight to see. He could knock them in all over the place and completely bully players on his day. He was never frightened of anything. There seemed to be no pressure on him at all when he played me that time. He destroyed me. He actually potted me off the table, starting with a break of 92 and ending with a break of 77. I did lead 4–3 – but that was before he won seven frames in a row to win 10–4!

It wasn't a nice feeling at all. This was the first time I had been out of the World Championship before the semi-finals since 1982. I drove home after the match and it took four long hours – listening to Radio 5 on the hour every hour announcing that I had been knocked out – to get there.

When I got home and went to bed I remember that I felt very tired. Yes, it had been a long day and a long drive home but I also felt quite old. I suppose that in the eyes of the game I was relatively old. I was only thirty-four but the game was changing so fast and Peter was just one of a new breed coming through.

It felt like I was slowly losing my game and there was a new generation waiting to mop up my tears. In fact, within a few years, Peter, Ronnie O'Sullivan, John Higgins and Mark Williams would all win the World Championship and many other major titles.

Peter went on to reach the World Championship quarter-finals in 1992, where he was beaten by Terry Griffiths. The final would be the first of three in a row between Stephen Hendry and Jimmy White – and this was probably the one that Jimmy should have won. He led 14–8 going into the final session but then sat and watched Stephen rattle off ten frames in a row for a startling 18–14 recovery.

I felt this was finally going to be Jimmy's time. The nation was willing the Whirlwind to win. But Stephen just pulled the rug from under his feet. Jimmy was his hero as well – but it didn't matter one bit. That is what a true winner has to have in his make-up.

Jimmy did recover to win both the Rothmans Grand Prix and the UK Championship that autumn, defeating Ken Doherty (who beat me in the quarter-finals) and John Parrott (who beat me in the semi-finals) respectively. My world ranking was now down to four but I reached the final of the World Matchplay in Doncaster again in December, where I lost 9–4 to James Wattana, and won the Indian Masters, beating Steve James 9–6 in the final in Delhi before the end of the year.

This good form continued into the early part of 1993 when I beat James Wattana 10–2 in the final of the British Open in Derby and Alan McManus 9–4 in the final of the Irish Masters at Goffs.

So while it might have seemed like the end of an era, I was still churning out results here and there. In the World Championship, Stephen met Jimmy again in the final and Stephen beat Jimmy again in the final by a crushing 18–5.

My participation in the tournament ended in the second round with a 13–11 defeat by Alan McManus. A few months later, on 16 July 1993, I became a father again when my second son, Jack Edward, was born. This was far better timing for the snooker season!

I actually played Alan McManus three times in 12 months in various finals around this time. He was another great player, as hard as granite. He was also the latest Scottish player to make his name in the game. He might have lived in Stephen Hendry's shadow a little bit but he had his moments, most notably beating his fellow countryman in the final of the Masters in 1994. Similar to Wales in the 1970s, Scotland was now unearthing some amazing talent with John Higgins also beginning to break through.

The second time I met Alan in a final was at the 1994 Regal Welsh Open in Newport. I played really well during that tournament and dropped just two frames on the way to the final. I beat Alan 9–6 to win the trophy. The highlight was a 125 break that won me the tenth frame but the 59 clearance that won me the match was even more pleasing. It was my first world ranking title of the season.

The following month, the two of us met again in a best-of-17-frames final at Goffs. Between us, we made three centuries in the first eight frames. We were level-pegging at 8–8 but a break of 69 in the final, sudden-death frame won me the Irish Masters title for an eighth time!

In addition to these two trophies, I also reached the final of the Dubai Classic (where I lost to Stephen Hendry, 9–3) and the Thailand Open (where I lost to James Wattana, 9–7). With the Welsh Open, these tournaments were part of the nine that now made up the list of world ranking events.

In the big one at the Crucible, I reached the semi-finals for the first time since 1991; there I came up against my old foe Stephen Hendry again.

Earlier in the tournament, I was standing outside the theatre when a fan came up to me and asked if I had heard the news about Stephen. Something about the way he said Stephen's name suggested this wasn't anything that had happened on a snooker table.

'He's broken his arm,' the fan told me.

'I hope it's his right one!' I didn't reply.

Instead I just said: 'Oh' and walked on, praying it would be his right one!

As it turned out, Stephen had broken his left arm, a hairline fracture just above his left elbow, after slipping in his hotel bathroom. Apparently, he hit it on something porcelain related. Unfortunately for the rest of us left in the tournament, he hadn't been booked into a room on the opposite side of the corridor – a mirror image of the one he was in! Things might have turned out differently if he had been.

He won the last eight frames in a row to come from 9–8 down to beat me 16–9. But, as a result of a fairly decent season, my world ranking was back up to number two for the forthcoming campaign. For the fifth successive season, Stephen remained world number one. He also beat Jimmy White 18–17 in their fourth world final.

This was Jimmy's sixth and last World Championship final defeat and it is probably the one that most people remember more than any of the others. It also came ten years after I had beaten him in his first world final. He certainly never had a better chance to win the championship. He was so close to the finishing line: 37–24 up in the final frame with the balls at his mercy when he inexplicably missed a straightforward black from its spot.

Stephen got up and proceeded to make one of the biggest pressure clearances in the history of the World Championship. It was perhaps not quite as amazing as Alex Higgins' break against Jimmy 12 years earlier but, arguably, it was more impressive. He never put a foot wrong – unlike his earlier bathroom blunder!

As you would expect, Stephen mopped up, showing no emotion at all. All that was on Jimmy's face; big close-ups filling the TV screen. The viewers at home no doubt felt his pain. The Whirlwind's chance of the big one would now be gone.

I think Jimmy always felt the weight of expectation. Every defeat in the world final made that expectation even greater the next time around. It was a shame he never won it. He had the game to do so.

Furthermore, I believe he played the right game to beat Stephen in that final and, of course, he came very close to it. He went 37–24 in front in the final frame. So near yet so far. Actually, it wasn't dissimilar to how Alex had miraculously turned the tables on him in 1982 when Jimmy was so close to winning their world semi-final. The Whirlwind might well have gone on to win the World Championship that year as well. Sliding doors and all that …

Jimmy was in his early thirties by the time he reached his sixth world final. It was a tremendous credit to his consistently high standard that he kept getting to all those finals. I hadn't made a world final since 1989 but Jimmy was still doing it year after year. He seemed to adapt to the new style of snooker better than me. So, anybody who dismisses his competitiveness, temperament or overall strength or standard of play is treading on thin ice. His record in the game only lacks one thing. Sadly that is the biggest thing of all.

But I think it is unfair to judge a player purely and simply on his performances at the World Championship. If you look at it from that angle only, Jimmy gets ripped to pieces: six finals, six defeats. But if you look at the snooker he produced and his staying power at the top level of a changing game, he deserves a lot of respect.

Moreover, Jimmy probably played a better game in the 1990s than he did in the 1980s. He was much more of a gambler when he was younger. Had he developed a more mature game earlier on in his career things might have turned out differently for him. By his own admission, he was a party animal and he has since said himself that maybe he paid the price. As he grew older, I think he began to wise up. He has certainly become a much more studious player with the passing of time.

Maybe because Jimmy was never world number one he found the emergence of super Stephen Hendry easier to handle than I did. I had been dethroned; he hadn't. I certainly don't remember the 1990s as a particularly happy time, despite the odd title. It was torture sometimes. I also felt somewhat of a failure because somebody else had come along, upped the general standard of play and I was left floundering without an answer.

If I was to look back at Jimmy's game from those days, the only area that might have made a difference was perhaps his technique. Keeping your body still is of paramount importance to a snooker player and, at crucial times, there was a little bit of movement with Jimmy. I am talking about minute percentages. But those are the ones than can make a big difference. One missed pot in a 35-frame match made a huge difference to his snooker CV.

The one constant with the most naturally gifted players is that they don't have to think about technique as much. But that can be a negative. In their youth, perhaps they were not as open to listening to a coach as somebody with less natural talent. In their careers, perhaps there was one moment when that lack of knowledge or method let them down. One thing I am certain about is that players who have won the most are absolutely solid on the shot with no body movement at all. Stephen Hendry and I both had that.

At around this time, American nine-ball pool was being covered by Sky. *The Hustler* had been a favourite film of mine since I was a teenager and some of the shots featured in it were superb. Paul Newman and Jackie Gleason, who starred in the film, could actually play a bit, too, even if some of the set-up trick shots were obviously done by a hired hand. That man was Willie Mosconi – the Joe Davis of pool – who was not only technical adviser on the film but also had a cameo role in it.

Twenty-five years after the release of the original, a sequel was made called *The Color of Money*. It featured a much older Paul Newman and a young pretender, played by Tom Cruise. Both of these films are essential viewing. Television interest in American pool started to rise and, while it never rivalled the soaring success of snooker, it did become popular. I played a couple of big names, such as Gentleman Jim Rempe and Steve Mizerak. While these were fun events, I was sent packing with my tail between my legs. I realised that while the pockets on an American pool table were like the Grand Canyon, there was a lot more to the game than the layman might think.

Then, in 1994, Barry Hearn had an idea of hosting a USA v Europe nine-ball pool event called the Mosconi Cup. It was shown on Sky and it went down a storm. It was a discipline new to UK viewers as well (where eight-ball pool is the pub game of choice). For the first two years, a mixture of Alex Higgins, Jimmy White, Allison Fisher and me represented Europe (even though we were by no means the cutting edge of European nine-ball pool) and came up against the best players in the States (or so we thought!). We shared the spoils.

However, the following year, the USA sent over the big guns. Some of these guys had starred in *The Color of Money*! They looked strong, assured and mean! The granite Johnny Archer and the volatile Earl Strickland particularly impressed me. I was still new to the game but I had enjoyed playing in a couple of lower profile individual events and had started to pick up some of the skills and nuances – although I never really got to grips with the explosive break-off shot or the spectacular 'Jump' shot. We got our asses 'whooped' – as the Americans succinctly put it – for the next six years!

The most embarrassing 'whooping' was the sixth in 2001 when we were drubbed 12–1 at York Hall in Bethnal Green. We had two German lads in our team – Oliver Ortmann and Ralf Souquet – and they were steaming. I had initially viewed the whole thing as a bit of a laugh but even I felt the humiliation that year.

Next time around, the European team met up a couple of days before the event and bonded. As usual, it was a race to 12 rubbers – a mixture of singles and doubles – but our team this time around (Oliver, Ralf, Marcus Chamat, Mika Immonen, Nick van den Berg and me) was a totally different proposition. By this time, I had played in numerous pool tournaments, including the new nine-ball World Championship in Cardiff.

We had the crowd on our side and we were leading 11–9 when I went into battle against the mercurial and temperamental legend that was the eight-time nine-ball world champion, Earl Strickland.

In normal circumstances, there would only have been one winner, but in a best-of-nine this turned out to be one of the most exciting matches I have ever experienced with a cue in my hand. It went down to 4–4 and sudden death.

Earl took control of the rack but an uncharacteristic error while playing from the five ball for position on the six meant he had a missable shot. Ironically, it was the same type of shot as my black against Dennis Taylor. Amazingly, he missed it. Suddenly, I was three balls away from beating one of the greats of the game and securing the first credible win for the Europeans against the mighty Americans. I knocked in the six and the eight to leave myself perfectly on the nine ball.

This was it. My team-mates were already celebrating and the crowd couldn't believe it. But I had one more thing to do – pot a simple nine ball into a huge American pool table pocket from two feet. It was unmissable – but nothing is ever certain. With my back arm shaking like a leaf, I remembered to keep my head perfectly still and watched it go in. The crowd erupted as I shook hands with Earl – and then the rest of the European team descended upon me. We were in a huddle, jumping for joy. Six years of humiliation had evaporated in one shot.

This wasn't even my sport but I was caught up in it all. We were all in tears. It was one of the best moments of my career – regardless of the fact that this wasn't even my career – and while we celebrated Team USA could only watch in disbelief.

After a much-deserved celebratory party at our hotel, I staggered on to a morning train back to Romford from Liverpool Street – still wearing my Team Europe shirt – and I was amazed how many people congratulated me, having watched Sky the previous night.

I enjoyed some great moments in pool, especially in the Mosconi Cup, but perhaps my proudest moment came against the greatest pool player ever, Filipino Efren Reyes, in the 2000 nine-ball pool World Championship, when I came from 8–1 down to win 9-8.

Both of these memorable and magical moments have been preserved for posterity on YouTube and looking at them once more while writing this book has brought a tear to my eye. It was great to relive those occasions and listen to the commentary of my old fellow snooker professional Jim Wych, alongside the inspirational Sid Waddell. For so many years, Sid weaved his magic as a darts commentator but he also carved out another endearing fan base when he became the voice of nine-ball pool. He was a great character and is sadly missed.

21. HOT STREAK!

I stand inside Wembley Conference Centre with my arm raised, soaking up the cheers from this once volatile crowd. It is a great feeling to win such a major prize at such a mature age – six months short of forty – and without doubt this is one of the best moments of my career. I am as proud as punch.

Out of nowhere, I am the Benson & Hedges Masters champion again. I can't believe it. The year is 1997. It is like turning the clock back with the celebrations in the hospitality area. It is fabulous and unexpected. But my opponent – the popular twenty-one-year-old genius that is Ronnie O'Sullivan – could be forgiven if he said that it was all down to the streaker ...

The world of snooker continued to change. Back in the middle of the decade, the 1994–5 snooker season – my seventeenth as a professional – saw a long list of different winners at various events: Ken Doherty won the Regal Scottish Masters; Alan McManus won the Dubai Classic; John

Higgins won the Skoda Grand Prix, the Castella British Open and the International Open (beating me in the final); Mark Williams won the Benson & Hedges Championship; John Parrott won the Malta Grand Prix; Ronnie O'Sullivan won the Benson & Hedges Masters; Peter Ebdon won the Benson & Hedges Irish Masters; James Wattana won the Thailand Open; and Stephen Hendry won the Embassy World Championship, the Royal Liver Assurance UK Championship, the European Open and the European League. And I won the Regal Welsh Open.

I was at war with my cue again. A bad workman blames his tools and it was time for me to blame mine. As I was now losing more than I was winning, I convinced myself that the reason was my cue. I believed it was bent – or, rather, the grain of the ash shaft was not perfectly straight. I was convinced I was being tricked into choosing the wrong line on the shot. Trying to improve my technique was always the driving force for my father and me. But it was now driving us mad. So, I decided I needed to get a piece of wood with a different grain.

The grain in my father's John Parris two-piece cue somehow seemed to make the shot look different to me. I had never messed around with cues before but I was desperate. I practised hard with it and, perhaps like a golfer with a new putter, found inspiration from somewhere. It seemed to suit me better and so I played with it for a while. I had nothing to lose.

I thought I had found the answer, too, when I beat John Higgins 9–3 in the final of the Welsh Open in Newport to win my first world ranking title of the season. It was the twenty-eighth ranking title of my career. Little did I know it would also be my last. But I lost to Terry Griffiths in the first round of the Masters the following week and when I also went out of the World Championship in the first round, losing 10–7 to qualifier Andy Hicks, it was back to the drawing board.

I wasn't playing well. My form dipped again. The 1995–6 season saw me reach the finals of the Guangzhou Masters in China and the Irish

Masters – for a record tenth time – in Co. Kildare, but I lost in both of them, to Tony Drago and Darren Morgan respectively. While Stephen Hendry secured a second Triple Crown, I slumped to number ten in the world rankings. It was not a happy time for me.

Every now and then I did get the occasional confirmation that I was still a force in the game but such experiences were becoming fewer as I got older. By the time I hit my fortieth year I had got to the stage where I didn't consider myself to be anything other than the underdog when I came up against the top players.

I started to play with yet another cue. John Parris was able to model it on the one I had played – and won with – in the 1980s. The cue got off to a flyer! The first time it really came to the fore was during the 1997 Benson & Hedges Masters at Wembley Conference Centre. It was to be a tournament I would never forget.

Actually, I had been laid low with flu the week before the event and as a result I didn't really pick up my new cue. But the human body can often feel stronger after a cold or a virus. I hadn't practised too much, and I felt fresh. Maybe that was because I hadn't beaten myself up so much on the practice table beforehand or perhaps it was my expectations being lowered and subsequently feeling less pressure? I beat Alan McManus 6–4 in the first round and then came up against Peter Ebdon in the quarter-finals.

My opponent had changed a bit since the days when he was known as a pony-tailed giant-killer who had knocked me out in Sheffield. He had been runner-up at the World Championship the previous year and he was now a very strong personality in the game. I felt I didn't deal with his intensity too well at that time. My recent record against him wasn't great either.

We were tied at 3–3 and 4–4 before I snatched the ninth frame to lead 5–4 and then took the tenth on the black to record a late-night 6–4 victory. The crowd rose to their feet at the end to applaud me. That was something else. I hadn't felt this good at Wembley for years. I struggled to remember whether I had ever received a standing ovation there before.

The following day, I beat Ken Doherty 6–1 to reach my first Masters final since 1988. My opponent was to be the new People's Champion, Ronnie O'Sullivan, who was already making his third successive appearance in the final at Wembley having won the title in 1995 and having finished runner-up to Stephen Hendry in 1996.

Playing Ronnie in that atmosphere at that time of my career was something else. We were like two generations colliding at the table. He was knocking them in off the lampshade and capable of embarrassing anybody on his day and I felt that I might have to rely on my tactical nous to stand any chance at all. It was a clash of titans from different eras and I must admit that I felt apprehensive, hoping that he wouldn't make me look like an old carthorse – just as he now seems to do regularly to some of the more talented players of today.

I received another warm reception from the Wembley crowd. Admittedly, Ronnie's went up by a few more decibels, but, all the same, there was no booing to be heard from either side. It was certainly a very different and much more positive rapport between the crowd and me than what I had been used to at this venue earlier in my career.

The Rocket immediately lived up to his nickname. Sensational back-to-back breaks of 116 and 113 won him the first two frames as I sat, watched and pondered. I knew that all I could do was to try and stay with him. I was helped no end in this quest by a streaker.

I was already feeling the heat in this projected two-session final when I played a safety shot and walked back to my seat. As I did so, I saw somebody out of the corner of my eye – I couldn't tell if it was a man or a woman at this stage – straddling the surrounding hoardings. In hindsight, considering that the interloper was only wearing a borrowed jacket, she was risking a nasty injury!

As I sat down, I heard laughter and wolf whistles ringing out from the crowd as the young woman bounced around in front of us for all she was worth – while Ronnie and I waited for security to come and rescue her, so to speak. I never looked up. I have always felt that the best way to deal with a streaker is for everybody concerned not to acknowledge their existence. As it was, I was struggling in the match and I didn't want to acknowledge the situation at all. So, I didn't even get to see her face at the time!

Once she had been escorted from the arena, play resumed and there was one of the most wonderful gestures ever when Ronnie walked up to John Street, who was refereeing his last final at the age of sixty-five, and wiped his brow of imaginary perspiration.

All in all, it had been a break from proceedings and somehow it helped me to regain enough composure to break Ronnie's spell of superiority. I managed to level the match at 4–4 at the interval.

However, Ronnie began the evening session wonderfully and polished off four frames in less than 50 minutes to lead 8–4, including another very strong break of 121. Slowly but surely, I managed to haul myself back into contention and when I made a 130 break in the fifteenth frame to get back to 8–7, I felt the crowd were willing it to go all the way.

That helped me. It also helped me that Ronnie started to misfire. A missed pink in the next frame let me in for a break of 63 to level the scores at 8–8. Just like the old days, I trundled off to the toilet to keep my concentration and focus.

Ronnie led by 28 in the following frame but I came back with a break of 56 to take it on the pink, and after he played a poor safety shot in the next frame I scrambled over the line with a break of 35 to clinch my third Masters title.

It was a moment to treasure. I think it is fair to say there was an element of nostalgia in the crowd that night. Without doubt, that win was one of the most satisfying moments of my career because I felt genuine warmth from the crowd at the end – something I'd never felt at that particular venue. I had never had a particularly good record at the Masters and I had to fight for everything I got there. It now felt like I was accepted at last.

To win such a major title in such a situation was very sweet indeed. But if I had a choice I would say that winning tournaments regularly – as I did in the 1980s – felt much sweeter. There is nothing quite like being the centre of attention. I missed the buzz of being the player everybody wanted to talk to. That was the best feeling in the world. Suddenly, somebody else comes along and nobody wants to talk to you …

The following week I was brought back down to earth when I lost 5–3 to Chris Small in the second round of the International Open in Aberdeen. In fairness, Chris did quite a nice job on me and suddenly I was back to square one. Within weeks, it felt like the Masters hadn't happened at all. I was struggling with my form again and locked in a seemingly daily struggle of trying to play the game to the same standard that I had shown at Wembley.

However, the Masters win did seem to put my name back in the frame in the forthcoming World Championship. It made a nice story anyway. A lot had been made of Stephen Hendry gunning for a record seventh world title in the modern era – he had beaten Nigel Bond 18–9 in the 1995 final and Peter Ebdon 18–12 in the 1996 final – but I was after a record seventh world title in the modern era as well and, while not overly confident, I still felt that on my day I could possibly do it.

It wasn't to be: Ken Doherty thrashed me 13–3 in the second round. He then went on to beat Stephen 18–12 in the final and therefore end the defending champion's amazing run of five successive world titles. A record seventh win at the Crucible was still there waiting for somebody …

The following season, I reached my last final of the 1990s – ranking or non-ranking – when I beat Jimmy White 7–4 in the final of the China International, later to be renamed the China Open, in Beijing. There were also some low points for me along the way and crashing out in the second round of the UK Championship in Preston 9–2 to Northern Irishman Gerard Greene in November 1997 would be among them.

It wasn't that Gerard wasn't a capable player. It was that there were growing signs that I was being turned over by more and more players further and further down the world ranking list. This was a sign of things to come for every player in the game – there were becoming fewer easy draws in the professional field.

I ended the 1990s ranked fifteenth in the world and hanging on to my place in the top 16. By now, John Higgins – who had won the 1998 World Championship, 1998 UK Championship and 1999 Masters – had replaced his fellow Scot Stephen Hendry as world number one after eight seasons.

Stephen did secure that seventh world title by beating Mark Williams 18–11 in the 1999 world final. This was revenge of sorts after losing to him in the final of the Masters the previous year when he missed the final black of the final frame as he tried to play the cue ball from under the opposite side cushion to sink the winning ball into the centre pocket. Mark lifted the trophy and his success suggested that the tide had turned once more and a new Rat Pack was now snapping at Stephen's heels.

Deep down, I think I knew that Stephen would one day set a new record for World Championship wins at the Crucible but I didn't suspect for one moment that his seventh world title would also be his last.

22. HOLDING BACK THE YEARS

The early years of the new millennium continued to be difficult for me. Out of the world's top 16, I now needed to qualify for the World Championship and I failed to do so in both 2001 and 2002.

The first cut was the deepest. A 10–6 defeat by Andy Hicks in the final qualifying round, held almost 200 miles from Sheffield in the rather less than salubrious surroundings of Newport, meant I wouldn't play at the Crucible for the first time in 23 years. This hurt a lot. But it also opened a new door for me with a late call-up by BBC Sport – it was to be my first regular job since stacking shelves in a supermarket back in my teens.

I also did some television work with ITV Sport at various events up and down the country. These programmes were hosted by Capital Radio disc jockey Russ Williams and the two of us had a great laugh together. On one occasion during a live highlights show featuring a Peter Ebdon match we decided to get in as many names of biscuits as possible into our chat:

'Well, that was a Nice shot, Steve,' Russ kicked off.

'Yes, Russ,' I replied. 'Of course, Peter Ebdon is sometimes coached by his brother-in-law, Gary Baldrey!'

And so it went on. I can't remember all the brand names we got out but I do remember that – with me one biscuit in front approaching the final question – this was the final crescendo:

'Well, the Wagon Wheels certainly fell off there, Steve,' Russ joked, drawing level.

'Yes, and that was all John Higgins needed to Breakaway,' I countered.

Game over: I was one biscuit up with only ten seconds of the show left. The beers were on Russ. Or so I thought.

'Yes, he truly is a Royal Scot,' he said. 'Goodnight.'

It was a draw. We were off air. And the crew were in tears …

Just like the beginning of the 1980s and the 1990s, the start of the 2000s was to herald a new era in snooker with the likes of John Higgins, Paul Hunter, Ronnie O'Sullivan, Matthew Stevens and Mark Williams dominating the game.

Stephen Hendry did reach a couple of finals in the 1999–2000 season – winning the unsponsored British Open and finishing runner-up in the Benson & Hedges Irish Masters and the Thailand Masters – but John Parrott, Jimmy White and I were nowhere.

I think Stephen had seen the change coming. He said in a press conference that Ronnie O'Sullivan was going to outplay him one day. Back in the 1990s, I would never have said anything like that about a rival, even if I thought it might be true.

To his credit, he might have resolved the looming problem in his own head better than I did by doing it this way. But he was looking ahead. I had been so busy not thinking about the future in the 1980s that when I was eventually replaced as world number one, I was left in a state of shock.

Stephen came to terms with the arrival of the new Rat Pack a lot better than the rest of us. I can still recall when Mark Williams started to regularly get the better of him and he suddenly began to look vulnerable for the first time. That was interesting to see. Ironically, Stephen and Mark became good friends at this time, something I couldn't get my head around. Mark was on his way to becoming the most dominant player in the world: he would go on to win the Triple Crown!

I certainly never wanted to be around anybody who was beating me. I used to like being around Terry Griffiths, because I usually got the better of him, but I hated being around Stephen, for obvious reasons! However, Mark is a good laugh and he just started taking the mickey out of Stephen. Nobody had ever done that before. It was quite funny to see it but Stephen almost seemed to enjoy it. They just got on well together and have remained good mates.

Stephen did seem to come to terms with it all and he looked a damn sight happier on the table than I ever did in the 1990s. In truth, he was probably going through the same turmoil in practice as I had, asking himself how he could stop the new brigade.

The answer is he couldn't. None of us can. We all have to go through it. It is called the circle of life. I still thought Stephen did a great job by hanging in there. His world ranking never dropped below the top ten in the 2000s and, amazingly, he returned briefly to the status of world number one in 2006. That shows how good he still was.

Both the Whirlwind and I lost our places in the top 16 in the world in 2000. However, I did win a match at the Crucible, beating Graeme Dott 10–6 in the first round. I remember it vividly for the fact that I went to the toilet a lot during the match and my opponent considered it to be a form of gamesmanship – which it certainly wasn't – and more or less went on to say so in his post-match interview.

Graeme is a gritty and tough player and, of course, no player gets to three World Championship finals – winning one of them – like he has unless they possess bundles of ability. But he isn't the quickest player on the block and, as you would expect in a contest between two methodical and tactical players, it was a very slow contest. To some degree, our styles were relatively similar at the time and we probably cancelled each other out.

For example, we only managed seven of the allotted nine frames in the first session. My regular need to go to the toilet had also hit overdrive. I was beginning to feel more nervous during matches as I got older and I found that my body – my bladder included – didn't cope as well with pressure. Either that or I was having trouble in the trouser department. I was now into my forties and had probably made my first visit to the doctors for the rubber-gloved finger by then! But I can understand how it might have looked to Graeme.

We had a laugh about it all during an interview we did together the following year when I deliberately kept on stopping our chat so that I could pop out to the toilet. Graeme saw the funny side. Despite some dour appearances during interviews, he has a great sense of humour. Although, to be fair, none of us are much fun on the days we lose!

After winning through my first-round match, I lost to number two seed and 1998 world champion John Higgins 13–11 in the last 16. John made breaks of 141, 129 and 127 but I pushed him hard: from 10–5 and 12–9 down in the match. New world number one Mark Williams beat the Masters champion Matthew Stevens 18–16 in an all-Welsh final.

I didn't qualify for the Benson & Hedges Masters in the early part of the decade and had to wait until late 2002 to play in the televised stages of the Power House UK Championship. I lost 9–7 to John Higgins in the third round there. My world ranking had now slumped to a new low of 25.

I found that I desperately needed a tonic of some description and what better place to find it than another trip to Buckingham Palace to meet the Queen! It was time for me to get an upgrade to OBE status. The letter had arrived and so off the family and I went. I knew the drill by now, although I decided against taking a flask and a packed lunch with me! I wondered if I would get to have another chat with the nation's biggest secret snooker fan ...

The Queen seemed to have her finger on the pulse. I am sure she didn't know about my inner turmoil or the fact that my world ranking was at an all-time low. But I was no longer the cutting-edge snooker player she had met in 1988. I knew that. The Queen confirmed it.

Once again, there I was in the queue of soon-to-be-honoured guests. When it was my turn, I bowed and walked towards her. The Queen pinned on my medal and shook my hand. This time her words went even deeper – and there were only a few of them:

'Tell me, do you still play?' she asked.

I was crestfallen. I muttered something about the players getting better but I had already been given the push ... I could hardly tell her how shot selection had become much more aggressive and that I thought I had been standing wrongly. That moment was effectively the end of my career as I knew it!

My two meetings with the Queen seemed to bookend my time at the top of the game. I am not saying that this latest experience drove me to drink but around that time I did start to take a double whisky before I went out to play; just to see if a stiff drink could calm my nerves.

Why not? I had tried most other things to find an answer to help with my troubles on the table and I felt that I needed something to steady my nerves over the opening frames of a match. I felt I wasn't settling down quickly when I played and, therefore, I was always playing catch-up. I chose whisky because I hated it. It was the first drink that got me drunk and therefore my logic saw it as medicine not pleasure.

The experiment proved inconclusive, so I stopped it. Obviously it could have been a dangerous road to go down if I had continued and I didn't want to do anything like that. But there is no doubt that it took the edge off my nerves a bit.

My form did pick up a little when I managed to reach the semi-finals of a new ranking event, the LG Cup, at the Guild Hall in Preston. I beat two of the current big names of the game – Mark Williams 5–1 and Paul Hunter 5–4 – on my way to losing 6–4 to Alan McManus, who subsequently lost 9–5 in an all-Scottish final to Chris Small. This was Chris's only world ranking title as he had to retire from the game a few years later due to a serious spinal condition.

I played in the Masters for the first time in four years in early 2003 as a wild card, coming through 6–3 against Joe Swail in a preliminary round at Wembley. But I lost 6–2 to John Higgins in the first round. I also reached the quarter-finals of the Benson & Hedges Irish Masters – now a world ranking event – for the nineteenth time at Goffs. John beat me there as well, 6–4.

John had won all the major honours in the game, but by his own standards he was now going through something of a lean spell. He would return stronger before the end of the decade, going on to win the World Championship again in 2007, 2009 and 2011 plus both the UK title and Masters again. John's strengths are that he has no weaknesses. He is of such a high standard in break-building, positional play and temperament. In the Top Trumps version of snooker, he would have massively high marks in all disciplines.

What I liked about him was that he always knew when he was in a match. I think he had the ability to sense danger better than anybody else around. He also understood when the time was right to attack. He was similar to me in that respect. He was also as solid as a rock when he hit the ball. He had a great all-round game, including a very strong B game.

That is important to mention. When things weren't going right for him, he could still dig in and play the right shot at the right time. That can make a big difference.

People often ask me who I consider the best snooker player of all time. As we will see later, for different reasons I would place both Stephen Hendry and Ronnie O'Sullivan on the podium. But there have also been times when I thought that John Higgins was perhaps the best match player of them all.

I qualified for the World Championship for the first time in three years in April 2003 but lost to seventh seed Stephen Lee 10–6 in the first round. Mark Williams defeated Ken Doherty 18–16 in the final to pick up the winner's cheque for £270,000. But rankings were my new target and my improved form during that season put me back in the world's top 16 at number 11.

This meant that at forty-six I was placed in the main draw in most events. In the Welsh Open in Cardiff in January 2004 I beat Mark King 5–3, John Higgins 5–1 and Robert Milkins 5–4 to set up a semi-final against Hong Kong's Marco Fu.

I beat him, too, 6–3 – including a break of 105 – to earn a final against the one and only Ronnie O'Sullivan. This was my first final in a world ranking event since I beat John Higgins in the same tournament nine years earlier. Furthermore, it was my first major final since I had shocked the Rocket at the Masters in 1997.

It was a best-of-17-frames final and I started magnificently, winning the first three frames. I also took the fifth frame on the black. But two sensational breaks of 125 and 139 from Ronnie at the end of the afternoon session underlined what I was up against as he levelled the match at 4–4 going into the evening session.

However, with all the pressure seemingly on Ronnie and a dogged approach from me, I managed to stick to a game plan and took the first two frames of the night. Back came Ronnie with a 103 break to make it 6–5, but I won the next two frames, both of which were close, to lead 8–5. One more frame and the title was mine. Seven years on from my shock win in the Masters, I was now on the verge of causing perhaps an even bigger surprise.

Ronnie then produced a break of 118 in five and a half minutes in the next frame – his fourth century of the match – and his mood was on the up again. I was into the balls early on in the next frame and made a good 40. But old habits die hard and instead of trying to smash into the pack off the black, I settled for trying to get on one of the two loose reds. It went wrong and, in the end, I wasn't even on the red properly. Ronnie responded with 77 to take the frame.

The next frame was a tight affair. I led 51–26 but I just couldn't get over the line. I knew that I had had my best opportunity in the previous frame but I had failed to go for the jugular. I had a chance of a long red but crucially missed it. This was followed by a courageous clearance of 48 by Ronnie to take the match into a sudden-death decider at 8–8.

The final frame was even edgier than the previous one. I led 18–0. Ronnie replied with 22 and soon led 33–18. I now attempted to pot a red into a middle pocket – with the black waiting – but it rattled in the jaws and refused to drop. Ronnie potted red and black but failed to continue his break. He later added another 16 points but then snookered himself with three reds remaining. Nerves were getting the better of both of us.

At 57–18 down, I was still in the match. However, the table wasn't too inviting. I potted a red into a corner pocket with the rest, the pink into a middle pocket and the penultimate red into the green pocket to score eight before having to play safe.

I was 31 behind with 35 left on the table. I had to make sure that I could follow the final red with a brown or better. There was an opportunity to try a long pot down the cushion. Sadly, I missed it and a double-kiss proved fatal.

The Rocket cleared the table to win the title. In fairness, he had won the last four frames under a lot of pressure, but it was a disappointing end to a great week for me. I had a very good chance against him in the final and I let him off the hook, really. But Ronnie produced the better snooker when it mattered.

Left-handed, right-handed, it didn't matter to him. He always has the ability and that is what makes him such a tough guy to beat. I came so very close, though, and it was such a shame that I was denied a twenty-ninth ranking title nine long years after I had won my twenty-eighth.

For a while afterwards I beat myself up a bit by wondering whether or not I could have beaten Ronnie by playing it another way in the fourteenth frame. I had gone to try and nick a few points instead of being more aggressive and it went wrong for me. Maybe I should have cut my losses and played safe? All sorts of things went through my head. But it is all what ifs now ...

The Welsh Open was one of only 15 tournaments that were played that season, half the number of the record high we had in the mid-1980s. The ban on tobacco sponsorship was beginning to hit the game hard. The 2004 Masters – won by Paul Hunter for a third time in four years in a thrilling final against Ronnie O'Sullivan 10–9 a fortnight later – was unsponsored. The most famous snooker sponsor of all, Embassy, wasn't allowed to continue to be associated with the World Championship after the end of the following season. As a result, the game had to find new sponsors quickly.

Someone who would have been very happy with this news was the one-man protest group that used to stand outside the stage-door entrance to the Crucible on his bicycle with a placard reading 'Smoking Kills'. People used to laugh at him but he was certainly ahead of his time.

In the meantime, probably the greatest snooker player anyone had yet seen was back in the world number one spot after his second World

Championship title – three years after he won his first with an 18–14 win over John Higgins – was achieved with a resounding 18–8 final victory over Graeme Dott.

Still in his twenties, Ronnie O'Sullivan had now won two World Championships, three UK Championships and one Masters. His talent was always supreme: he made a 147 in competition at the age of fifteen and won the UK title at seventeen.

The argument that he could have won so much more isn't even worth raising. When he was at one with himself and his game, he could be untouchable and a joy to watch. Before the decade was out, he would go on and win another world title, another UK one and three more Masters. Again, it could have been so much more. But as we all know, it often seemed that the only player who could beat the Rocket at times was himself.

I had some sympathy for him. Ronnie is a perfectionist: I think all top snooker players are to a degree. When he was in his supreme winning-machine mode, nobody could touch him. But he often felt the strain of trying to achieve that level all the time.

A two-week event like the World Championship can take a lot out of a player and trying to get yourself into the right frame of mind and maintain a certain level of concentration can be a real struggle, particularly when you play a match and then have four or five days off. You need to relax but you can't relax properly; you need to focus but you can't focus properly. If you know you have a chance of winning the top prize, the nervous energy is at its worst. I know all about it – I regularly lost half a stone in weight up there – and I went on to win it! At the end, you are absolutely knackered. And then it is over …

Ronnie was now undoubtedly the new People's Champion, having taken over from his hero Jimmy White in much the same way as the

Whirlwind took over from his hero Alex Higgins. But I would say that Ronnie is the most naturally gifted player of them all.

If I had to try and sum the three of them up: Ronnie would be the one who was born with a cue in his hand – he is the epitome of Tommy, the pinball wizard on a snooker table; Jimmy would be the daredevil with flair; and I think Alex was truly a genius. But you can easily put them all in the same bracket, even though they are all different in many ways.

All three have entertained millions with their swashbuckling styles and for all the tournament victories of Stephen Hendry, John Higgins and myself, I bet we would have loved to have had the panache that Alex, Jimmy and Ronnie brought to the table.

My own participation in the 2004 World Championship didn't extend beyond the first round after a 10–7 defeat by qualifier Anthony Hamilton. However, I had done enough during the season to keep my place in the top 16 at world number 13.

I maintained that top 16 ranking for another season – albeit slipping down to number 15 – after some decent performances the following season here and there, including quarter-final appearances in both the Malta Cup and the Masters.

To some degree, my world ranking was kept high by a level of built-in insurance that the top 16 were afforded by the powers that be. Events were structured to ensure that the top 16 entered at the last-32 stage, even though there were attempts to negate this advantage by not awarding them the full allotment of points if they lost their first match.

All the time this procedure continued meant that the top 16 only had to win, say, one match per tournament and, by the end of the season, they would probably have racked up enough points to stay in the elite places and therefore thwart an up and coming player, who was arguably knocking on doors but might also have been somewhat inconsistent. At the very least, it slowed down the rate of change of the top 16 in the game.

At the 2005 Masters, I was overjoyed to beat the 'Beckham of the Baize' and defending champion Paul Hunter 6–5 in the first round. Paul was a star. He was snooker's pin-up boy: blond, good-looking and a great player. He was very popular wherever he played but particularly at Wembley. His appeal also had the potential to cross over into other areas of the media's attention and that was good for snooker, too.

I started the match with a break of 70 against him and ended it with one of 81. It was a big achievement for me to beat him, especially in that competition and at that venue.

Paul was tipped to be a future world champion and few would have argued with that prediction. He amazed the Wembley crowds with his tightrope walks in matches there. He won three thrilling Masters finals in four years between 2001 and 2004 and each one of them went down to a deciding frame.

In 2001, he memorably fought back from 6–2 down at the interval to beat Fergal O'Brien 10–9, making four centuries in six frames on the way. He subsequently famously confessed in his post-match press conference that his remarkable recovery was down to his very own 'Plan B' during the mid-session interval with his girlfriend and future wife, Lindsey.

Obviously, this made the headlines and the snooker authorities seemed delighted that Paul had spilled the beans about what he and Lindsey had been up to in the afternoon. It was even claimed by some that this was just what the game needed in order to negate the criticism that there were no longer any characters around.

I wonder what Tony Knowles felt like reading those headlines the next day? When he had mentioned his bedroom antics to the press in the snooker boom years during the 1980s, the WPBSA hit him with that fine! I reckon Tony is due a refund – that way I might finally get my hands on the £70 he owes me from our room share in Canada back in the 1970s.

As always, Paul was gracious in defeat when I beat him that day in 2005. Just a month later, he was diagnosed with malignant neuroendocrine tumours in his intestine. Tragically, there was to be no cure. In October 2006, Paul died at the young age of twenty-seven. He is sadly missed. The German Open, held in Fürth, an event which Paul won in its inaugural season in 2004, was subsequently renamed the Paul Hunter Classic in his memory.

At the last-ever World Championship to be sponsored by Embassy, I beat Gerard Greene 10–9 and Michael Holt 13–10 to reach my first quarter-final at the Crucible since 1996. I was now up against a twenty-two-year-old qualifier in the last eight who had been a 150–1 outsider for the title before the tournament began.

But Shaun Murphy blew me away just as he blew everybody else away that year, including two other world champions in John Higgins and Peter Ebdon. He crushed me 13–4. He went on to beat Matthew Stevens 18–16 in the final to become the first qualifier to win the world title since Terry Griffiths 26 years before.

Like Terry, Shaun was a popular world champion. He played the part well, too, and brought a little bit of showmanship to it all, which was really nice to see. Shaun is a larger than life character with the air of a champion around the table. He is also a great spokesperson and a true ambassador for the game.

Back in 2005, Shaun didn't seem to think too much about it all and was knocking them in for fun. He has remained at the top of the game without getting his hands on the trophy for a second time. But he hasn't stopped trying to look for the next step up the improvement ladder in order to win it again.

The UK Championship had been one of the most successful tournaments of my career in my heyday. I won it six times and appeared in the final nine times. In December 2005, at the age of forty-eight, it provided me with another moment to cherish.

At the new venue at the Barbican Centre in York I reached the semi-finals with some hard-fought victories over Mark Allen (9–7), Stephen Maguire (9–8) and Ken Doherty (9–7). I was playing some great stuff and apparently rolling back the years. There to meet me for a place in the final was my old foe, Stephen Hendry.

It was always important for me to start well against Stephen. Otherwise, I felt that he just started to dominate proceedings. However, on this occasion, the two of us were in for a shock as I pulverised him early on by winning the first five frames.

I also won three of the following five frames to lead 8–2 in our best-of-17-frames encounter and required just one more for victory. Stephen managed to pull four frames back but no more. I won the match on the black with a break of 66 to win 9–6: I was in my tenth UK Championship final!

My opponent would be Ding Junhui, an eighteen-year-old Chinese player destined for great things in the game. Ding wasn't even born when Dennis Taylor and I made our ground-breaking trip to China in 1985 but he grew up with the game and started playing at the age of nine.

Ding beat Stephen Hendry in the final of the China Open earlier in the year but at the start of the season he still had a world ranking of 62. Within two years, he would be in the top ten.

I already knew that Ding was a great player. Peter Ebdon had helped to welcome him to the UK as a result of his involvement with Gary Baldrey, who had started to move into management and became a representative for the Chinese players. Subsequently, Peter had informed anybody who would listen that Ding was special.

So, even though I was in the UK final, I still felt that I was probably the underdog. I held Ding after six frames at 3–3 but then he broke away, winning five of the next six frames. The lead proved too much and he beat me 10–6.

I knew that Ding was going to be strong and perhaps I was a bit weak when it came to the crunch. I didn't play as fluently or solidly as I had in the previous rounds and in the end it was a bit of an anti-climax to what had been a very exciting week for me. But it was the highlight of my season and I had once again proved that on the day I could still compete with the best on the biggest stage.

In the newly named 888.com World Championship at Sheffield, I reached the second round – after beating Andy Hicks 10–4 – and another meeting with defending champion Shaun Murphy. The match was a closer contest this time around. But it wasn't close enough. Shaun beat me 13–7.

There was some excitement at the end of frame 11 when the fire alarm went off and we had to be escorted outside. By all accounts, the Crucible audience were longing for something similar during the longest world final on record as Graeme Dott continued Scotland's fine recent record in the tournament by eventually defeating Peter Ebdon 18–14 in an otherwise forgettable final that ended at 12.53 a.m. – over half an hour longer than even Dennis Taylor and I had managed in 1985, back in the days of the old interpretation of the miss rule!

With my world ranking back up to 11, my goal of being ranked in the top 16 at the time of my fiftieth birthday was now well within reach. I won important ranking points at the UK Championship in York again the following season, where I reached the quarter-finals before losing to second seed Graeme Dott. I also did reasonably well in the Welsh Open in Newport, where I lost to eventual champion Neil Robertson in the semi-finals.

In the 2007 World Championship I came up against somebody I was now much more used to meeting in the BBC commentary box or presentation studio than around the snooker table. John Parrott and I hadn't played a serious competitive match against each other for seven years and he was now a presenter on *A Question of Sport*.

John fought through two rounds of qualifiers to reach the Crucible and then drew me in the first round. We both received a lovely ovation from the crowd. It was a good match, too. We both hit centuries, John had the better of it early on and led 9–6 but I fought back to level at 9–9.

In the final frame, I potted the final red only to see the cue ball career into the middle pocket. Right on cue, the cameras flashed to my mugshot and thousands of lip-readers up and down the country got a full blast from me!

John clinched the final frame to record victory in a match played by two former world champions with an aggregate age of over ninety. However, I had done enough over the whole campaign to keep my place in the top 16 in the world for the following season – which would see me turn fifty – at number 15. I had reached my target. It was a proud achievement.

I was a first-round loser at the World Championship again the following year, when I was beaten 10–8 by Stuart Bingham. Ronnie O'Sullivan went on to win the crown for the third time and claim the twentieth world ranking title of his career. But my place in the top 16 was gone.

Sadly, with the passing of time, appearances in the latter stages of world ranking events became less and less for me as I passed fifty. I did reach the quarter-finals of the Shanghai Masters in September 2008 and qualified for the World Championship in 2009, only to lose 10–2 to Neil Robertson. I felt that time was finally catching up with me.

But there was to be one more exciting chapter.

23. AN UNLIKELY ADVENTURE

The rather low-key English Institute of Sport is a multi-sport facility in Sheffield, used as a training venue for sports as diverse as fencing and futsal. The main feature there is a 200m indoor running track.

It was this place – where I had to play over a few days in March 2010 in the hope of making it through to the Betfred.com World Championship a few miles down the road at the famous Crucible theatre for a record thirtieth time – that was the springboard to an extraordinary and unlikely adventure for me.

In total, seventy-two players were present, including former world champions Ken Doherty and Graeme Dott plus an up and coming youngster called Judd Trump. My world ranking of 23 meant that I came into the competition at the fifth and final qualifying round.

I was up against Adrian Gunnell, who had been around since the early 1990s and reached a career high of 36 on the world ranking list. Adrian was known on the circuit for once achieving three 147 maximums in four frames in practice. He was also a player who could one minute look unbeatable and the next be completely off the pace. Adrian produced two centuries against me but, in front of what felt like one man and his dog at times, he wasn't at his best and I had enough in my locker to beat him 10–4 and qualify for the World Championship for a record thirtieth time.

To put that figure in context: those 30 appearances spanned five different decades – from my Crucible debut way back in 1979! Five decades at the age of fifty-two. How does that work? It meant something to reach that milestone – it still stands as a record and it is unlikely to get beaten anytime soon …

When I reached my early fifties, I decided to try and enjoy playing snooker. I made a conscious effort not to beat myself up as much – although that was easier said than done. I tried to treat snooker as a hobby. As it was, I developed something of a love/hate relationship with the game.

Going into the 2010 World Championship, the latest concern regarding my technique was that I felt I wasn't hitting the ball positively. As a result, I decided to focus on keeping my head down a little longer after the shot. I hoped that would make me a bit more consistent and solid on the shot. My nerve endings weren't those of the twenty-one-year-old who had first turned up in Sheffield back in the late 1970s.

I was absolutely determined not to just go along to the Crucible and make up the numbers. I was fed up with doing that; the old pro turning up at half a dozen world ranking tournaments feeling like something of a part-timer. So, I made a determined effort to get myself into a better frame of mind ahead of the tournament. I wanted to go there and give it my best shot. My form hadn't been too good since I'd played Stephen Hendry in the UK Championship in Telford the previous year – being level at 6–6 before losing 9–6. I also wanted to enjoy the occasion. At my ripe old age of fifty-two, I couldn't be sure if this was going to be the last time I ever played there.

I was drawn against the number 16 seed, Mark King, in the first round. I knew Mark well. He hails from Romford and we practised together a lot over the years. He never gives up. I nicknamed him 'Weeble' early on in his career after the famous catchphrase. He might have wobbled from time to time but he never completely fell down. Incidentally, Mark is one of the few players who have dropped out of the world's top 16 only to recover and return to it – twice!

The reception I received when I walked down those famous steps into the arena at the Crucible took my breath away. I had a lump in my throat. It was an amazing and emotional experience and one that I wanted to savour. But I was there to play a match.

In the first few frames I felt I was playing OK – but I still found myself 3–1 down at the interval. I did manage to get into something of a stride when we returned. A break of 77 won me the fifth frame but after ten frames I was still two adrift at 6–4 behind. I had a lot of work to do.

I also wasn't helped by a sudden bout of ocular migraine, which resulted in kaleidoscopic vision. I could see the cue ball and the object ball and everything to the left of them – but anything to the right was a fuzzy blur. It would have been easy for me to have panicked and, had it been the first time in my life that this had happened to me, I might have been concerned. But it had occurred once before at home, after which I spoke to a doctor who explained what was happening.

So, I kept calm and trusted my cue action, even though it was quite disorientating not to be able to see the pocket on a right-handed cut. At the mid-evening interval I led 7–6. I realised that I might also have been playing on an empty tank so I wolfed down a couple of bananas and had a decent swig of water in my dressing room. I returned to the arena to produce not only my best spell of the match but, arguably, the best snooker I had played that season.

I also sensed as never before that the crowd were on my side. I made a season-best break of 91 – a simple statistic that shows how much of a struggle the game had become for me – to go 9–8 up. But in one of those real ding-dong first-round battles at the old theatre it was perhaps inevitable that it was going to go to the wire. A break of 48 by Mark in the eighteenth frame ensured that was the case.

The support I got from the crowd during the final frame was awesome. But it was torture out there. It went all the way down to the pink and black. I was so pumped up that I was shaking at the end. The emotion showed as I walked around the table puffing out my cheeks – with the majority of the hooked crowd rooting for me to get over the line. With two balls remaining, Mark required a snooker and lost the match after potting the pink by mistake.

I was a relieved man. At times during the last frame I feared I had thrown it away. But I pulled off an excellent, unexpected victory in the end. I saluted the crowd and they gave me an amazing standing ovation. It was an extraordinary experience for me, the polar opposite to what I had once experienced in the same arena back in the 1980s.

But it had been a tough match. It felt like I had been out there for 17 days, never mind two sessions. My prize was a meeting with the defending world champion and top seed, John Higgins. I hadn't bothered to look beyond the first-round draw before the tournament, but I was relieved to hear that my best of-25-frames second-round match against John was going to be played over three sessions and three days. I expected three sessions and three days of pure granite.

I knew that I needed to raise my standard even higher. But the feelings in my heart remained the same: I had nothing to lose and I just had to go out there and give it my best. I didn't think about whether or not I could beat him. I considered that my best way to have any further success in the tournament was to keep the heat off myself and just concentrate on the one thing I had been working on in practice: trying to keep my head still for an extra couple of seconds after I had hit the cue ball.

My match against John began in a similar atmosphere to how my first-round had finished, with the crowd well behind me. I couldn't have wished for better support from the Sheffield faithful. The Romford Roar had long since become a thing of the past but I reckon they were still all there in spirit, tuned into a television set and remembering the good old days that we had there!

I started well, too, winning the first frame with a break of 53, the third with one of 48 and the fifth with one of 72. I also won the next three frames on the trot, including my first century at the Crucible since my first-round match against John Parrott in 2007. I led 6–2 at the end of the session.

My concentration was good. My mood was good. My tactics were good. But, as I have said before, John's strengths are that he has no weaknesses. He had overturned bigger leads before. To win 13 frames before he did remained a massive task for me, but I managed to stick with him in the second session, despite a break of 106 helping him to edge it by five frames to three and reduce my overall lead to 9–7 going into the third and final day.

It was the third frame of the final day before I managed to get my next points on the board – and that came courtesy of a foul! Breaks of 70 and 115 by John – his 100th century at the Crucible – levelled the match at 9–9, but he missed two crucial blues in the next two frames and breaks of 46 and 49 were enough for me to regain a two-frame advantage at 11–9 going into the mid-session interval.

My mind was clear at the break. It was less so within an hour as John recorded two half-century breaks to level the match at 11–11. The next frame would be crucial and I was delighted to grab it with a break of 35.

John led 43–0 in the following frame but missed a very easy red. I got back with it, and it came down to a fight on the colours.

Eventually, I get to the colours. With five balls left, I am one point behind. I can pot the green – but I can't get position on the brown.

But this time I am prepared. Instead of the negative way I had lost to Ronnie O'Sullivan in the Welsh Open a few years before, I am going to go for it. I actually mutter the words 'Go for Gold' under my breath! I decide to play position for the double and – at the same time – the cannon on the blue.

Perhaps I should have said those words a few more times to myself during the beginning of the twenty-first century! I play the shot to perfection. And I now know that this is the potential match winner. I double the brown into the middle pocket and watch the cue ball nicely develop the blue over the top right corner pocket.

The crowd go ballistic. I am on the verge of knocking out the world champion! A few more blows of my cheeks and I cut the blue in with the extended rest. All I have to do now is knock the pink into the centre pocket.

I am shaking like a leaf – far more than I was in the 1985 black ball final against Dennis Taylor – and so I take a deep breath to compose myself. I concentrate on keeping my head still. But I still deliver the cue as if it was truly somebody else's arm. It actually feels like I am using a conger eel to hit the cue ball instead of an old wooden cue! Regardless, I stay down on the shot and I hit it accurately enough. As soon as I hit it, I know that it is in! I have won 13–11.

I put my hand to my head in disbelief. Always the perfect gentleman, John is the first to shake my hand and, above the roar from the crowd, says the kindest words he could have said to me: 'You're still the man!'

How he has the magnanimity to say that at this time is beyond me. Had I been in his shoes, I doubt I would have been able to have got a single word out! His words mean a great deal to me. As I walk off the stage, I am on cloud nine.

It was such a sweet feeling. When the wins were coming one after the other for me, back in the glory days, it was great but it was also expected. This win was totally unexpected. As a result, there was something very, very special about this day.

I will always remember until the day I die my walk from the Crucible theatre up to the Winter Garden just 100 yards or so away for a live TV interview with BBC presenter Hazel Irvine in the studio there. It was so surreal – I was usually sat here with her analysing the action!

This time, I had to walk through a mass of cheering, waving people, who had been watching the match unfold on the big screens outside the Crucible. Everybody loves an underdog and everybody seemed to love a former world champion coming good again in such style over 20 years after he had last lifted the world trophy even more!

I made my way across the paved area outside the theatre – with the giant screen that had just shown my match against John – and entered the complex to yet more applause. That walk in itself was out of this world, the nearest experience I have ever had to what it must feel like to be a golfer walking up to the eighteenth green on the final day leading the Open at St Andrews. It was one of the most emotional moments of my life.

The Winter Garden is a great setting for a TV studio with people standing all around us. But that almost backfired on the day. Behind Hazel was some greenery – I was still away in my own little world trying to take everything in as I sat down to speak to her and John Parrott, alongside whom I had, bizarrely, been working as a pundit just a few days before – and suddenly some bloke representing Fathers4Justice appeared from out of the jungle and jumped over the tiny barrier that separated our studio from the packed crowd. He started shouting out 'Fathers 4 Justice' at the top of his voice during my big interview. Everything quickly disintegrated before my eyes as I tried to make sense of where I was and my feeling at that precise moment. All hell broke loose around me and the studio.

I tried to continue talking to Hazel and John live on BBC 2 while Frank Baker, our giant and trusted security man, dropped his Kentucky fried chicken to wrestle this protestor to the floor in front of me. It was hard to keep a straight face as I watched big Frank's trousers slip down around his knees with pieces of KFC strewn all around him on the floor!

My win over John Higgins has been talked about as the biggest shock ever recorded at the Crucible. I would say that in terms of personal pride in my performance it was possibly my greatest of all time. Not because it was my best performance – it wasn't – but because nobody can expect to beat the world champion when they are fifty-two and supposedly past it.

I knew how good I was and I had faith in my abilities. But I also knew that John was such a great player and still at the top of his game. (And remember that he won the world and UK titles again the following season!) So, to pull off something like this was an incredible achievement for me. It came 25 years after my black ball world final against Dennis Taylor and 21 years after my last world title. I felt like the Duracell bunny!

After two emotional and exhausting World Championship matches – totalling 43 out of a possible 46 frames – I had to remind myself that I was only in the quarter-finals. My opponent was the Australian Neil Robertson, who had already won four world ranking titles.

In the quarter-final I allowed myself to play with more inhibitions and that was a mistake. Neil came out and took the game by the scruff of the neck. I was immediately on the back foot and I froze: I had lost the match after two sessions, really. Neil only required one more frame from the final session to win, so beat me 13–5. It was a minor consolation to have recorded my highest break at the Crucible since 1994 in this match with a 128 in the eleventh frame.

Neil went on to beat Graeme Dott 18–13 in the final. If I was going to lose to anybody, I suppose it was at least something that it turned out to be the player who went on to win the World Championship. But after beating John Higgins so memorably I would be lying if I didn't say it was also a huge disappointment to bow out so weakly in the very next round. It didn't matter how well I had played in the previous round. That counted for nothing now.

'You are only as good as your last performance,' so the saying goes, but every professional snooker player knows that is not entirely accurate. You are, actually, only as good as your next performance!

24. UNFINISHED BUSINESS

The 2010 Betfred.com World Championship was marred during the final weekend by shock revelations that John Higgins – who suddenly had the whole of the second week of the tournament off after his shock defeat by me – was persuaded to go out to Kiev, in Ukraine, with his then manager, Pat Mooney. The resulting *News of the World* sting, led by the undercover reporter Mazher Mahmood, was to send shockwaves throughout the game of snooker.

John had apparently been caught on video agreeing to throw a frame at a future World Series showcase event that he and his manager had previously co-promoted and were planning again for the forthcoming season. I was sitting in the BBC TV studio when Barry Hearn telephoned me on my mobile to warn me about what was going to be in the Sunday newspapers on the first day of the world final. Nobody could talk about anything else when the news broke. It made headlines all over the world. Film footage was also uploaded to the internet. It made for depressing reading and viewing.

Television crews started to arrive in Sheffield by the busload. They were not coming up to South Yorkshire to report on the snooker either. They were focusing on this scandal. I was interviewed and quoted as saying this could be the game's darkest hour. In the past, players had been found out for cheating. But none of them had the profile of John Higgins.

As it was, John hadn't thrown any match. It hadn't happened. It was all about the sting and nothing else. Rumour had it that the real sting was to try and discredit Pat Mooney – and John had got caught in the crossfire. Regardless, the game was tarnished and John's reputation also took a big knock. He was banned from professional competitions for six months and fined £75,000.

Overall, snooker was in the doldrums. We hadn't really recovered from the change of legislation concerning tobacco sponsorship in the early 2000s. As a result, we were now down to six world ranking events and the game was almost on its knees.

Thankfully, Barry Hearn was voted – by the players – to take control of World Snooker's business interests in June 2010 and things began to change for the better. Barry actually phoned me up beforehand to ask for my advice. I asked him if he needed the aggravation! The decision was his alone and I was delighted that he decided to go for it because, in my view, he was the only one who could save us.

Barry has a true passion for snooker. Furthermore, nobody can sell the game as well as him. The really nice part for him is to get the chance to finish off a job he felt he started back in the 1980s. So, this was an emotional journey for him – and I know that it meant a lot to him to be given the vote of confidence.

He had to overcome a lot of prejudice to get there. For far too long some people in the game wanted to be big fish in a very small pond and do without him. The problem was the pond was getting smaller and still some people lobbied against him.

Finally, the majority realised that we needed him. But he was voted in by a very slim majority. If three or four people had changed their minds there might well have been a different outcome. In the end, enough of the 'independent' players recognised that we were simply not fit to continue without somebody like Barry at the helm. It was a cry for help and, fortunately, he accepted the challenge – with the understanding that the membership was behind him and gave him the reins to the financial side of the game.

It was always going to be a hard decision for the players to make. Ever since the early 1980s, when Mike Watterson was eased out of snooker, the WPBSA had promoted the game as well as run it. Therefore, the players owned the commercial rights. After many years of hard evidence that the WPBSA, in all of its current and previous guises, was not fit for purpose the game was at a crossroads.

Players were calling for drastic action. They had seen what Barry had done for darts; they were aware that he could still put on great snooker events, such as the Premier League, which enjoyed superb coverage on Sky; and more and more of them were now asking the question: why isn't he doing this for snooker?

Historically, of course, the WPBSA board wouldn't let him because of their fear of losing control of the game. Barry was viewed as a competitor rather than somebody to work alongside. But with the game effectively on its knees and him no longer being seen as having a vested interest – by this time he was managing me out of sentiment more than anything else – the new players (not as brainwashed as previous generations) got on the bat phone!

There still seemed to be as many players who were sceptical about it as those who were prepared to take the risk – if you could even call it that! The sceptics believed we shouldn't give away our commercial rights while those in favour could see that the game was imploding around them and began to ask how much these rights were actually worth in our hands. What did we have to lose? Even if the commercial rights are worth something in the future, while Barry and Matchroom would benefit, so, too, would the players.

Barry guaranteed minimum prize money with a clause that if he didn't increase it year on year by a certain percentage he would be in breach of the deal and, consequently, the players could have their game and their commercial rights back. As it turned out, Barry has dramatically increased the prize money as I knew he would. He told me he felt it would be a piece of cake to up it and that he was aiming to increase the total money on the tour from £3 million to £10 million.

Before the all-important EGM vote it seemed factions within the game continued to put self-interest before the ultimate good of the game. We still had a management team of 110 Sport in place at the time. Ian Doyle had passed control to his son, Lee, who had continued to do what his father had done from the time he owned Cuemasters in the 1990s. And what Ian had done was not only try and get the best players in his stable – as Barry had done with Matchroom before him – but also, it seemed to me, get as many players as he possibly could onside so that – while he knew he could never take control of the game, for exactly the same reasons that Barry could not – at the very least he could try have a block vote within the game. Subsequently, this could be used for a number of reasons, the main one being – as far as I saw it, anyway – to vote members on to the board who were sympathetic to his cause. Any moves to change the constitution that 110 Sport thought detrimental to the game could then theoretically also be blocked. In the end, the WPBSA still held a majority as they increased the voting power further down the world ranking list. This maintained the status quo even though at times the top players appeared to become frustrated that the tail was wagging the dog!

By the time Barry decided to throw his hat into the ring, Lee was struggling. He did at least have large parts of the emerging Chinese market as an ace in the pack and he seemed to be very keen to protect this one good source of income.

What Barry proposed was destined to take all that away, so 110 Sport did all it could to persuade as many players as possible to vote against him. They even put up a counter-candidate, who was proposing to roll out a similar but seemingly more attractive version of Barry's plan. In reality, I think he was probably nothing more than a puppet.

The other source of 'no' votes came from the people that had been put in charge of the Snooker Academy at the English Institute of Sport in Sheffield. The head coach there, Del Hill, had coached both Ronnie O'Sullivan and Graeme Dott to World Championship success in the past. He had influence over a number of players. Many of the new Chinese players were based at the Academy and used it as a practice facility. Their UK management – together with Del Hill – therefore had a potential block vote. I reckon they believed that if Barry took over at the helm their roles might change. If so, they were right.

So, from the start, Barry was fighting an uphill battle. However, it wasn't all doom and gloom. The more forward-thinking managers and those who had already had run-ins with 110 Sport considered Barry to be a far safer and much more professional pair of hands than anybody else around.

These people worked just as tirelessly at the scaremongering tactics of those on the other side. The whole situation had become a case of them against us. Behind the scenes, it was Brandon Parker – who was Paul Hunter's manager and is currently with Shaun Murphy – who was the catalyst in securing a positive outcome for Barry at the Extraordinary General Meeting.

The membership invited Barry and a faceless guy called John Davison to appear at the EGM to state their cases. Barry turned up – but, crucially, John didn't. A number of players later stated that this helped them make their minds up – during the very last minutes of voting!

Barry's presentation was, as we had come to expect from him, forthright! He pulled no punches, he was professional and he spoke from the heart. He was also a little confrontational in so much as he said that he didn't need the job and, if he wasn't successful, there would be no second chance – life is too short!

In the end it was perhaps the most exciting and nerve-wracking vote in the game's history. And, trust me, I have been involved in a few of them over the years as we floundered around getting rid of one chairman, only to install another one and realise it was the system at fault more than the individual ...

The old chairman and board members of the WPBSA didn't hang around. It doesn't really matter who they were now! The fact is they couldn't run the game for exactly the same reasons why, in my view, politicians shouldn't run the country: it wasn't that they were bad people, it was that their skill base – although maybe good in one area – wasn't actually required for the real job in hand.

Over the years I believe that every WPBSA board member has tried to do a good job for snooker. But, along the way, with all the infighting and general mismanagement, they got voted out with bad feelings surrounding them. Their replacements were their critics, who quickly discovered the same hot potatoes once when they got into office!

Barry gave a very emotional speech afterwards. I was close to tears myself. In fact, perhaps I was actually in tears at one point as Barry told the membership what he had told me the week before:

'Stevie boy,' he said (he did use my first name sometimes!). 'We started in this game together. This was my first sport. I still love it. I am still passionate about it. I know I don't need the hassle in my life but I can't help it. It's unfinished business!'

The other big story in snooker in the summer of 2010 was the death of Alex Higgins, in July, at the age of sixty-one. He suffered from throat cancer for many years but also lost his love of life in later years. Malnutrition was the cause of death in the end. So many people had tried to aid Alex – but he shunned a lot of help. It was a very sad end to the life of an incredible performer. The Hurricane entertained millions with his cavalier style of play. I will always remember the excitement that came with a match against him. My own life would not have been as rich if he hadn't been around.

In what felt like no time at all, more ranking tournaments were being added to the snooker calendar, including the innovative Players Tour Championship (PTC), which in its first year alone generated an extra 12 weekend events!

Admittedly, there wasn't much prize money at stake at first but it gave the players an idea of the shape of things to come. There are now a more manageable six PTC events with double the amounts of money on offer at each individual competition. Players had a reason to get up in the morning and practise once again.

Barry's other main objective was to make the game a level playing field for the 128 players on the main tour. He, like many others, felt the need to remove any insurance and future proofing reward that the higher ranked players got year on year by being constantly seeded through to the latter stages, and make every event a flat 128 draw with the world ranking list changing after every single event. Furthermore, the ranking list would become a prize money list for the buzz it would generate in the media.

Barry's reasons were based purely around the fairness of sport and his belief that unless the game could spread its roots far and wide there was no real hope of it surviving long term. He also felt that while the British public still watched the game in their millions on TV, it was now better to spread the eggs around different baskets.

The biggest problem with the old structure was that while it wasn't impossible for a young player to break through the ranks, it was getting very hard. The top players were excellent and, to some degree, that meant further down the pecking order good kids were beating each other's brains out and then coming unstuck when they reached the unfamiliar TV stages.

We had to make sure that there was no dead wood being protected by the system. I was a case in point: I stayed in the world's top 16 far longer than my form actually warranted. Just a few good results each year could keep me afloat! Changing things didn't just help the British-based youngsters either – there were now going to be more opportunities for overseas players to chance their arms as well.

The main argument against a flat 128 draw is that sponsors, television and the host city or country may not get to see their favourite players should they get knocked out in the pre-TV stages. As it stands, the Australian Masters and Shanghai Masters still use a tiered system. So does the World Championship – where the top 16 players in the world still go through to the final stages in Sheffield – and this has been the case since the early 1980s.

Of course, many fans don't care about any of this. All they want is to see Ronnie O'Sullivan and the other big names in action. To some degree, that is the catch-22 situation in which snooker finds itself. Hopefully, one day the game will be able to break free of these constraints.

I must also say that if this idea had been sprung on me at various times during the 1980s and 1990s, I would probably have been very much against it. The vast majority of those who vote will always put personal circumstances before the good of the collective. That's life!

Barry also had to get to grips quickly with the disciplinary situation within the sport. John Higgins was suspended at the time, following the incident in Kiev. He was later banned and fined for his decision not to inform the authorities of the illegal approach made to him by an outside party within the allotted 24-hour period.

A former member of Scotland Yard was brought on to the World Snooker board and Barry laid down the law to the players regarding what the future of the game would now hold for anybody who was found guilty of match fixing in the future.

We all hoped that would be the end of it. But, sadly, in the last couple of years there have been occasional matches that have looked suspect, some of them involving former world number five Stephen Lee. He was subsequently banned by an independent tribunal for 12 years for match fixing. It was a very sad day for snooker. Here was a player, who was still capable of winning events, found guilty of such dishonesty.

Players are now regularly informed of the lengths to which the authorities and the police will go regarding monitoring betting. This happens in all sports. Sport and betting are inextricably linked and it is fair to say that considering the profile of snooker, the isolated incidents of match fixing have been relatively few. If there is any wrongdoing, it generally sticks out like a sore thumb anyway.

It is more or less impossible to make any real money from throwing a sporting event without the authorities suspecting as much. Of course, the next step is actually proving it in a court of law. While that course of action must be taken to protect the integrity of any sport, the costs in legal fees can be horrendous. The Stephen Lee case cost the WPBSA £150,000 with no chance of reclaiming the costs.

When a player in any sport is bent, the consequences are enormous. Not only has the person involved betrayed the trust and loyalty of his friends, who may have unsuspectingly had a flutter on their man, but they have ultimately betrayed their sport as well, including the other members of their association, by not only tarnishing the image but costing money. In both cases, the villain has crapped on his own doorstep and, apparently, among thieves that is a worse crime than thieving itself!

Ultimately, snooker is no more fixed than any other sport. You will always have people who, for a variety of reasons, stray off the path – but I know that the heart and core of snooker is solid and not rotten at all. Of course, there will always be rumours and there will always be people who are very willing to believe these rumours.

Ironically, World Snooker is now heralded as a sport with its finger very much on the pulse of integrity within sport. Other sports are looking at our model as something they could adopt. How crazy is that for the game associated with a misspent youth?

As we all know, if players get caught it is their own stupid fault and something they will live to regret. The game may have got a bit of bad press but, ultimately, the next generation will think twice having seen the penalty dished out to Stephen Lee. Technology is now everywhere and with Big Brother watching I do believe that, ultimately, fixing in sport will become, if not a thing of the past, a very risky business indeed for those who attempt it.

Back to the future: there has undoubtedly been a fresh optimism for the game since Barry returned. This feeling has grown with every year that has passed. He loves the challenge and he is constantly working on ways to get it right. We have a bright future ahead of us.

Barry runs the business side at World Snooker and former world number 28 Jason Ferguson is now the chairman of the WPBSA, which has become more like the Royal and Ancient in golf, dealing with rules and regulations. The two sides are still inextricably linked and should there ever be a major fallout, the new set-up would become unworkable.

But, with the promotional and administrative sides separated, the world of snooker is a far happier environment to be around.

In general, the players have no hidden agenda. They don't have people whispering in their ears any more, feeding them misinformation and untruths. Furthermore, staff are no longer fearful for their jobs and don't need to look over their shoulders to make sure that an unguarded comment isn't being monitored. In Barry, the TV companies and sponsors have somebody who speaks their language and delivers on his promises.

Jason is perfect for his role, too. No disrespect to anybody who has done the job before him, but he is the best chairman we have had by miles in my opinion. Previously, the role was linked with promoting the game and making money as well – which is now Barry's job – so it was perhaps more difficult in the past but, in Jason, we undoubtedly have a really good egg who is also a great diplomat. I think we have two great men at the helm.

As a result, we now work alongside organisations such as the International Billiards and Snooker Federation rather than considering them to be some form of competitor, as we once did. Everything is totally different nowadays. Everybody is trying to build bridges and in some cases rebuild them. We have seen rapid change and Jason deserves credit for that. The game seems to be a happy ship once more. We are definitely moving in the right direction again and it is far more comfortable to be involved all round. Compared to what we had not so long ago, it is the difference between getting off a slave ship and boarding a luxury liner …

The biggest change in snooker in recent years has been the global growth of the game and the biggest growth market of them all has been China. Five of the eleven world ranking events in 2013–14 were held in China (at venues in Beijing, Chengdu, Haikou, Shanghai and Wuxi).

The future is bright. The future might be Chinese. It will certainly be worldwide. China alone is a country with a population of 1.3 billion people and participation in snooker is popular among youngsters out there. A growing percentage of the best up and coming players seems to be Chinese, apart from one or two coming through in the UK and a few bright prospects elsewhere in Europe.

In time, I think the game will eventually be dominated by Chinese players – as long as they retain their interest levels. They have started up academies over there, putting the game on the school curriculum in a sense. Any child who shows any talent is now recognised and fast-tracked through the system.

Beijing has become the epicentre of snooker with around 1,000 clubs in that city alone. I think parents take their children to such places from a very young age. That is not happening in Britain any more because, culturally, we have gone down an entirely different road where kids – armed with PlayStations, mobile phones and computers – now have a different social lifestyle from the one that I had in the 1960s and 1970s. That said, even if, eventually, things are no different in China, the sheer size of the population will still mean a large amount of good young players will come through.

While snooker continues to enjoy better than most TV audiences in the world of sport in our country, participation is certainly down. If parents no longer take their children down to a snooker club for a game, there will be no world snooker champions of the future. In the history of our own little world, it could effectively be the end of the Roman Empire ...

But I think it is a fascinating development. In my day we went to Prestatyn and Preston; now the tour is off to Chengdu and Wuxi. The British players have come to terms with it all as well as could be expected. To make it on the tour, they now have to treat it like a business more than ever before. The vast majority of them have already realised they are better off looking after themselves – arranging their own flights and hotel bookings – to cut costs when they play abroad rather than employing a manager basically to babysit them.

As a result, players talk to each other much more nowadays. Some of them even room together. There is a much more professional attitude all round. Players are away from home for longer and that means their overheads are higher. However, that doesn't guarantee they will pick up prize money out there, even if some decent money is being pumped into some events in China.

The next step might be for everybody to have to qualify for Chinese events over in China. At the moment, these early stages are held in the UK, but I think it is only a matter of time before we get to the point where there are enough quality Chinese players around to question why qualifying competitions for events in China are being held in towns in England. Some of the players at the lower end of the pay scale will have to do their sums carefully to see if they can justify carrying on with the game or whether they need to get a proper job!

The last event I played out in China was the International Championship in Chengdu in October 2013, where I came up against a fourteen-year-old boy called Zhao Xintong, who received a wild card into the competition. Taking out of the equation the concession to the sponsors to allow wild cards to come into the event at the last-32 stage, this boy was astonishingly good and better than anybody I have ever seen at that age – and that includes Ronnie O'Sullivan! He beat me 6–1 and outplayed me. I won the first frame as well.

I didn't see anybody jumping up and down in the air when he beat me. It didn't seem to come as a surprise to anybody. He certainly wasn't fazed about playing me. If his father knew who I was beforehand and told him about me I am sure he would have just shrugged his shoulders and said: 'So what? He can't play any shot better than I can!' He would have been right, too. He went on to beat Craig Steadman and Barry Hawkins – who was ranked in the top ten in the world at the time – as well. In total, he dropped four frames against three professionals in three matches.

It took the experience and standard of Marco Fu to stop his advance and any further embarrassment to other adults.

A thirteen-year-old boy called Yuan Sijun also took four frames off Jimmy White in the same tournament. Jimmy had to pull out all the stops to beat him 6–4. It was an extraordinary experience for both of us. It was ridiculous and fascinating in equal measure. Never mind that these kids weren't even born when I played Dennis Taylor in 1985; there is a chance that their parents weren't born either!

The surge in knowledge, participation and talent in China since the day Dennis and I made snooker's maiden voyage out there is unbelievable. I genuinely think we should celebrate it all. For us to have sold snooker around the world is a massive success story. Whatever happens next is for future generations ...

The standard is obviously going through the roof out there and the UK will possibly struggle to compete with China relatively soon. We are, arguably, thin on the ground when it comes to an up and coming talent and the thinnest we have been for many years, too. It is a totally different story over there.

Ding Junhui is the star name in China. He has over four million Chinese followers on their version of Twitter. I wonder how he deals with the fame; to me he comes across as being relatively shy and only interested in snooker. Maybe the whole personality thing doesn't matter to the Chinese as much – unless that is just a misconception by the media? The British public, though, seem to want even more from their sports stars nowadays. But where does it end? What do we actually want in this country: world champions or *Big Brother* performers?

Ding is an inspiration in his home country. I have heard that something like 60 million people in China watch him when he plays in the World Championship – that is almost the population of the UK!

He has already won eleven world ranking events – including five in the 2013–14 season (three of them held in China) – but the irony is that he hasn't yet really impressed at the World Championship, only getting past the quarter-finals once.

Some in the game think Ding might not win the world title unless it moves to China, which of course might never happen. It is an interesting thought. Maybe Ding has something of a Chinese albatross around his neck? I guess that the weight of 60 million people watching you would be pretty heavy.

The big Chinese cities are now trying to stage the biggest and richest events. It may be that there will soon be an event in China that has similar prize money to the World Championship. But the debate about whether the World Championship should move there is a non-starter for me. As long as the BBC wishes to show the tournament there is absolutely no point in it moving from Sheffield. Furthermore, all the recent talk about the World Championship leaving the city didn't come from the snooker world.

I think the biggest worry for the game in our country is if the BBC ever decides that it doesn't want to show snooker any more. It currently shows the big three tournaments and, hopefully, that will continue. I don't worry about it too much because I think the BBC really values the sport. But who knows what the future may hold?

It is not just the BBC that shows snooker, but it currently has the cream. The power of terrestrial TV coverage is also very big in the UK. However, internet streaming has become very popular and, of course, satellite television is very well established. In fact, Eurosport does a great service for the sport across the whole of Europe. World Snooker has also developed its own TV channel.

But the BBC is very important and so, too, I believe, is the Crucible theatre. Nobody should ever undervalue the special bond the game has with that place. It gives us an identity and a home: it is our Wembley,

Wimbledon and Lord's. Sheffield used to be known for steel; knives and forks. It is probably almost as well known for snooker nowadays. And who knows what the game has brought to the city financially over the years as well? It is somewhat ironic for theatre lovers and performers alike that the Crucible is now, first and foremost, known as a snooker venue and not the brilliant theatre in the round as it was when Mike Watterson's wife once went to see a play!

The casual snooker viewers in the UK – the ones who claim there are no characters in the sport any more – cannot begin to understand how much attention the game has received around the globe in recent years. I have always been bowled over by how many countries I have visited that have embraced the game and know my name – and I am talking about relatively new territories where I would have thought my mugshot and one-time Rear of the Year hadn't had too much attention of late!

Back to the baize and there were big changes to the UK Championship in York in 2013. I missed out on all the fun when it happened on account of eating bugs in the Australian jungle. But Barry Hearn's plan to introduce a fairer competition with 128 players taking part in a multi-table format was a success.

The multi-table set-up is exciting in its own way and it allows fans to look around the arena to watch different matches featuring a variety of top players. But I do think it is important for us to keep the one-table or two-table set-up that we have at events such as the Masters and the World Championship. The Masters is unique, anyway – fans generally go along to Alexandra Palace to watch a shoot-out between two top players. Generally, good snooker is guaranteed because only the best 16 players in the world are invited to take part.

The best multi-table set-up I have seen so far is at the German Masters in Berlin. There are five tables in the Tempodrom amphitheatre and 2,500 seats. The event is always a sell-out. Germany is another big growth area for snooker. The desire for the game over there is immense and it reminds me a lot of the scene in the UK in the late 1970s. The Paul Hunter Classic in Fürth is also very popular and it has become something of a pilgrimage for snooker fans in recent years; similar to the feeling the fans used to get when they went to Pontin's in Prestatyn all those years ago.

The Germans like what they see on TV and have turned up in their droves to watch the action live. Furthermore, a happy atmosphere is guaranteed. There is a real passion for the game and I find it particularly exciting that a lot of young people attend these events. The same is true about many other European countries that are now hosting competitions. The excitement in Eastern Europe also replicates what we experienced in the UK back in our heyday. The home audience is a lot harder to please than it was and that is understandable – the game is no longer a new phenomenon here and everything in life has a time frame – but in a lot of other European countries the game is fresh and we are reaping the rewards once more.

Further afield, there are also some good players in Afghanistan, Brazil, India, Iran and Pakistan. In fact, they seem to be popping up everywhere. Perhaps not in great numbers – but maybe that will change one day.

As an older player, it is nice to visit new countries and feel genuinely appreciated for what I have done for the game. A lot of younger fans still come up to me and ask for my autograph, having just watched the 1985 World Championship final on YouTube. It can be a bitter pill to swallow, that one losing world final is more famous than my six winning world finals. But that is still the one match that most people remember – or watch on YouTube – and remind me about.

There is also demand for good coaches all over the world. The WPBSA has finally become free of the politics that were strangling snooker. Therefore, its coaching scheme has received a shot in the arm. Terry Griffiths, the man who started off the WPBSA coaching badge back in the 1990s – but was then elbowed out for political reasons – is an integral part once more. Along with our new Head of Coaching, Chris Lovell, Terry and I have overseen a new wave of enthusiastic coaches in ever-growing numbers worldwide, all eager to put something back into the game they love.

Under the coaching banner, we are also taking snooker into schools. From the WPBSA's perspective, this is a good, forward-thinking policy: if children are not being taken to snooker clubs by parents, as I was, perhaps we should bring the snooker clubs to them? From the schools' perspective, the maths demanded of the game can offer another tool in their teaching armoury. After showcasing our 'Cue Zone into Schools' programme, teachers have been amazed at how previously difficult or unruly kids who have struggled to learn in a classroom have knuckled down to get involved academically. So, the game that started off with associations of a misspent youth is now being valued as an innovative method of learning. You couldn't make it up!

World Snooker now has a full calendar of events. That is a phenomenal turnaround from where we were just a few years ago. Barry has been the catalyst. He is the man who kick-started it all. Only the biggest cynics would think we don't have a safe pair of hands at the helm.

The game is also fast becoming a truly worldwide sport. Players are not forced to have to move to Britain to survive any more. That is how a world game should be. Some of the players may sometimes moan that the only real winners are the hotels and airlines but, as the old saying goes: 'You have to be in it to win it!'

It sounds so simple but before Barry took over snooker didn't have the infrastructure to enable it to achieve any of this. It all came down to somebody who understood business being prepared to put a bit of money up front and take a risk. I have always defended Barry when people have criticised him for being all about money. I know him better than that. I also know that he splits opinions. But he is a fair fighter in business. He has always been on the side of the boxer, the darts player or the snooker player, but he is also about fair competition and giving fans value for money. He has a market trader mentality and knows the value of a pound coin.

Some people will never understand what snooker means to him. As much as we owe him a debt of gratitude, it is also important to say that he would never betray the game – because of what it means to his whole life. He knows it is a much harder sell this time around. But he will keep up the fight – until he finally retires. Yes, he will be exasperated by the knockers and the moaners within the game – but he will still fight for them.

Sadly, Barry and I don't see as much of each other nowadays. He remains a workaholic and is much more of a grafter than I have ever been. But we still enjoy some good times together, mostly spent fishing down at his pond. Naturally, he calls it a lake!

25. WILD CARD

Stephen Hendry doesn't believe the standard of snooker – especially at the top end – has improved over the years. I vehemently disagree with him. I think it has gone through the roof.

A lot of snooker players from the 1980s and 1990s are now involved in TV work. As a group backstage we are like something off *The Muppets*. We don't praise the good shots too often but we will nit-pick over small mistakes all night long. It is quite funny for us 'experts' to be commentating about the latest generation of 'experts' who are, in my opinion, better than we ever were. I suppose it was the same when the previous set of 'experts' used to commentate on us! Although, I don't ever remember it being so critical!

However, I have spent my life analysing and criticising my own game and I don't think for one minute that I am on my own. Snooker players are tough on themselves so I think harsh criticism is accepted in the game by and large.

I also find that I spot things as a commentator that I missed as a player. For instance, I can spot how a game is unfolding much more easily from the commentary box. The vast majority of frames are won by somebody making a mistake and the other guy mopping up the tears. It is very rare for a frame to be won without some mistake being made somewhere and, many times, the mistake is not so much an attempted pot as a bad decision!

The whole nature of kill or be killed nowadays is that players have to take more risks to be able to get that first punch in. The percentage shot has moved in a far more aggressive direction. The first chance a player gets, he goes for it. It is a much more positive, attacking mentality than anything that was around in the 1980s and that is because of the evolution of the species.

One thing that has become apparent is how many frames are lost by players who do not commit totally to clinching the frame there and then. The number of frames I class as 'what if frames' are much higher than I ever thought was the case when I was in my pomp. Poor decisions as opposed to actual errors can be frame-defining moments and that is now the nature of the game. Perhaps that is because more mistakes are now punished? A common one is when a player doesn't open up the pack when he has a chance to do so; it invariably comes back to haunt him.

I do think that our commentaries can border on being a little negative. As players and former players, I think we all expect total excellence on the table at all times and, if a player makes the slightest error, we can't help but pick up on it. If the likes of Willie Thorne or John Virgo had been commentating on themselves back in the 1980s, they would have ripped themselves to pieces. It would actually be quite funny to get them to do that one day! It would also be quite interesting – based on what they now know after commentating on the modern game.

Willie epitomises the modern-day commentator. He majors on the positional side of the game and I am sure he has helped to educate the next generation about its importance. Strangely enough, I don't think he actually played like that himself. But he has been able to provide a fabulous view of it all from the commentary box.

It is quite tough to be a good commentator and give a balanced opinion. I try not to use clichés and my pet hate is the careless use of the word ... 'careless'. So, while the commentators are criticising players, the commentary could be better at times as well.

We all have a good laugh at each other's expense. We know each other very well and, funnily enough, because we are no longer rivals, we have much more fun together than we ever did as players. The banter flows backwards and forwards from the studio to commentary box. The camaraderie is good. We are like a big family.

For me, Hazel Irvine is the jewel in the BBC's crown of sports presenters. She is always incredibly well prepared and her notes on the players resemble a CIA dossier from the Cold War! Furthermore, I think snooker fans have taken her to their hearts in the same way as they did David Vine – perhaps even more so! She is the perfect host; a brilliant journalist who never seems to put a foot wrong.

None of what Hazel says is on autocue – beloved of so many television presenters – and after watching her deliver some of her links John Parrott and I often bow in her direction in awe and deference. I have been lucky to have seen some of the best TV sports presenters at close hand over the last 30 years or more and since John and I have now effectively learned the ropes as analysts – with the occasional piece to camera thrown in – it makes us appreciate how hard the job can be.

Dave Bowden was the first floor manager John and I ever worked with and he is still around today. Dave nicknamed us 'the Citrus Twins' and that is how we are now known on the road by the crew, who have since endearingly shortened it to 'the Citri'. The joke is that Hazel does all the talking while John and I just stand or sit there looking like lemons.

I never really watched the World Championship or other tournaments until I started working in TV. It wasn't something that I got out of the game. If I wasn't in the world final, obviously I was in a sulk. I might have switched on to watch the end of the match but not much more than that. It wasn't a case of not wanting to watch anybody else win it. Well, it might have been …

I just wasn't as interested if I wasn't in it. I think most players are the same. I know full well that Stephen Hendry would have gone and lived on Mars for a couple of weeks rather than watch somebody else win the world title.

One aspect of the game I have noticed from high up is why some players are prolific century-break makers and others aren't. One reason players such as Ronnie O'Sullivan are so good at it is down to expertise in choosing the right positional shot; when to open up the pack and when not to open up the pack and so on …

The 147 is about the ultimate control of the cue ball to keep on the black every time. Some of them have been easier than others. There have been some 147s where there hasn't been one ball on a cushion throughout the frame. But, even so, to keep control of that cue ball as the number of reds decreases, and to hold it together on the colours, is a massive test of nerve.

It took Ronnie just over five minutes to make one at the Crucible once. But my televised 147 included a really bad positional shot which meant that the only option I had was to play a double. I wasn't on any one of the colours properly either. So, I certainly couldn't consider it a pure 147. But, of course, the significance of it was massive – and that is what makes it so special for me.

If there was one part of my game that I would like to do all over again from the start it would be the percentage of time I devoted in practice to break-building as opposed to that of technique. If I could have found a like-minded professional to sit down with and have days of break-building analysis, rather than just following my instincts about what I had picked up from playing the game, I think I would have become a much better player. But I didn't. I kept myself to myself in my practice room with my father … admittedly the outcome wasn't that bad but perhaps it could have been even better.

As I have said, I think snooker coverage is a lot more educational nowadays. If you had been a snooker fan back in the 1980s, you probably had to do the analysis for yourself. Today, you can receive a lesson from a professional or, at the very least, a former professional. You can also pick up a lot from just studying your favourite players and copying their patterns.

My memory of the level of critical analysis we got in the 1980s was Ted Lowe going: 'Oh dear!' That is probably a little unfair because former world champion John Pulman was around at that time, too. But they certainly didn't go into as much detail as we do today and, of course, the technology for analysis wasn't around to help them either.

As players' knowledge of break-building has improved, we have seen the benefits of calculated risks. I was fortunate enough to play in the 1980s, when the general standard of play wasn't as high as it is today. I didn't have to take too many out-and-out risks because I was presented with so many opportunities that I could play risk-free; even if I did make a mistake and leave my opponent among the balls, I would invariably get another chance.

Fast-forward ten years and I was out of my comfort zone. Stephen Hendry arrived and punished players' mistakes – with more frame-winning breaks than anybody before him. I tried to go with the flow and learn but it was difficult for me to do so. I now play a far more aggressive and risk-taking game than I ever did in the 1980s. Otherwise, I would have been left in the slow lane.

But it is getting harder to compete with the very best. Ronnie O'Sullivan has become a phenomenon. What makes Ronnie unique is that he is now so strong in every area of his game: potting, break-building, tactical play, safety play and mental strength. The last one has taken a while for him to master but since he has been using a sports psychiatrist to good effect, he seems so much happier within himself.

To have the right mental attitude is important in any sport and snooker is no different. Potting the frame or match ball can be a problem at the best of times and if you should be in the wrong frame of mind it can be doubly difficult. It is called 'clinchers disease'. It is understandable that while some of us are naturally gifted competitors, others might find they need help in that area. I was one of the lucky ones: I never needed any help to mentally reach the level I required to be a winning machine.

The use of sports psychology in snooker is relatively new and I find it an interesting subject. I would like to talk to a sports psychologist myself in one respect but I also think there is a concern for the new kid on the block considering this path to find a good one – a bit like separating a good builder from a cowboy but, potentially, even worse! At least with a bad builder you can spot the flaws. How do you judge a poor sports psychologist?

Once I was past my best I am not sure that I would have accepted the views of a sports psychologist anyway. I would probably have argued with them too much! However, I accept that I might come from an old school of thinking that using a sports psychologist is a sign of weakness. Thankfully, I was never in need of one during my prime and while I might have had a more successful time of it in the 1990s especially, had I used one, I hung on in there pretty well! I am pleased I never wanted to go down that road.

In every sport there is an age at which players seem to go off the boil. In snooker, it has tended to be around forty. I won my last major title at thirty-nine. Ronnie O'Sullivan is already the oldest player – at the age of thirty-seven in 2013 – to win the World Championship since Ray Reardon did it in his forties back in 1978. I was thirty-one when I was last crowned world champion and Stephen Hendry was thirty when he did it. So, it will be interesting to see what happens over the next few years. But the Rocket might well be the one who raises the bar.

In addition to all his talents, I think another reason why Ronnie has done so well at the World Championship is his physical condition. Seventeen days of a long, hard tournament are going to suit a fit man much more than somebody who is out of shape. What the older players have over the younger ones is experience. But that counts for nothing if your body is not up to the pressure that the game can place on your central nervous system. Ronnie has both fitness and experience.

As players get closer to a ceiling of achievement, the margins become important. Regardless of the sports psychologist or the coach, a fit body gives the mind the best chance to operate efficiently. If a player can't respect his body, I would suggest there is a mental weakness there. If you can't get fit, you're not paying the price. If you like the pies, what does that say about you? You can't beat talent. But if two players have roughly the same talent, who would you bet on? Lean and Mean or XX Large? Fitness has been a key strength for Ronnie.

I didn't do a bad job of paying the price. Neither did Stephen Hendry. Alex Higgins never paid the price one little bit – so that shows you how brilliant he actually was. One of the other things about exercise is that it releases endorphins that stop you from getting depressed. Running has helped Ronnie and he has set an example by being able to overcome his personal demons and setting his life on track.

There are more ripped snooker players around today than ever before. The only things that used to rip in the 1980s were Bill Werbeniuk's trousers.

At thirty-nine, Ronnie doesn't look his age. He keeps himself in good physical condition. One of the current top players in the world came up to me recently and asked for my advice regarding his game. He had concerns going forward because he had hit the age of thirty. If a player who is involved at the top level of the game today is beginning to feel old at thirty, it is probably true to say that snooker is becoming a younger man's game. In some ways, though, Ronnie is improving with age …

I think Ronnie will be the first player since Ray Reardon – at the age of forty-five in 1978 – to win the World Championship in his forties. Should he still be enjoying and playing the game by the time he gets there, I also think he is the only player capable of winning a world ranking event after he turns fifty!

I won the World Championship six times in the 1980s, Stephen Hendry won it seven times in the 1990s and Ray Reardon won it six times in the 1970s. It is a total fluke that we each dominated during a single decade. Ronnie has bucked that trend as well. He won it in 2001, 2004, 2008, 2012 and 2013. For a player to win the world title having not played on the tour for a whole year – as he did in 2013 – is also remarkable.

He currently has five World Championship titles to his name. His longevity at the top of the game has lasted for more than 20 years since he won the UK Championship in 1993 at the age of seventeen. Such prowess over such a length of time is astonishing – particularly given the standard of the game – and it may never be seen again.

There are no slow matches with Ronnie. He has something about him that doesn't allow him to get dragged into that type of contest. He plays the game differently from the others. That is why he is so special and probably why he is so popular.

Ronnie also seems to have this ability to play telling safety shots, which puts his opponents in so much trouble that it forces them to take risks. Invariably, Ronnie gets the better of the safety exchanges these days – and that makes him an even harder nut to crack!

While there is an analytical and technical side to the game of getting the ball into the hole, there is also a psychological side to how desperate you are to want to do that. Is it absolutely everything to you or are there other things going on in your life that matter more? Would you rather be on holiday with your family, for instance? Just how badly do you want to get that ball in the hole? The same applies to every sport. It is what separates champions from the rest.

I think it helps to have a bit of edge, too. It is usually the younger man who has a chip on the shoulder. A young lion has more fight than an old lion. Men certainly mellow as they get older, so self-centred aggression, the hunter instinct, ruthlessness and selfishness are an advantage.

I love snooker. I practise for the purity of the game and to try and improve my technique to make it as good as it can be so I can, therefore, enjoy occasional moments of great beauty when everything is working perfectly. I would imagine that somebody like Ronnie O'Sullivan experiences even greater moments of purity. But when it comes down to it the only reason we do it, after a certain number of years, is for the purpose of competing against somebody else in a tournament.

Some years ago, we opened up the game to 'pay and play' and lots of good amateurs tried to make a go of it on the tour. We had up to 600 players paying a yearly membership of around £500. These hopefuls turned up in Blackpool for three months of the year, and the vast majority of them soon realised they weren't good enough to turn professional. They all loved the game but sometimes that is not enough.

One of the reasons for loving the game has to be that you are good enough to handle it competitively. Nobody is besotted with the game when they are losing! I loved the game in the 1980s and I hated it in the 1990s. Stephen Hendry loved it in the 1990s but, despite having a better attitude than I did about younger players coming through, he was still left beating himself up left, right and centre when he started losing later on. The fact is that, at a professional level, the game is all about winning.

Ronnie O'Sullivan is also the best pressure player I have ever seen in my life. Regardless of what is being heaped upon him, he can still play his game naturally. He strikes the ball so beautifully under the severest of pressure. He never tightens up and he never quits on the shot. Stephen Hendry and John Higgins were both brilliant under pressure but I don't think either of them got to be as good as the Rocket is now.

Ronnie's whole game is just the best we have ever seen. When Stephen came along, I thought nobody was ever going to be better than him. When John surpassed him with better all-round match prowess, I thought nobody was ever going to be better than him. But now Ronnie has surpassed even that great standard.

It is hard to imagine that anybody in the future will be more breathtaking than Ronnie, but history tells you that there probably will be. I think a player from China will probably be the next one to raise the standard yet again. If the game continues to be so popular out there, I think that is almost inevitable. But, as we move closer to the ceiling of what a human being can realistically achieve on a snooker table, the next generation are going to find it harder to prove they are actually better than their predecessors.

So, what about the distant future? Back in the 1980s, I was invited to Bristol University to watch a robot arm with a camera attached to it attempting to play snooker. This was funded by some higher power for research into artificial intelligence. At that time, the university was just about coming to grips with the computer recognising and discriminating between the coloured balls. Obviously, we have come a long way since then but I wonder how long it will be before the world snooker champion is challenged to a game by the scientists?

Back to Ronnie: some wonder if he can go on and break Stephen's record of seven world titles. Well, he is running out of time unless he can push the barriers back even further and win it well into his forties, as I think he will. I certainly think he'll have a crack at it in the future, and I can't see anybody who is going to be able to out-Ronnie Ronnie at the moment.

I think it also helps him a little bit that he can now afford to pick and choose his events. I reckon he resented having to play in certain tournaments and that is why he took some time out. But he does need to make sure that he generates enough prize money to stay in the top 16. If he was to have a couple of years where he didn't get anywhere in the tournaments he enters, there is a possibility that he might have to go through the qualifiers to play in the World Championship. So he could come unstuck.

The thing is, when the end approaches for a player, it does seem to happen overnight. One minute you are winning everything, and the next minute the wheels have fallen off and you can't buy a trophy! It happened to me. It happened to Stephen Hendry as well. John Higgins is now the latest player to look vulnerable. Time will tell, Ronnie!

There is no doubt that the Rocket is blessed. If ever a man found his role in life the day he discovered he could put a small ball into a slightly bigger hole with a pointed stick, that was Ronnie! He fell on his feet. For him to become an eight-time winner of the toughest event of all over what would be a very long period at the top of the game would be proof-positive that he is the most astonishing player the game has ever seen.

However, there was one man who did manage to stop the new, improved Ronnie – 2014 world champion Mark Selby. The Jester from Leicester inflicted the Rocket's first defeat in three years at the Crucible with an amazing performance and a fabulous comeback in the final from 8–3 and 10–5 down to win it 18–14.

It was a monstrous performance by Mark on the biggest stage of all. He is a monumental player – clinical among the balls, mentally strong and blessed with a fantastic temperament. Some of the shots he played in that final were magnificent. He was also the only player who seemed to be able to play his own game against Ronnie and not allow the Rocket to dictate the match.

Mark waited patiently for his chance to come again at the Crucible after losing 18–13 to John Higgins in the 2007 world final. Since that day, he has won three Masters titles and the UK Championship. He has so much determination that it is very hard to break him down. He is another one who is made of granite and he is fit as well. He slugged it out with Neil Robertson late into the night in their 2014 World Championship semi-final while Ronnie had a day off after breezing into the final. But Mark showed no signs of fatigue at all.

In some ways, Mark is like an upgraded version of Cliff Thorburn: a modern-day Grinder of the highest order. I say an upgraded version because I think the older generation lacked the cue power or technique of today's generation. Technique has improved so much that players have a much larger range of shots nowadays and everybody has upgraded their cue action. Mark's game is perfectly balanced between aggressive and defensive. I make the comparison with Cliff only because, to some degree, he has a robotic quality to his game. I wonder who started all that off?

Even though nothing is certain, I imagine that Judd Trump will also be crowned world champion one day as well. He has strengths that Mark hasn't. But Mark has that World Championship title in the bag! Judd has reached the world final where he also lost to John Higgins – 18–15 in 2011 – and he has been world number one as well. He is another aggressive player with great potting prowess and he is also a true entertainer.

Judd is still quite a few years away from turning thirty so age is on his side as well. Somewhere down the line he will find that there is a younger player who is better than him – but he has time on his side at the moment. At some stage soon, I think it is all going to kick into place for Judd. He has been under a lot of scrutiny since he reached that world final. But all the speculation of him one day becoming the youngest world champion has now gone. It is no longer an issue and that will help him.

In fact, unless an astonishing player breaks through, you could argue that we may have seen the last of the early-twenty-somethings – and even teenagers – winning events. It may be that the game has now reached a critical mass of quality players that means every player has to be more patient and wait in the queue to get their name on the winner's board. There is an apprenticeship to be served and a level of experience and maturity that needs to develop. Judd is still bubbling under at the moment.

The astonishing and relentless power potting Judd brought to the world final has eased off a bit over the past few years. I don't know if he ever sat down and thought about that or if it just naturally happened but his game has changed and I like it better. I don't think he is the type to play rash shots – even though it might look like it at times – and there isn't any impatience there.

Judd's astonishing but so-near-yet-so-far comeback against Ronnie O'Sullivan in the final of the 2014 Coral UK Championship underlined his true potential and just how amazing he is in his own right. I don't think I have ever seen such a jaw-dropping player as Judd.

The shots he takes on are from no textbook that was ever in my local library. It would be fun to put Joe Davis into a time machine and whisk him into the future, and watch his disbelief at the standard that he had put down all those years ago when he helped to set up the first ever World Championship.

Another aggressive player is Neil Robertson. He is one of the big shot makers. He struts around the table with true confidence and once again epitomises the young testosterone-fuelled lion. He has already won the world title, of course, and I expect he will do so again. He is also in that current group of astonishing players.

The rest of us just grow old gracefully. The long-overdue improvements to tournaments and the ranking system speeded up my exit from the top 64 players in the world. The game is also more 'have cue, will travel' than ever before. As well as changes to snooker, there has also been a change in me with less of a commitment to play on the circuit full-time. I regard the game as more of a hobby than ever nowadays.

My decision to miss out on the UK Championship in York in 2013 and go on *I'm a Celebrity …* instead was probably a statement of intent from me in some ways. I risked the pride involved of staying on the tour for perhaps another year by opting out of the second biggest event in the calendar. But it was only pride. It had nothing to do with my professional career because that wasn't going anywhere by that stage. I was very much getting to the point where I wanted to pick and choose.

The expansion of the game overseas also influenced me, too. I don't have the desire to jump on a plane to China with absolutely no guarantee of getting through the first round of whatever event I am playing in before having to jump on another plane to come back home, even if I could get through the qualifying matches – which is by no means certain. Regardless of the fact that snooker is hot-wired into my DNA, I am sure I can find a better use of my time.

I think the 2013–14 season really defined for me what I should be doing to enjoy myself. I had to admit that I would rather be at home than travelling around the world. Maybe losing so often had worn me down. And I was losing in somewhat brilliant style quite often in 2013 and 2014 – with my ability to hit the cushions on the long pots (and even on the short pots) becoming better and better year on year.

After coming out of the jungle, I quickly realised that I was getting ever closer to losing my place in the top 64. I started to reassess my views on it all and the conclusion I reached was … so what? As the whole scenario got closer to its inevitable conclusion – at the World Championship qualifiers at the Ponds Forge International Sports Centre in Sheffield – I grew calmer thinking about the possible outcomes.

Ponds Forge was built for the 1991 World Student Games. Its main feature is an Olympic-sized swimming pool, but it was turned into a multi-table snooker arena for a few days as over 140 of us slugged it out for the honour of taking one of the 16 qualifying places at the Crucible, which is probably within reach of a Judd Trump screwback from there.

I played Craig Steadman in my first match, which was in the second of four best-of-19-frames qualifying rounds. Sadly, my wheels came off before I had even got into gear. I trailed 7–2 overnight after an agonising first session. I went back to my hotel feeling pretty demoralised. During the night, there was a fire alarm and I couldn't sleep. I walked down to a café as early as I could the next morning and sat there for a while with a friend, mulling it all over. I mentally regrouped as best I could and went down to the venue with the proverbial mountain to climb.

I did actually slowly pull the match around a little bit and managed to cut Craig's lead to 8–5. But once he won another frame – to go 9–5 in front – the pressure was really on me. I was now staring the guillotine in the face – or should that be the basket! I fought like the champion I still am inside to come back again to 9–8 but it was too much for me to make up in the end. I went out of the competition 10–8.

Had I managed to somehow scrape over that second qualifying round hurdle, I would still have needed to have got through two more matches to reach the Crucible. I failed. But I was in good company: Graeme Dott, Peter Ebdon, Matthew Stevens and Mark Williams all missed out as well.

With that defeat I also lost my place in the top 64 in the world and, therefore, my place on the professional tour as well. As it turned out I was absolutely fine about it. In truth, it was my form over two whole seasons that had lost me my place in the top 64 anyway, not a defeat in one event.

If I had entered the UK Championship and a couple of PTC events that clashed with my time on *I'm a Celebrity ...*, I might have scraped into the top 64. But perhaps that would have only been for one more year; especially given that I had already decided not to travel the world in search of mediocrity.

So, as things stand, my World Championship quarter-final match against Neil Robertson in 2010 was my last appearance at the Crucible – for at least five years anyway! As my world ranking got lower and lower, the requirement for me to win more qualifying matches to reach the Crucible increased. There is now a strong possibility that I might never play there again. To do so would arguably be my greatest ever achievement.

In my sixtieth birthday year – which, between you and me, will be 2017 – for an absolute last hurrah I might see if I can qualify for the professional tour again just for the fun of it and enter Q School. The possibility that I could get to sixty and create a small milestone does appeal to me. I don't sit and think about it – but it would be an interesting target to see if I could do it.

In the meantime, I have been fortunate enough to be handed a wild card – along with Stephen Hendry and James Wattana – an opportunity to participate in all the tour events on a tournament-to-tournament basis, should the full contingent of 128 players on the tour not take up their chance to enter an event.

My plan is to stay away from the long-distance trips to events in Australia, China or India but I remain attracted to the PTC events in Europe. I also intend to play in the World Championship qualifying competition again – which I am able to do as a former world champion – plus the World Seniors, which I was pleased to win in 2013 when I beat Nigel Bond in Portsmouth.

I took up my wild-card entry option to enter the Coral UK Championship in 2014 and was drawn to play Ricky Walden, a fantastic cueist and already a winner of world ranking events overseas, in the first round. I don't think I went into the match with much resolve but I still turned a trick or two and at 2–2 perhaps I had him concerned, at least fractionally. I lost 6–2 in the end.

In my press conference afterwards – attended by the usual small amount of reporters who are present for a loser of a last 128 round – somebody had got wind of an interview I had done with Ronnie O'Sullivan on Eurosport where I had been quite candid about my future within the competitive game.

I think they thought I was alluding to my retirement. They were at a loss as to how to proceed with the interview when I made a Peter Sellers comparison, saying that my brain had retired but my body hadn't. I said I felt like Dr Strangelove, when his hand did things independently of the rest of his body. (My left hand filling out the forms to enter the tournaments and my right hand wondering why it was still playing in them!) It wasn't the press announcement they had been expecting or perhaps hoping for but, throughout my career, I have always tried to be far more interesting than my *Spitting Image* puppet would have managed!

Barry Hearn's other brainchild sounded much more fun. Instead of having the 2015 World Championship with the top 16 players in the world already through to the Crucible and 112 other professionals playing to make up the remaining 16 places, he has announced that he will increase the 112 by 16 special invitations to 128.

These invitations will go to all previous world champions plus a mixture of still-to-be-confirmed others. At the time of writing, the excitement is unbearable. Whose left hands will fill out the forms to be there: Ray Reardon, Cliff Thorburn, Joe Johnson, John Parrott, Stephen Hendry, me? Furthermore, could Allison Fisher, Reanne Evans (the current ten-time women's world champion), Earl Strickland or even Rui Chapéu also be invited to attend?

I am glad I never retired from the game when it was perhaps expected of me to do so. Stephen Hendry retired far too early in my opinion – but that was his decision. As for me, even though most of the 1990s were tough and the 2000s were awful, had I retired I wouldn't have had that fabulous moment against John Higgins at the World Championship in 2010. That still remains a special memory for me.

It just might be that I have played the game for so long now that I am actually unable to get the words 'I retire' out of my mouth! I still want to see if I can try and improve and even though, in my heart of hearts, I know I am probably not going to be able to achieve that, I think I continue for the agonising fun of it. I still hate losing. I still flirt with the idea with genuine optimism until it all goes wrong. I must have some sort of masochistic streak in me. The snooker table has been a constant in my life. I say it is a hobby. It might just be a habit …

Jimmy White is still on the tour. He still manages to do it somehow. He says he still believes that he can win the world title that eluded him for so many years. Recently he also spoke publicly about how he feels that his problems with drugs were to blame for him not winning it much earlier in his career.

It is certainly true that Jimmy used to go on benders between events, from time to time. The two of us shared the same driver for a while – namely one Robert 'Robbo' Brazier – and on more than one occasion he had to go off and try and find Jimmy to pick him up and take him to an exhibition. All he ever discovered was that nobody knew where he was. Robbo soon learned skills he never knew he possessed, similar to those of a bounty hunter tracking down his prey.

If the Whirlwind had his time again, I think he might approach it all a little more professionally from a younger age than he did – but I think he would still enjoy himself because that was his nature. I managed to separate my personal enjoyment from my professional life. By doing that, I believe I had the best of both worlds. But Jimmy was a different character. Could he have done things differently? The only person who really knows that – and even he may not know – is Jimmy himself.

It is admirable that he doesn't seem to have too many regrets about how it all panned out. It can't be easy always having the words 'six-time world finalist' hanging over your head but he manages it well. I think he probably has the same masochistic streak as me. The two of us were like the Last of the Mohicans. At the time of writing, we are down to one. Jimmy is still in there fighting and his competitive spirit has been extraordinary. What a fantastic achievement it is for him to still be on the tour.

The love and respect Jimmy receives from snooker fans is well deserved. He continues to tour and travel. He went over to play in China recently. Unlike me, I think he sees that it can be the difference between staying in the top 64 or not at the end of the season and that still seems to matter to him.

Over the years, I have seen him go from a cheeky Jack the Lad whiz kid to one of the top players in the game who, perhaps, let his potential slip because he partied too hard and was maybe not as dedicated as others. But I have great admiration for the fact that in his fifties he now seems to approach being a tour player much more professionally than ever before. So, it might be unfinished business for him.

Tony Drago is another incredible warrior who is still around. It is interesting to note that the last eighties men standing are, arguably and most probably, also the most gifted.

Stephen Hendry retired from snooker in 2012. In the end I think the game began to eat him up in the same way it did me. The big difference between us was that no longer being a winning machine drove him to such distraction that he didn't even want to play the game any more. He was still in the top 16 in the world when he retired and he made a 147 during his last tournament, which just happened to be the 2012 World Championship!

Many felt that he probably had another major tournament win in him, but losing was driving him crazy to the nth degree. So he decided to retire at the age of forty-three. Maybe retirement was more preferable to him than getting bashed up on the table – where he used to win all the time.

There will always be a debate about who is the greatest player of all time. For me, inevitably the tide has turned in favour of the Rocket, but I would love to be able to go back to the time of Joe Davis at his peak and play him to see what he was like and to see what his standard was. I don't believe the game has ever gone backwards. Every era has improved on the standards of the previous one. If Ronnie had been around when Stephen was at his peak, Stephen wouldn't have been at his peak. And if Stephen had been around when I was at my peak, I wouldn't have been at my peak – not in the same way, or, at least, not to the same degree. I don't think I would have won six World Championships.

But the beauty of the guessing game is it is just that: nobody actually knows. If we were able to pick everybody up in that time machine and put us all in the same era, I think that Joe Davis probably wouldn't make it to the professional ranks. The same applies to Ray Reardon to a large degree. But if they had grown up in another era, it might well be a different story. Projecting even further, what if Earl Strickland or Efren Reyes had been born in the UK instead of the USA and the Philippines respectively? As for me, I think it might be difficult for me to make the top eight in the world in my time machine. It would certainly be a hard job to do so. Obviously, I haven't got a clue! Answers on a postcard, please …

When I look back at my career, I just think that while I lived in an era in which I didn't always have everything my own way, I did have quite a decent run at it. I am not trying to be magnanimous or self-deprecating, I am just trying to tell it like I see it.

The city of Sheffield has become a second home to me. I have travelled up there, either to play or watch snooker, since the late 1970s. It has changed a lot and it is fair to say that when I go up there nowadays I am in a much more relaxed state than in days past. I no longer walk over the cellar doors outside the Brown Bear pub either!

During my career there have been plenty of sliding doors moments. If I hadn't signed with Barry Hearn, I wouldn't have been fast-tracked into turning professional by him back in 1978. Therefore, I wouldn't have been ready to win the World Championship in 1981. And so on ...

And if my father hadn't been snooker-mad? Well, who knows?

He is eighty-eight now. The two of us have been through it all. Snooker is our habit. Whenever I go over to my parents' house he always asks when I am going to start practising properly again, even though I am, effectively, semi-retired.

We both know where I am at with the game. But we still get locked into this all-too-familiar world of ours; one that only we really know. My father will continue to check if my back arm is straight or my grip is correct and I will still stop and ask him: 'Really?' Nothing changes in that respect. Although he has accepted that I just do it for enjoyment nowadays. We have finally come to that conclusion.

We haven't had a normal father-son relationship. We have never discussed a job application, for instance. But he has been there for all the highs and all the lows. So, while mentally I might have just about given up, physically I find that my body keeps turning up at events.

My father no longer comes to watch me but he does continue to watch snooker on television or via the internet. He also continues to knock the balls around every day, while I struggle to practise if there is nothing on the horizon. The two of us have a relationship that is so involved with snooker that if we take the game out of it we would probably struggle to know what to say to each other.

We both know that I am never going to win the World Championship again. But we still think that we might win a match! So, I think I will always go over there and dabble in snooker with him while he is still happy to pick the balls out of the pockets!

The pleasure any hobby gives is unquantifiable. If you are lucky enough to find something in your life that not only gets you up in the morning but also entertains you and pays your wages, then you have had a right result!

I have been very lucky. What else would I have done? My life in snooker has been everything and more than I ever thought could be possible. You really couldn't have made it up. As a famous puppet once said on national television back in the 1980s, it has been mad, devil-may-care and interesting ...

ACKNOWLEDGEMENTS

My thanks go to Lance Hardy, Andrew Goodfellow, Anna Mrowiec, Richard Collins, Lijana Sutich and Clive Everton.

PHOTO CREDITS